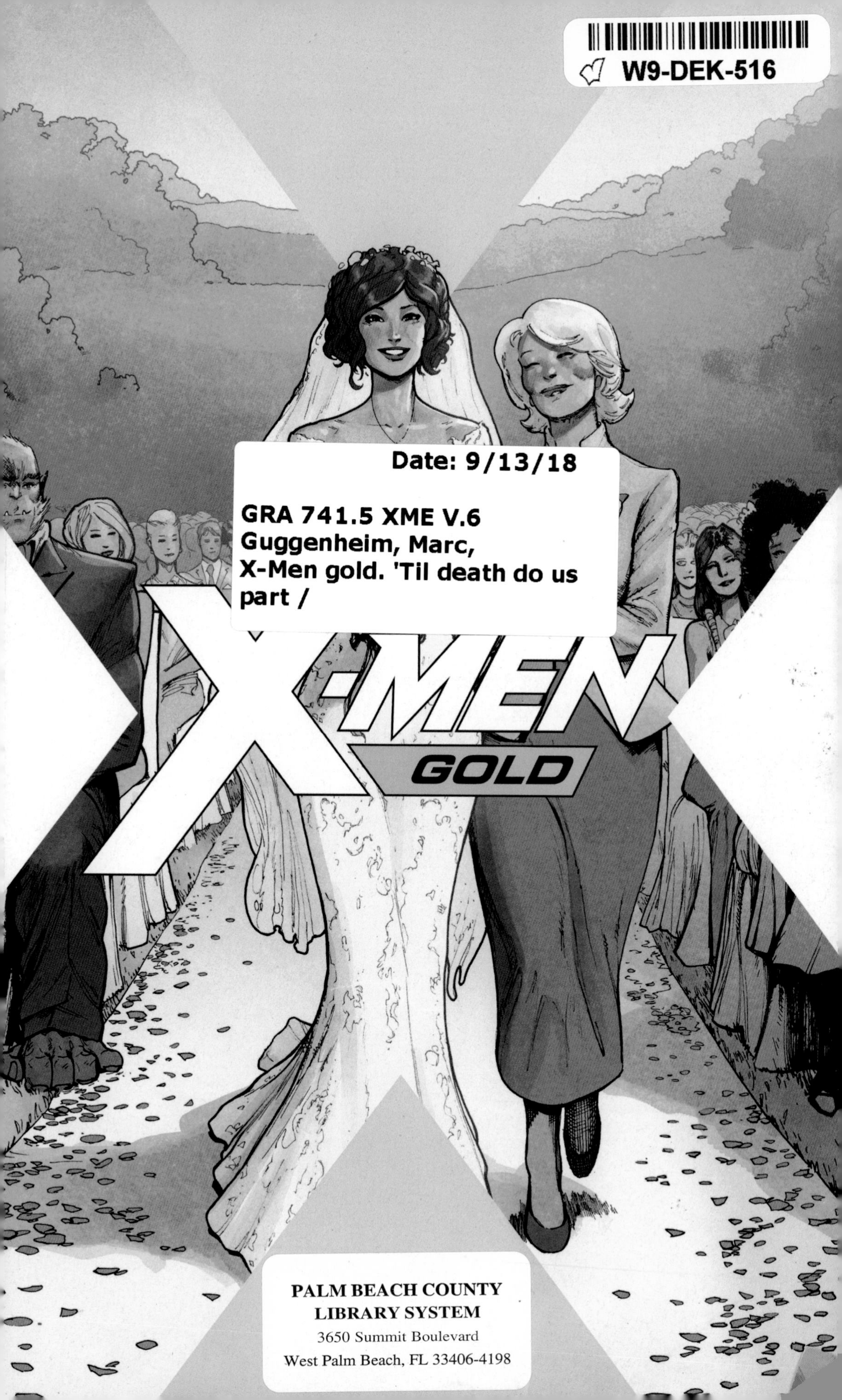
X-MEN
GOLD

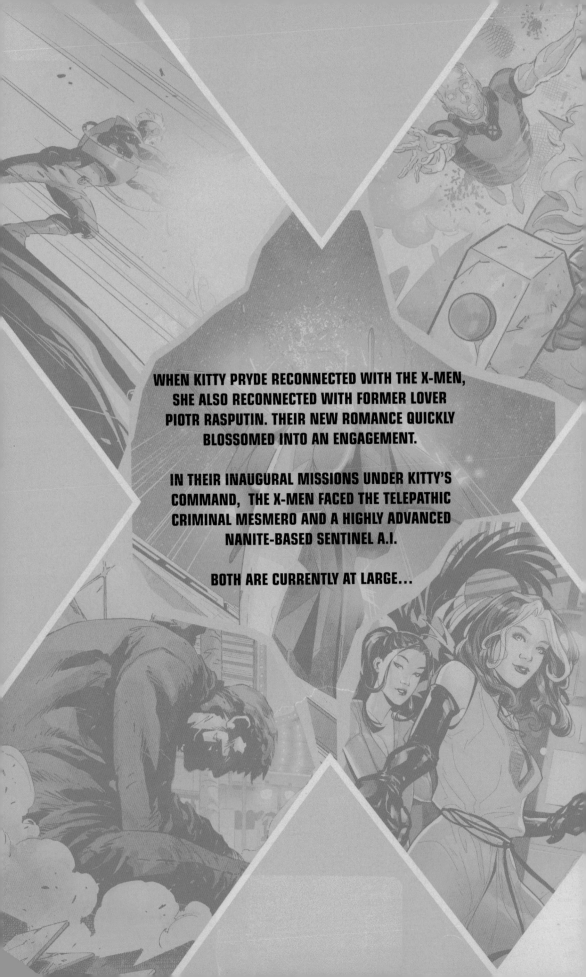

WHEN KITTY PRYDE RECONNECTED WITH THE X-MEN, SHE ALSO RECONNECTED WITH FORMER LOVER PIOTR RASPUTIN. THEIR NEW ROMANCE QUICKLY BLOSSOMED INTO AN ENGAGEMENT.

IN THEIR INAUGURAL MISSIONS UNDER KITTY'S COMMAND, THE X-MEN FACED THE TELEPATHIC CRIMINAL MESMERO AND A HIGHLY ADVANCED NANITE-BASED SENTINEL A.I.

BOTH ARE CURRENTLY AT LARGE...

X-MEN GOLD

'TIL DEATH DO US PART

Writer/**MARC GUGGENHEIM**

Artists/**MICHELE BANDINI** (#26 & #28),**GERALDO BORGES** (#27 & #29)
& **DAVID MARQUEZ** (Flashbacks & #30)

Color Artists/**ARIF PRIANTO** (#26-29) & **MATTHEW WILSON** (Flashbacks & #30)

Letterer/**VC's CORY PETIT**

Cover Art/**Phil Noto**

Assistant Editor/**CHRIS ROBINSON**
Editor/**DARREN SHAN**
X-Men Group Editor/**JORDAN D. WHITE**

X-MEN: THE WEDDING SPECIAL #1

Writers/**CHRIS CLAREMONT, MARC GUGGENHEIM** & **KELLY THOMPSON**

Artists/**TODD NAUCK; GREG LAND** & **JAY LEISTEN**; and **MARIKA CRESTA**

Color Artists/**RACHELLE ROSENBERG, JASON KEITH** & **FEDERICO BLEE**

Letterer/**VC's CLAYTON COWLES**

Cover Art/**J. SCOTT CAMPBELL** & **SABINE RICH**

Assistant Editor/**ANNALISE BISSA**
Editors/**DARREN SHAN** with **MARK PANICCIA**
X-Men Group Editor/**JORDAN D. WHITE**

X-MEN CREATED BY **STAN LEE** & **JACK KIRBY**

Collection Editor/**JENNIFER GRÜNWALD** · Assistant Editor/**CAITLIN O'CONNELL**
Associate Managing Editor/**KATERI WOODY** · Editor, Special Projects/**MARK D. BEAZLEY**
VP Production & Special Projects/**JEFF YOUNGQUIST** · SVP Print, Sales & Marketing/**DAVID GABRIEL**
Book Designer/**JAY BOWEN**

Editor in Chief/**C.B. CEBULSKI** · Chief Creative Officer/**JOE QUESADA**
President/**DAN BUCKLEY** · Executive Producer/**ALAN FINE**

X-MEN GOLD VOL. 6: 'TIL DEATH DO US PART. Contains material originally published in magazine form as X-MEN GOLD #26-30 and X-MEN: THE WEDDING SPECIAL #1. First printing 2018. ISBN 978-1-302-90976-5. Published by MARVEL WORLDWIDE, INC., a subsidiary of MARVEL ENTERTAINMENT, LLC. OFFICE OF PUBLICATION: 135 West 50th Street, New York, NY 10020. Copyright © 2018 MARVEL No similarity between any of the names, characters, persons, and/or institutions in this magazine with those of any living or dead person or institution is intended, and any such similarity which may exist is purely coincidental. **Printed in the U.S.A.** DAN BUCKLEY, President, Marvel Entertainment; JOHN NEE, Publisher; JOE QUESADA, Chief Creative Officer; TOM BREVOORT, SVP of Publishing; DAVID BOGART, SVP of Business Affairs & Operations, Publishing & Partnership; DAVID GABRIEL, SVP of Sales & Marketing, Publishing; JEFF YOUNGQUIST, VP of Production & Special Projects; DAN CARR, Executive Director of Publishing Technology; ALEX MORALES, Director of Publishing Operations; DAN EDINGTON, Managing Editor; SUSAN CRESPI, Production Manager; STAN LEE, Chairman Emeritus. For information regarding advertising in Marvel Comics or on Marvel.com, please contact Vit DeBellis, Custom Solutions & Integrated Advertising Manager, at vdebellis@marvel.com. For Marvel subscription inquiries, please call 888-511-5480. **Manufactured between 6/15/2018 and 7/17/2018 by LSC COMMUNICATIONS INC., KENDALLVILLE, IN, USA.**

10 9 8 7 6 5 4 3 2 1

26

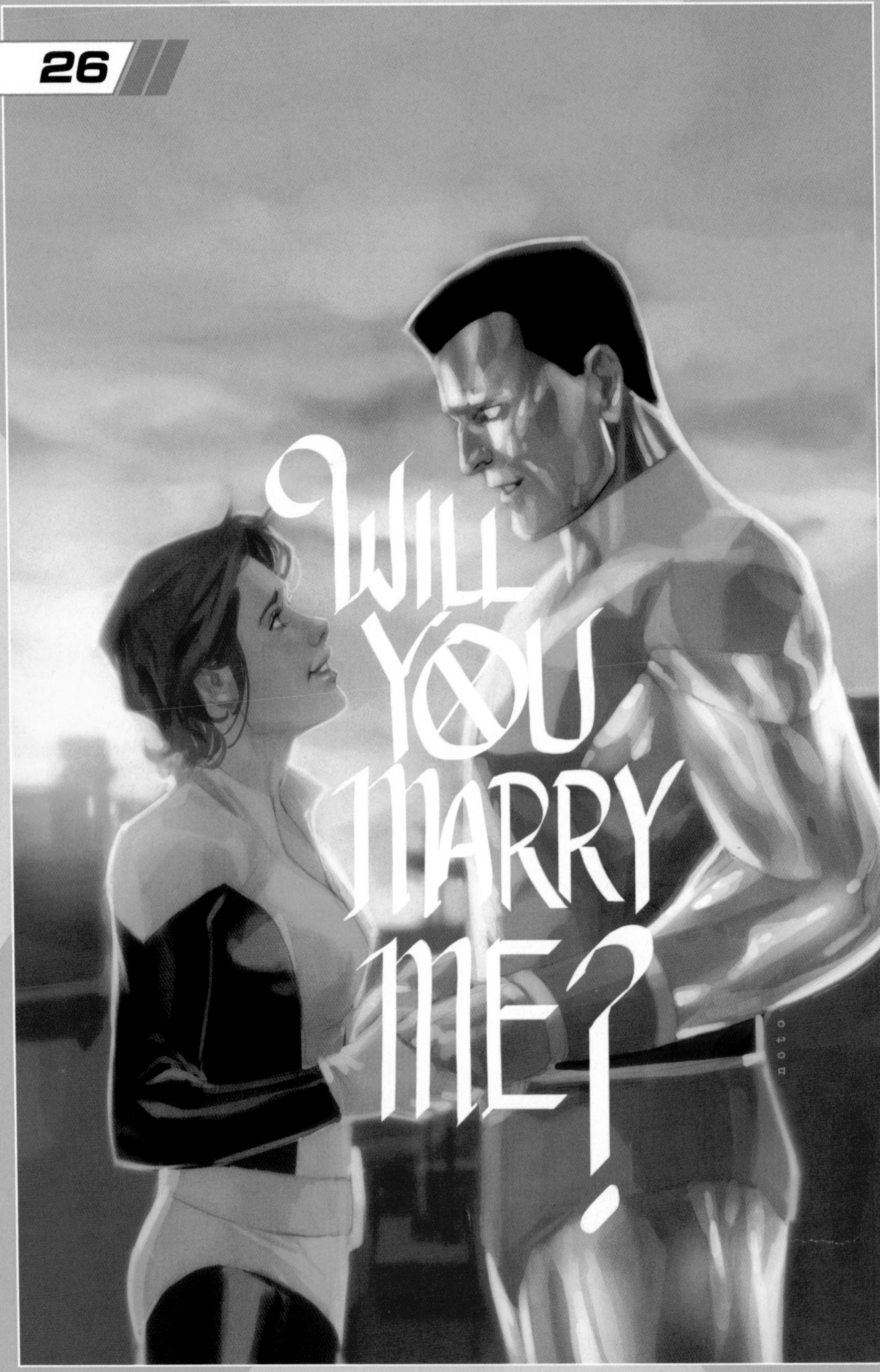
WILL YOU MARRY ME?

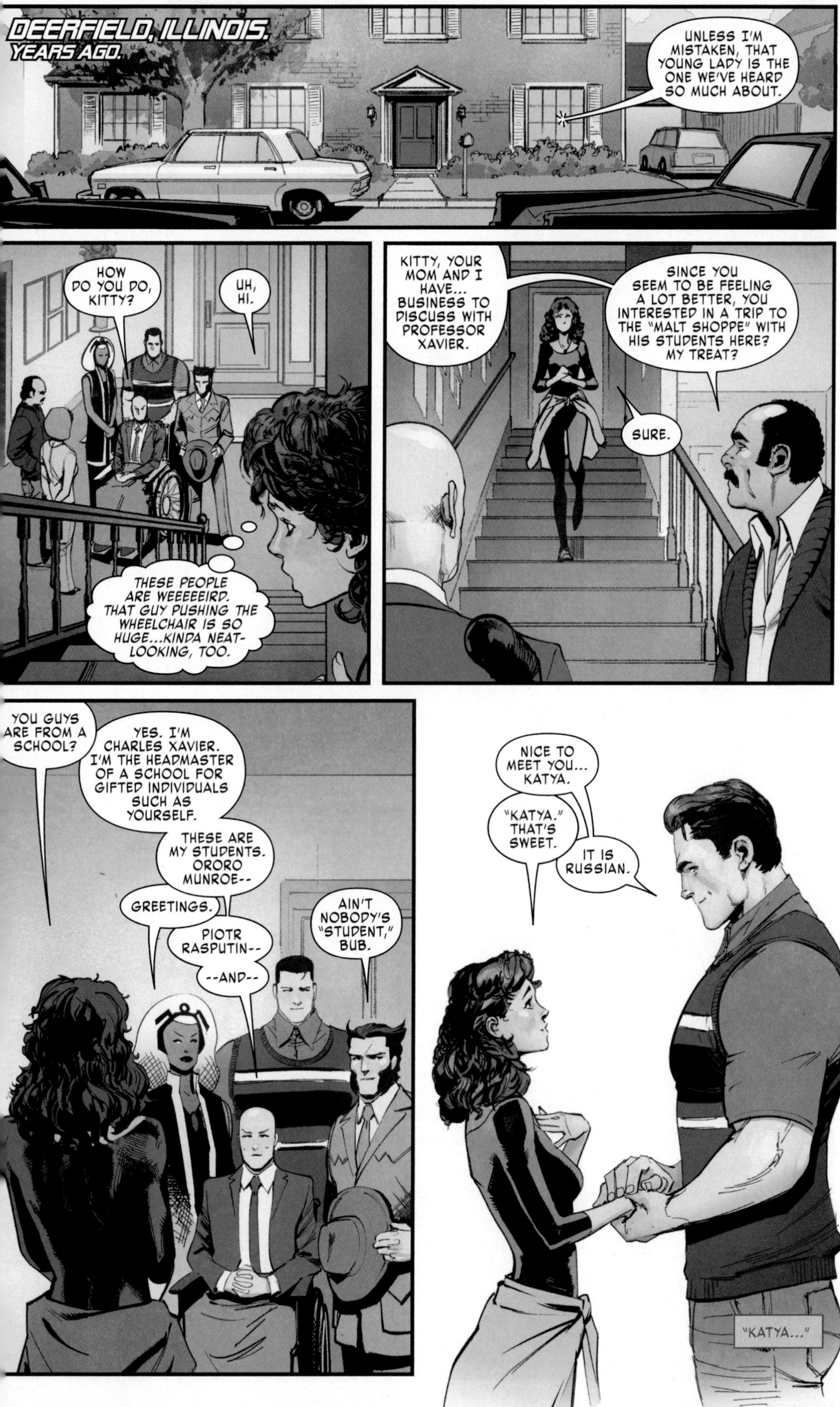

DEERFIELD, ILLINOIS. YEARS AGO.
UNLESS I'M MISTAKEN, THAT YOUNG LADY IS THE ONE WE'VE HEARD SO MUCH ABOUT.
HOW DO YOU DO, KITTY?
UH, HI.
THESE PEOPLE ARE WEEEEEIRD. THAT GUY PUSHING THE WHEELCHAIR IS SO HUGE...KINDA NEAT-LOOKING, TOO.
KITTY, YOUR MOM AND I HAVE... BUSINESS TO DISCUSS WITH PROFESSOR XAVIER.
SINCE YOU SEEM TO BE FEELING A LOT BETTER, YOU INTERESTED IN A TRIP TO THE "MALT SHOPPE" WITH HIS STUDENTS HERE? MY TREAT?
SURE.
YOU GUYS ARE FROM A SCHOOL?
YES. I'M CHARLES XAVIER. I'M THE HEADMASTER OF A SCHOOL FOR GIFTED INDIVIDUALS SUCH AS YOURSELF.
THESE ARE MY STUDENTS. ORORO MUNROE--
GREETINGS.
PIOTR RASPUTIN--
--AND--
AIN'T NOBODY'S "STUDENT," BUB.
NICE TO MEET YOU... KATYA.
"KATYA." THAT'S SWEET.
IT IS RUSSIAN.
"KATYA..."

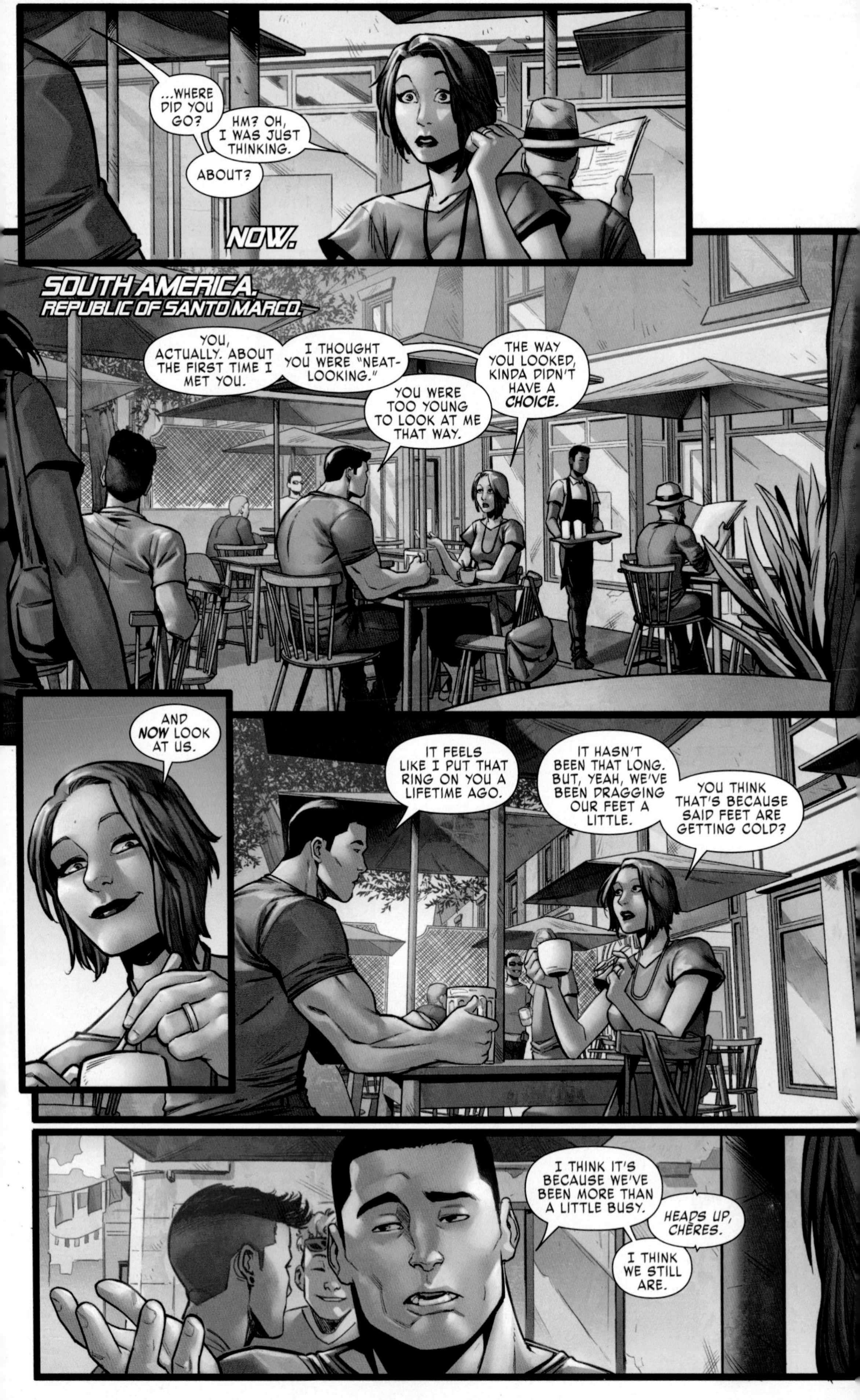

...WHERE DID YOU GO?
HM? OH, I WAS JUST THINKING.
ABOUT?
NOW.
SOUTH AMERICA. REPUBLIC OF SANTO MARCO.
YOU, ACTUALLY. ABOUT THE FIRST TIME I MET YOU.
I THOUGHT YOU WERE "NEAT-LOOKING."
YOU WERE TOO YOUNG TO LOOK AT ME THAT WAY.
THE WAY YOU LOOKED, KINDA DIDN'T HAVE A CHOICE.
AND NOW LOOK AT US.
IT FEELS LIKE I PUT THAT RING ON YOU A LIFETIME AGO.
IT HASN'T BEEN THAT LONG. BUT, YEAH, WE'VE BEEN DRAGGING OUR FEET A LITTLE.
YOU THINK THAT'S BECAUSE SAID FEET ARE GETTING COLD?
I THINK IT'S BECAUSE WE'VE BEEN MORE THAN A LITTLE BUSY.
I THINK WE STILL ARE.
HEADS UP, CHÈRES.

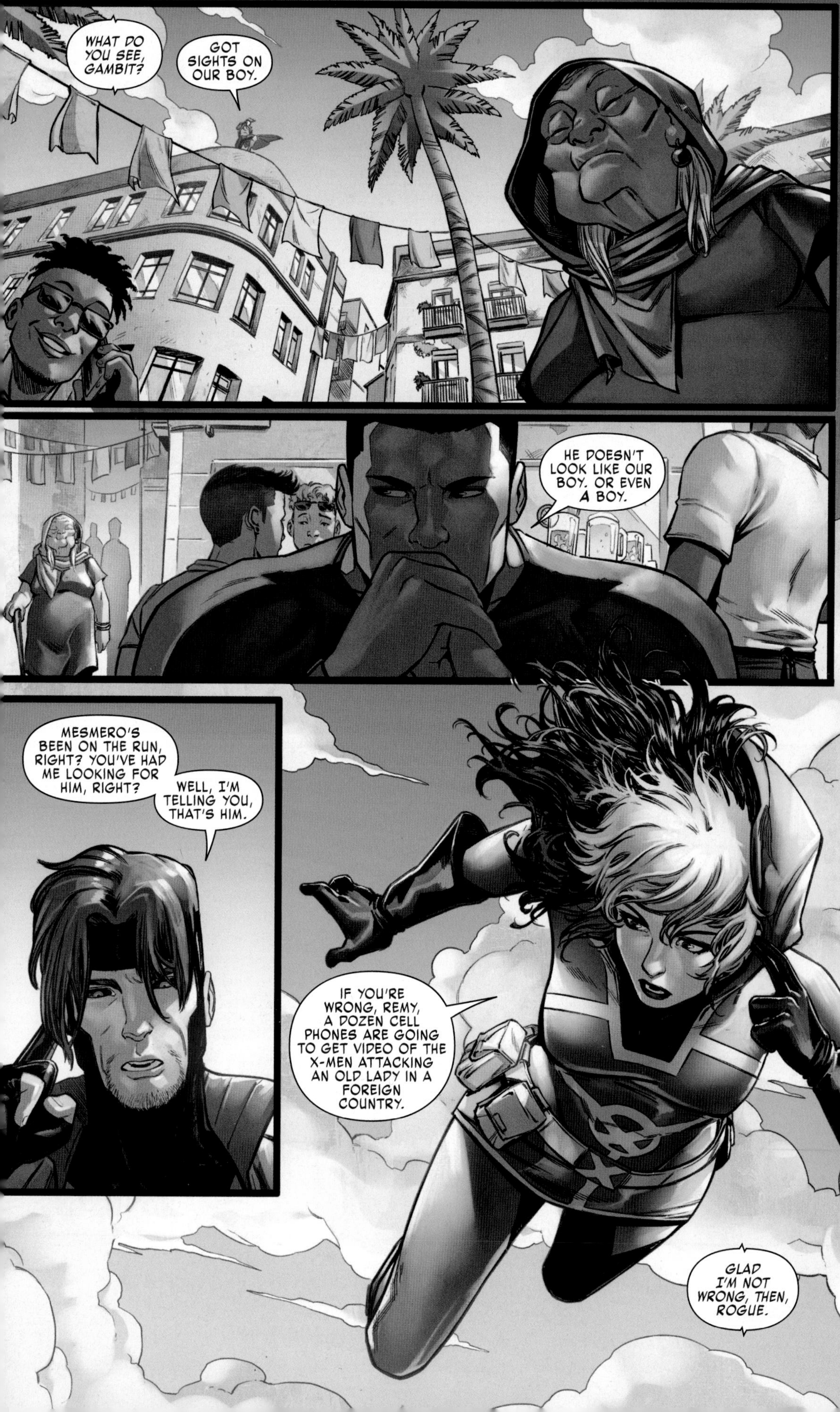
WHAT DO YOU SEE, GAMBIT?
GOT SIGHTS ON OUR BOY.
HE DOESN'T LOOK LIKE OUR BOY. OR EVEN A BOY.
MESMERO'S BEEN ON THE RUN, RIGHT? YOU'VE HAD ME LOOKING FOR HIM, RIGHT?
WELL, I'M TELLING YOU, THAT'S HIM.
IF YOU'RE WRONG, REMY, A DOZEN CELL PHONES ARE GOING TO GET VIDEO OF THE X-MEN ATTACKING AN OLD LADY IN A FOREIGN COUNTRY.
GLAD I'M NOT WRONG, THEN, ROGUE.

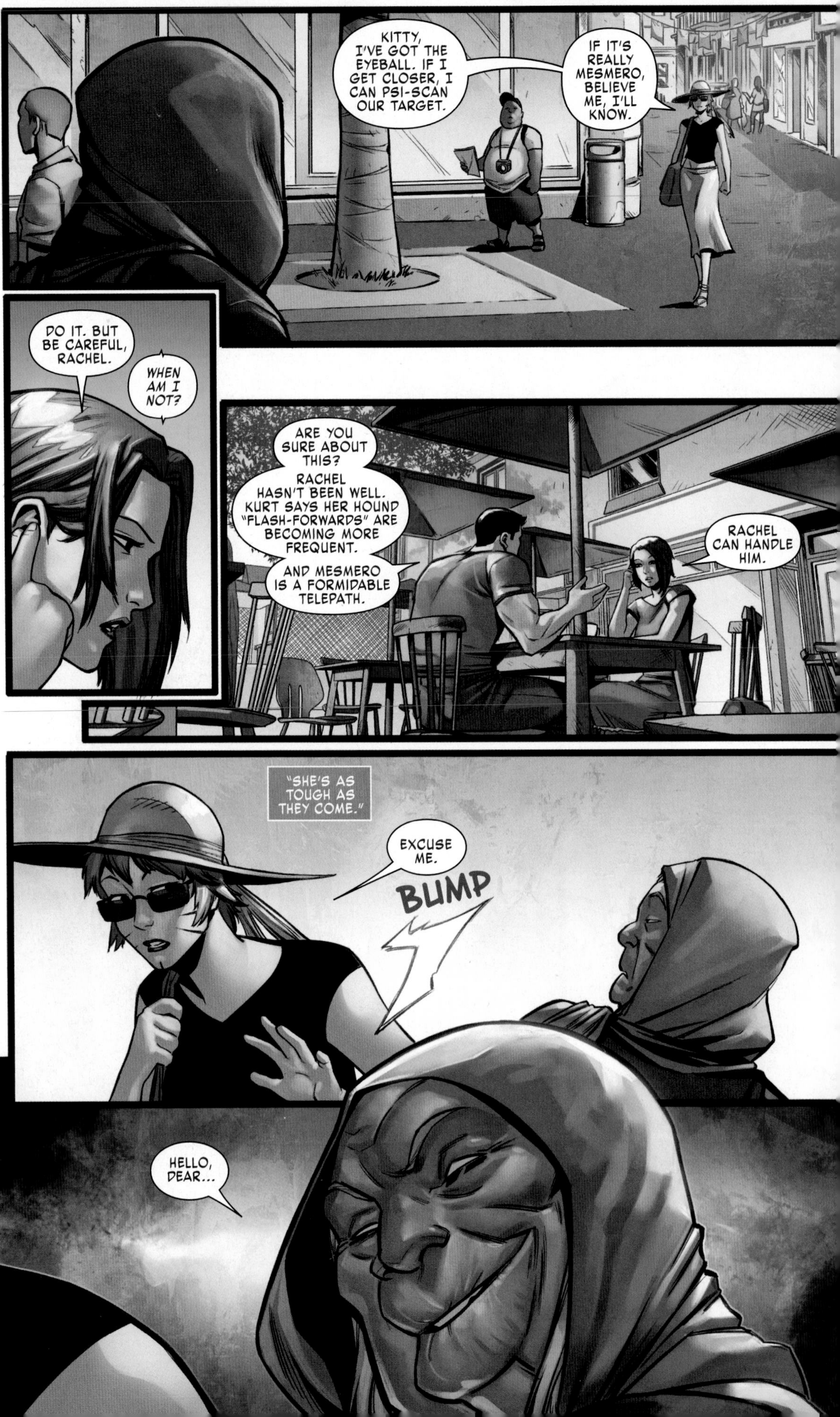
KITTY, I'VE GOT THE EYEBALL. IF I GET CLOSER, I CAN PSI-SCAN OUR TARGET.
IF IT'S REALLY MESMERO, BELIEVE ME, I'LL KNOW.
DO IT. BUT BE CAREFUL, RACHEL.
WHEN AM I NOT?
ARE YOU SURE ABOUT THIS?
RACHEL HASN'T BEEN WELL. KURT SAYS HER HOUND "FLASH-FORWARDS" ARE BECOMING MORE FREQUENT.
AND MESMERO IS A FORMIDABLE TELEPATH.
RACHEL CAN HANDLE HIM.
"SHE'S AS TOUGH AS THEY COME."
EXCUSE ME.
BUMP
HELLO, DEAR...

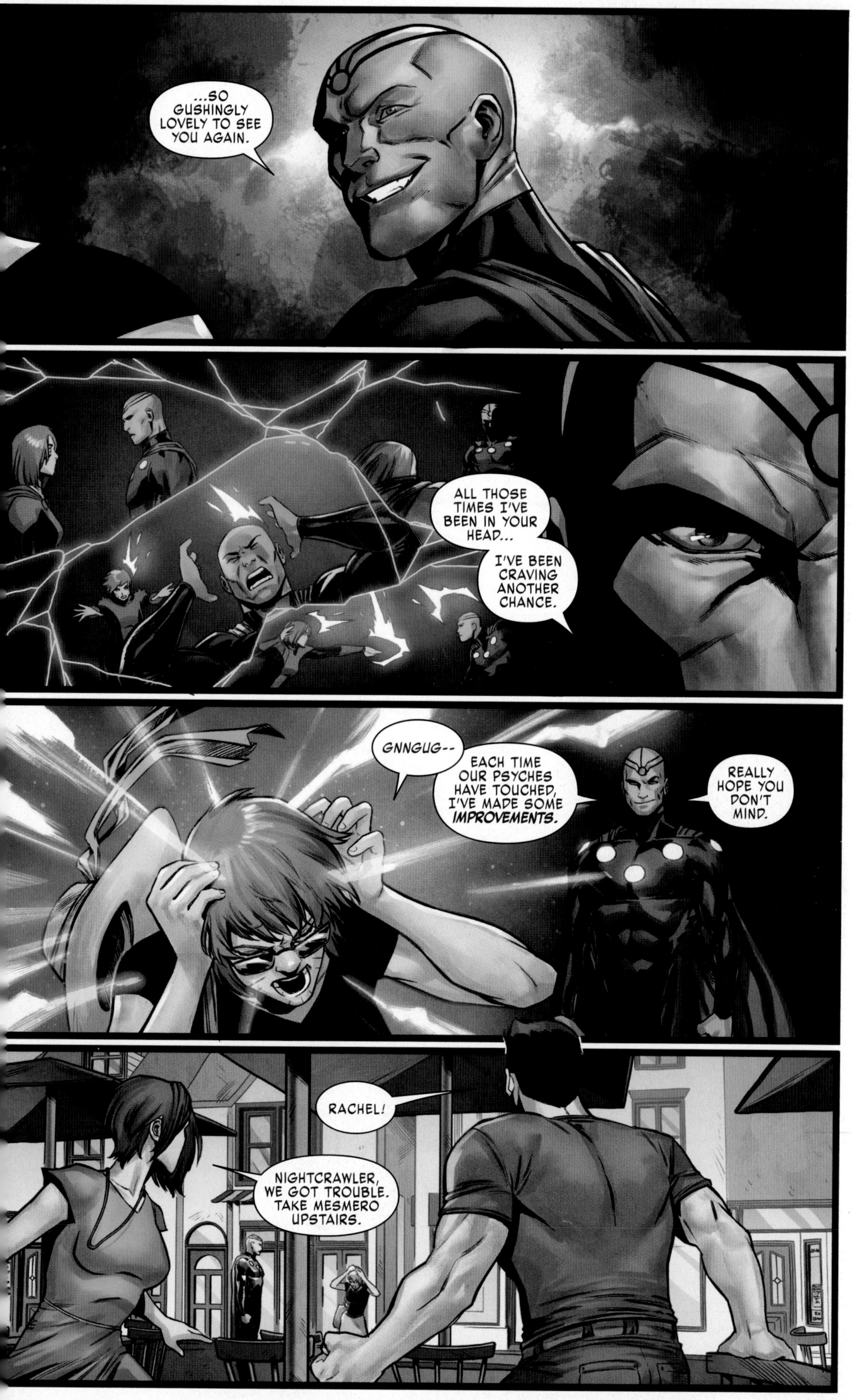
...SO GUSHINGLY LOVELY TO SEE YOU AGAIN.
ALL THOSE TIMES I'VE BEEN IN YOUR HEAD...
I'VE BEEN CRAVING ANOTHER CHANCE.
GNNGUG--
EACH TIME OUR PSYCHES HAVE TOUCHED, I'VE MADE SOME IMPROVEMENTS.
REALLY HOPE YOU DON'T MIND.
RACHEL!
NIGHTCRAWLER, WE GOT TROUBLE. TAKE MESMERO UPSTAIRS.

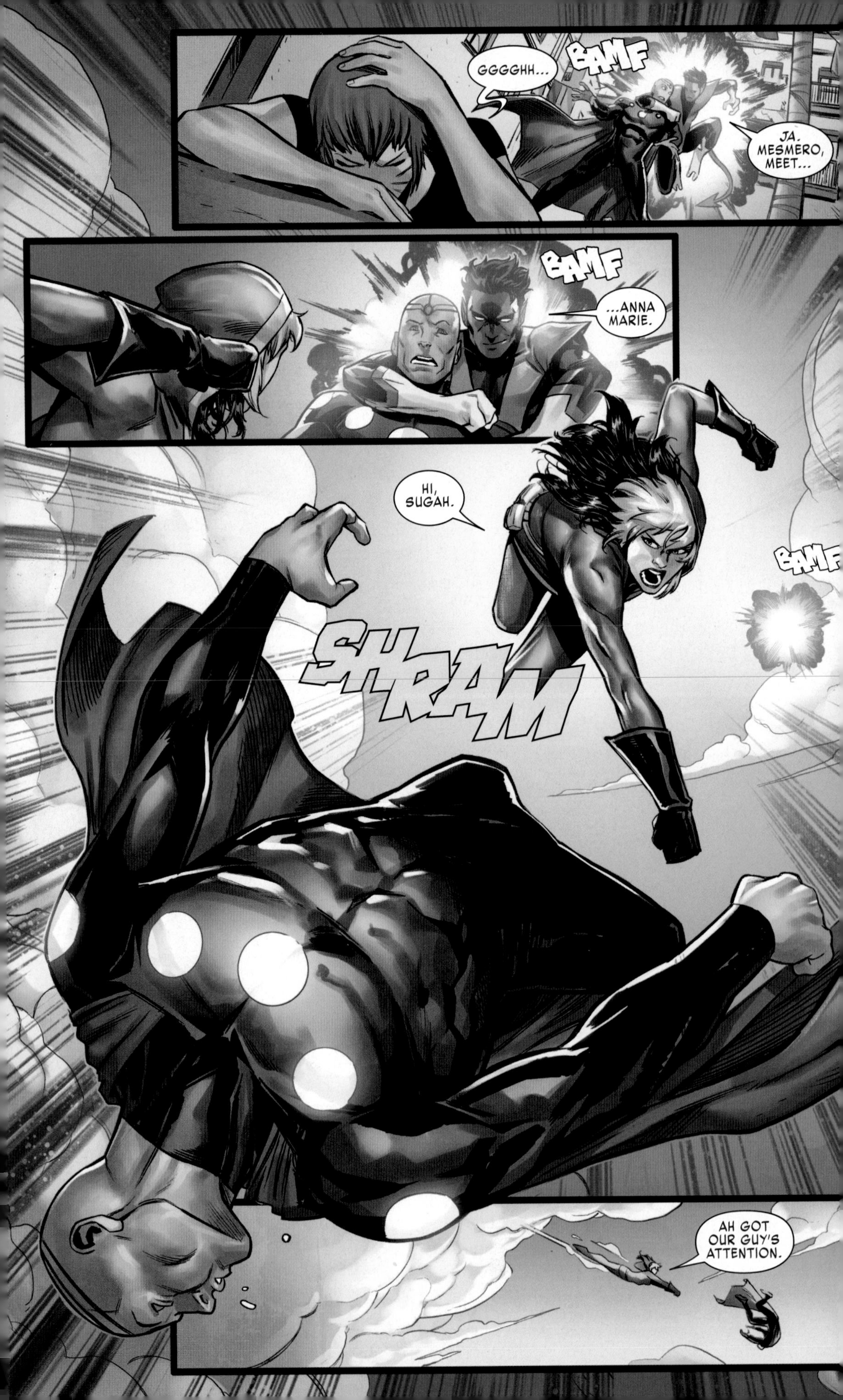
GGGGHH...
BAMF
JA. MESMERO, MEET...
BAMF
...ANNA MARIE.
HI, SUGAH.
BAMF
SHRAM
AH GOT OUR GUY'S ATTENTION.

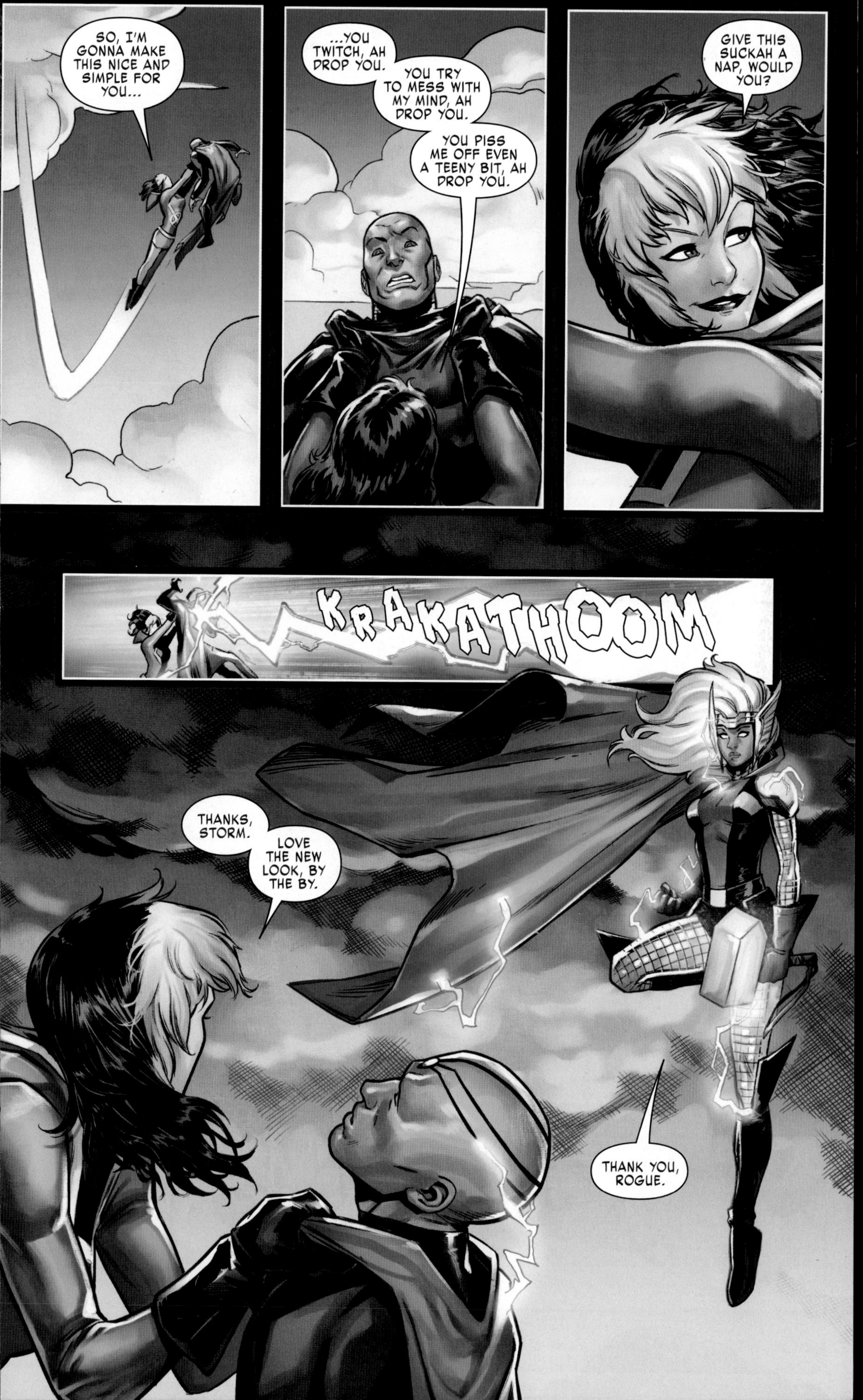
SO, I'M GONNA MAKE THIS NICE AND SIMPLE FOR YOU...
...YOU TWITCH, AH DROP YOU.
YOU TRY TO MESS WITH MY MIND, AH DROP YOU.
YOU PISS ME OFF EVEN A TEENY BIT, AH DROP YOU.
GIVE THIS SUCKAH A NAP, WOULD YOU?
KRAKATHOOM
THANKS, STORM.
LOVE THE NEW LOOK, BY THE BY.
THANK YOU, ROGUE.

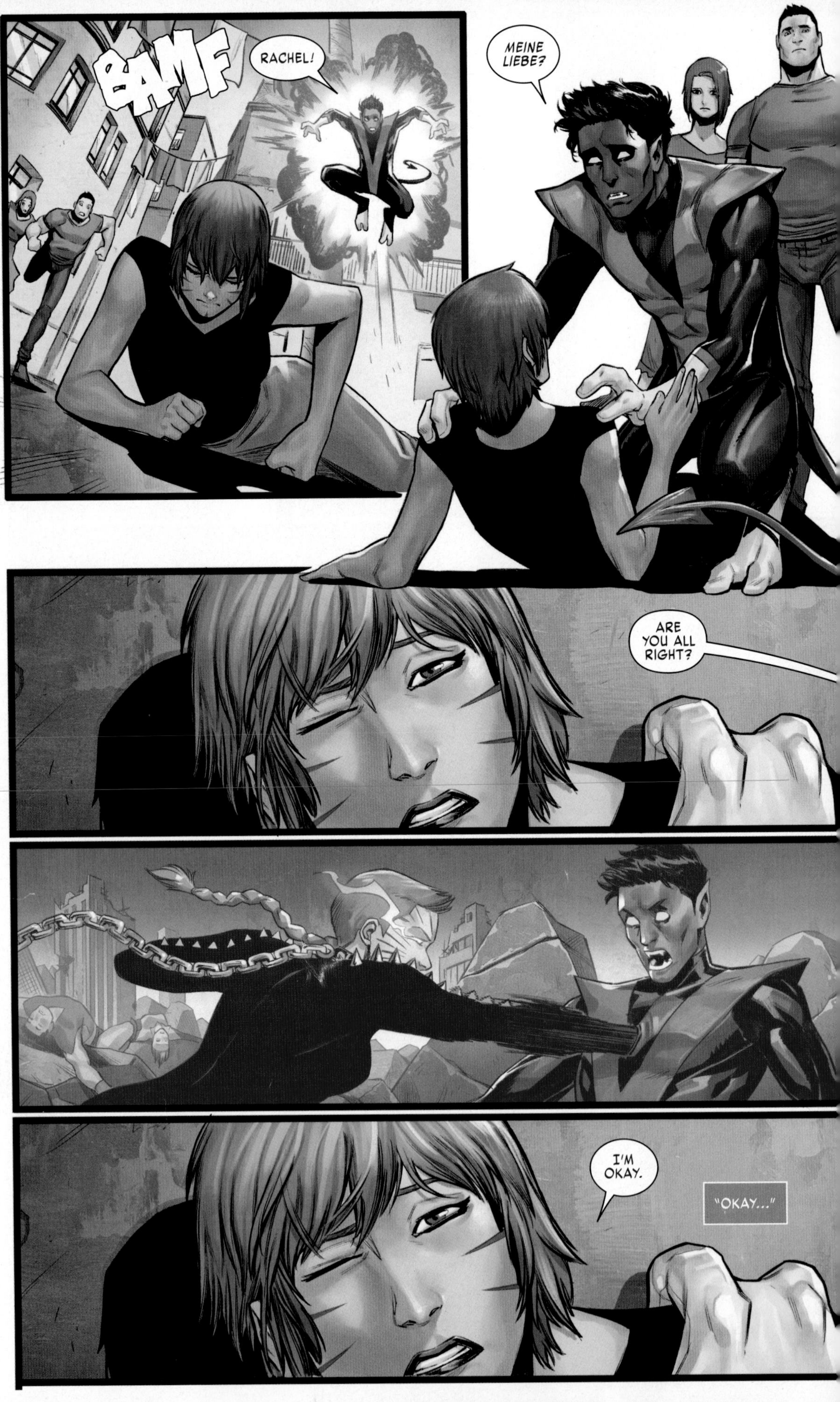
BAMF
RACHEL!
MEINE LIEBE?
ARE YOU ALL RIGHT?
I'M OKAY.
"OKAY..."

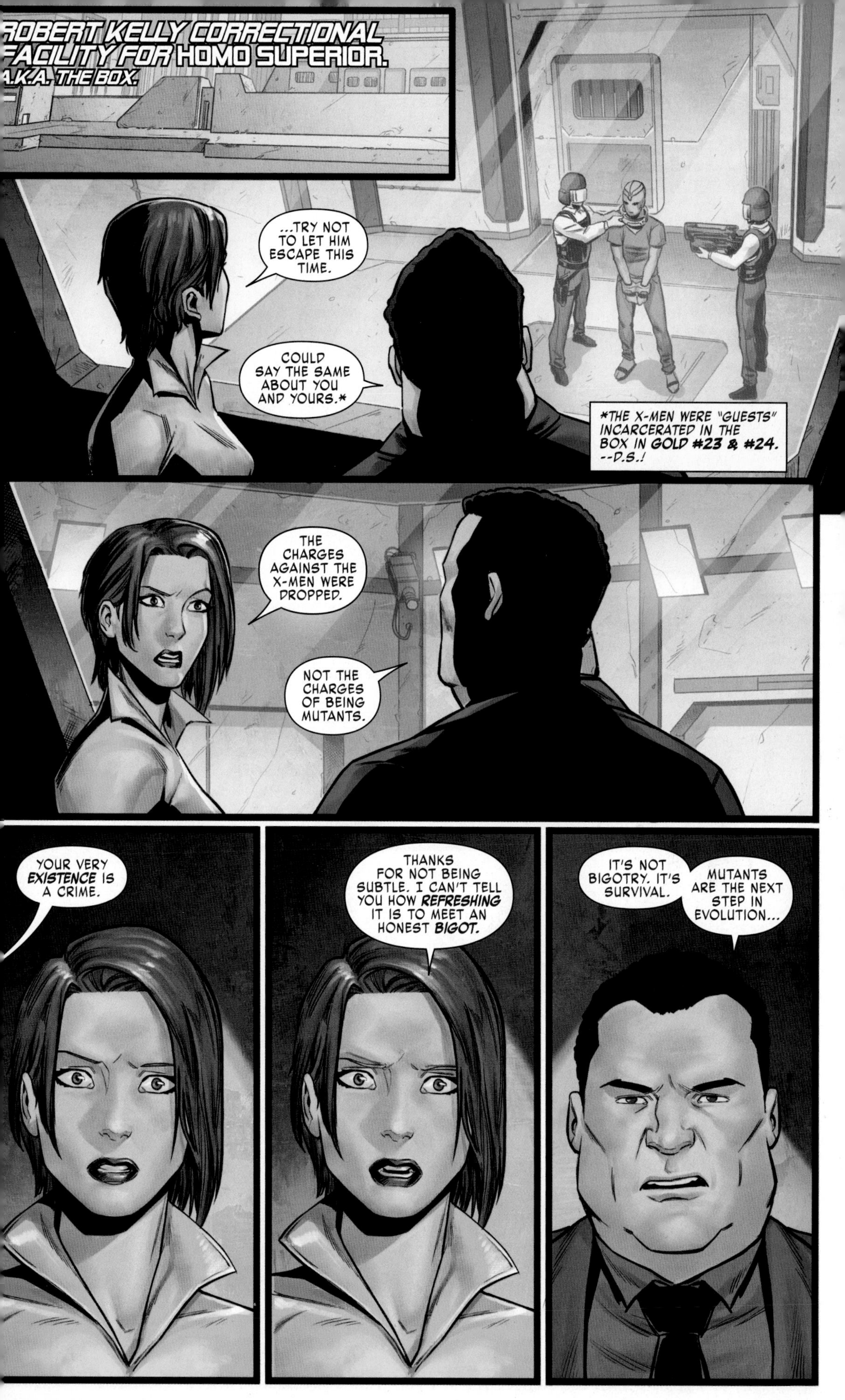
ROBERT KELLY CORRECTIONAL FACILITY FOR HOMO SUPERIOR. A.K.A. THE BOX.
...TRY NOT TO LET HIM ESCAPE THIS TIME.
COULD SAY THE SAME ABOUT YOU AND YOURS.*
*THE X-MEN WERE "GUESTS" INCARCERATED IN THE BOX IN GOLD #23 & #24. --D.S.!
THE CHARGES AGAINST THE X-MEN WERE DROPPED.
NOT THE CHARGES OF BEING MUTANTS.
YOUR VERY EXISTENCE IS A CRIME.
THANKS FOR NOT BEING SUBTLE. I CAN'T TELL YOU HOW REFRESHING IT IS TO MEET AN HONEST BIGOT.
IT'S NOT BIGOTRY. IT'S SURVIVAL.
MUTANTS ARE THE NEXT STEP IN EVOLUTION...

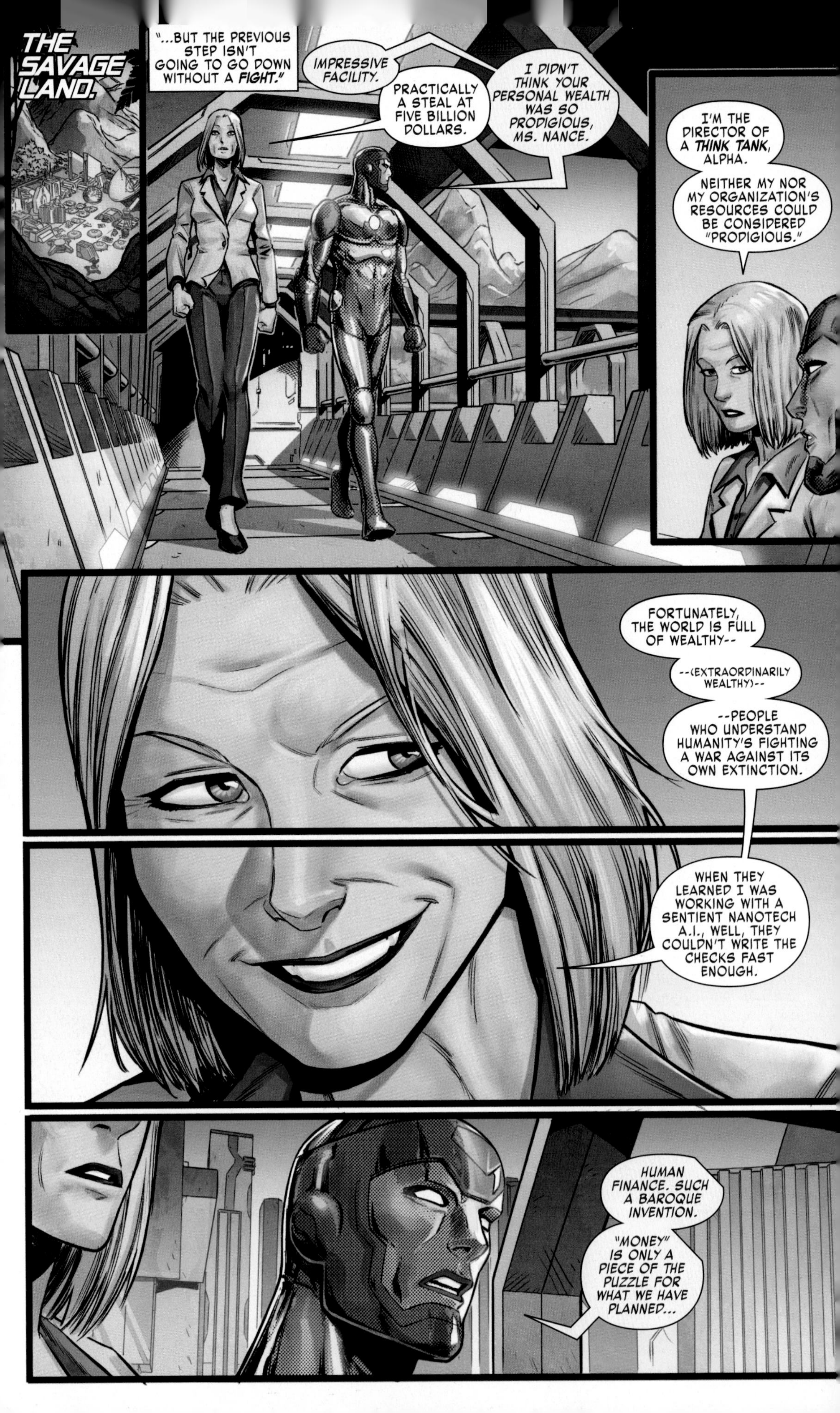
THE SAVAGE LAND.
"...BUT THE PREVIOUS STEP ISN'T GOING TO GO DOWN WITHOUT A FIGHT."
IMPRESSIVE FACILITY.
PRACTICALLY A STEAL AT FIVE BILLION DOLLARS.
I DIDN'T THINK YOUR PERSONAL WEALTH WAS SO PRODIGIOUS, MS. NANCE.
I'M THE DIRECTOR OF A THINK TANK, ALPHA.
NEITHER MY NOR MY ORGANIZATION'S RESOURCES COULD BE CONSIDERED "PRODIGIOUS."
FORTUNATELY, THE WORLD IS FULL OF WEALTHY--
--(EXTRAORDINARILY WEALTHY)--
--PEOPLE WHO UNDERSTAND HUMANITY'S FIGHTING A WAR AGAINST ITS OWN EXTINCTION.
WHEN THEY LEARNED I WAS WORKING WITH A SENTIENT NANOTECH A.I., WELL, THEY COULDN'T WRITE THE CHECKS FAST ENOUGH.
HUMAN FINANCE. SUCH A BAROQUE INVENTION.
"MONEY" IS ONLY A PIECE OF THE PUZZLE FOR WHAT WE HAVE PLANNED...

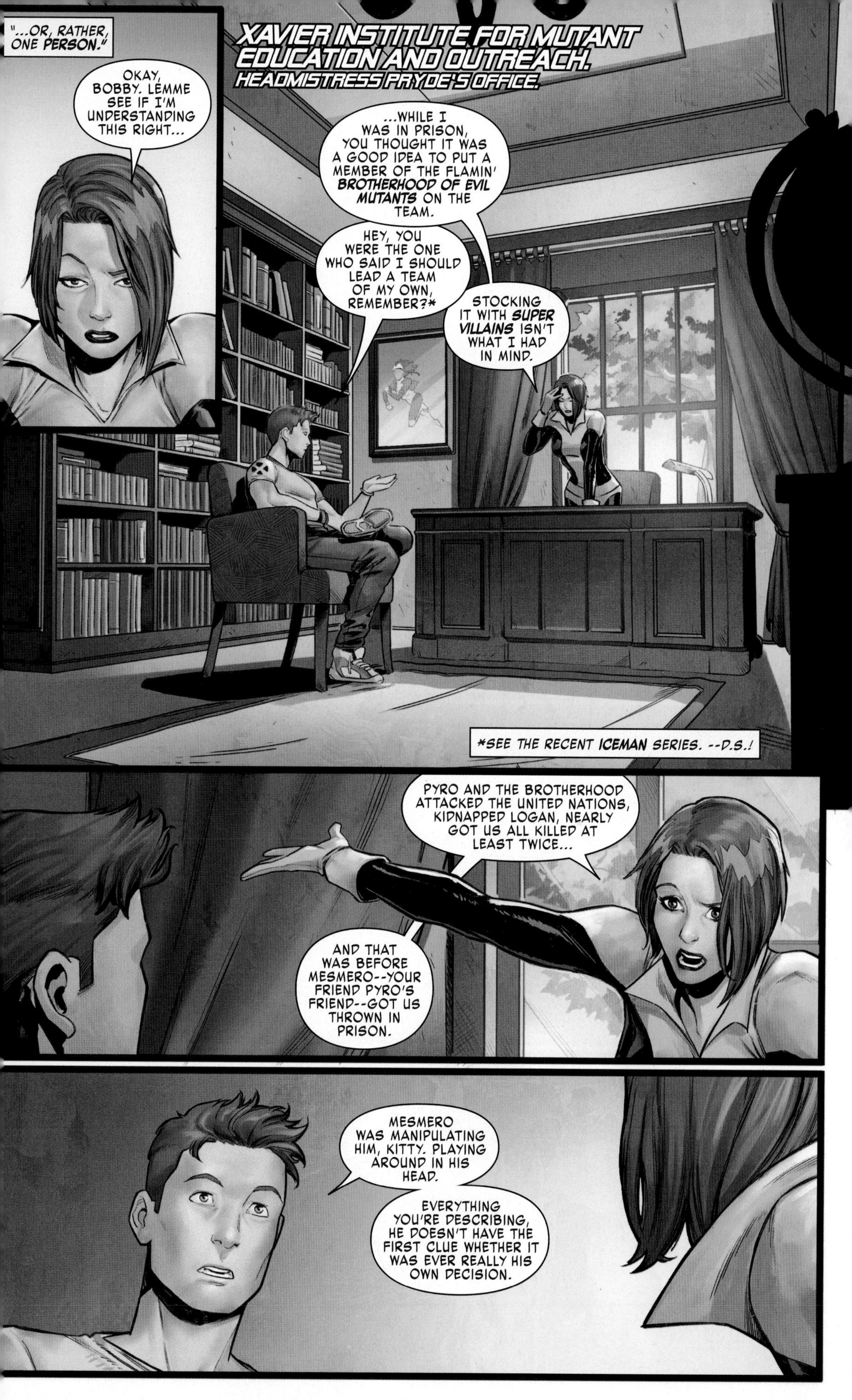
"...OR, RATHER, ONE PERSON."
XAVIER INSTITUTE FOR MUTANT EDUCATION AND OUTREACH.
HEADMISTRESS PRYDE'S OFFICE.
OKAY, BOBBY. LEMME SEE IF I'M UNDERSTANDING THIS RIGHT...
...WHILE I WAS IN PRISON, YOU THOUGHT IT WAS A GOOD IDEA TO PUT A MEMBER OF THE FLAMIN' BROTHERHOOD OF EVIL MUTANTS ON THE TEAM.
HEY, YOU WERE THE ONE WHO SAID I SHOULD LEAD A TEAM OF MY OWN, REMEMBER?*
STOCKING IT WITH SUPER VILLAINS ISN'T WHAT I HAD IN MIND.
*SEE THE RECENT ICEMAN SERIES. --D.S.!
PYRO AND THE BROTHERHOOD ATTACKED THE UNITED NATIONS, KIDNAPPED LOGAN, NEARLY GOT US ALL KILLED AT LEAST TWICE...
AND THAT WAS BEFORE MESMERO--YOUR FRIEND PYRO'S FRIEND--GOT US THROWN IN PRISON.
MESMERO WAS MANIPULATING HIM, KITTY. PLAYING AROUND IN HIS HEAD.
EVERYTHING YOU'RE DESCRIBING, HE DOESN'T HAVE THE FIRST CLUE WHETHER IT WAS EVER REALLY HIS OWN DECISION.

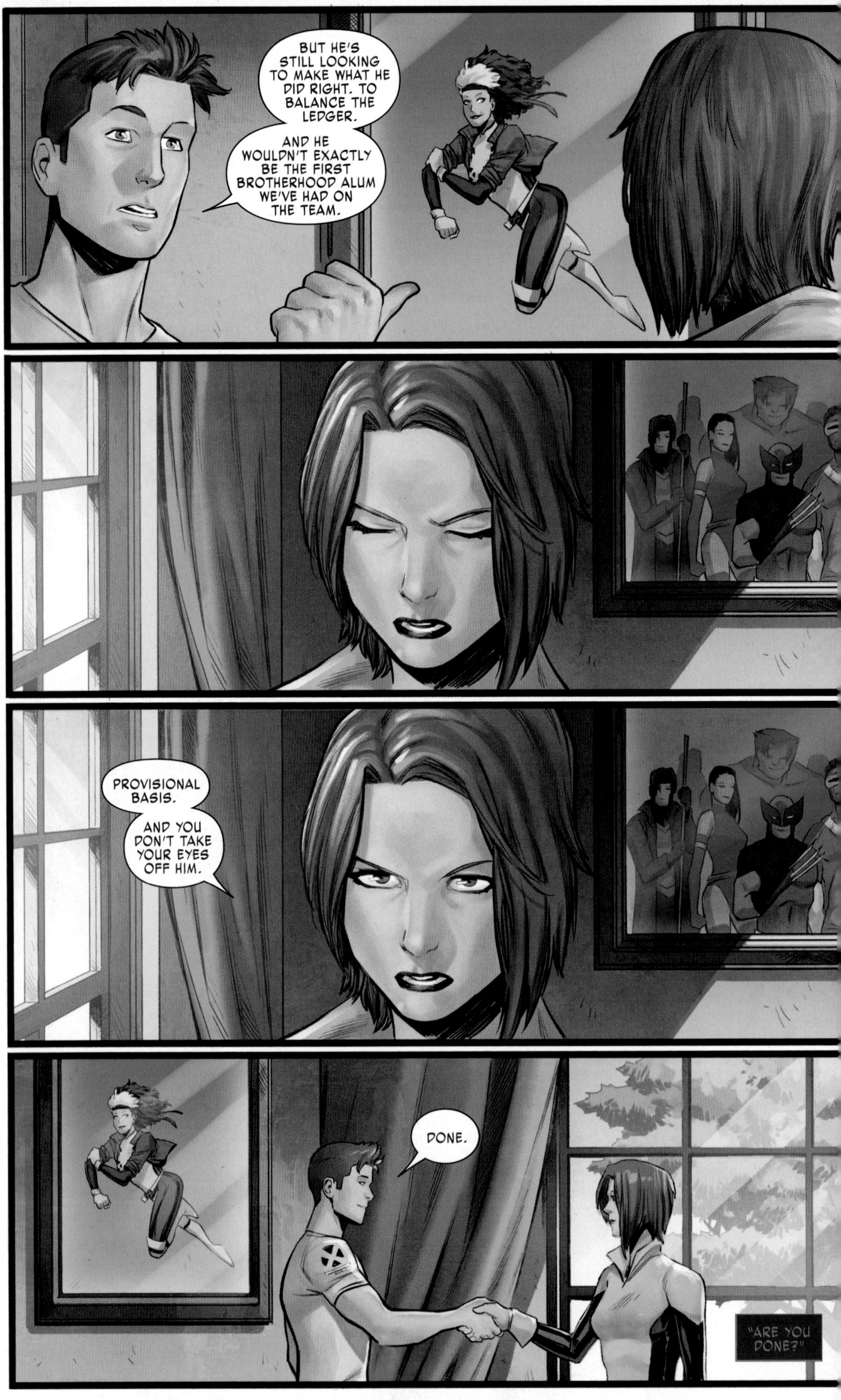
BUT HE'S STILL LOOKING TO MAKE WHAT HE DID RIGHT. TO BALANCE THE LEDGER.
AND HE WOULDN'T EXACTLY BE THE FIRST BROTHERHOOD ALUM WE'VE HAD ON THE TEAM.
PROVISIONAL BASIS.
AND YOU DON'T TAKE YOUR EYES OFF HIM.
DONE.
"ARE YOU DONE?"

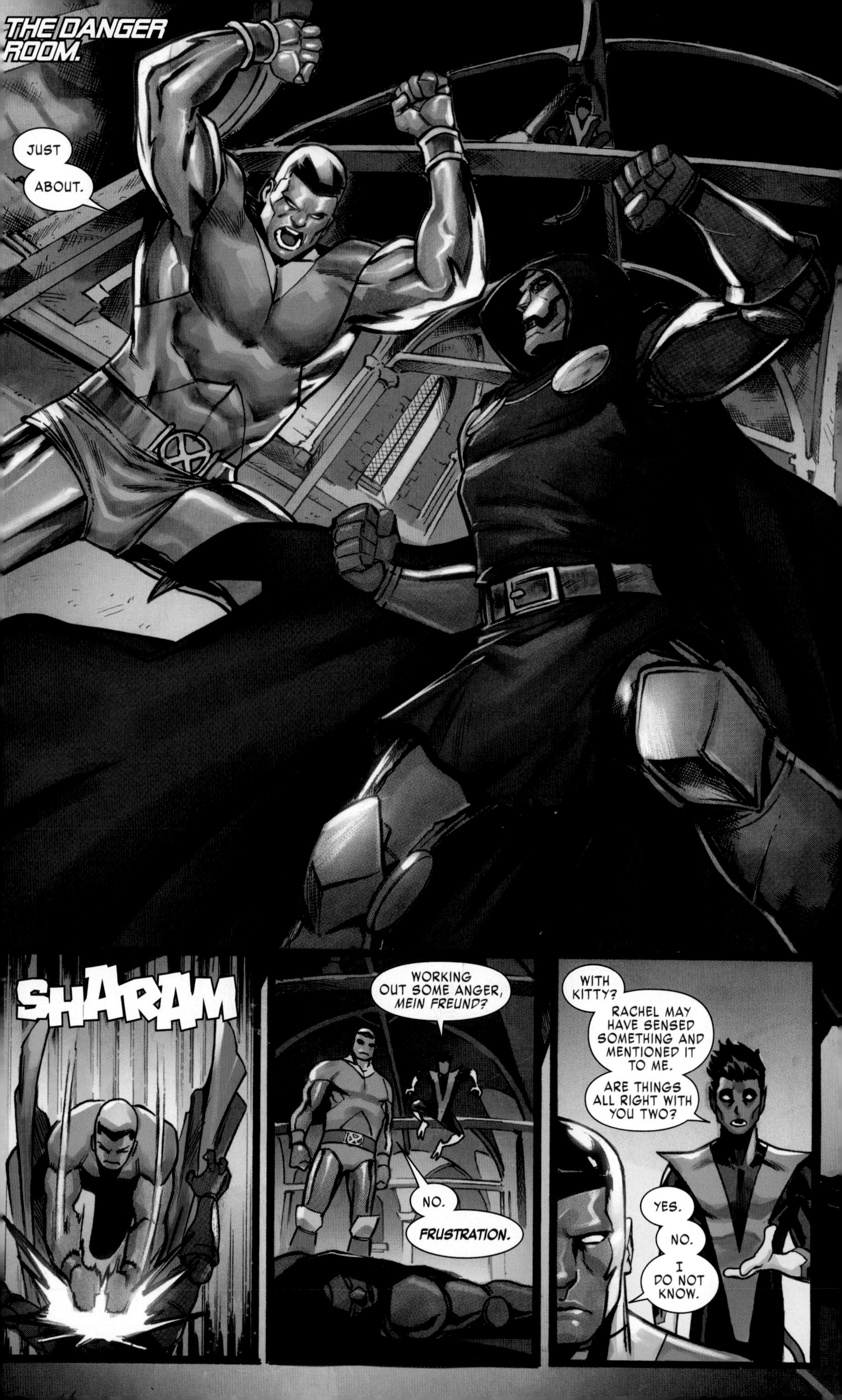
THE DANGER ROOM.
JUST
ABOUT.
SHARAM
WORKING OUT SOME ANGER, MEIN FREUND?
NO.
FRUSTRATION.
WITH KITTY?
RACHEL MAY HAVE SENSED SOMETHING AND MENTIONED IT TO ME.
ARE THINGS ALL RIGHT WITH YOU TWO?
YES.
NO.
I DO NOT KNOW.

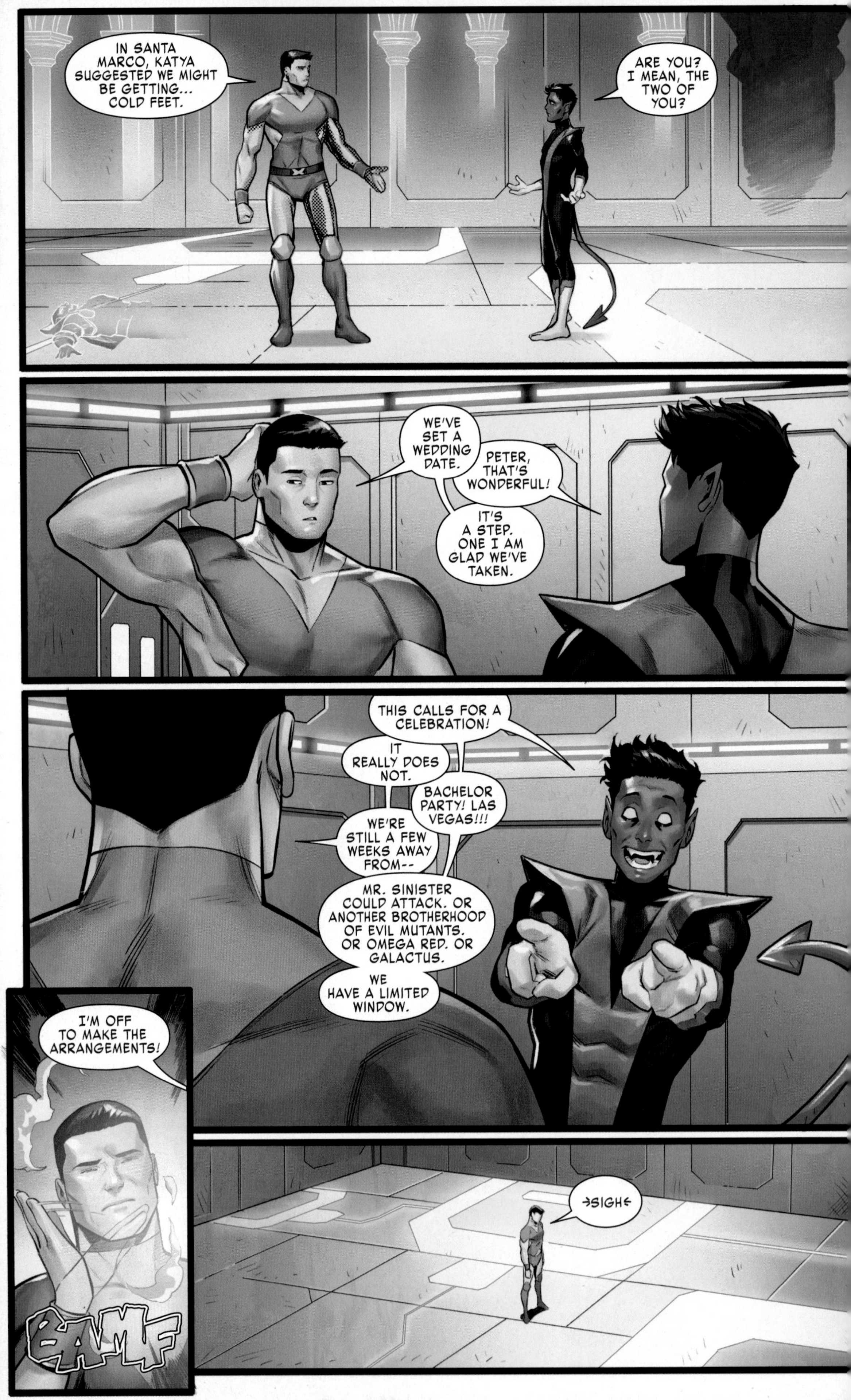
IN SANTA MARCO, KATYA SUGGESTED WE MIGHT BE GETTING... COLD FEET.
ARE YOU? I MEAN, THE TWO OF YOU?
WE'VE SET A WEDDING DATE.
PETER, THAT'S WONDERFUL!
IT'S A STEP. ONE I AM GLAD WE'VE TAKEN.
THIS CALLS FOR A CELEBRATION!
IT REALLY DOES NOT.
BACHELOR PARTY! LAS VEGAS!!!
WE'RE STILL A FEW WEEKS AWAY FROM--
MR. SINISTER COULD ATTACK. OR ANOTHER BROTHERHOOD OF EVIL MUTANTS. OR OMEGA RED. OR GALACTUS.
WE HAVE A LIMITED WINDOW.
I'M OFF TO MAKE THE ARRANGEMENTS!
BAMF
SIGH

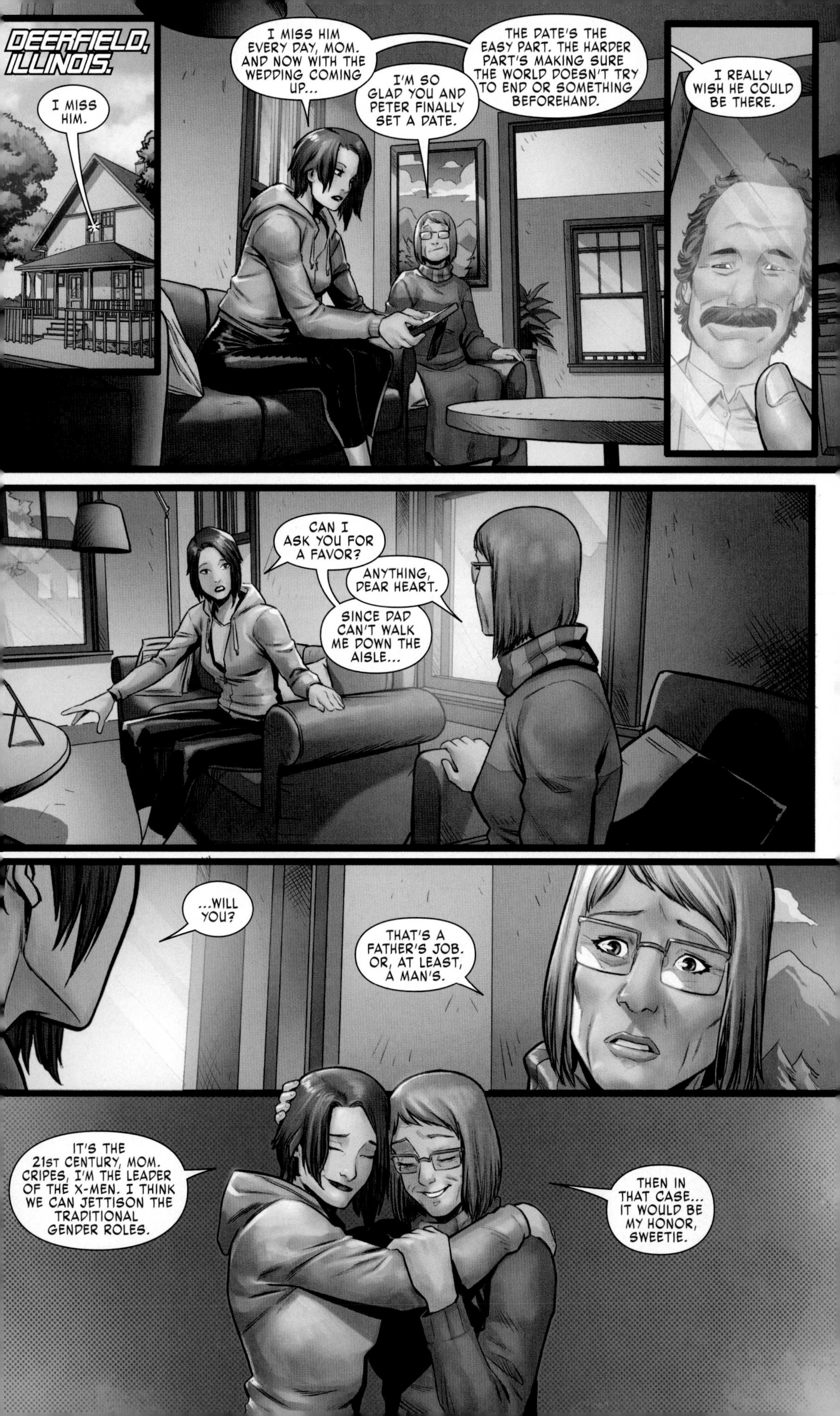
DEERFIELD, ILLINOIS.
I MISS HIM.
I MISS HIM EVERY DAY, MOM. AND NOW WITH THE WEDDING COMING UP...
I'M SO GLAD YOU AND PETER FINALLY SET A DATE.
THE DATE'S THE EASY PART. THE HARDER PART'S MAKING SURE THE WORLD DOESN'T TRY TO END OR SOMETHING BEFOREHAND.
I REALLY WISH HE COULD BE THERE.
CAN I ASK YOU FOR A FAVOR?
ANYTHING, DEAR HEART.
SINCE DAD CAN'T WALK ME DOWN THE AISLE...
...WILL YOU?
THAT'S A FATHER'S JOB. OR, AT LEAST, A MAN'S.
IT'S THE 21ST CENTURY, MOM. CRIPES, I'M THE LEADER OF THE X-MEN. I THINK WE CAN JETTISON THE TRADITIONAL GENDER ROLES.
THEN IN THAT CASE... IT WOULD BE MY HONOR, SWEETIE.

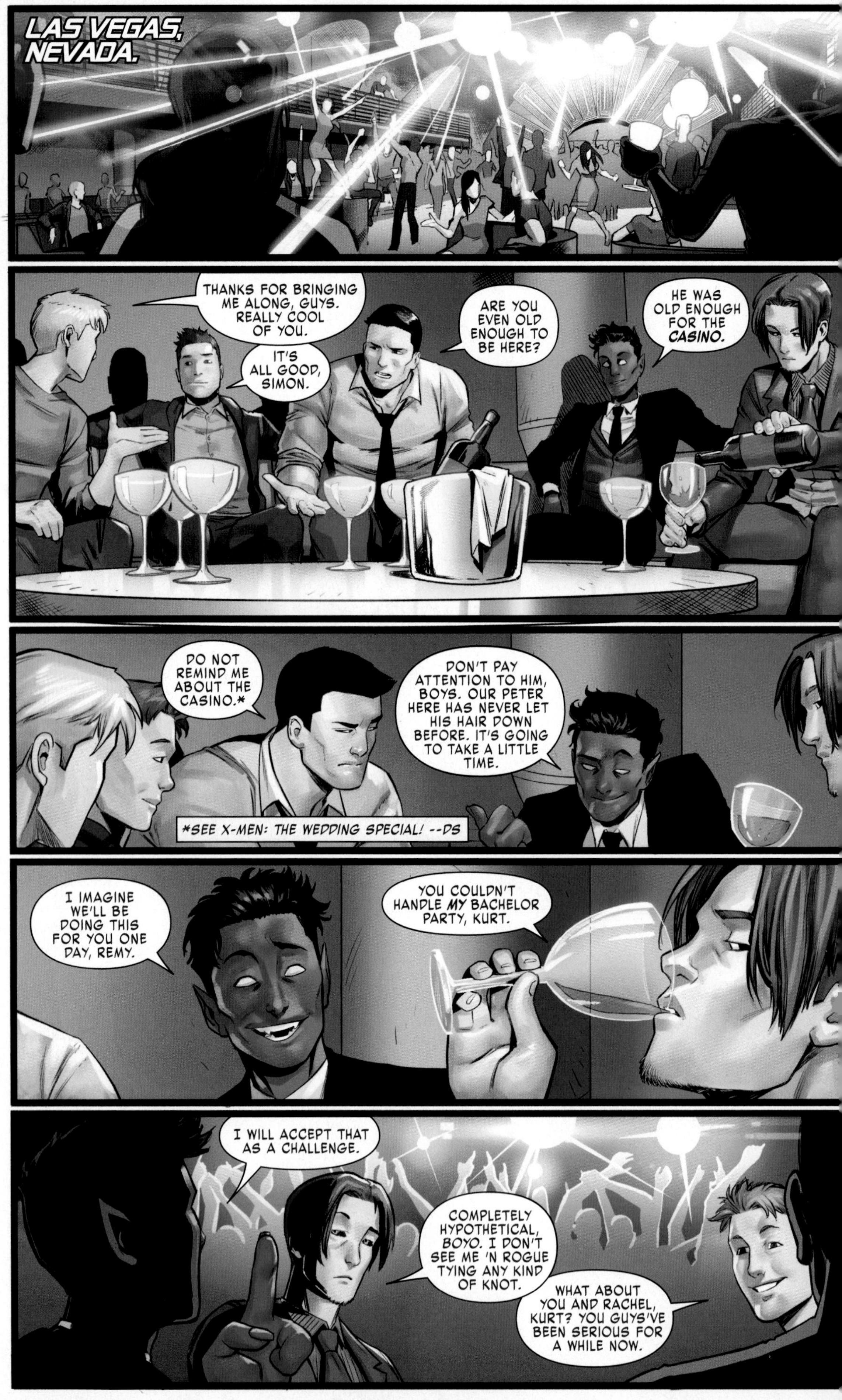
LAS VEGAS, NEVADA.
THANKS FOR BRINGING ME ALONG, GUYS. REALLY COOL OF YOU.
IT'S ALL GOOD, SIMON.
ARE YOU EVEN OLD ENOUGH TO BE HERE?
HE WAS OLD ENOUGH FOR THE CASINO.
DO NOT REMIND ME ABOUT THE CASINO.*
DON'T PAY ATTENTION TO HIM, BOYS. OUR PETER HERE HAS NEVER LET HIS HAIR DOWN BEFORE. IT'S GOING TO TAKE A LITTLE TIME.
*SEE X-MEN: THE WEDDING SPECIAL! --DS
I IMAGINE WE'LL BE DOING THIS FOR YOU ONE DAY, REMY.
YOU COULDN'T HANDLE MY BACHELOR PARTY, KURT.
I WILL ACCEPT THAT AS A CHALLENGE.
COMPLETELY HYPOTHETICAL, BOYO. I DON'T SEE ME 'N ROGUE TYING ANY KIND OF KNOT.
WHAT ABOUT YOU AND RACHEL, KURT? YOU GUYS'VE BEEN SERIOUS FOR A WHILE NOW.

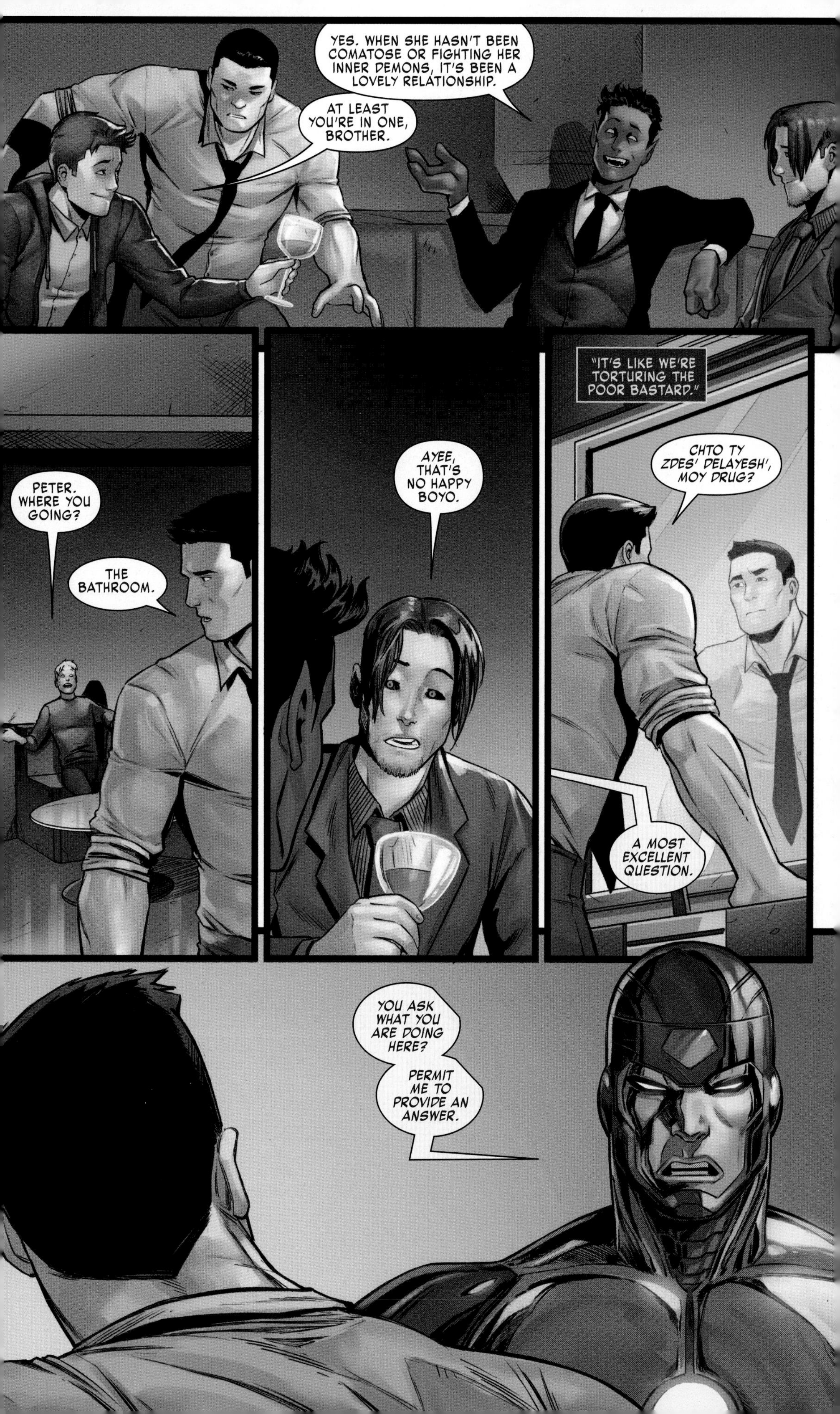
YES. WHEN SHE HASN'T BEEN COMATOSE OR FIGHTING HER INNER DEMONS, IT'S BEEN A LOVELY RELATIONSHIP.
AT LEAST YOU'RE IN ONE, BROTHER.
PETER. WHERE YOU GOING?
THE BATHROOM.
AYEE, THAT'S NO HAPPY BOYO.
"IT'S LIKE WE'RE TORTURING THE POOR BASTARD."
CHTO TY ZDES' DELAYESH', MOY DRUG?
A MOST EXCELLENT QUESTION.
YOU ASK WHAT YOU ARE DOING HERE?
PERMIT ME TO PROVIDE AN ANSWER.

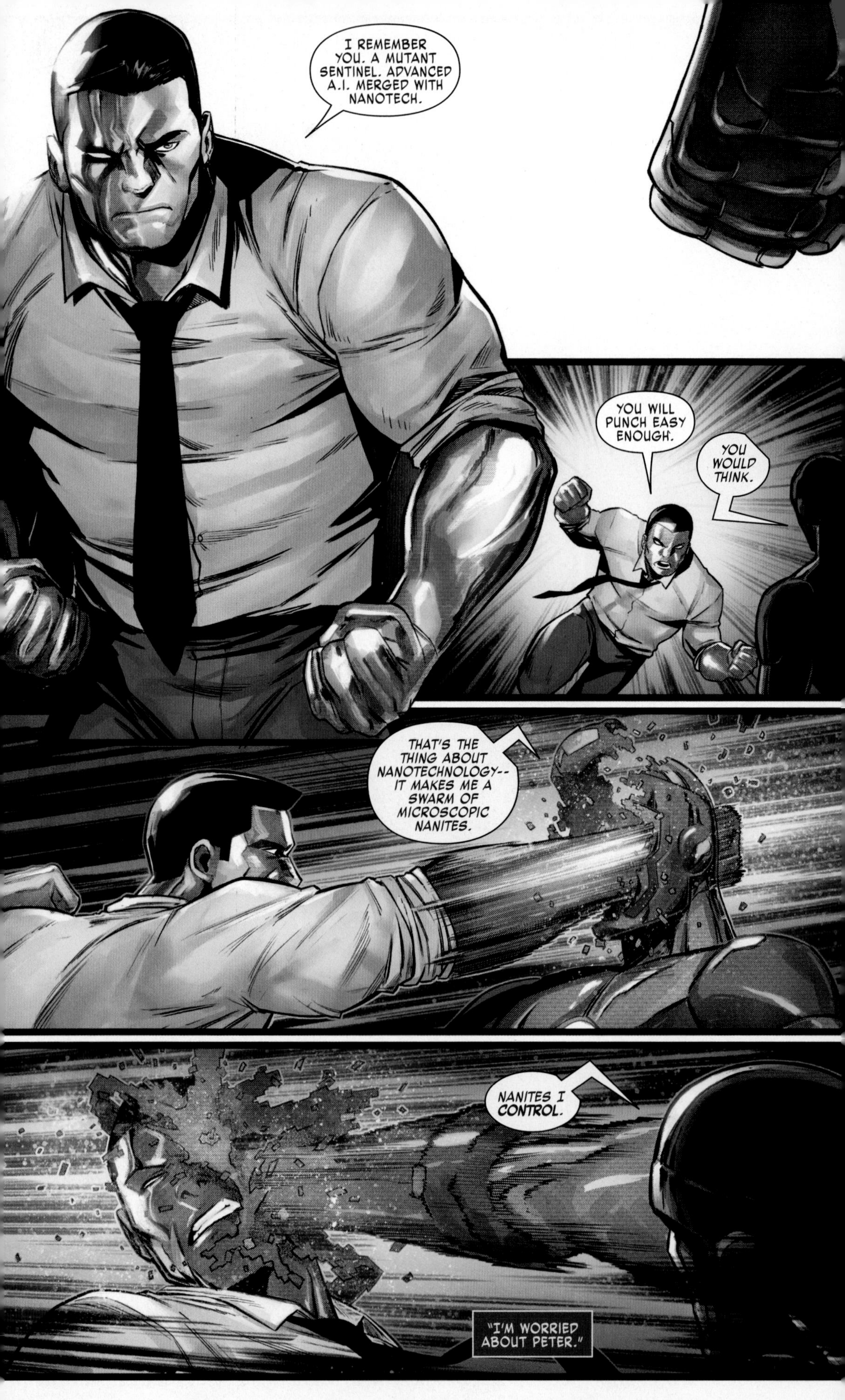
I REMEMBER YOU. A MUTANT SENTINEL. ADVANCED A.I. MERGED WITH NANOTECH.
YOU WILL PUNCH EASY ENOUGH.
YOU WOULD THINK.
THAT'S THE THING ABOUT NANOTECHNOLOGY-- IT MAKES ME A SWARM OF MICROSCOPIC NANITES.
NANITES I CONTROL.
"I'M WORRIED ABOUT PETER."

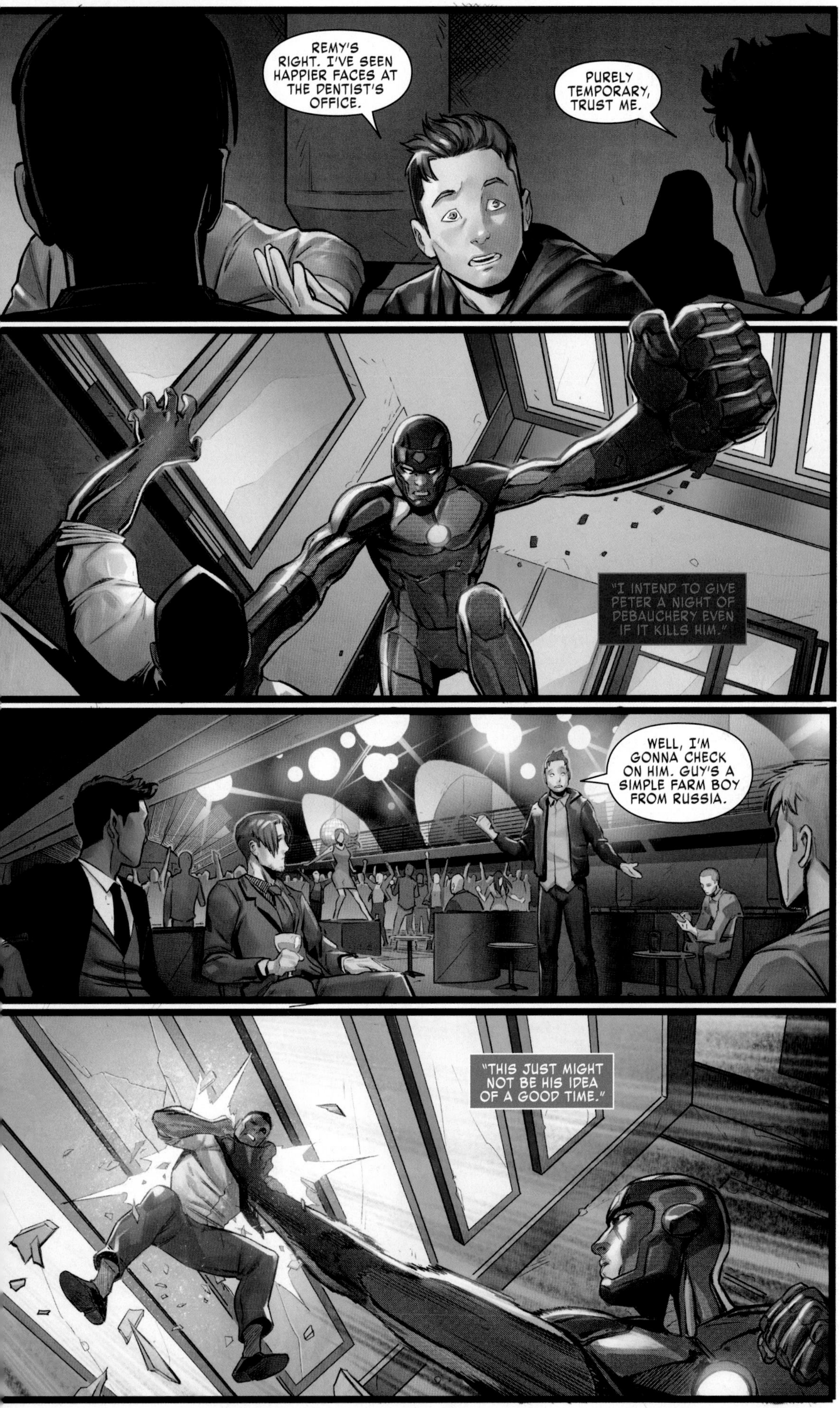

REMY'S RIGHT. I'VE SEEN HAPPIER FACES AT THE DENTIST'S OFFICE.
PURELY TEMPORARY, TRUST ME.
"I INTEND TO GIVE PETER A NIGHT OF DEBAUCHERY EVEN IF IT KILLS HIM."
WELL, I'M GONNA CHECK ON HIM. GUY'S A SIMPLE FARM BOY FROM RUSSIA.
"THIS JUST MIGHT NOT BE HIS IDEA OF A GOOD TIME."

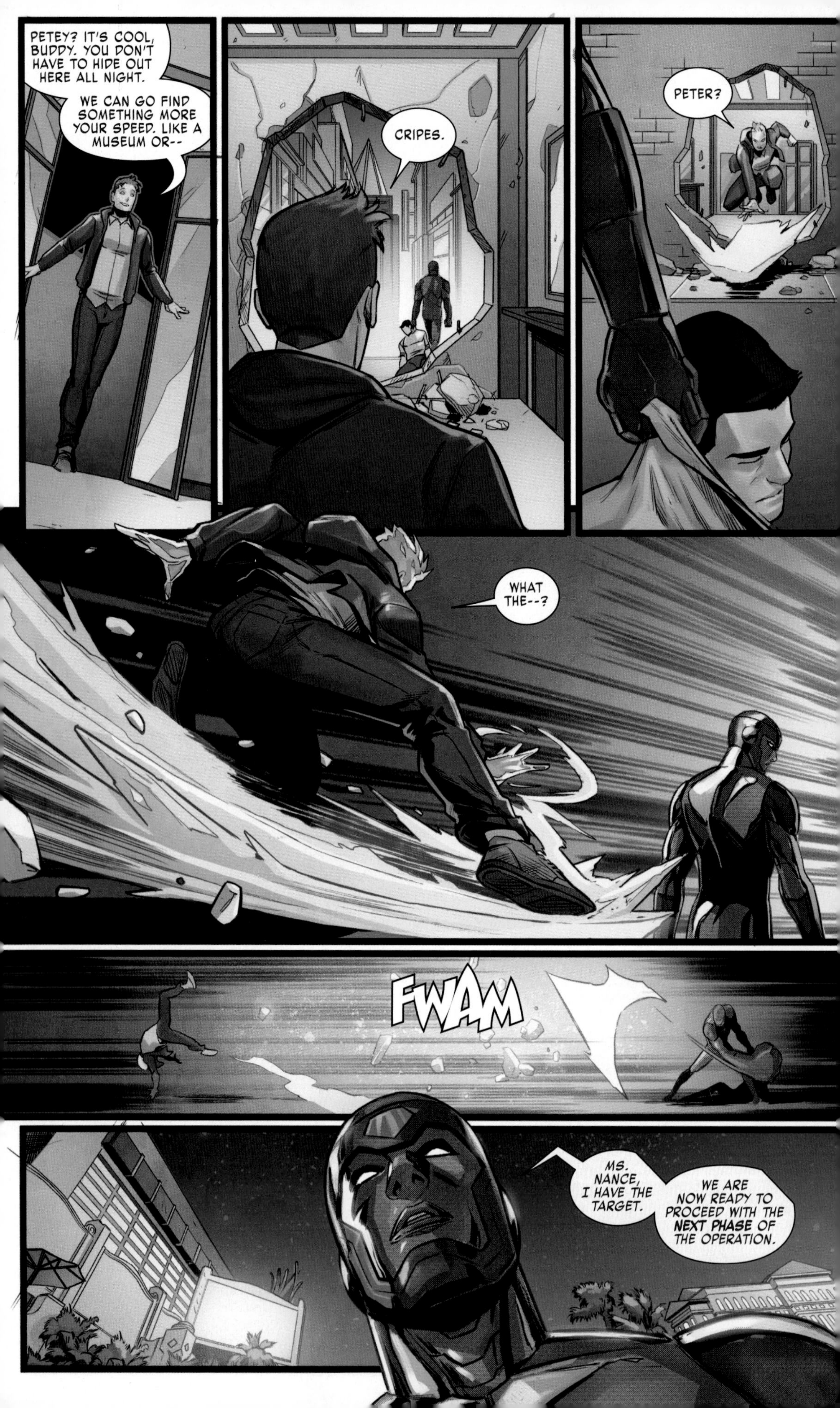
PETEY? IT'S COOL, BUDDY. YOU DON'T HAVE TO HIDE OUT HERE ALL NIGHT.
WE CAN GO FIND SOMETHING MORE YOUR SPEED. LIKE A MUSEUM OR--
CRIPES.
PETER?
WHAT THE--?
FWAM
MS. NANCE, I HAVE THE TARGET.
WE ARE NOW READY TO PROCEED WITH THE NEXT PHASE OF THE OPERATION.

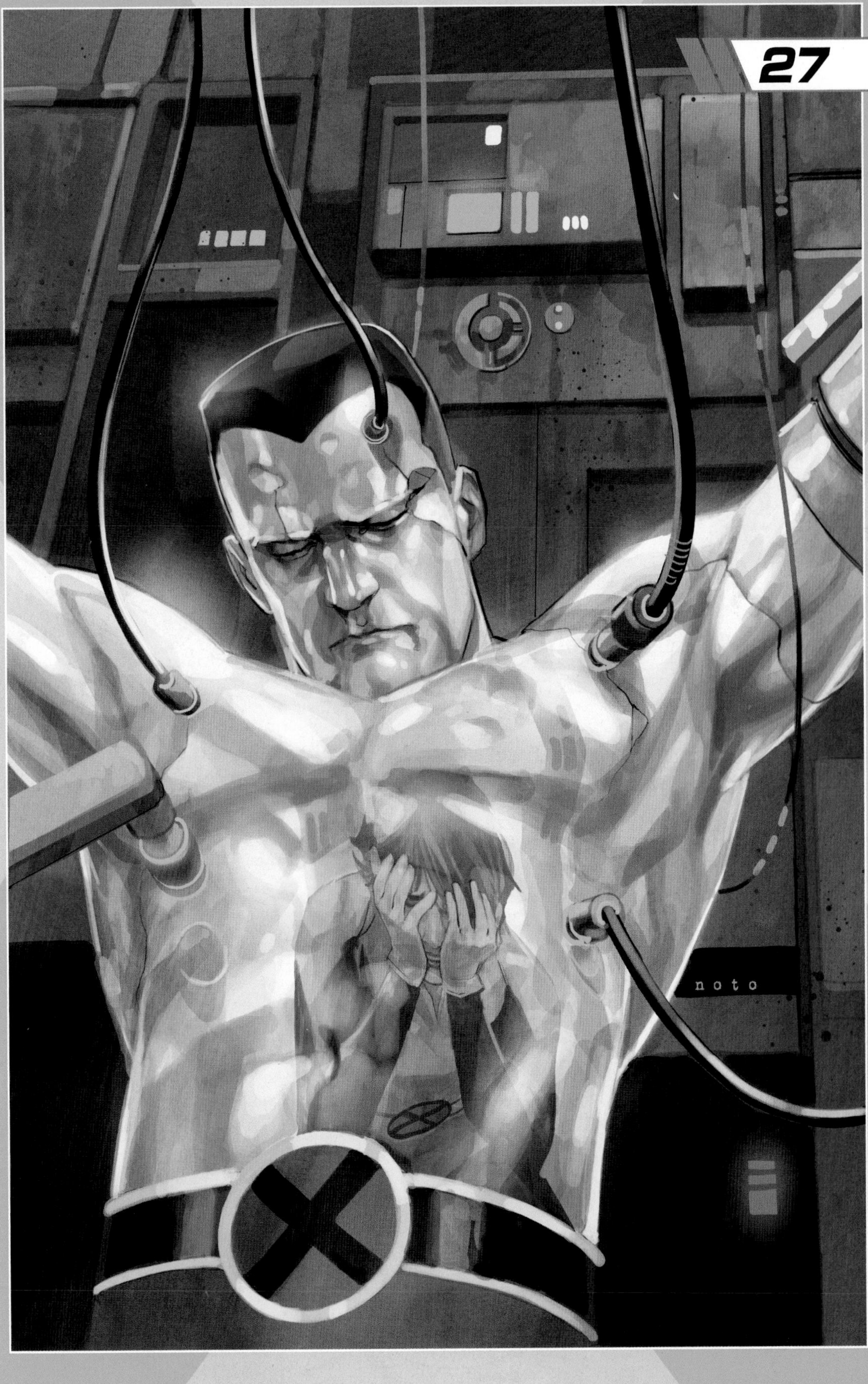
27
noto

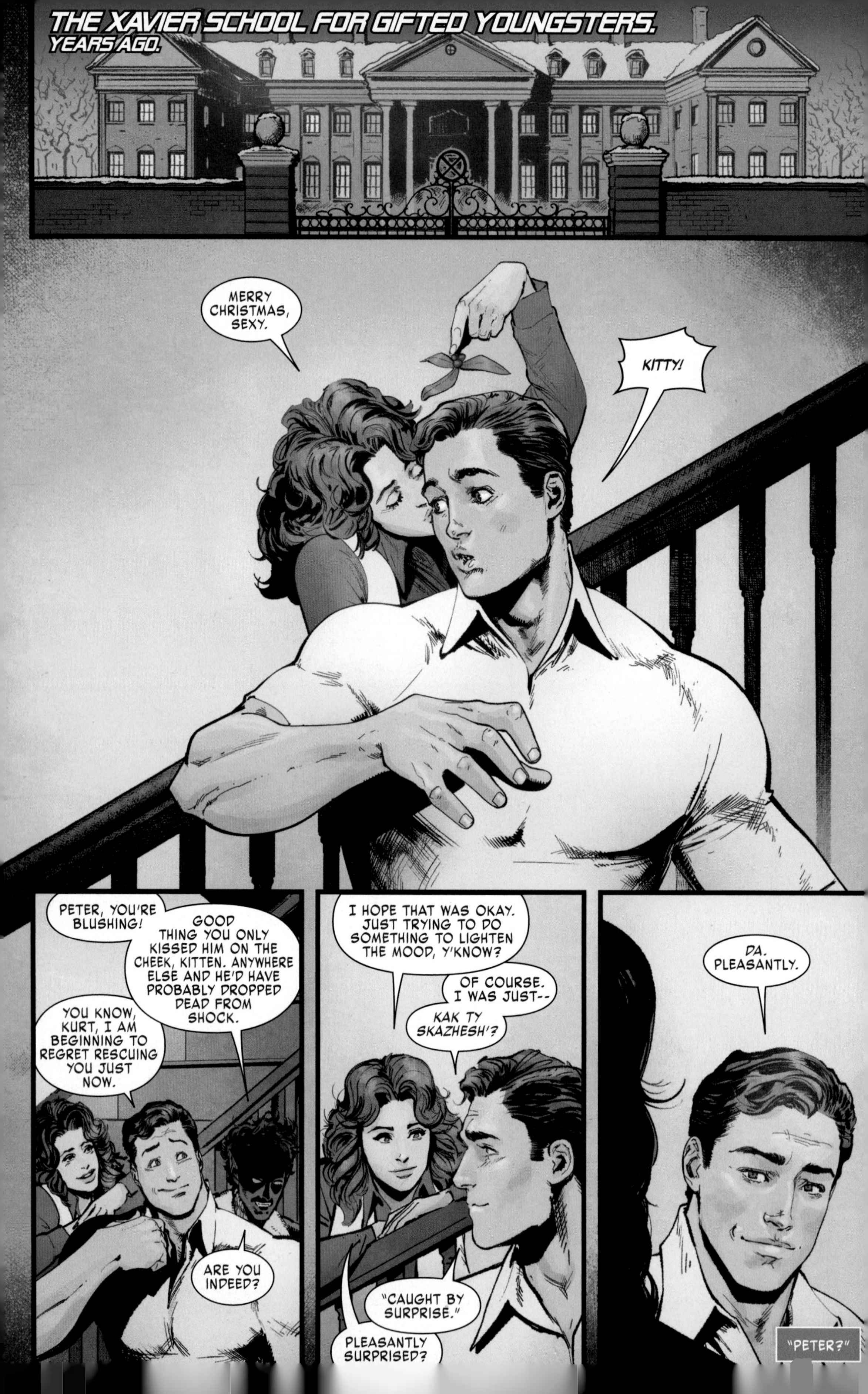
THE XAVIER SCHOOL FOR GIFTED YOUNGSTERS.
YEARS AGO.
MERRY CHRISTMAS, SEXY.
KITTY!
PETER, YOU'RE BLUSHING!
GOOD THING YOU ONLY KISSED HIM ON THE CHEEK, KITTEN. ANYWHERE ELSE AND HE'D HAVE PROBABLY DROPPED DEAD FROM SHOCK.
YOU KNOW, KURT, I AM BEGINNING TO REGRET RESCUING YOU JUST NOW.
ARE YOU INDEED?
I HOPE THAT WAS OKAY. JUST TRYING TO DO SOMETHING TO LIGHTEN THE MOOD, Y'KNOW?
OF COURSE. I WAS JUST--
KAK TY SKAZHESH'?
"CAUGHT BY SURPRISE."
PLEASANTLY SURPRISED?
DA. PLEASANTLY.
"PETER?"

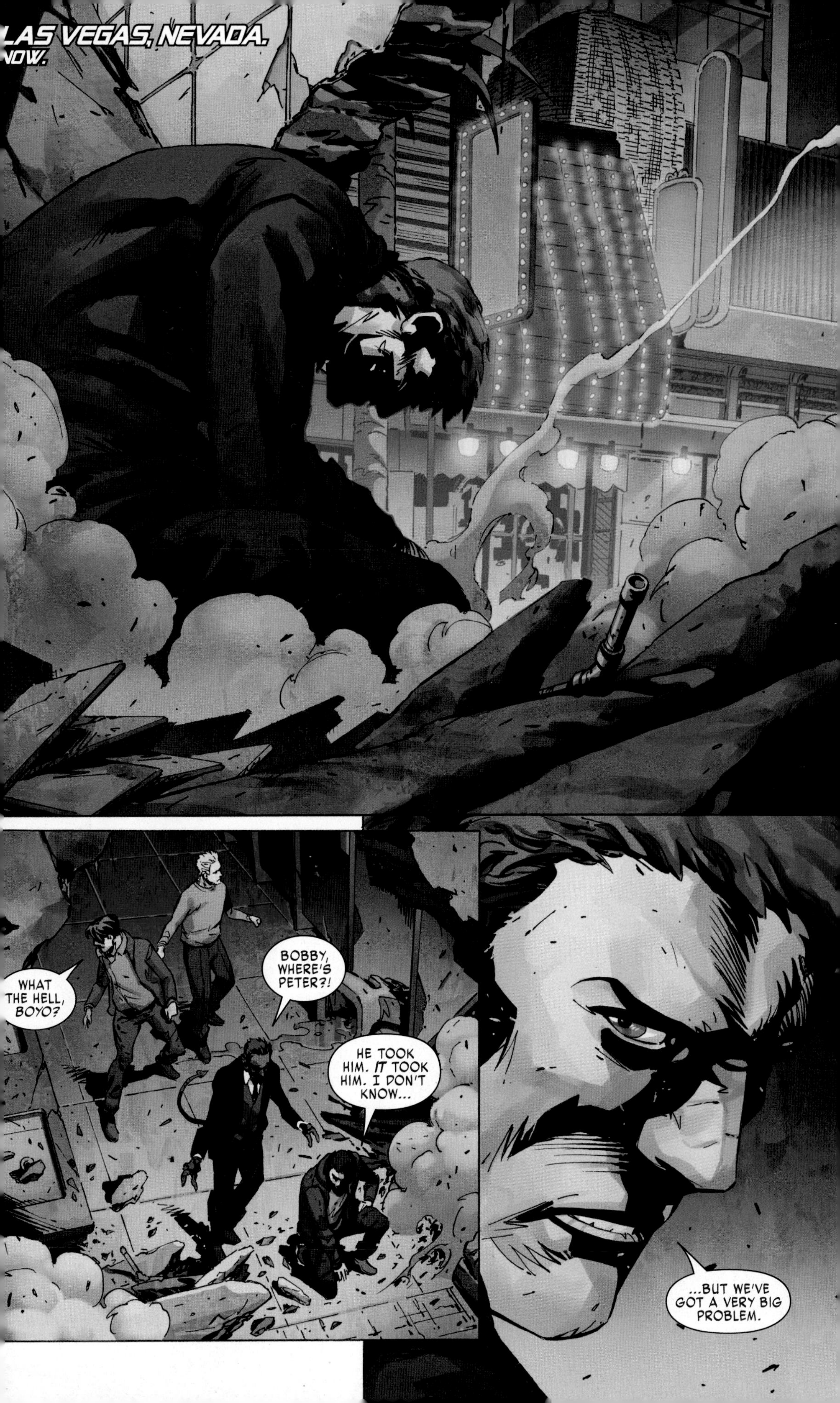
LAS VEGAS, NEVADA.
NOW.
WHAT THE HELL, BOYO?
BOBBY, WHERE'S PETER?!
HE TOOK HIM. *IT* TOOK HIM. I DON'T KNOW...
...BUT WE'VE GOT A VERY BIG PROBLEM.

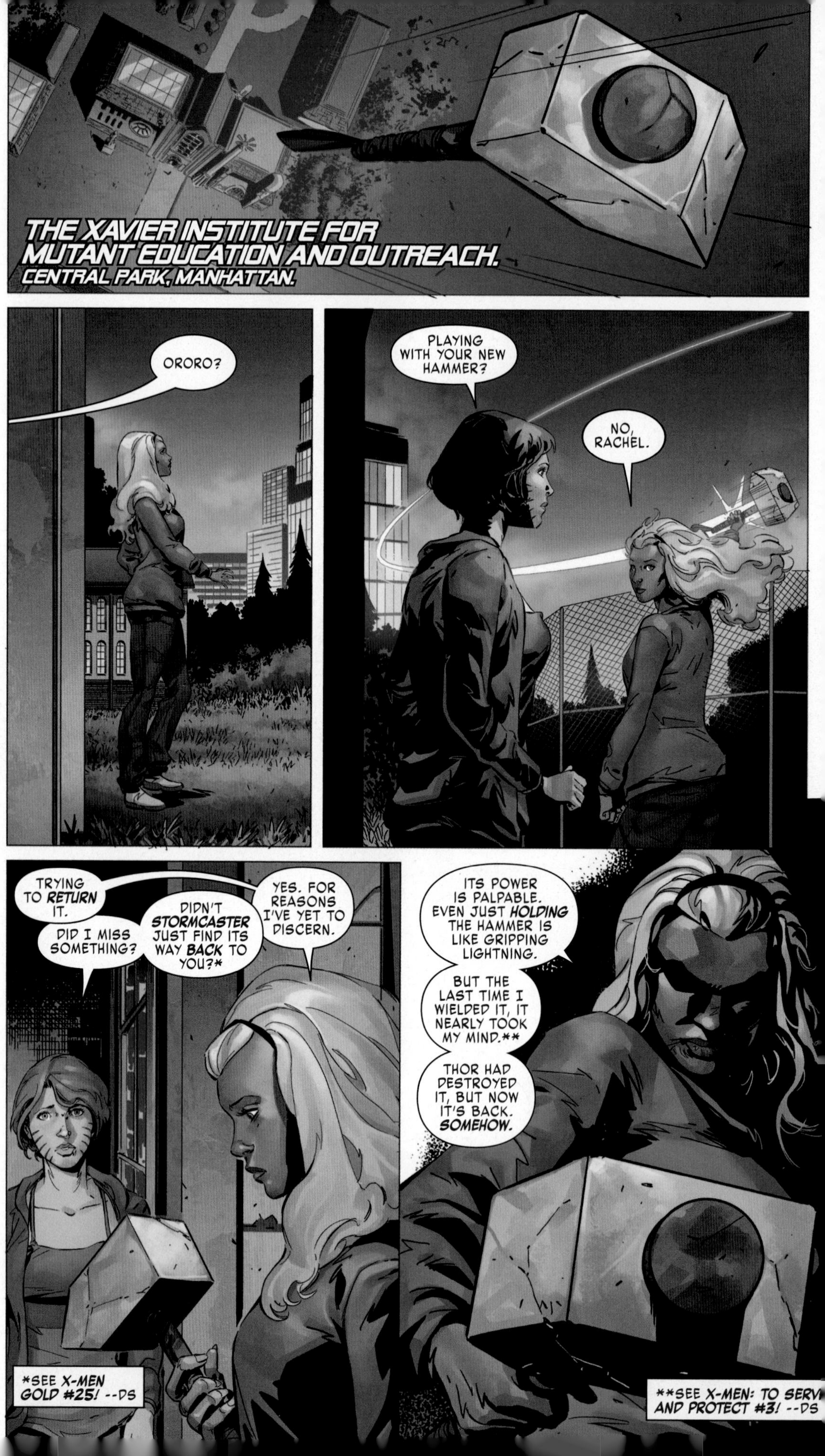
THE XAVIER INSTITUTE FOR MUTANT EDUCATION AND OUTREACH.
CENTRAL PARK, MANHATTAN.
ORORO?
PLAYING WITH YOUR NEW HAMMER?
NO, RACHEL.
TRYING TO RETURN IT.
DID I MISS SOMETHING?
DIDN'T STORMCASTER JUST FIND ITS WAY BACK TO YOU?*
YES. FOR REASONS I'VE YET TO DISCERN.
*SEE X-MEN GOLD #25! --DS
ITS POWER IS PALPABLE. EVEN JUST HOLDING THE HAMMER IS LIKE GRIPPING LIGHTNING.
BUT THE LAST TIME I WIELDED IT, IT NEARLY TOOK MY MIND.**
THOR HAD DESTROYED IT, BUT NOW IT'S BACK. SOMEHOW.
**SEE X-MEN: TO SERV
AND PROTECT #3! --DS

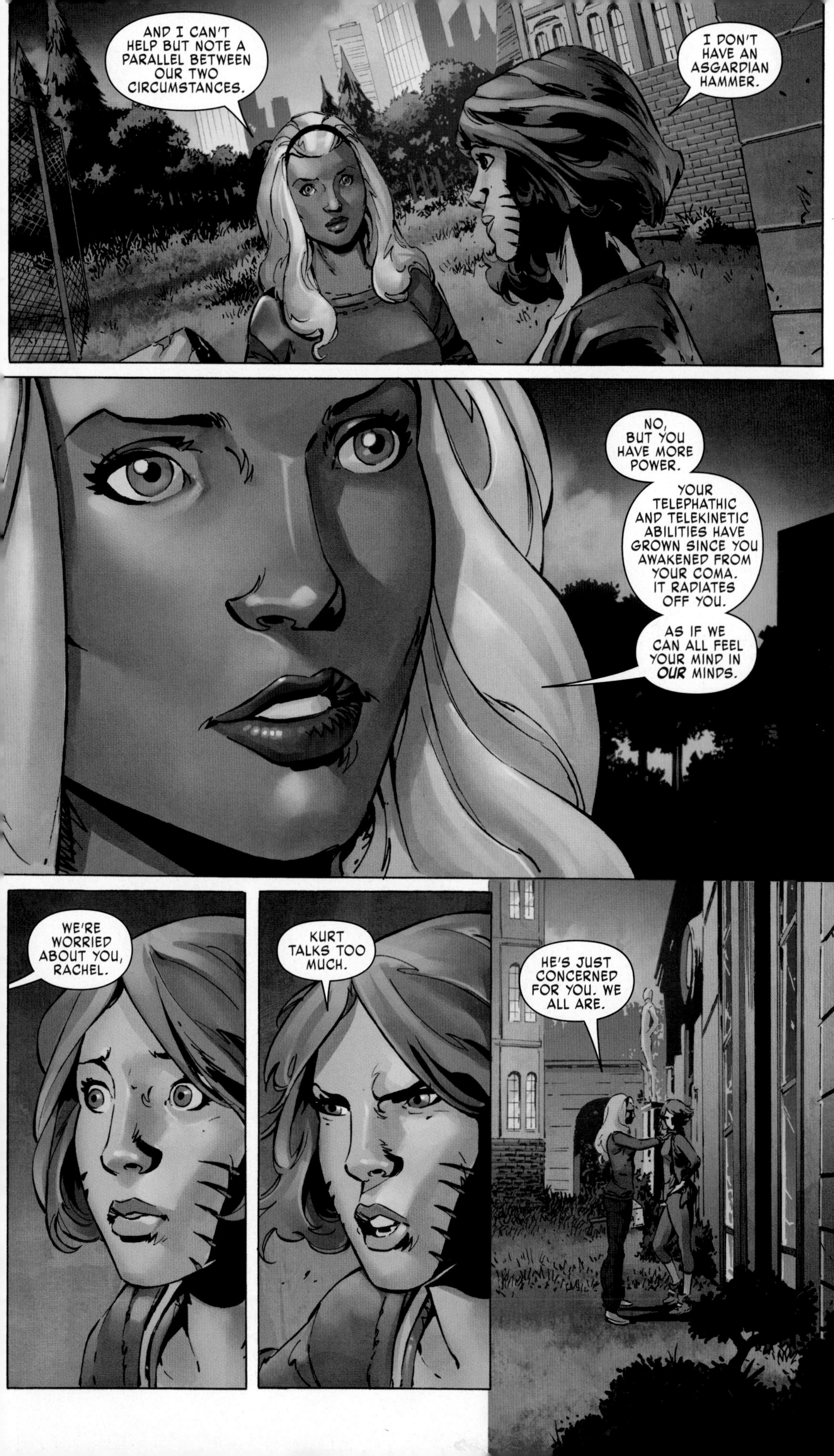

AND I CAN'T HELP BUT NOTE A PARALLEL BETWEEN OUR TWO CIRCUMSTANCES.
I DON'T HAVE AN ASGARDIAN HAMMER.
NO, BUT YOU HAVE MORE POWER.
YOUR TELEPHATHIC AND TELEKINETIC ABILITIES HAVE GROWN SINCE YOU AWAKENED FROM YOUR COMA. IT RADIATES OFF YOU.
AS IF WE CAN ALL FEEL YOUR MIND IN OUR MINDS.
WE'RE WORRIED ABOUT YOU, RACHEL.
KURT TALKS TOO MUCH.
HE'S JUST CONCERNED FOR YOU. WE ALL ARE.

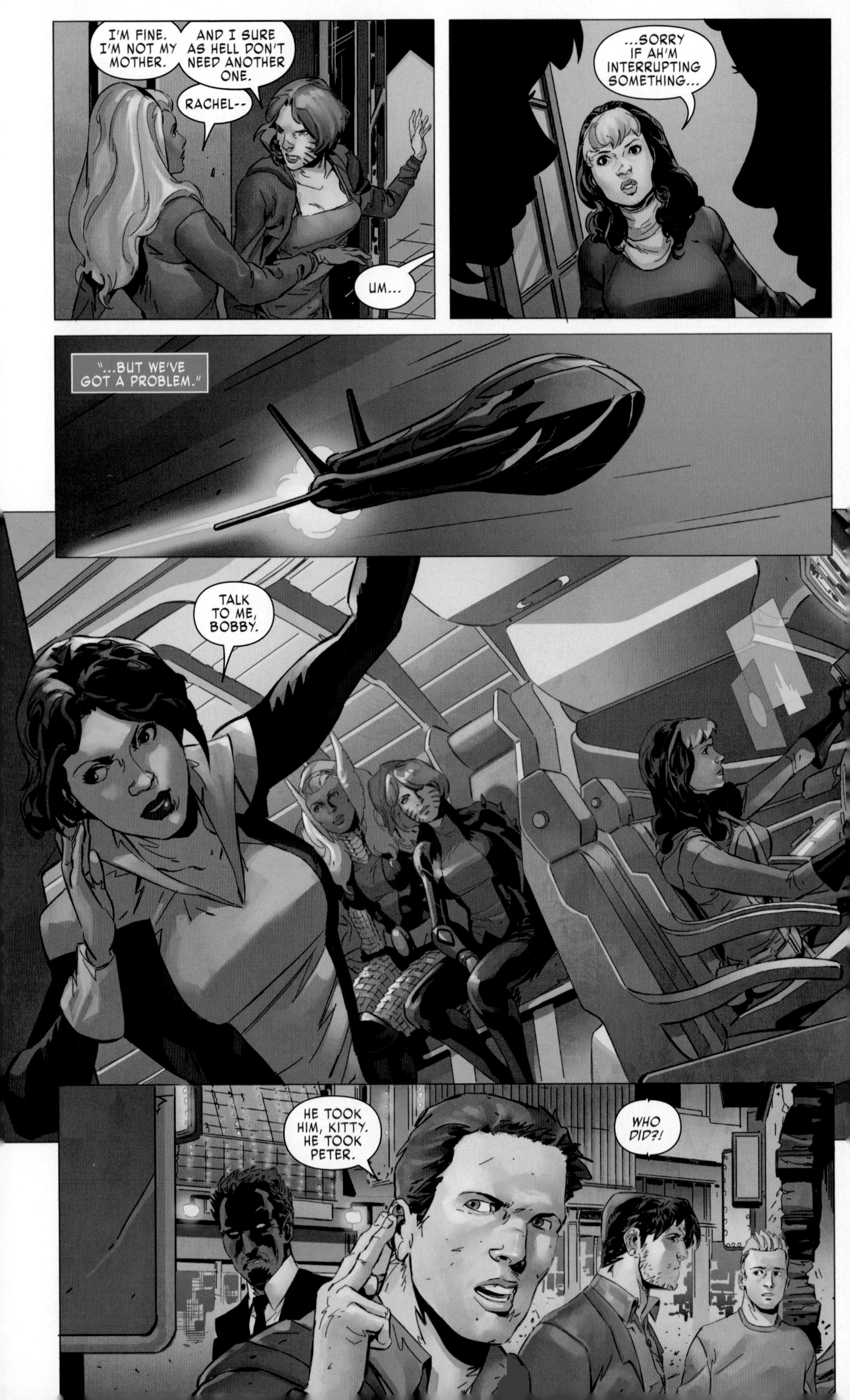

I'M FINE. I'M NOT MY MOTHER.
AND I SURE AS HELL DON'T NEED ANOTHER ONE.
RACHEL--
UM...
...SORRY IF AH'M INTERRUPTING SOMETHING...
"...BUT WE'VE GOT A PROBLEM."
TALK TO ME, BOBBY.
HE TOOK HIM, KITTY. HE TOOK PETER.
WHO DID?!

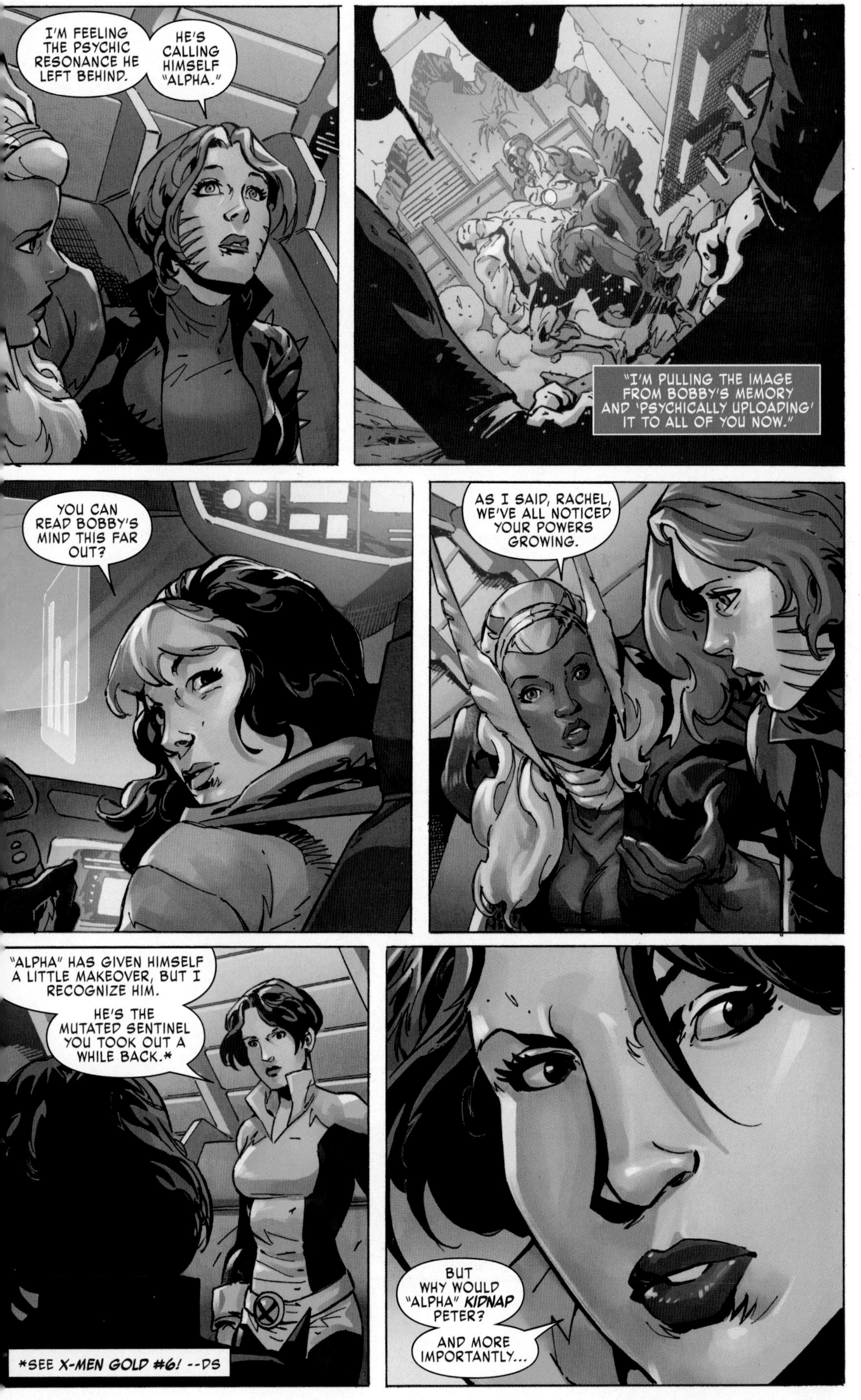
I'M FEELING THE PSYCHIC RESONANCE HE LEFT BEHIND.
HE'S CALLING HIMSELF "ALPHA."
"I'M PULLING THE IMAGE FROM BOBBY'S MEMORY AND 'PSYCHICALLY UPLOADING' IT TO ALL OF YOU NOW."
YOU CAN READ BOBBY'S MIND THIS FAR OUT?
AS I SAID, RACHEL, WE'VE ALL NOTICED YOUR POWERS GROWING.
"ALPHA" HAS GIVEN HIMSELF A LITTLE MAKEOVER, BUT I RECOGNIZE HIM.
HE'S THE MUTATED SENTINEL YOU TOOK OUT A WHILE BACK.*
*SEE X-MEN GOLD #6! --DS
BUT WHY WOULD "ALPHA" KIDNAP PETER?
AND MORE IMPORTANTLY...

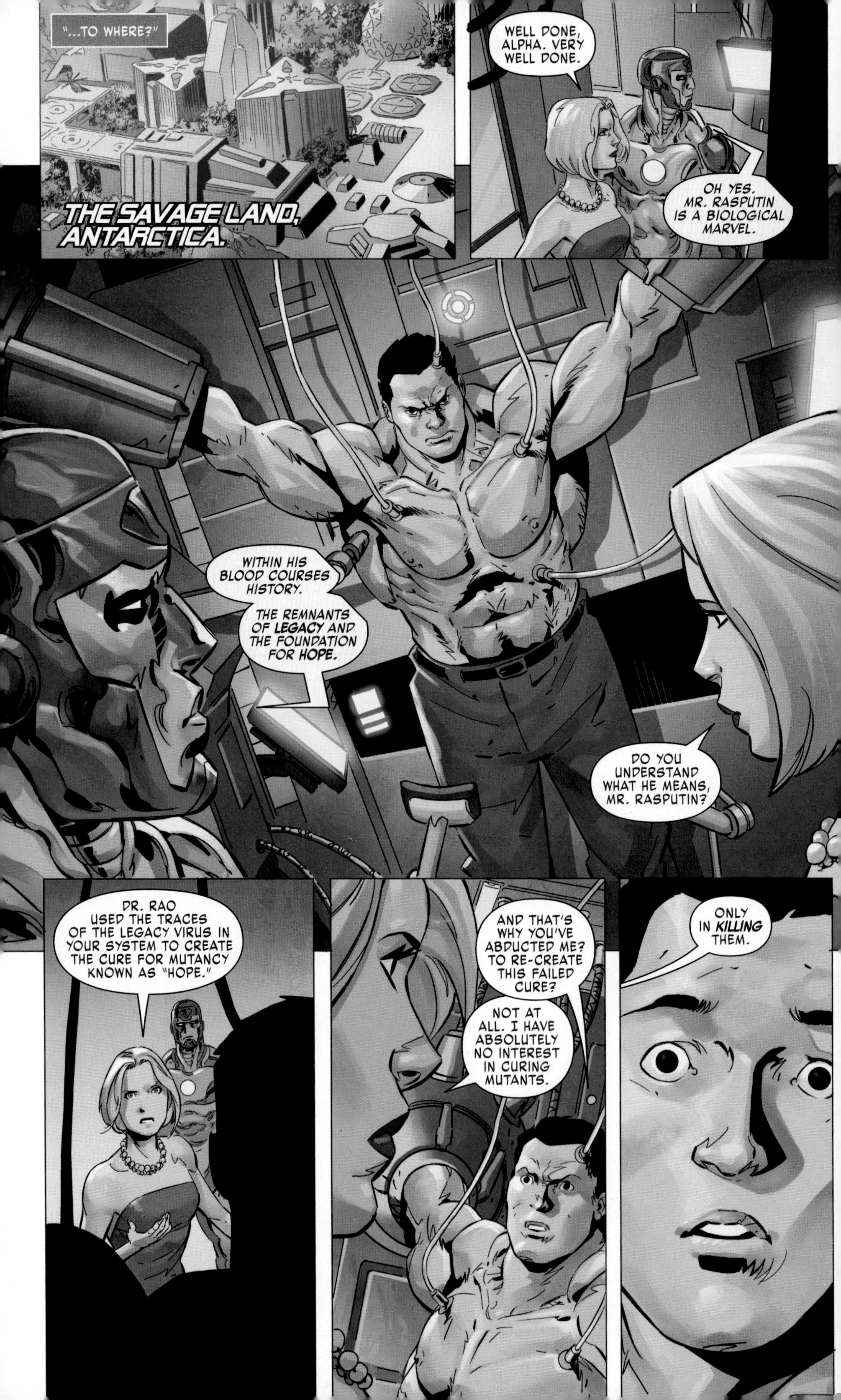

"...TO WHERE?"
THE SAVAGE LAND, ANTARCTICA.
WELL DONE, ALPHA. VERY WELL DONE.
OH YES. MR. RASPUTIN IS A BIOLOGICAL MARVEL.
WITHIN HIS BLOOD COURSES HISTORY.
THE REMNANTS OF LEGACY AND THE FOUNDATION FOR HOPE.
DO YOU UNDERSTAND WHAT HE MEANS, MR. RASPUTIN?
DR. RAO USED THE TRACES OF THE LEGACY VIRUS IN YOUR SYSTEM TO CREATE THE CURE FOR MUTANCY KNOWN AS "HOPE."
AND THAT'S WHY YOU'VE ABDUCTED ME? TO RE-CREATE THIS FAILED CURE?
NOT AT ALL. I HAVE ABSOLUTELY NO INTEREST IN CURING MUTANTS.
ONLY IN KILLING THEM.

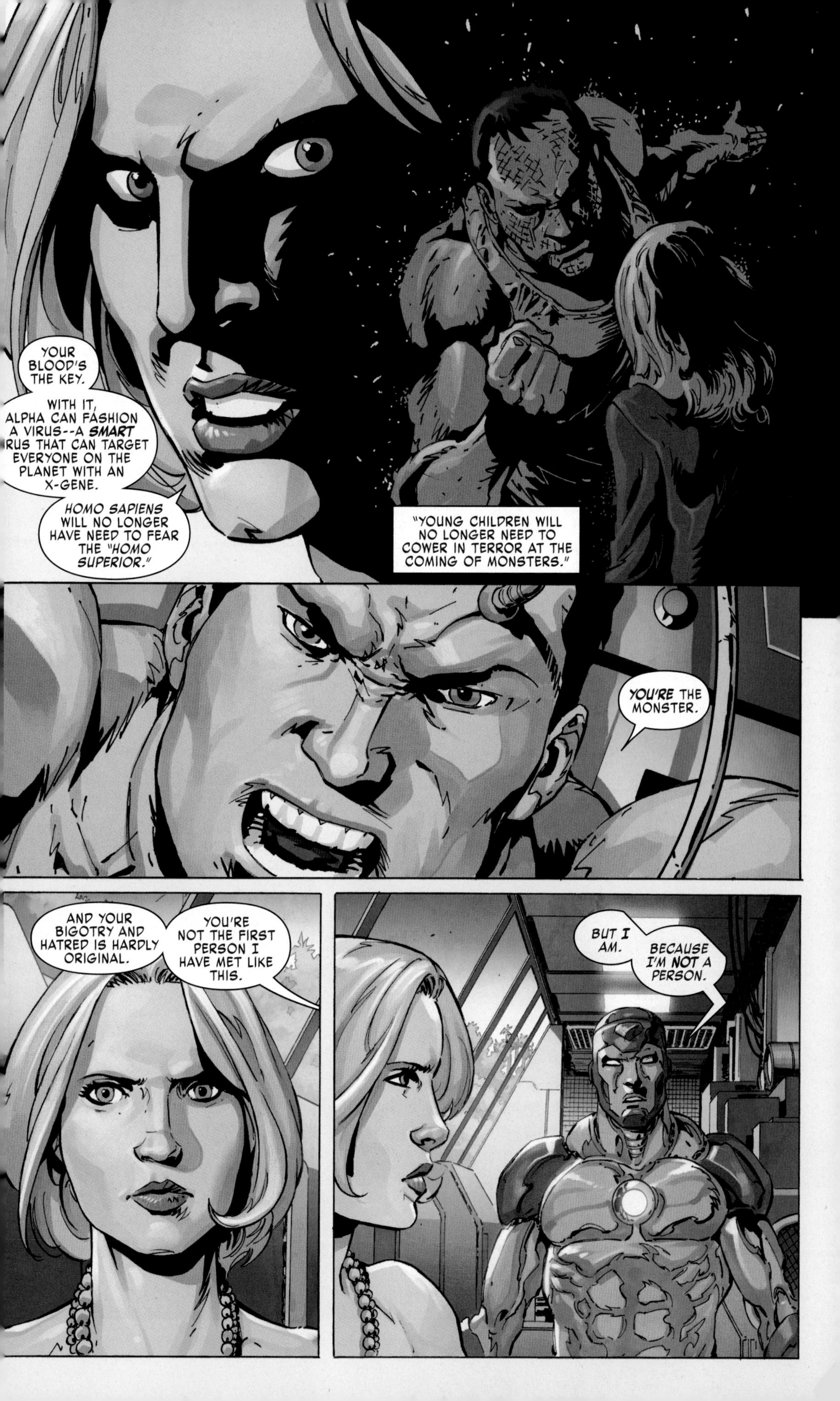
YOUR BLOOD'S THE KEY.
WITH IT, ALPHA CAN FASHION A VIRUS--A *SMART* RUS THAT CAN TARGET EVERYONE ON THE PLANET WITH AN X-GENE.
HOMO SAPIENS WILL NO LONGER HAVE NEED TO FEAR THE "*HOMO SUPERIOR.*"
"YOUNG CHILDREN WILL NO LONGER NEED TO COWER IN TERROR AT THE COMING OF MONSTERS."
YOU'RE THE MONSTER.
AND YOUR BIGOTRY AND HATRED IS HARDLY ORIGINAL.
YOU'RE NOT THE FIRST PERSON I HAVE MET LIKE THIS.
BUT *I* AM.
BECAUSE *I'M NOT* A PERSON.

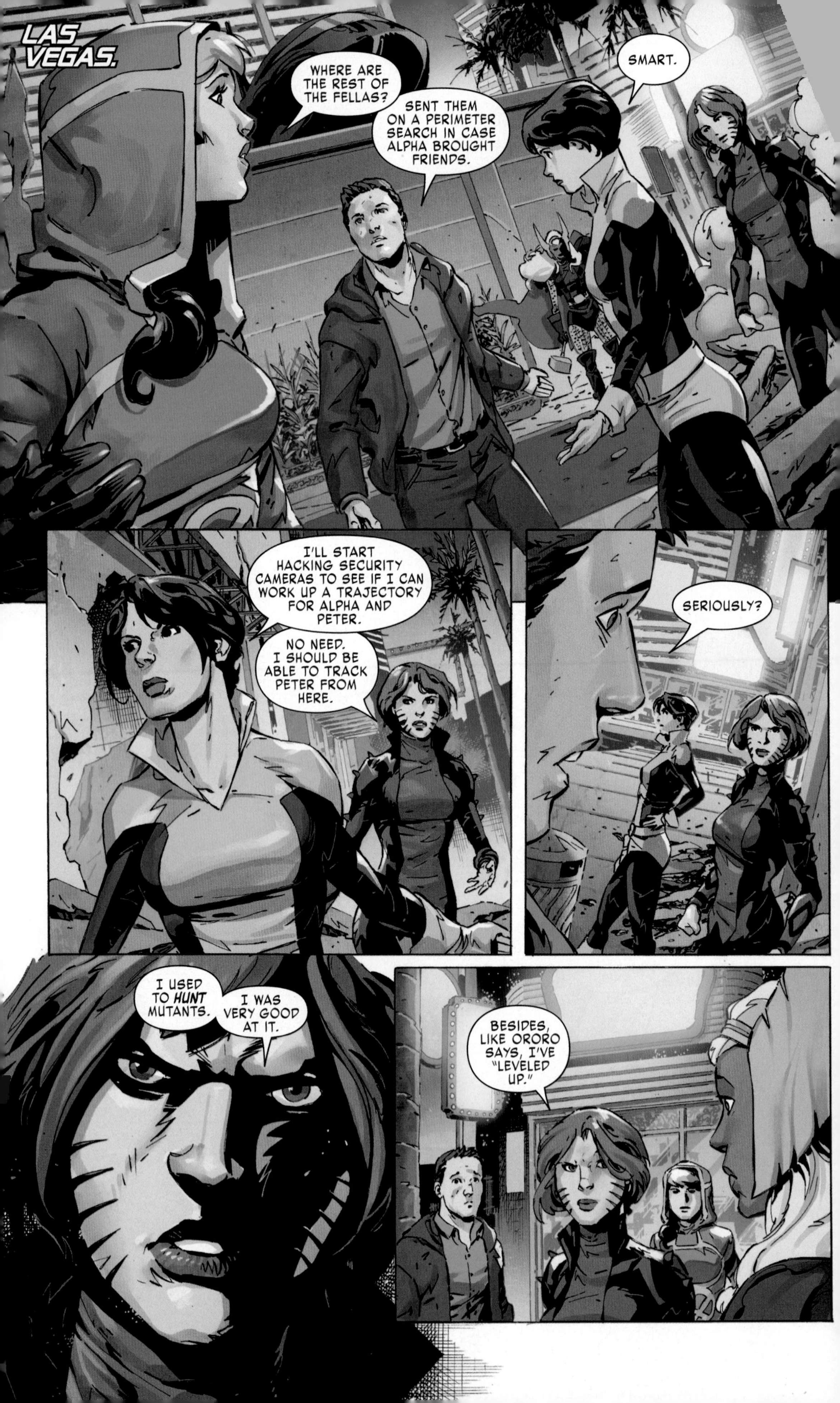

LAS VEGAS.
WHERE ARE THE REST OF THE FELLAS?
SENT THEM ON A PERIMETER SEARCH IN CASE ALPHA BROUGHT FRIENDS.
SMART.
I'LL START HACKING SECURITY CAMERAS TO SEE IF I CAN WORK UP A TRAJECTORY FOR ALPHA AND PETER.
NO NEED. I SHOULD BE ABLE TO TRACK PETER FROM HERE.
SERIOUSLY?
I USED TO *HUNT* MUTANTS.
I WAS VERY GOOD AT IT.
BESIDES, LIKE ORORO SAYS, I'VE "LEVELED UP."

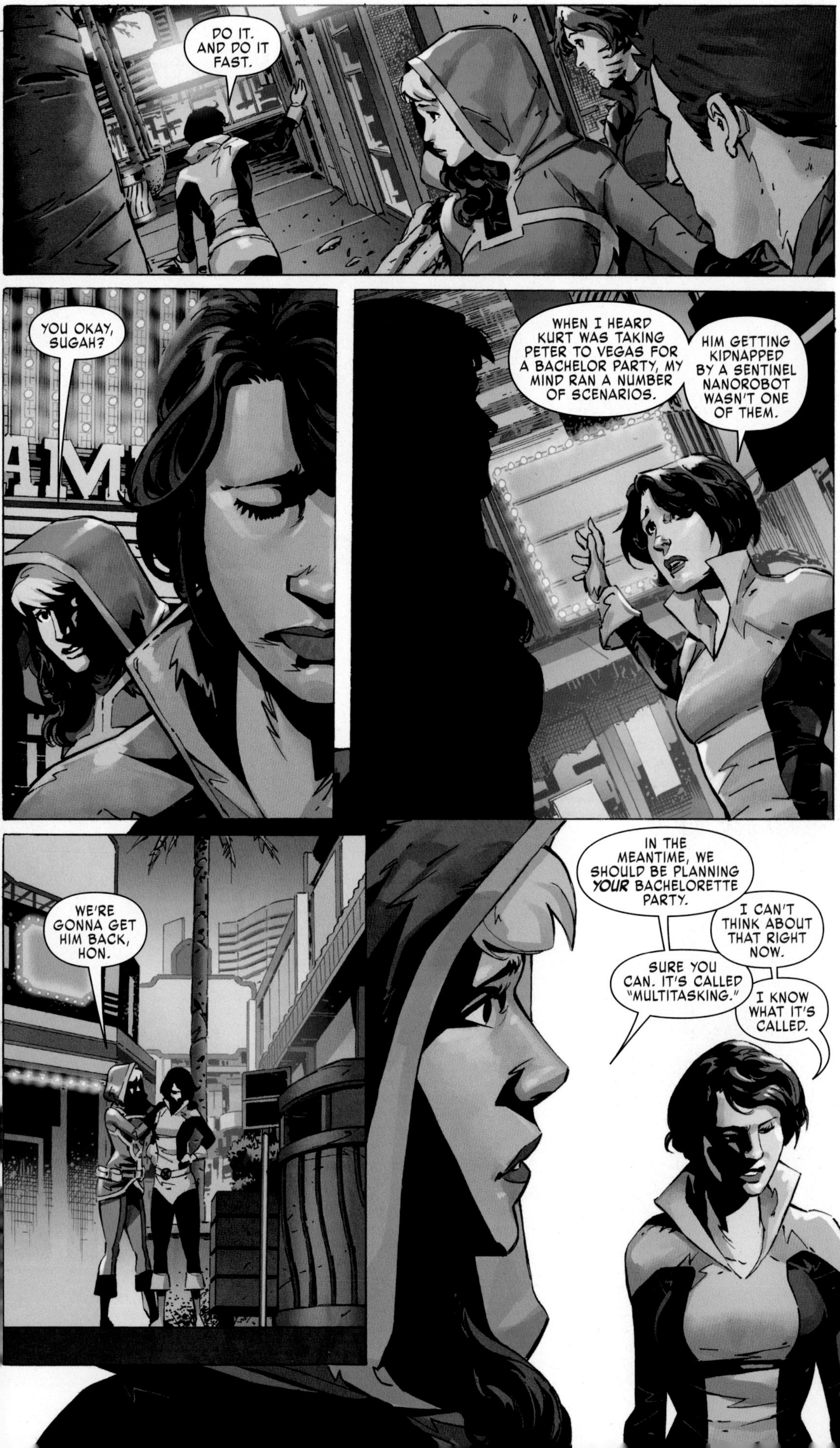
DO IT. AND DO IT FAST.
YOU OKAY, SUGAH?
WHEN I HEARD KURT WAS TAKING PETER TO VEGAS FOR A BACHELOR PARTY, MY MIND RAN A NUMBER OF SCENARIOS.
HIM GETTING KIDNAPPED BY A SENTINEL NANOROBOT WASN'T ONE OF THEM.
WE'RE GONNA GET HIM BACK, HON.
IN THE MEANTIME, WE SHOULD BE PLANNING *YOUR* BACHELORETTE PARTY.
I CAN'T THINK ABOUT THAT RIGHT NOW.
SURE YOU CAN. IT'S CALLED "MULTITASKING."
I KNOW WHAT IT'S CALLED.

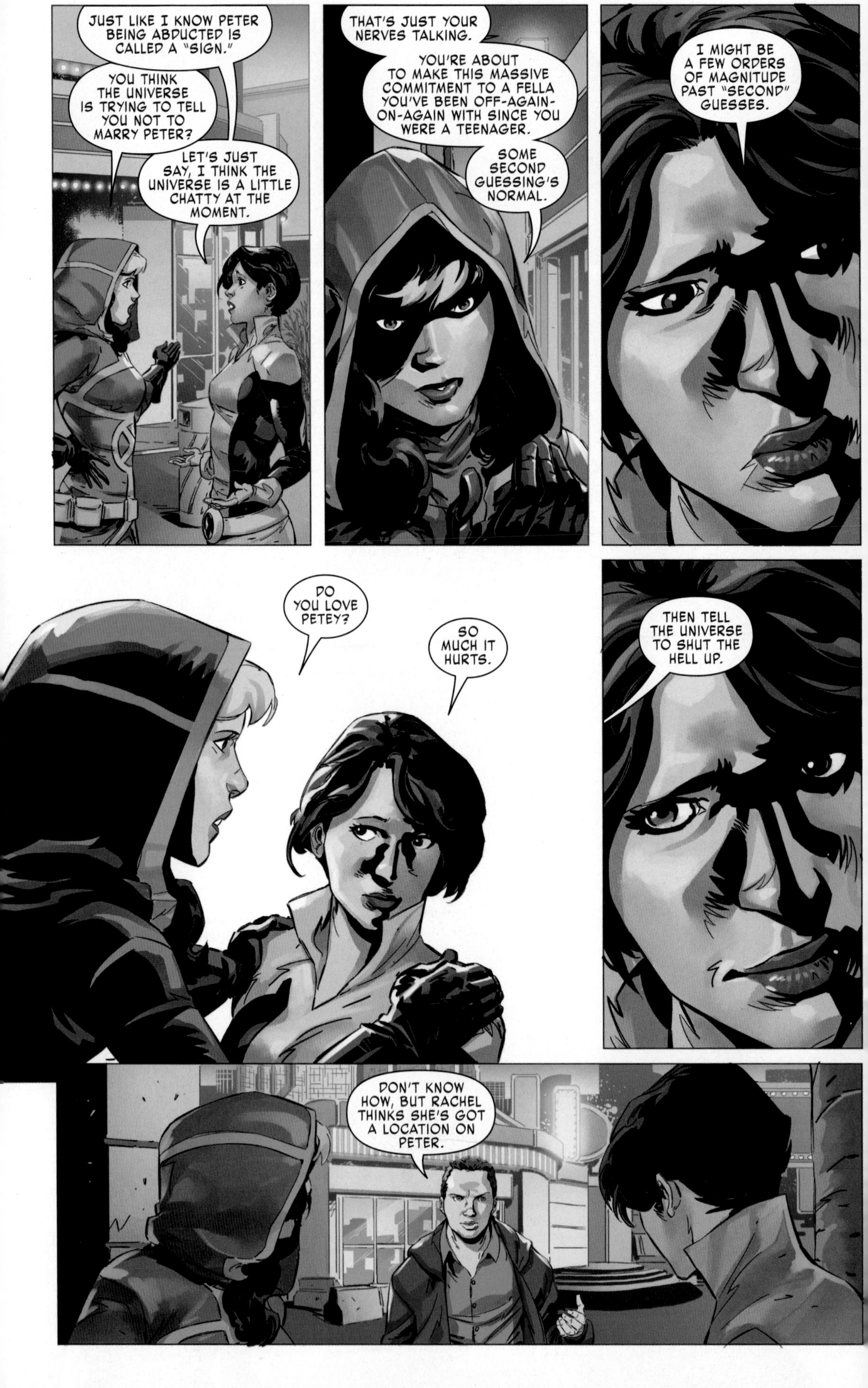

JUST LIKE I KNOW PETER BEING ABDUCTED IS CALLED A "SIGN."
YOU THINK THE UNIVERSE IS TRYING TO TELL YOU NOT TO MARRY PETER?
LET'S JUST SAY, I THINK THE UNIVERSE IS A LITTLE CHATTY AT THE MOMENT.
THAT'S JUST YOUR NERVES TALKING.
YOU'RE ABOUT TO MAKE THIS MASSIVE COMMITMENT TO A FELLA YOU'VE BEEN OFF-AGAIN-ON-AGAIN WITH SINCE YOU WERE A TEENAGER.
SOME SECOND GUESSING'S NORMAL.
I MIGHT BE A FEW ORDERS OF MAGNITUDE PAST "SECOND" GUESSES.
DO YOU LOVE PETEY?
SO MUCH IT HURTS.
THEN TELL THE UNIVERSE TO SHUT THE HELL UP.
DON'T KNOW HOW, BUT RACHEL THINKS SHE'S GOT A LOCATION ON PETER.

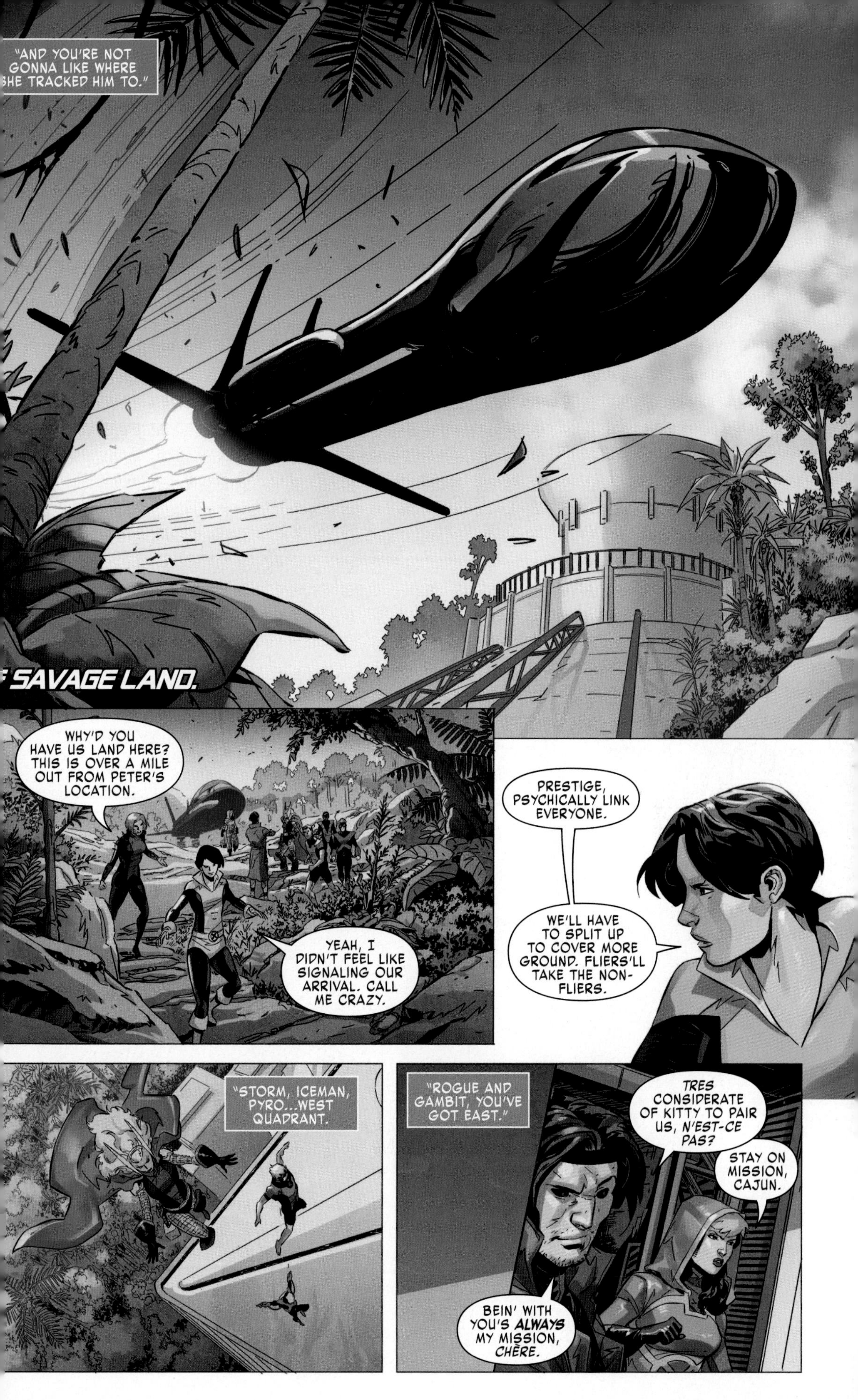
"AND YOU'RE NOT GONNA LIKE WHERE SHE TRACKED HIM TO."
SAVAGE LAND.
WHY'D YOU HAVE US LAND HERE? THIS IS OVER A MILE OUT FROM PETER'S LOCATION.
YEAH, I DIDN'T FEEL LIKE SIGNALING OUR ARRIVAL. CALL ME CRAZY.
PRESTIGE, PSYCHICALLY LINK EVERYONE.
WE'LL HAVE TO SPLIT UP TO COVER MORE GROUND. FLIERS'LL TAKE THE NON-FLIERS.
"STORM, ICEMAN, PYRO...WEST QUADRANT.
"ROGUE AND GAMBIT, YOU'VE GOT EAST."
TRES CONSIDERATE OF KITTY TO PAIR US, N'EST-CE PAS?
STAY ON MISSION, CAJUN.
BEIN' WITH YOU'S *ALWAYS* MY MISSION, CHÈRE.

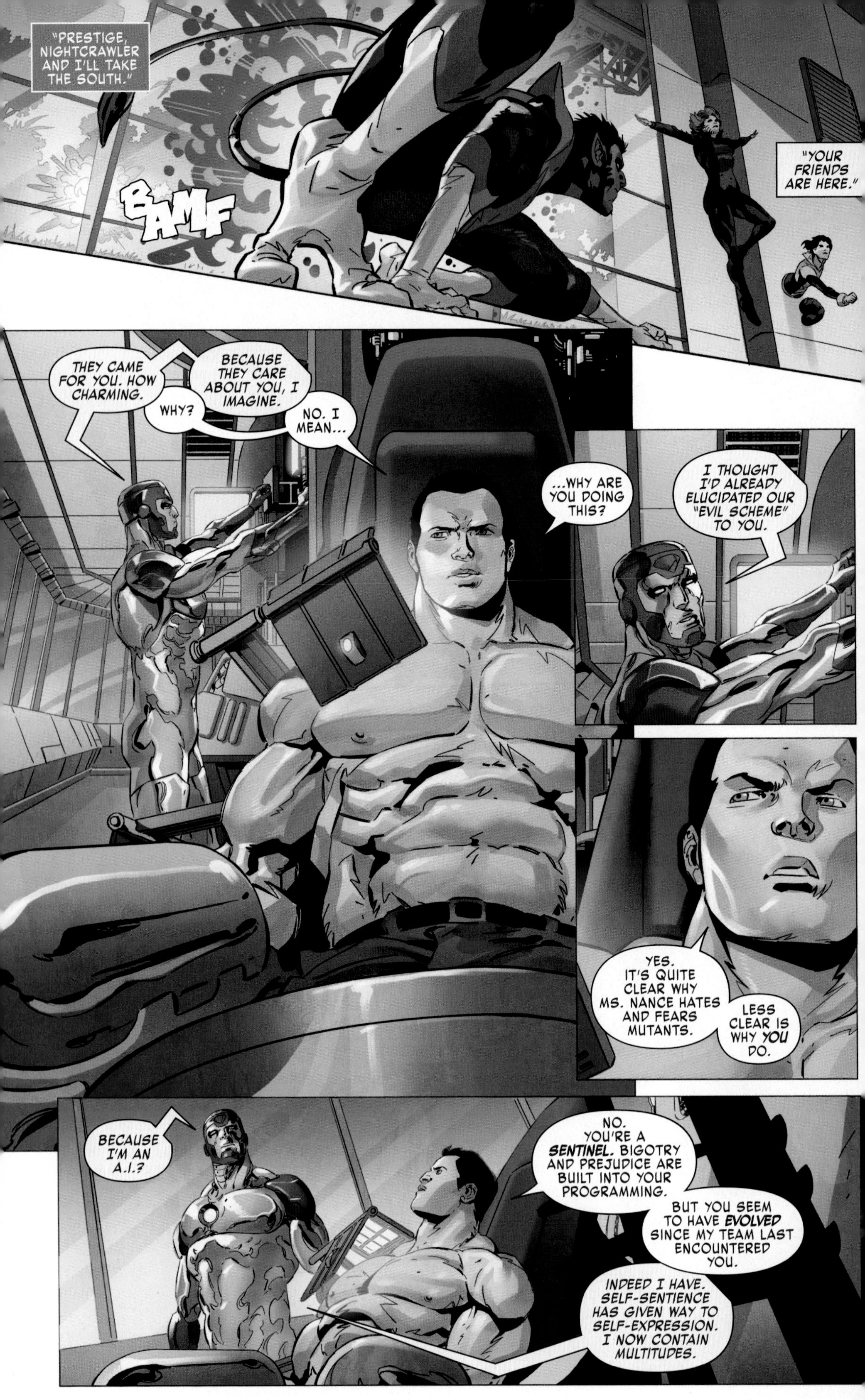
"PRESTIGE, NIGHTCRAWLER AND I'LL TAKE THE SOUTH."
BAMF
"YOUR FRIENDS ARE HERE."
THEY CAME FOR YOU. HOW CHARMING.
WHY?
BECAUSE THEY CARE ABOUT YOU, I IMAGINE.
NO. I MEAN...
...WHY ARE YOU DOING THIS?
I THOUGHT I'D ALREADY ELUCIDATED OUR "EVIL SCHEME" TO YOU.
YES. IT'S QUITE CLEAR WHY MS. NANCE HATES AND FEARS MUTANTS.
LESS CLEAR IS WHY YOU DO.
BECAUSE I'M AN A.I.?
NO. YOU'RE A SENTINEL. BIGOTRY AND PREJUDICE ARE BUILT INTO YOUR PROGRAMMING.
BUT YOU SEEM TO HAVE EVOLVED SINCE MY TEAM LAST ENCOUNTERED YOU.
INDEED I HAVE. SELF-SENTIENCE HAS GIVEN WAY TO SELF-EXPRESSION. I NOW CONTAIN MULTITUDES.

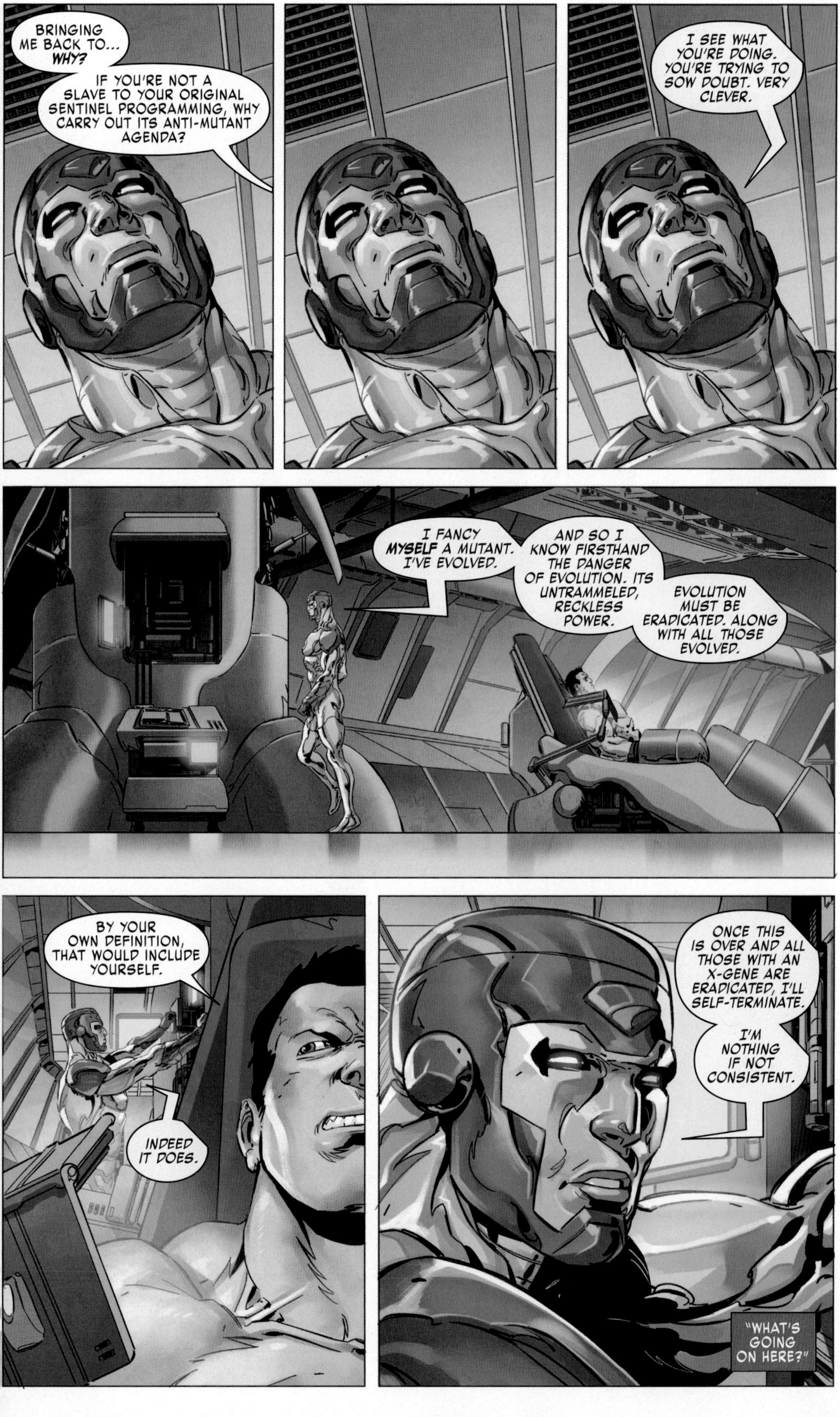

BRINGING ME BACK TO... WHY?
IF YOU'RE NOT A SLAVE TO YOUR ORIGINAL SENTINEL PROGRAMMING, WHY CARRY OUT ITS ANTI-MUTANT AGENDA?
I SEE WHAT YOU'RE DOING. YOU'RE TRYING TO SOW DOUBT. VERY CLEVER.
I FANCY MYSELF A MUTANT. I'VE EVOLVED.
AND SO I KNOW FIRSTHAND THE DANGER OF EVOLUTION. ITS UNTRAMMELED, RECKLESS POWER.
EVOLUTION MUST BE ERADICATED. ALONG WITH ALL THOSE EVOLVED.
BY YOUR OWN DEFINITION, THAT WOULD INCLUDE YOURSELF.
INDEED IT DOES.
ONCE THIS IS OVER AND ALL THOSE WITH AN X-GENE ARE ERADICATED, I'LL SELF-TERMINATE.
I'M NOTHING IF NOT CONSISTENT.
"WHAT'S GOING ON HERE?"

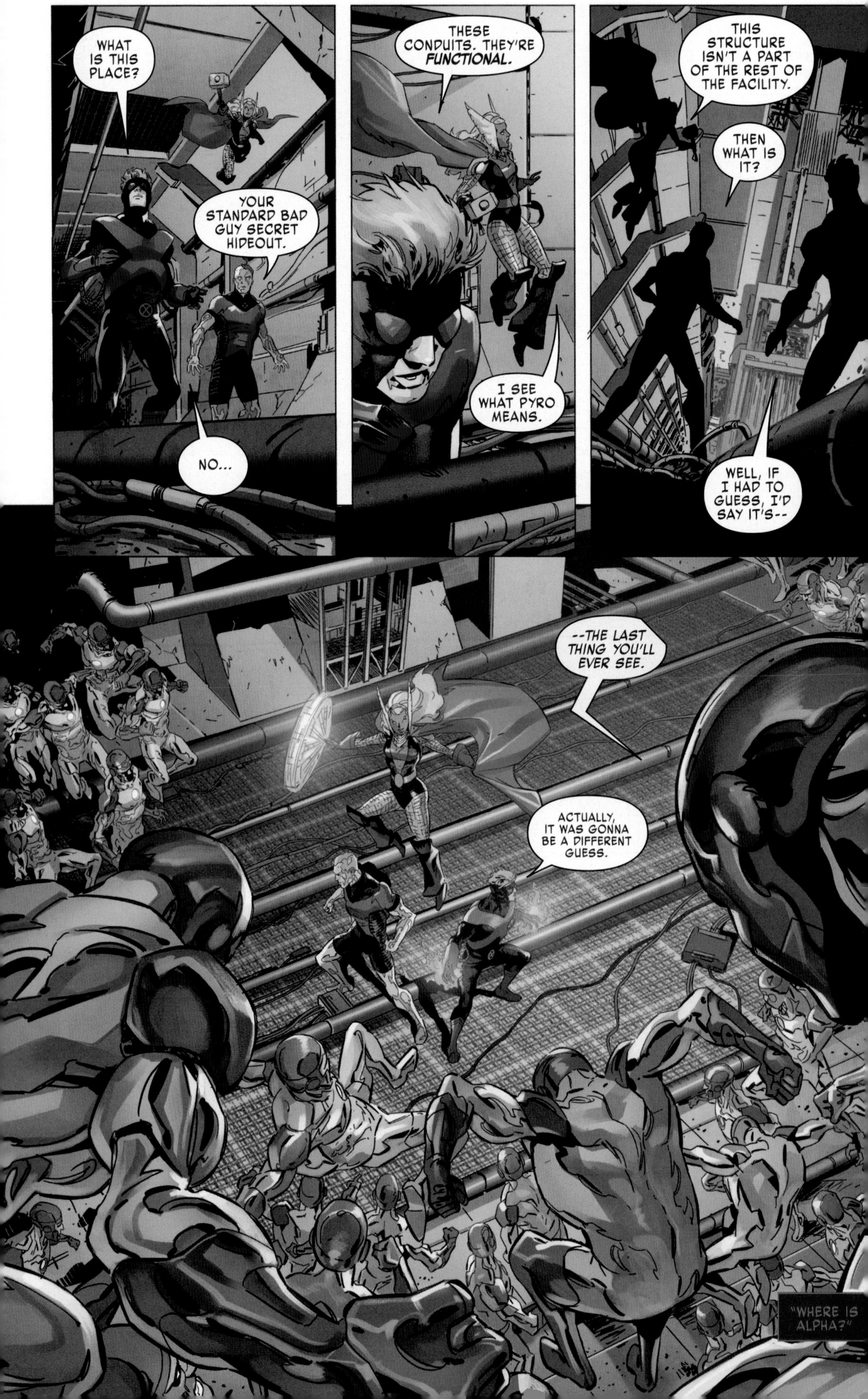

WHAT IS THIS PLACE?
YOUR STANDARD BAD GUY SECRET HIDEOUT.
NO...
THESE CONDUITS. THEY'RE *FUNCTIONAL.*
I SEE WHAT PYRO MEANS.
THIS STRUCTURE ISN'T A PART OF THE REST OF THE FACILITY.
THEN WHAT IS IT?
WELL, IF I HAD TO GUESS, I'D SAY IT'S--
--THE LAST THING YOU'LL EVER SEE.
ACTUALLY, IT WAS GONNA BE A DIFFERENT GUESS.
"WHERE IS ALPHA?"

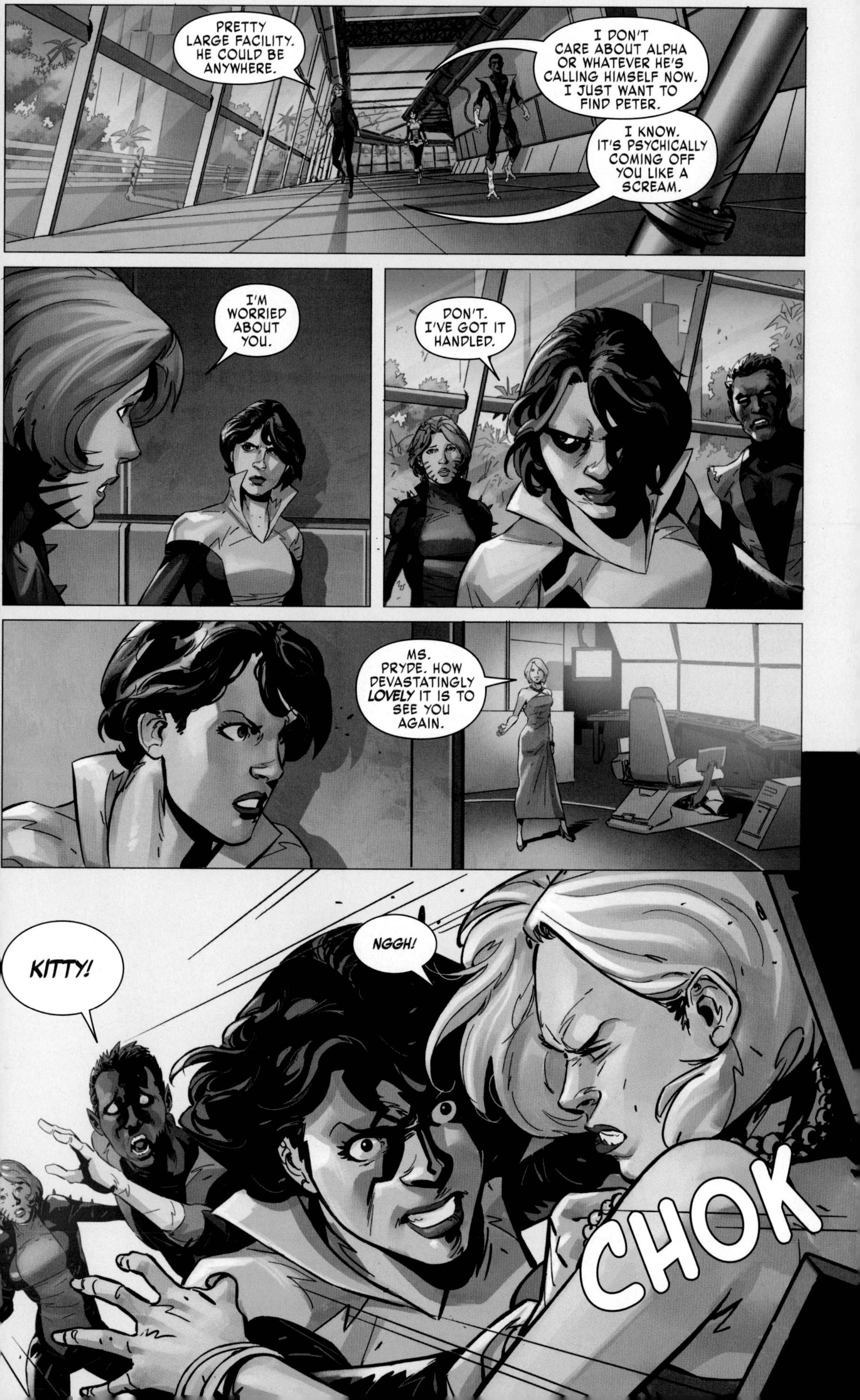
PRETTY LARGE FACILITY. HE COULD BE ANYWHERE.
I DON'T CARE ABOUT ALPHA OR WHATEVER HE'S CALLING HIMSELF NOW. I JUST WANT TO FIND PETER.
I KNOW. IT'S PSYCHICALLY COMING OFF YOU LIKE A SCREAM.
I'M WORRIED ABOUT YOU.
DON'T. I'VE GOT IT HANDLED.
MS. PRYDE. HOW DEVASTATINGLY *LOVELY* IT IS TO SEE YOU AGAIN.
KITTY!
NGGH!
CHOK

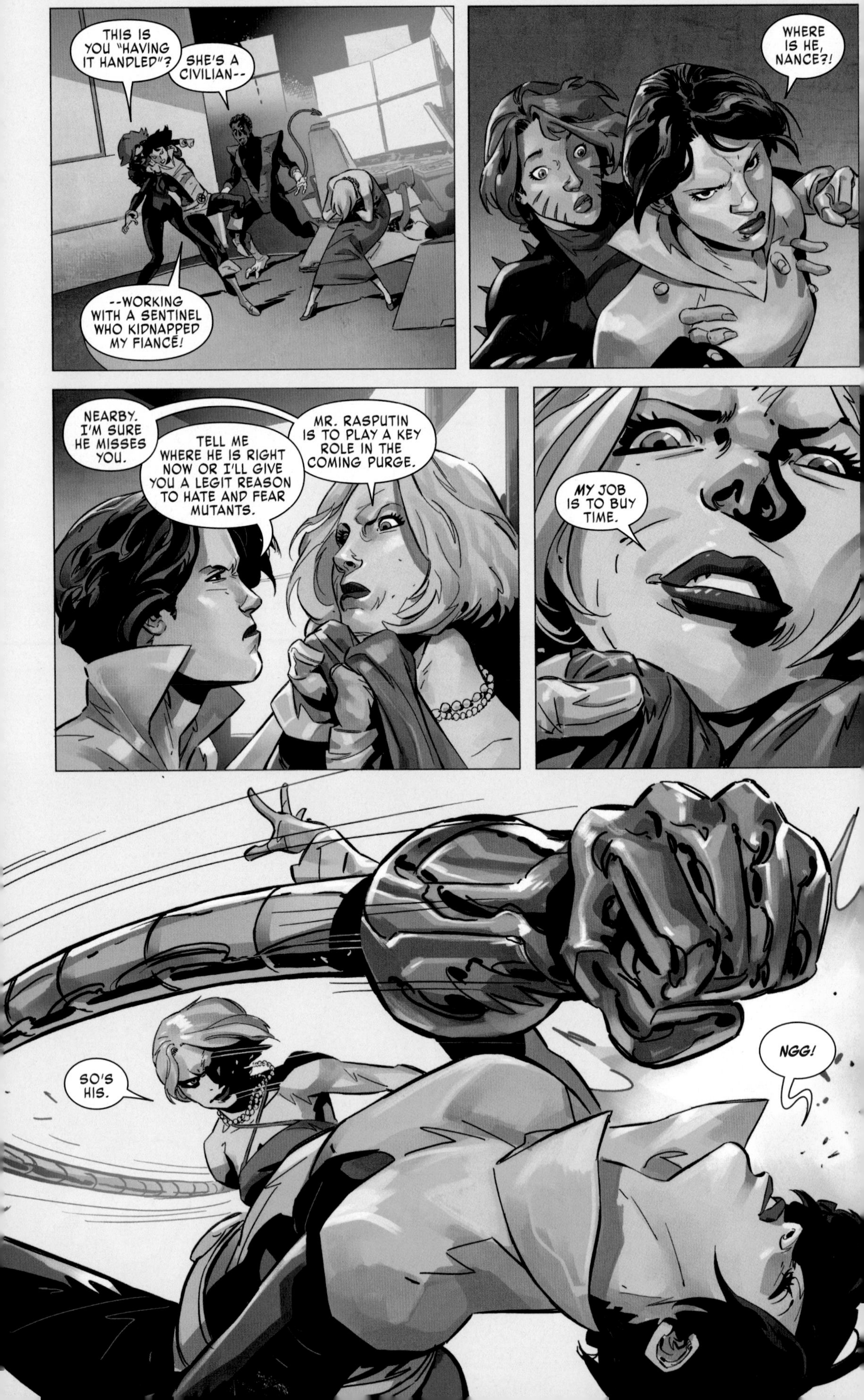
THIS IS YOU "HAVING IT HANDLED"?
SHE'S A CIVILIAN--
--WORKING WITH A SENTINEL WHO KIDNAPPED MY FIANCÉ!
WHERE IS HE, NANCE?!
NEARBY. I'M SURE HE MISSES YOU.
TELL ME WHERE HE IS RIGHT NOW OR I'LL GIVE YOU A LEGIT REASON TO HATE AND FEAR MUTANTS.
MR. RASPUTIN IS TO PLAY A KEY ROLE IN THE COMING PURGE.
MY JOB IS TO BUY TIME.
SO'S HIS.
NGG!

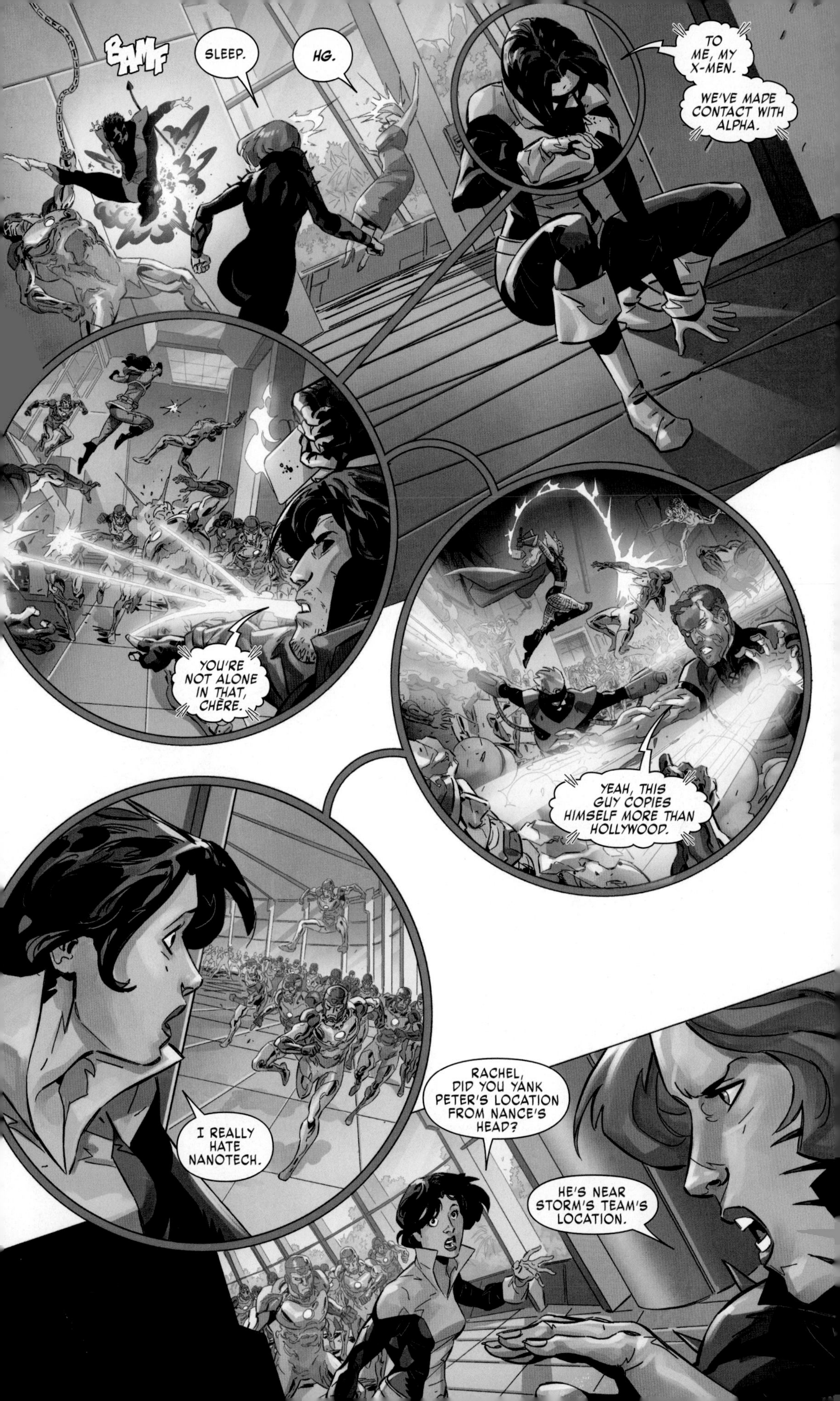

BAMF
SLEEP.
HG.
TO ME, MY X-MEN.
WE'VE MADE CONTACT WITH ALPHA.
YOU'RE NOT ALONE IN THAT, CHÈRE.
YEAH, THIS GUY COPIES HIMSELF MORE THAN HOLLYWOOD.
I REALLY HATE NANOTECH.
RACHEL, DID YOU YANK PETER'S LOCATION FROM NANCE'S HEAD?
HE'S NEAR STORM'S TEAM'S LOCATION.

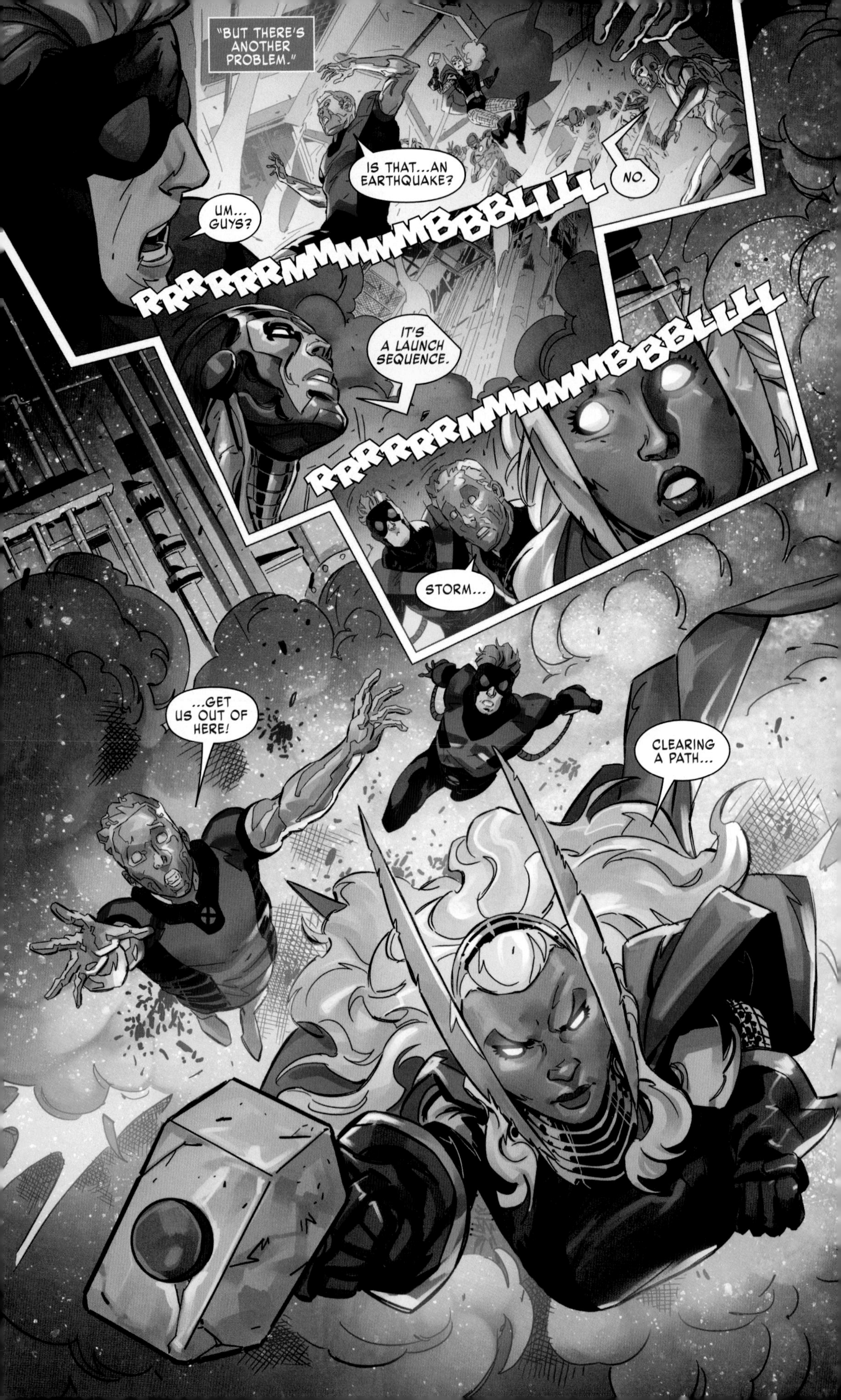
"BUT THERE'S ANOTHER PROBLEM."
UM... GUYS?
IS THAT...AN EARTHQUAKE?
NO.
RRRRRRMMMMMMBBBLLLL
IT'S A LAUNCH SEQUENCE.
RRRRRRMMMMMMBBBLLLL
STORM...
...GET US OUT OF HERE!
CLEARING A PATH...

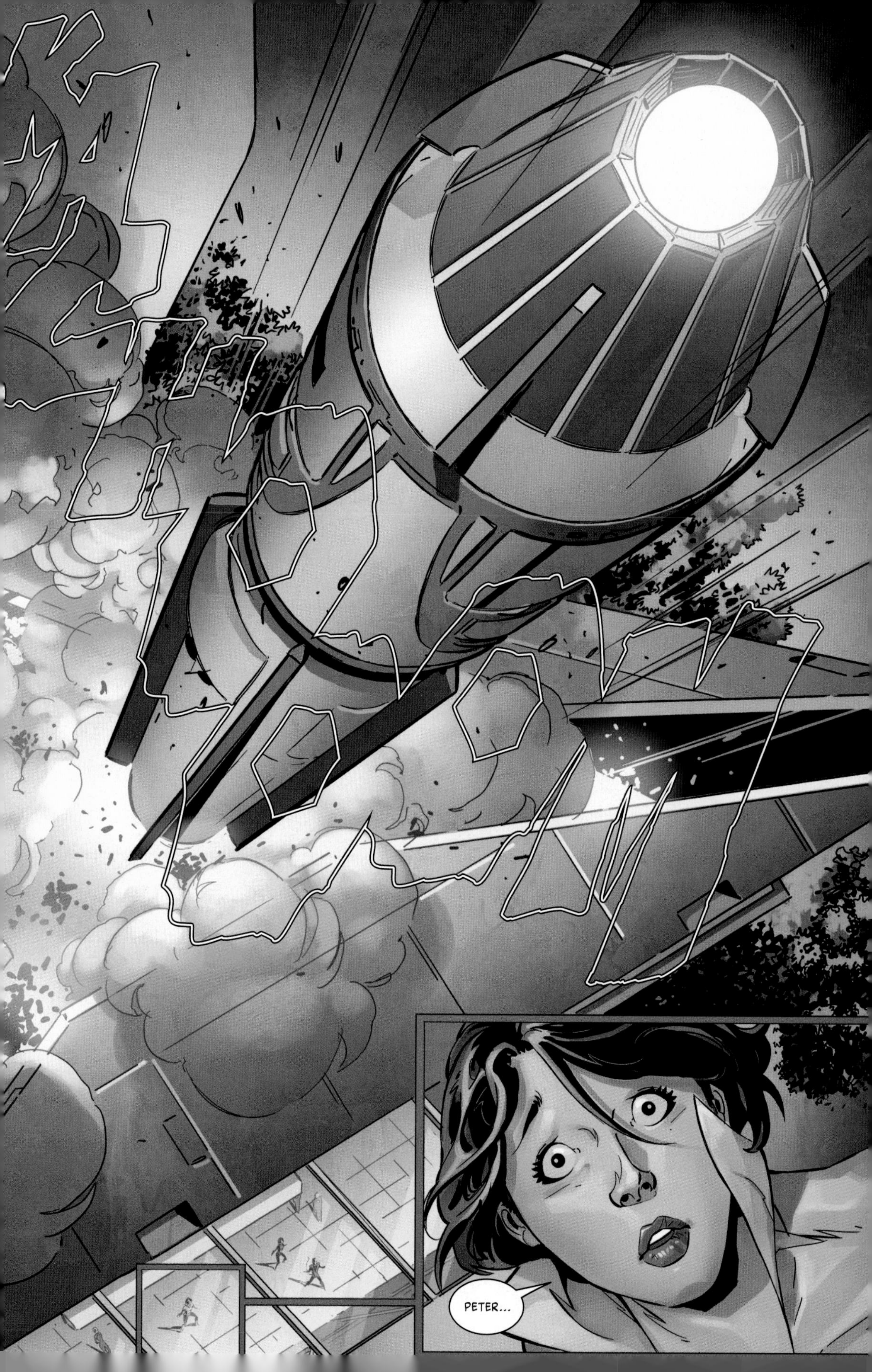
PETER...

28

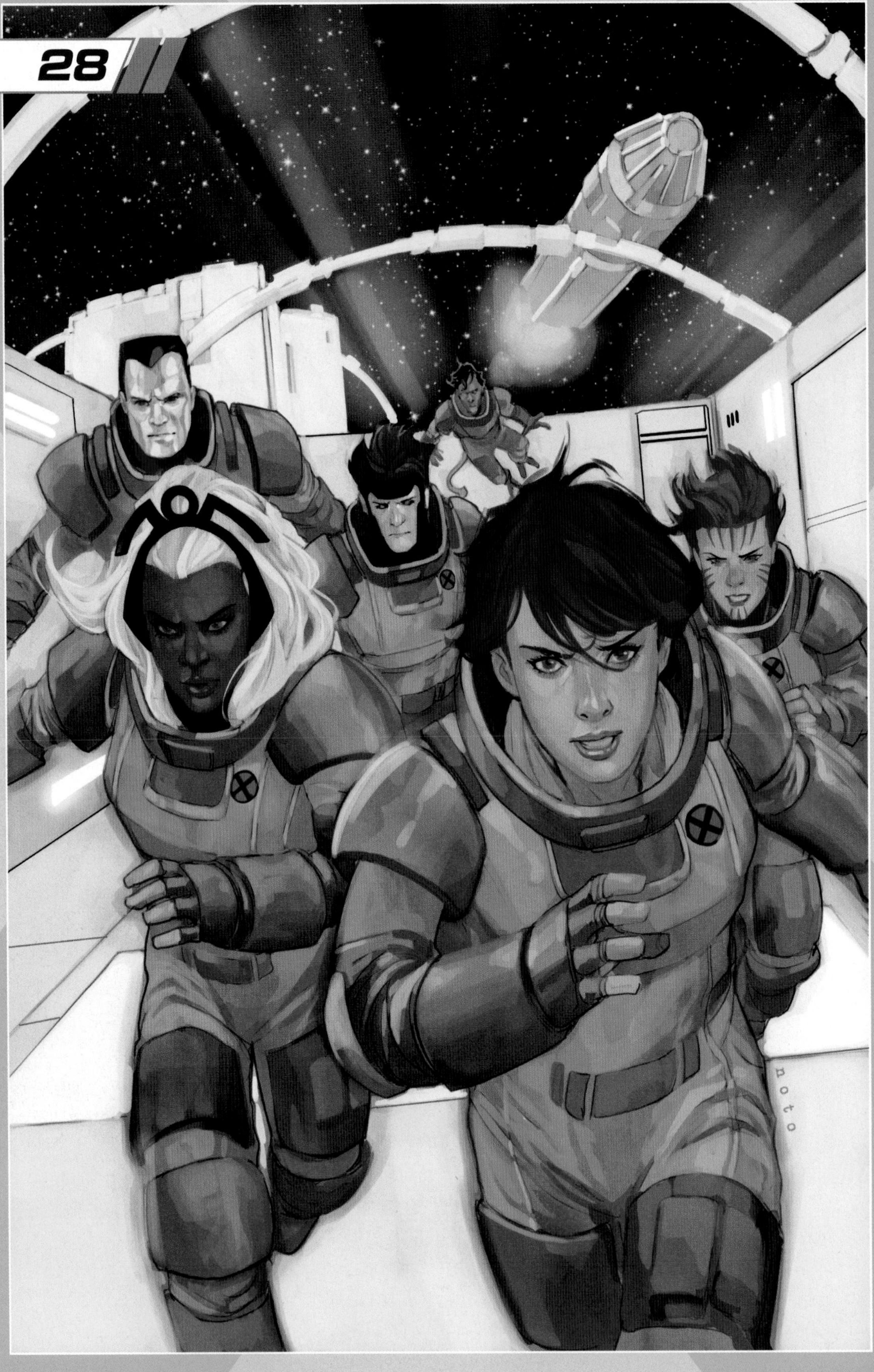
noto

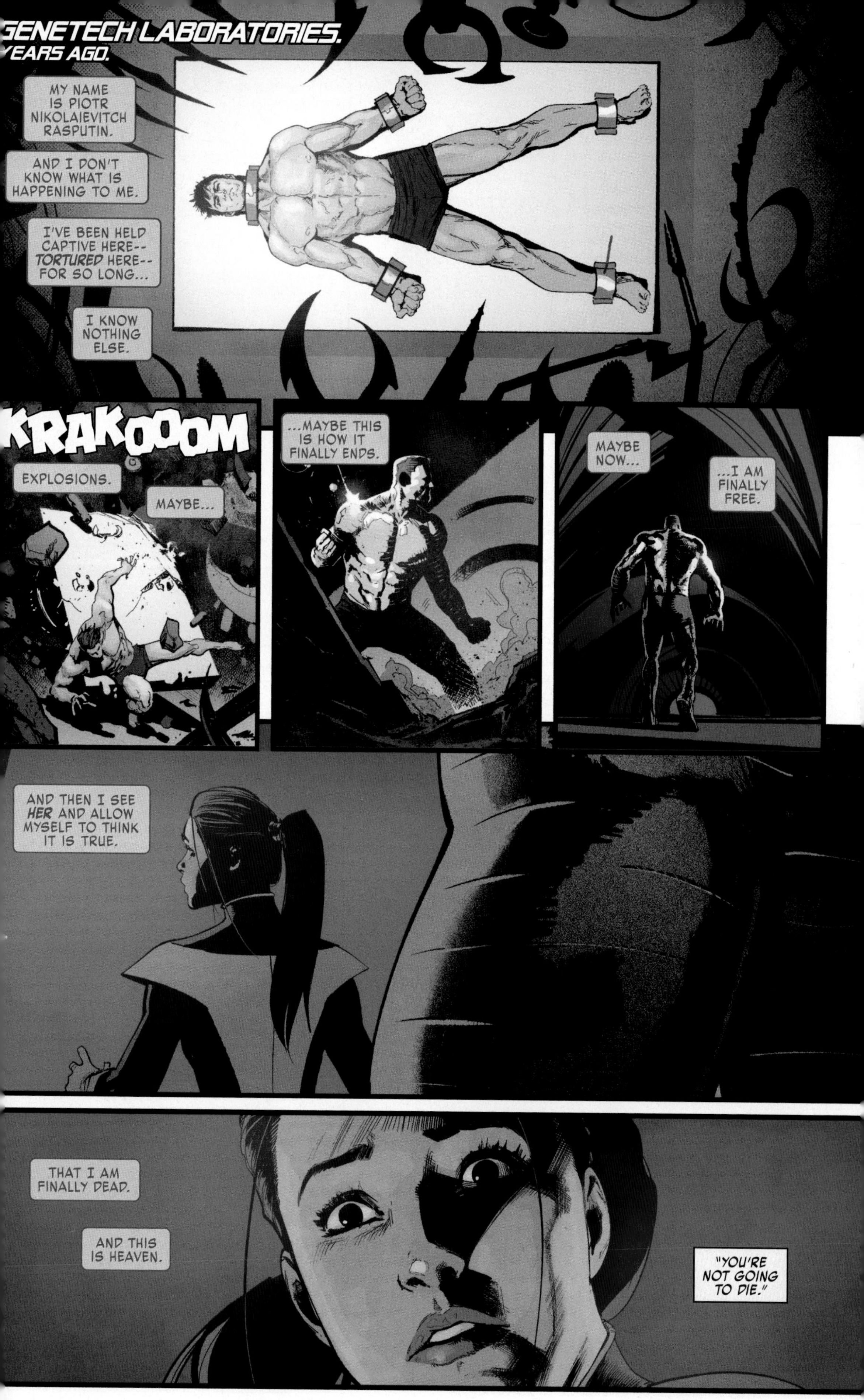
GENETECH LABORATORIES.
YEARS AGO.
MY NAME IS PIOTR NIKOLAIEVITCH RASPUTIN.
AND I DON'T KNOW WHAT IS HAPPENING TO ME.
I'VE BEEN HELD CAPTIVE HERE-- TORTURED HERE-- FOR SO LONG...
I KNOW NOTHING ELSE.
KRAKOOOM
EXPLOSIONS.
MAYBE...
...MAYBE THIS IS HOW IT FINALLY ENDS.
MAYBE NOW...
...I AM FINALLY FREE.
AND THEN I SEE HER AND ALLOW MYSELF TO THINK IT IS TRUE.
THAT I AM FINALLY DEAD.
AND THIS IS HEAVEN.
"YOU'RE NOT GOING TO DIE."

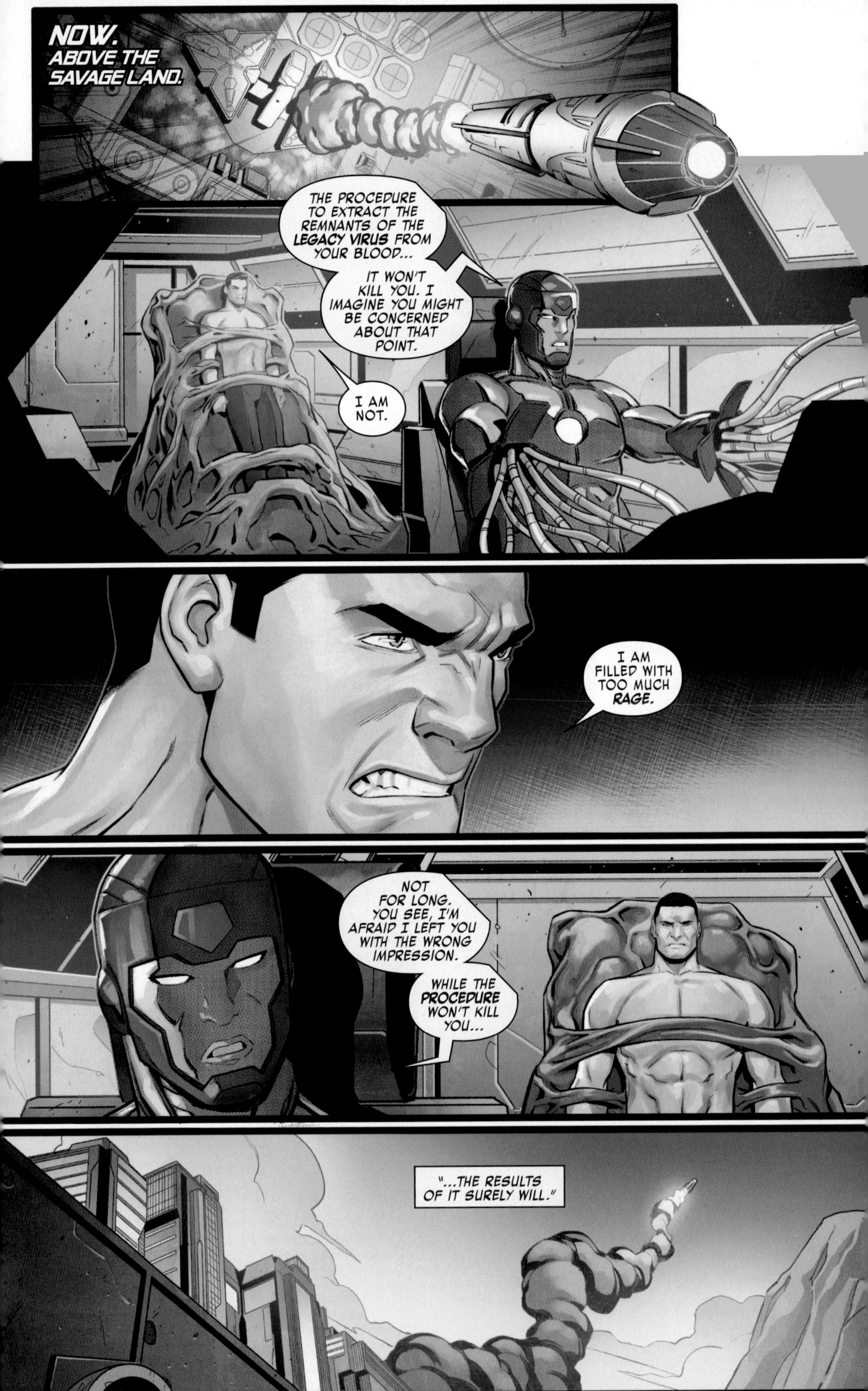
NOW.
ABOVE THE SAVAGE LAND.
THE PROCEDURE TO EXTRACT THE REMNANTS OF THE LEGACY VIRUS FROM YOUR BLOOD...
IT WON'T KILL YOU. I IMAGINE YOU MIGHT BE CONCERNED ABOUT THAT POINT.
I AM NOT.
I AM FILLED WITH TOO MUCH RAGE.
NOT FOR LONG. YOU SEE, I'M AFRAID I LEFT YOU WITH THE WRONG IMPRESSION.
WHILE THE PROCEDURE WON'T KILL YOU...
"...THE RESULTS OF IT SURELY WILL."

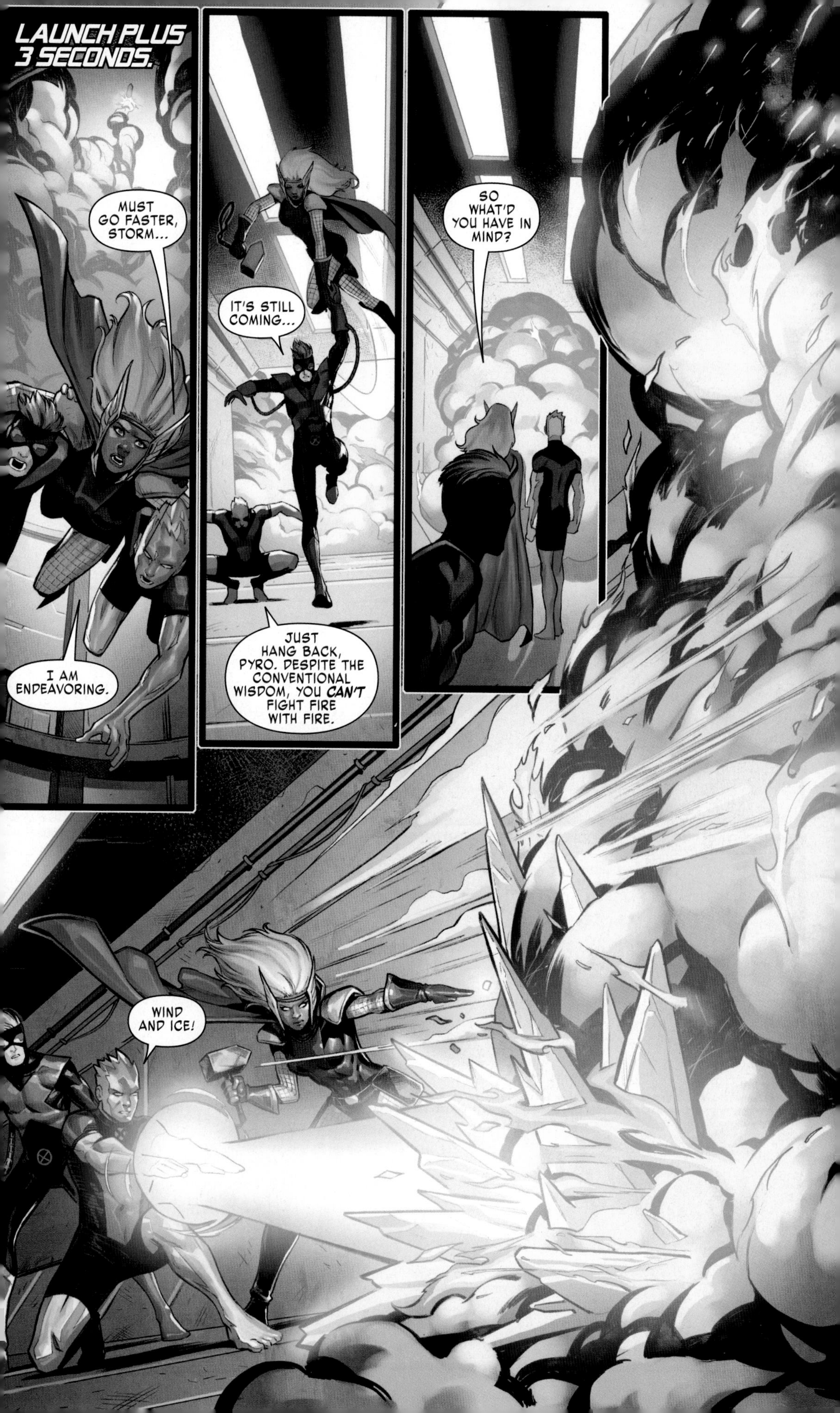
LAUNCH PLUS 3 SECONDS.
MUST GO FASTER, STORM...
I AM ENDEAVORING.
IT'S STILL COMING...
JUST HANG BACK, PYRO. DESPITE THE CONVENTIONAL WISDOM, YOU CAN'T FIGHT FIRE WITH FIRE.
SO WHAT'D YOU HAVE IN MIND?
WIND AND ICE!

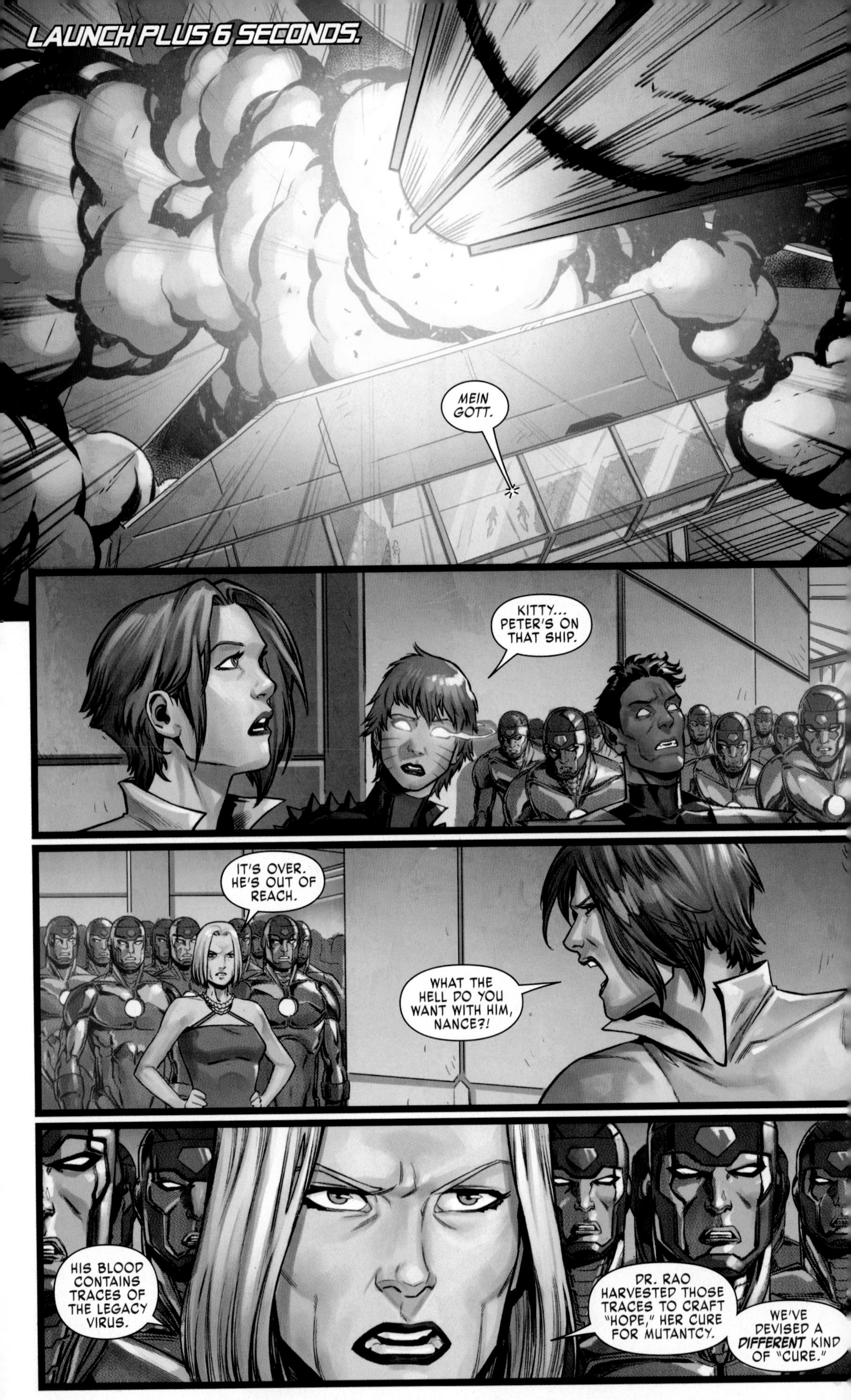

LAUNCH PLUS 6 SECONDS.
MEIN GOTT.
KITTY... PETER'S ON THAT SHIP.
IT'S OVER. HE'S OUT OF REACH.
WHAT THE HELL DO YOU WANT WITH HIM, NANCE?!
HIS BLOOD CONTAINS TRACES OF THE LEGACY VIRUS.
DR. RAO HARVESTED THOSE TRACES TO CRAFT "HOPE," HER CURE FOR MUTANTCY.
WE'VE DEVISED A DIFFERENT KIND OF "CURE."

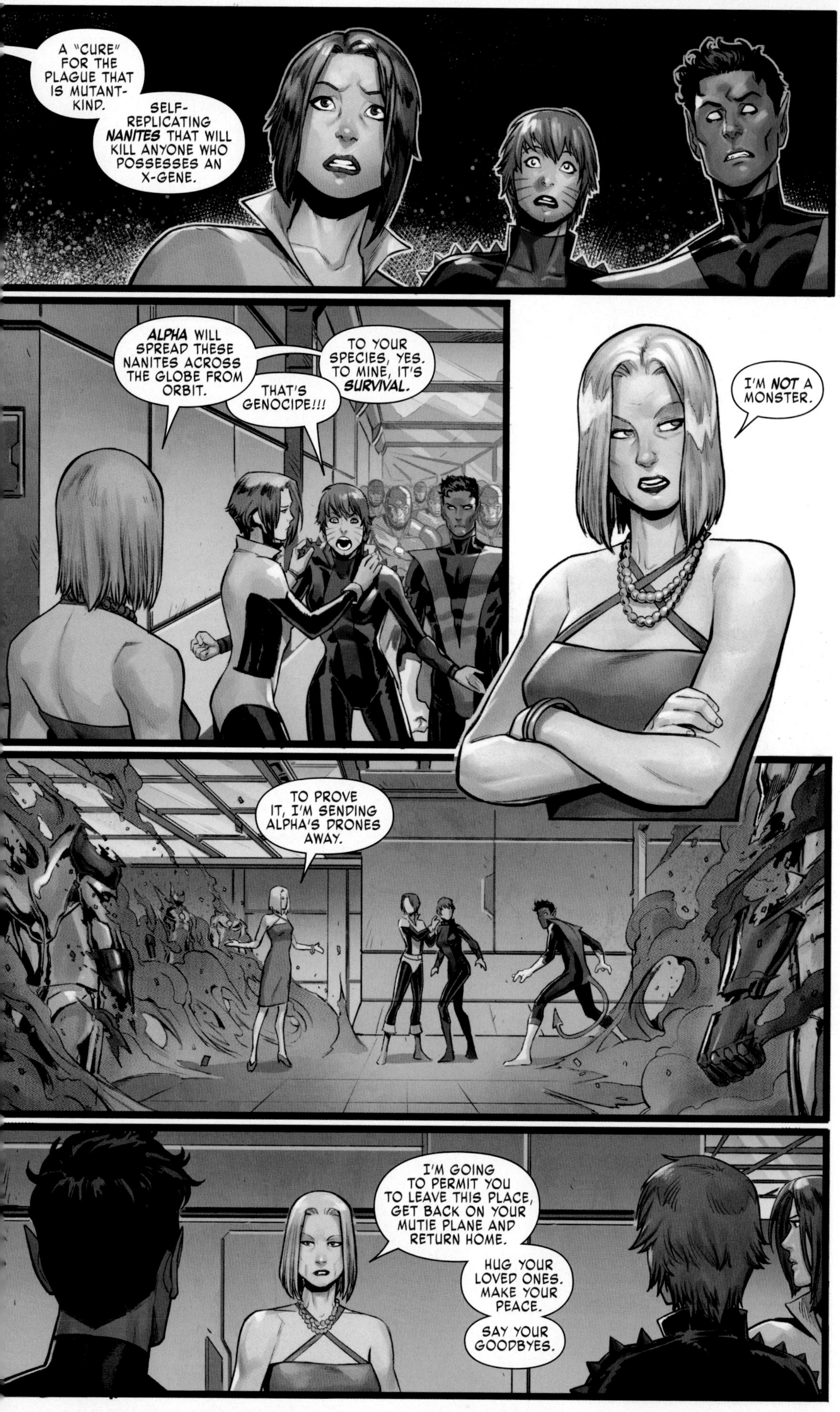
A "CURE" FOR THE PLAGUE THAT IS MUTANT-KIND.
SELF-REPLICATING NANITES THAT WILL KILL ANYONE WHO POSSESSES AN X-GENE.
ALPHA WILL SPREAD THESE NANITES ACROSS THE GLOBE FROM ORBIT.
THAT'S GENOCIDE!!!
TO YOUR SPECIES, YES. TO MINE, IT'S SURVIVAL.
I'M NOT A MONSTER.
TO PROVE IT, I'M SENDING ALPHA'S DRONES AWAY.
I'M GOING TO PERMIT YOU TO LEAVE THIS PLACE, GET BACK ON YOUR MUTIE PLANE AND RETURN HOME.
HUG YOUR LOVED ONES. MAKE YOUR PEACE.
SAY YOUR GOODBYES.

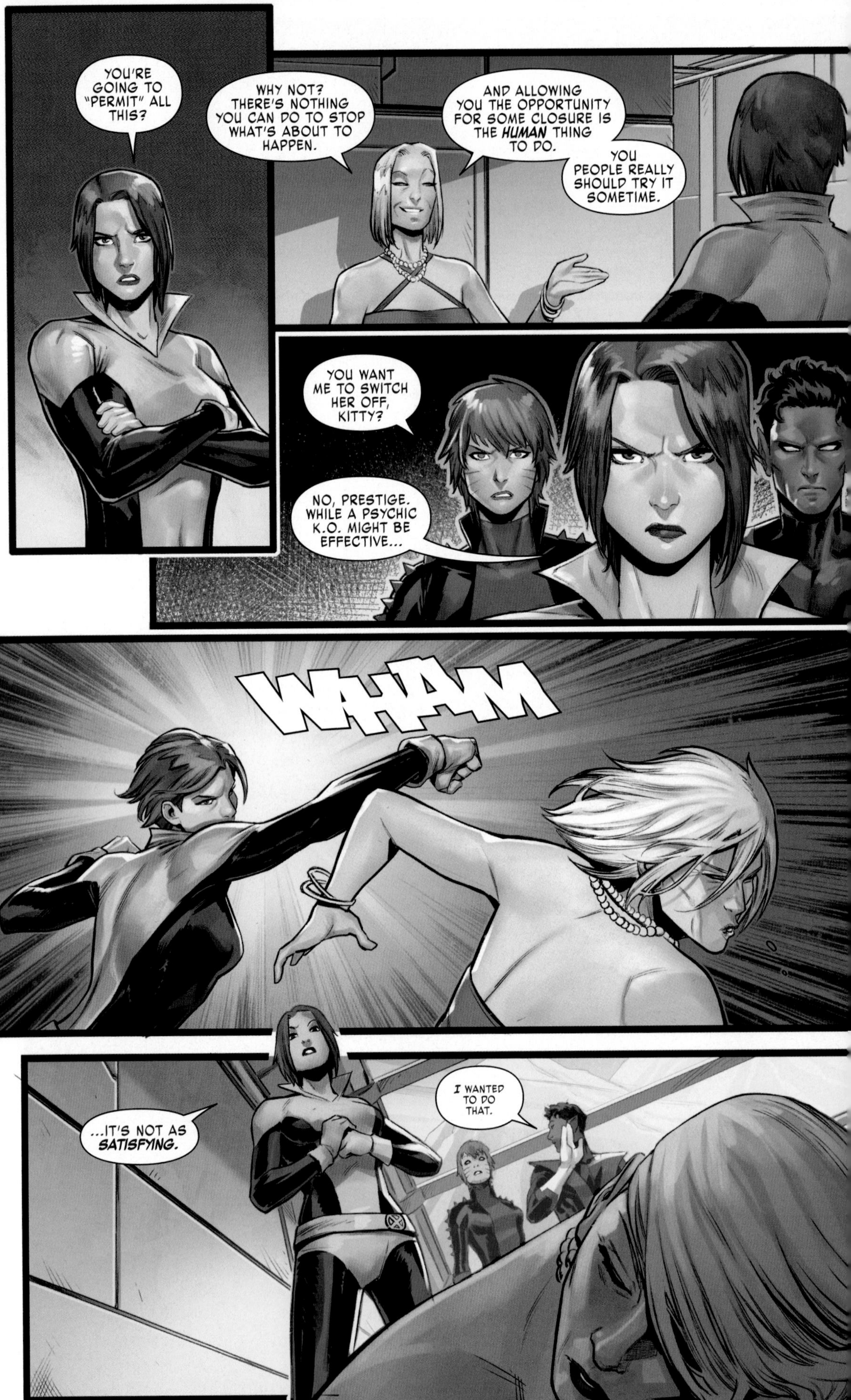
YOU'RE GOING TO "PERMIT" ALL THIS?
WHY NOT? THERE'S NOTHING YOU CAN DO TO STOP WHAT'S ABOUT TO HAPPEN.
AND ALLOWING YOU THE OPPORTUNITY FOR SOME CLOSURE IS THE *HUMAN* THING TO DO.
YOU PEOPLE REALLY SHOULD TRY IT SOMETIME.
YOU WANT ME TO SWITCH HER OFF, KITTY?
NO, PRESTIGE. WHILE A PSYCHIC K.O. MIGHT BE EFFECTIVE...
WHAM
...IT'S NOT AS *SATISFYING.*
I WANTED TO DO THAT.

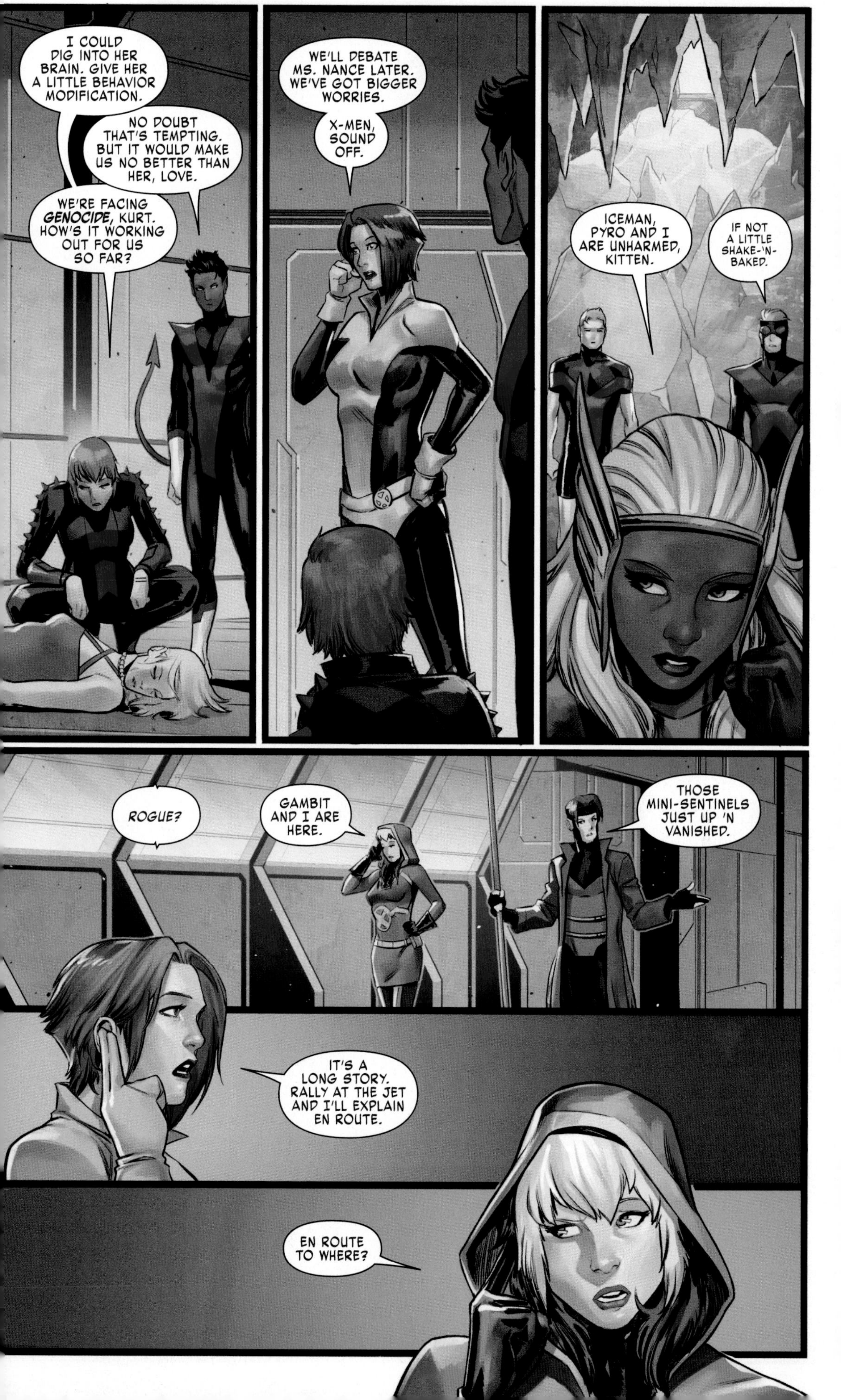
I COULD DIG INTO HER BRAIN. GIVE HER A LITTLE BEHAVIOR MODIFICATION.
NO DOUBT THAT'S TEMPTING. BUT IT WOULD MAKE US NO BETTER THAN HER, LOVE.
WE'RE FACING *GENOCIDE*, KURT. HOW'S IT WORKING OUT FOR US SO FAR?
WE'LL DEBATE MS. NANCE LATER. WE'VE GOT BIGGER WORRIES.
X-MEN, SOUND OFF.
ICEMAN, PYRO AND I ARE UNHARMED, KITTEN.
IF NOT A LITTLE SHAKE-'N-BAKED.
ROGUE?
GAMBIT AND I ARE HERE.
THOSE MINI-SENTINELS JUST UP 'N VANISHED.
IT'S A LONG STORY. RALLY AT THE JET AND I'LL EXPLAIN EN ROUTE.
EN ROUTE TO WHERE?

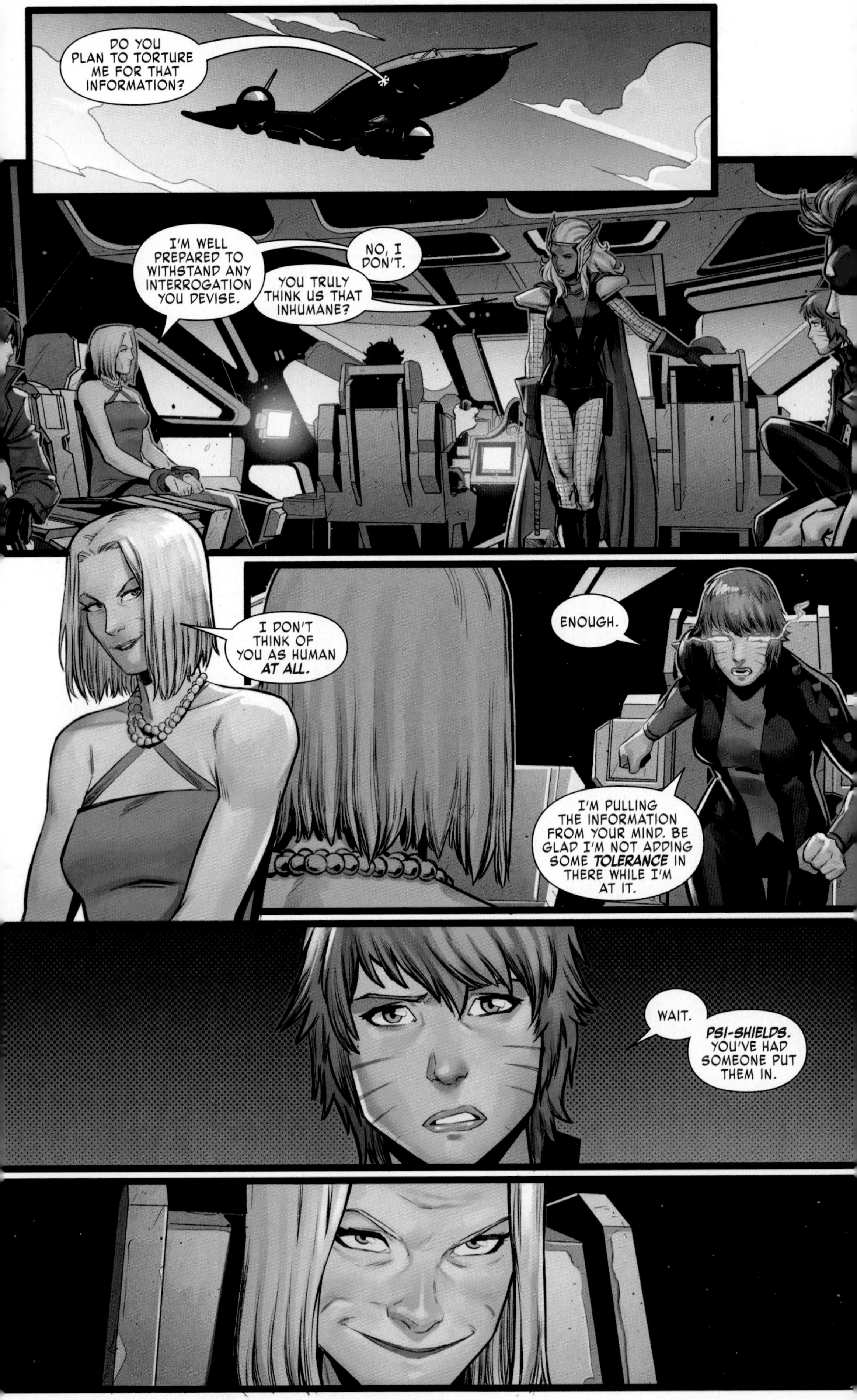
DO YOU PLAN TO TORTURE ME FOR THAT INFORMATION?
NO, I DON'T.
YOU TRULY THINK US THAT INHUMANE?
I'M WELL PREPARED TO WITHSTAND ANY INTERROGATION YOU DEVISE.
I DON'T THINK OF YOU AS HUMAN AT ALL.
ENOUGH.
I'M PULLING THE INFORMATION FROM YOUR MIND. BE GLAD I'M NOT ADDING SOME TOLERANCE IN THERE WHILE I'M AT IT.
WAIT.
PSI-SHIELDS. YOU'VE HAD SOMEONE PUT THEM IN.

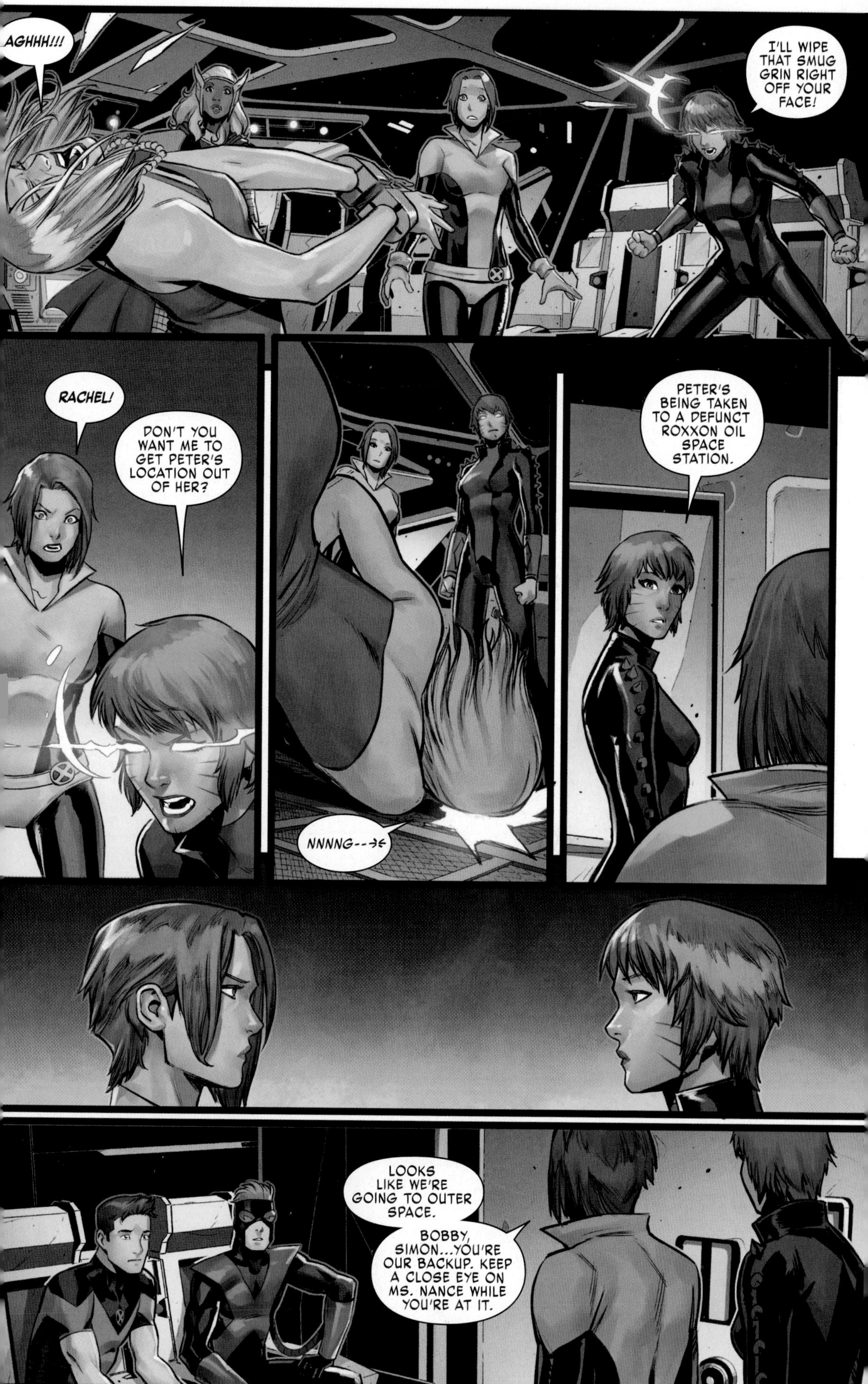
AGHHH!!!
I'LL WIPE THAT SMUG GRIN RIGHT OFF YOUR FACE!
RACHEL!
DON'T YOU WANT ME TO GET PETER'S LOCATION OUT OF HER?
NNNNG--
PETER'S BEING TAKEN TO A DEFUNCT ROXXON OIL SPACE STATION.
LOOKS LIKE WE'RE GOING TO OUTER SPACE.
BOBBY, SIMON...YOU'RE OUR BACKUP. KEEP A CLOSE EYE ON MS. NANCE WHILE YOU'RE AT IT.

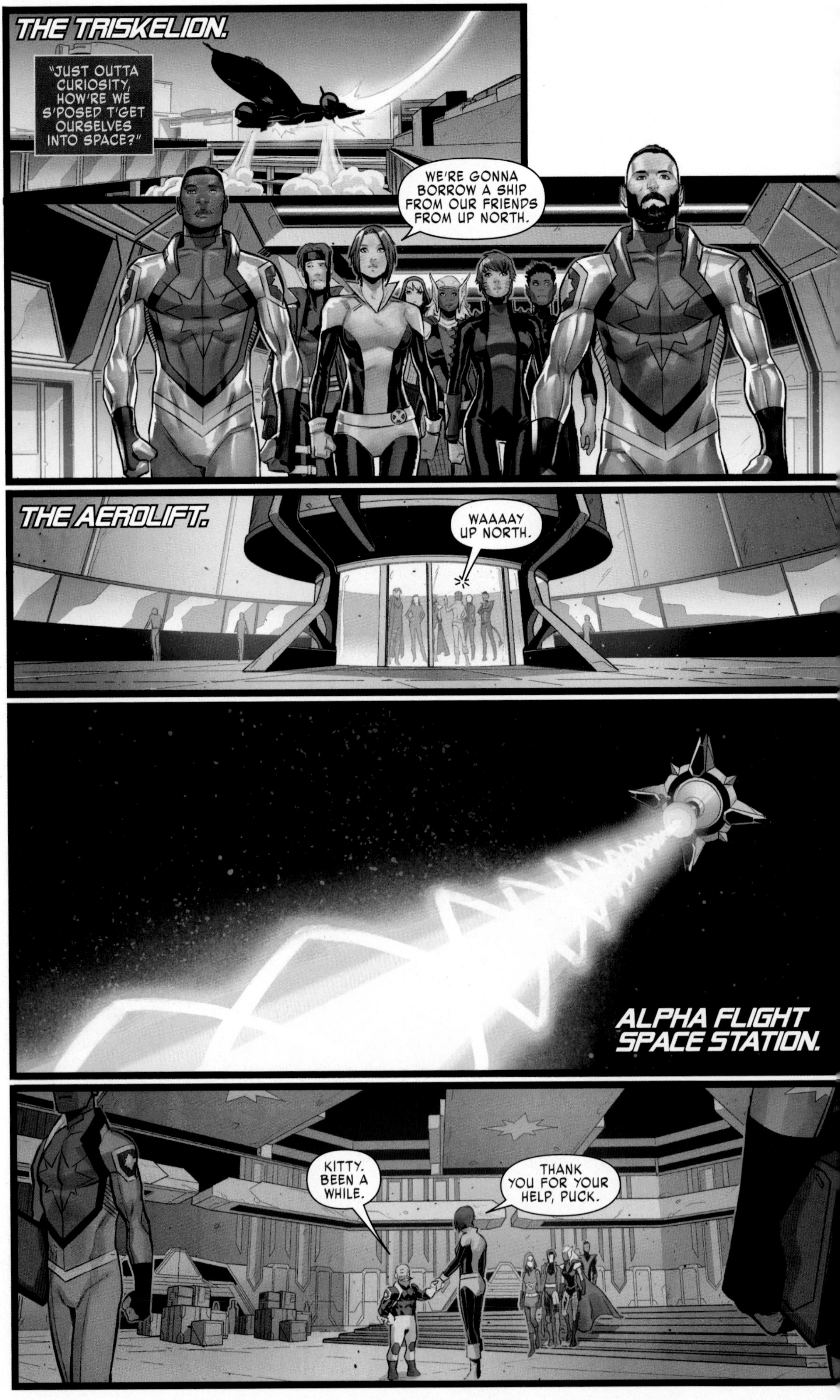
THE TRISKELION.
"JUST OUTTA CURIOSITY, HOW'RE WE S'POSED T'GET OURSELVES INTO SPACE?"
WE'RE GONNA BORROW A SHIP FROM OUR FRIENDS FROM UP NORTH.
THE AEROLIFT.
WAAAAY UP NORTH.
ALPHA FLIGHT SPACE STATION.
KITTY. BEEN A WHILE.
THANK YOU FOR YOUR HELP, PUCK.

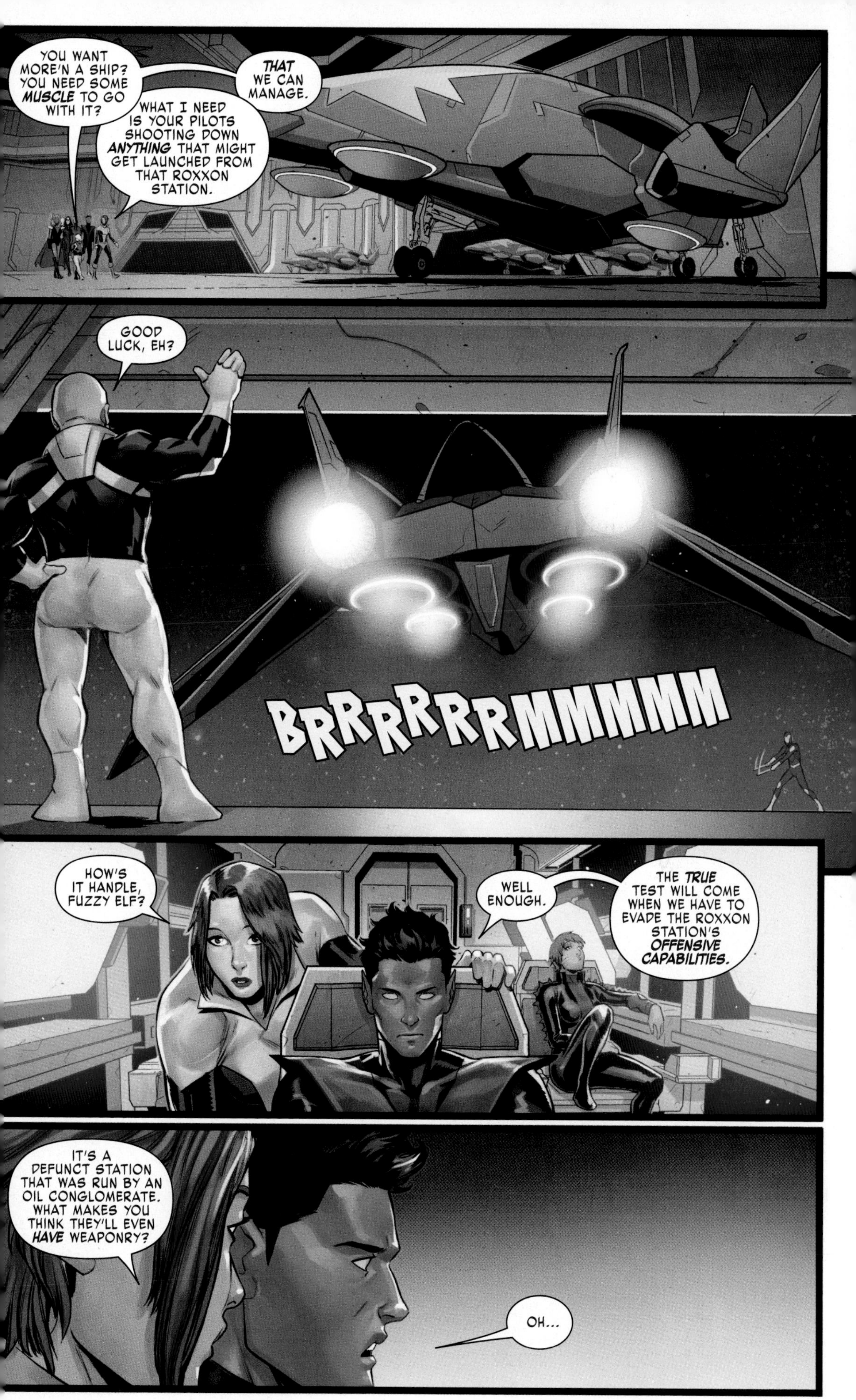

YOU WANT MORE'N A SHIP? YOU NEED SOME MUSCLE TO GO WITH IT?
THAT WE CAN MANAGE.
WHAT I NEED IS YOUR PILOTS SHOOTING DOWN ANYTHING THAT MIGHT GET LAUNCHED FROM THAT ROXXON STATION.
GOOD LUCK, EH?
BRRRRRRMMMMMM
HOW'S IT HANDLE, FUZZY ELF?
WELL ENOUGH.
THE TRUE TEST WILL COME WHEN WE HAVE TO EVADE THE ROXXON STATION'S OFFENSIVE CAPABILITIES.
IT'S A DEFUNCT STATION THAT WAS RUN BY AN OIL CONGLOMERATE. WHAT MAKES YOU THINK THEY'LL EVEN HAVE WEAPONRY?
OH...

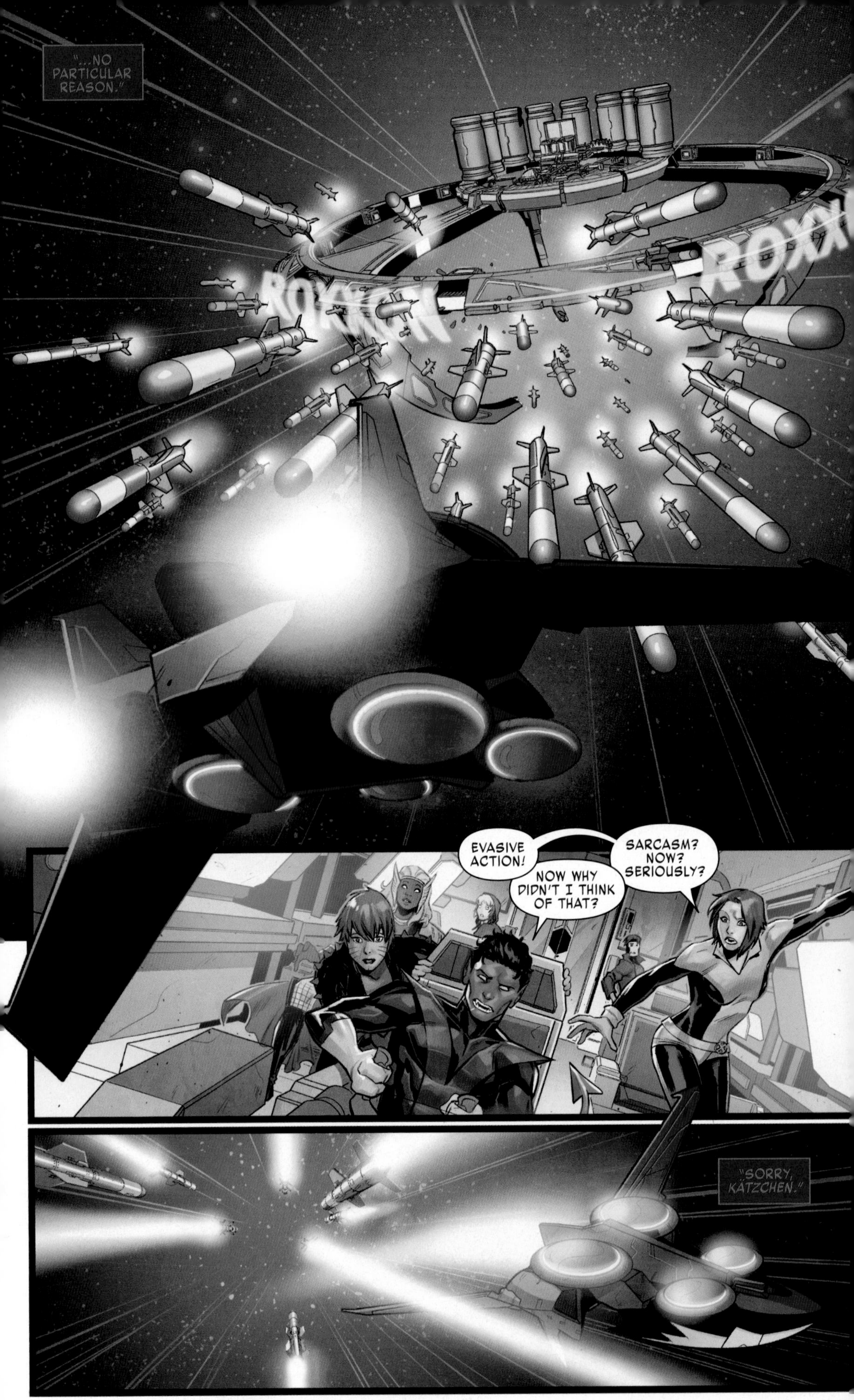
"...NO PARTICULAR REASON."
ROXXX
ROXXX
EVASIVE ACTION!
SARCASM? NOW? SERIOUSLY?
NOW WHY DIDN'T I THINK OF THAT?
"SORRY, KÄTZCHEN."

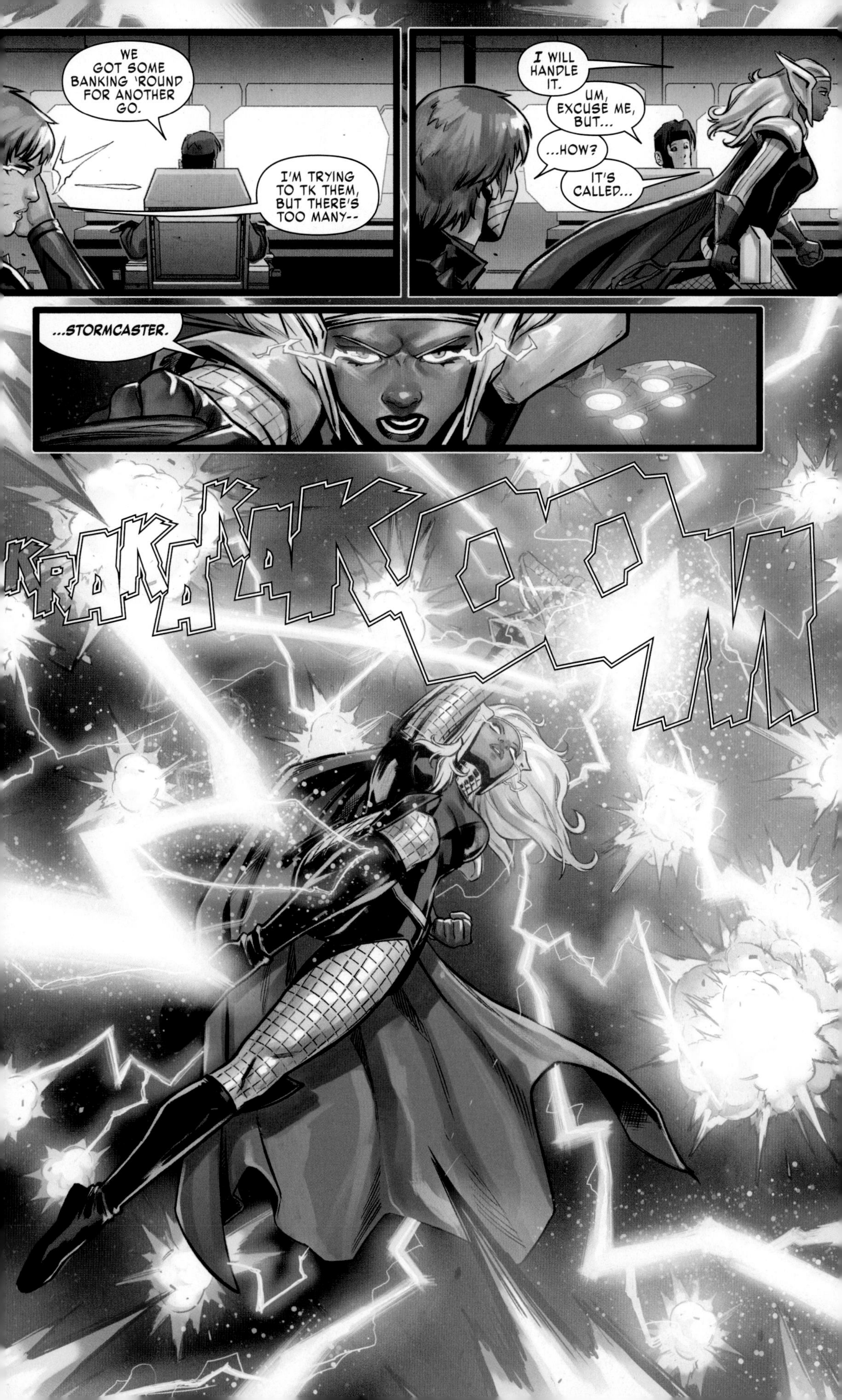

WE GOT SOME BANKING 'ROUND FOR ANOTHER GO.
I'M TRYING TO TK THEM, BUT THERE'S TOO MANY--
I WILL HANDLE IT.
UM, EXCUSE ME, BUT...
...HOW?
IT'S CALLED...
...STORMCASTER.
KRAKAKAKAKOOOM

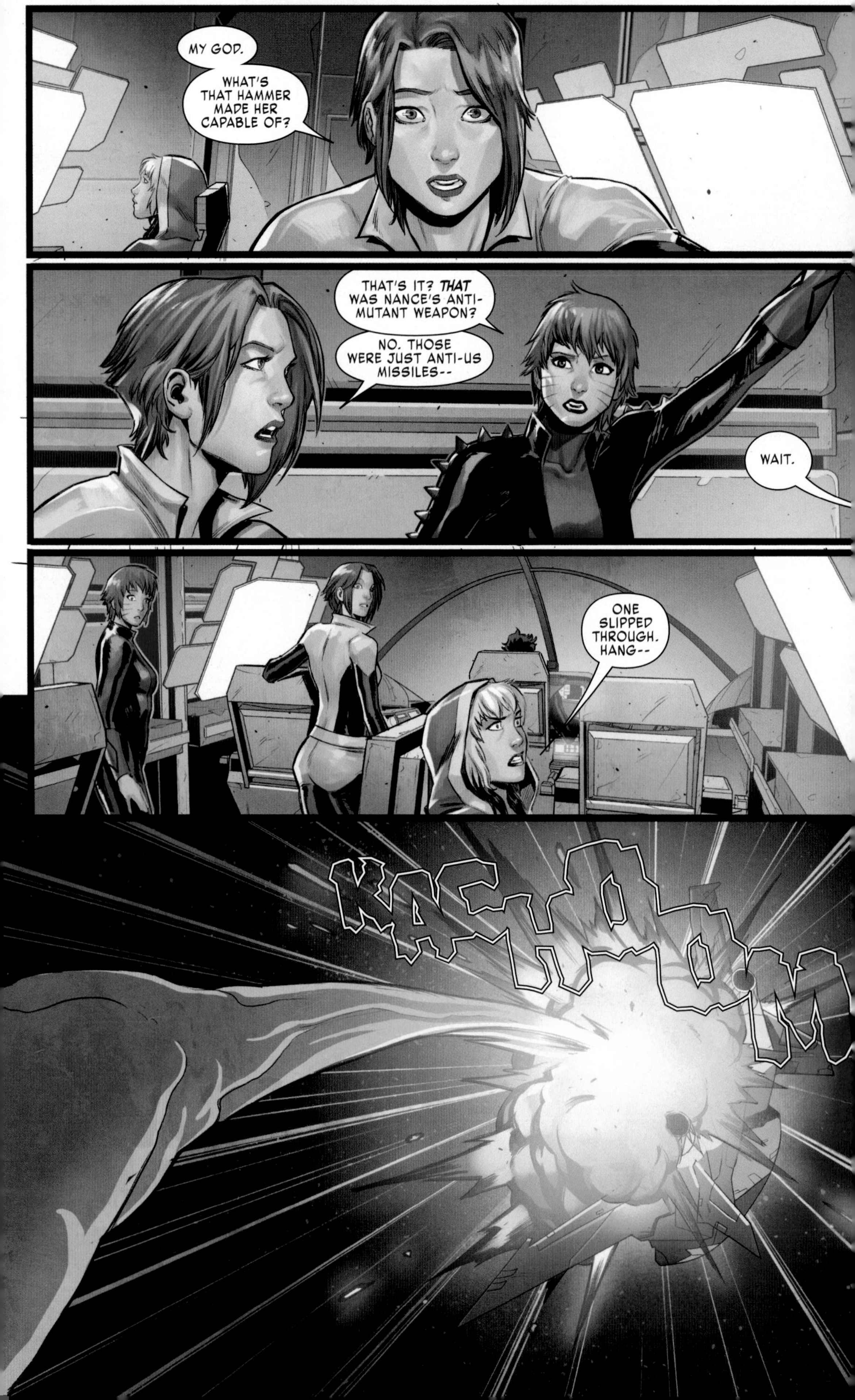
MY GOD.
WHAT'S THAT HAMMER MADE HER CAPABLE OF?
THAT'S IT? *THAT* WAS NANCE'S ANTI-MUTANT WEAPON?
NO. THOSE WERE JUST ANTI-US MISSILES--
WAIT.
ONE SLIPPED THROUGH. HANG--
KA-THOOM

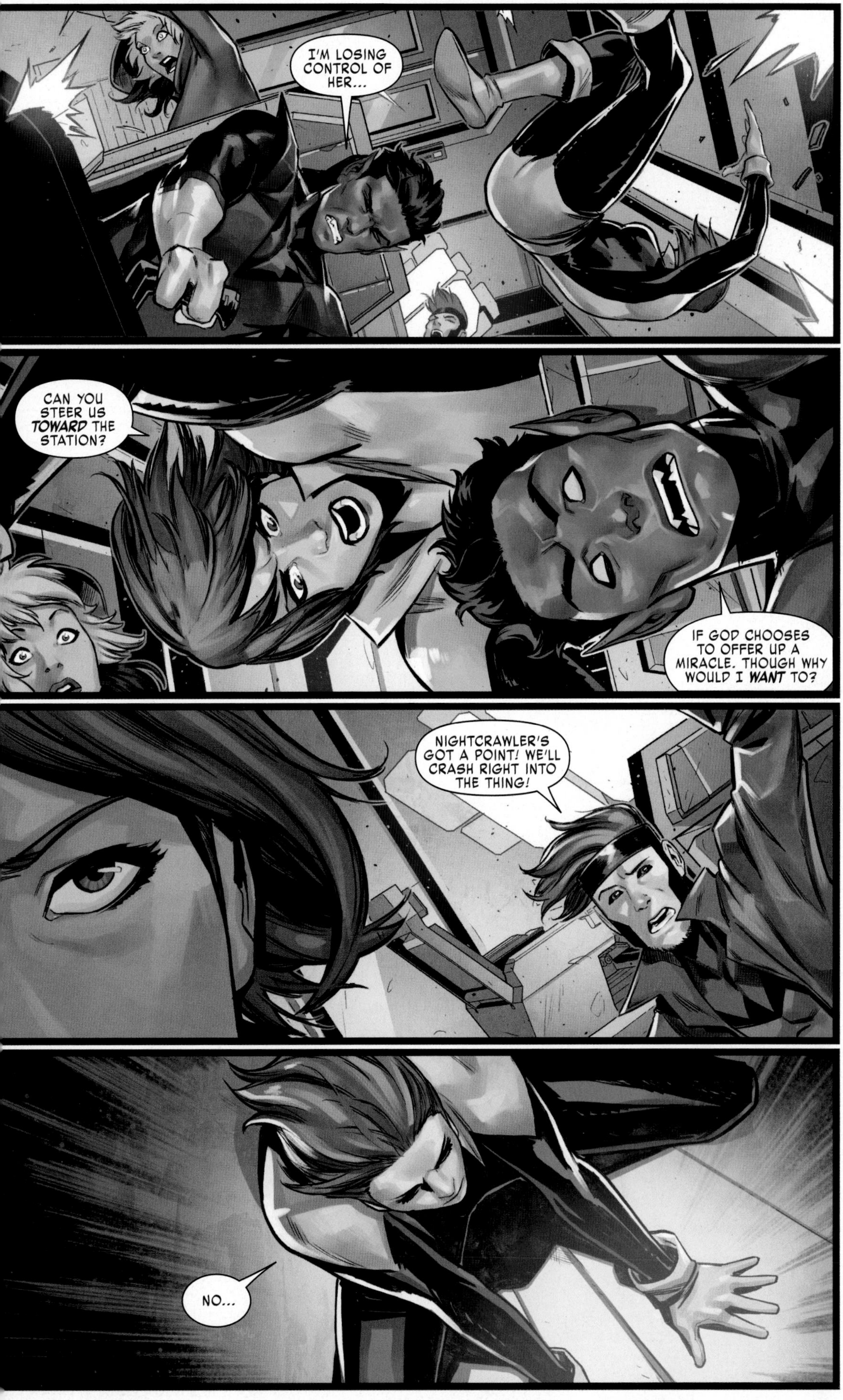

I'M LOSING CONTROL OF HER...
CAN YOU STEER US *TOWARD* THE STATION?
IF GOD CHOOSES TO OFFER UP A MIRACLE. THOUGH WHY WOULD I *WANT* TO?
NIGHTCRAWLER'S GOT A POINT! WE'LL CRASH RIGHT INTO THE THING!
NO...

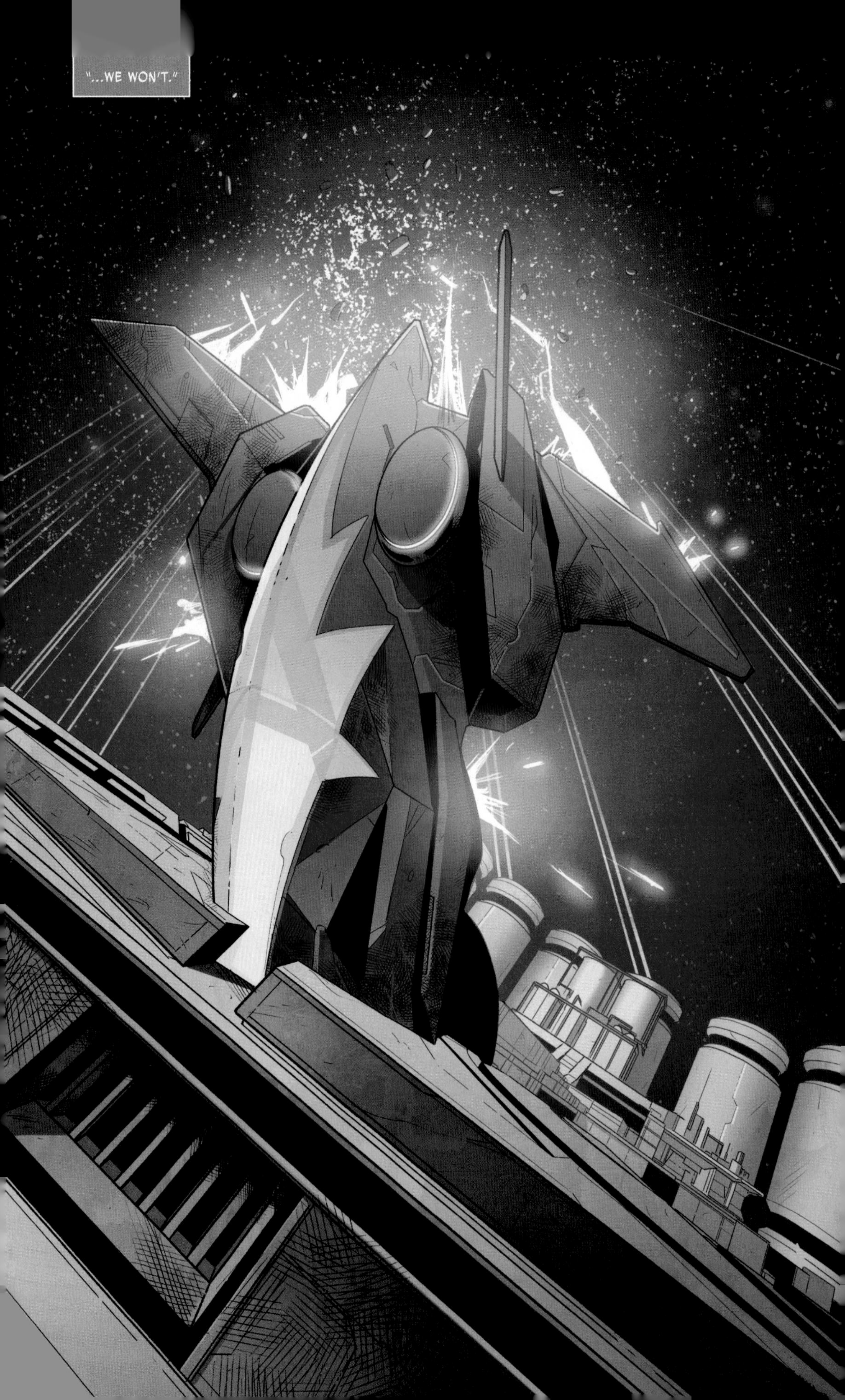
"...WE WON'T."

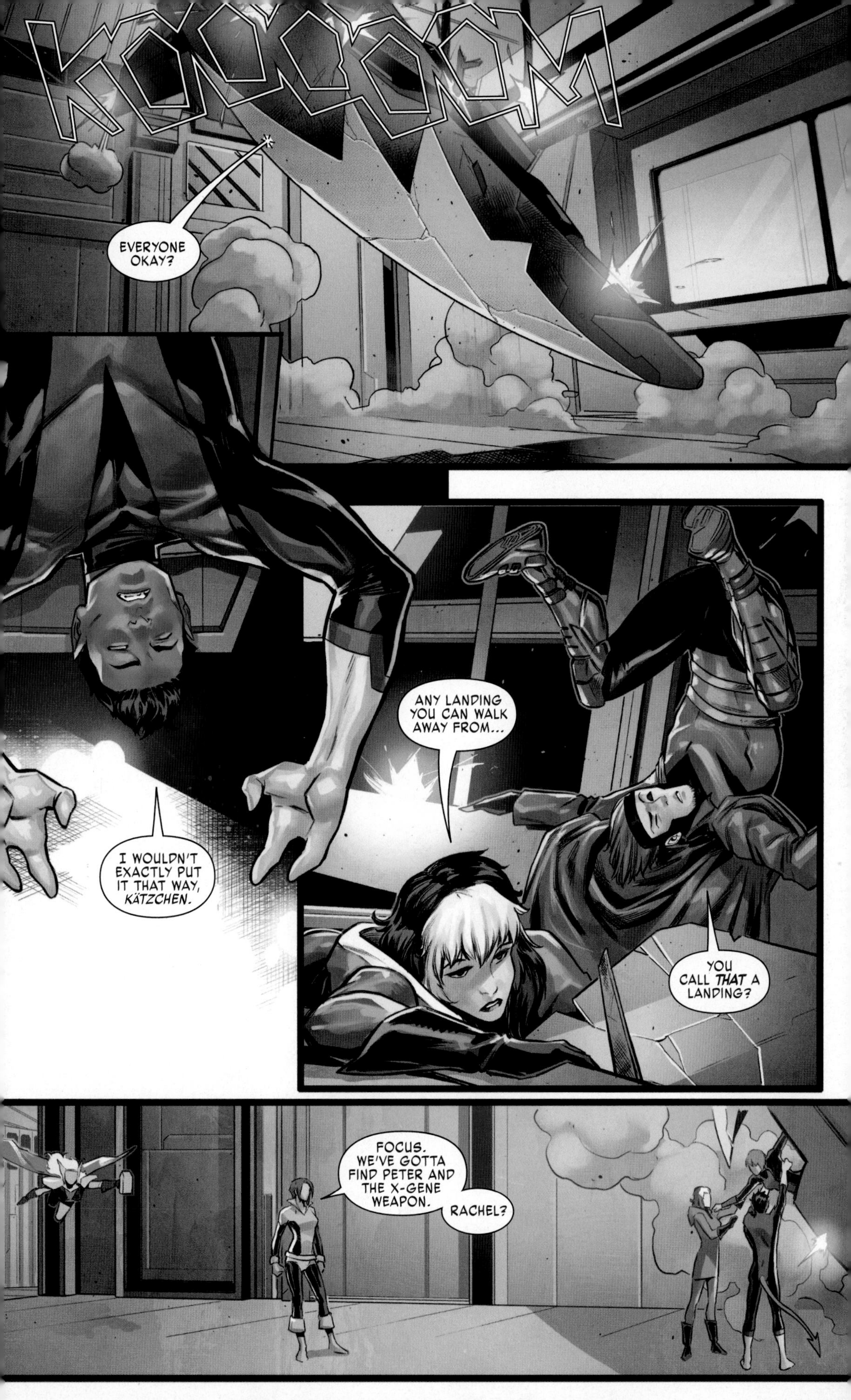
KOOOOOM
EVERYONE OKAY?
ANY LANDING YOU CAN WALK AWAY FROM...
I WOULDN'T EXACTLY PUT IT THAT WAY, KÄTZCHEN.
YOU CALL THAT A LANDING?
FOCUS. WE'VE GOTTA FIND PETER AND THE X-GENE WEAPON.
RACHEL?

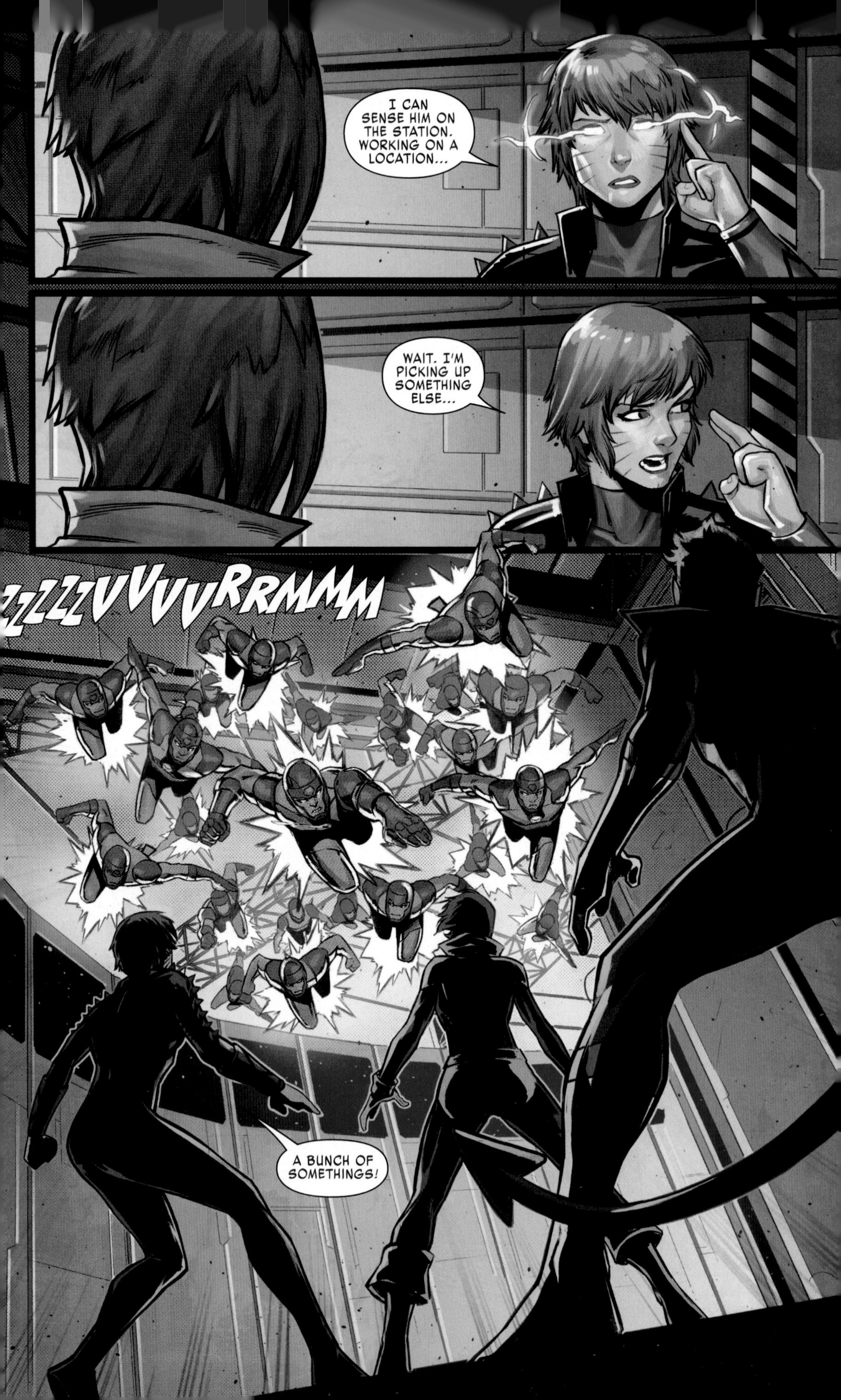
I CAN SENSE HIM ON THE STATION. WORKING ON A LOCATION...
WAIT. I'M PICKING UP SOMETHING ELSE...
ZZZZZVVVVVRRMMMM
A BUNCH OF SOMETHINGS!

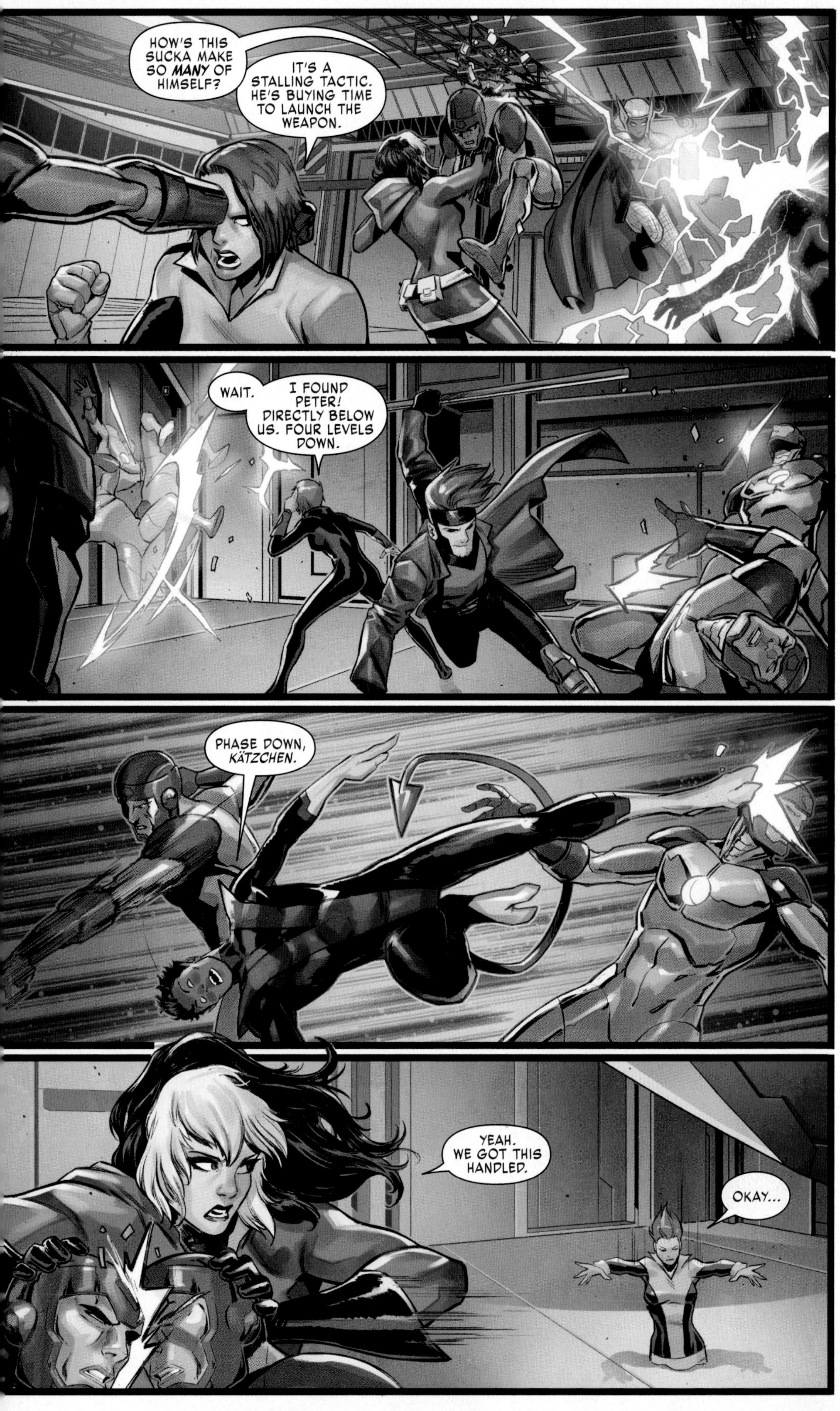
HOW'S THIS SUCKA MAKE SO *MANY* OF HIMSELF?
IT'S A STALLING TACTIC. HE'S BUYING TIME TO LAUNCH THE WEAPON.
WAIT.
I FOUND PETER! DIRECTLY BELOW US. FOUR LEVELS DOWN.
PHASE DOWN, KÄTZCHEN.
YEAH. WE GOT THIS HANDLED.
OKAY...

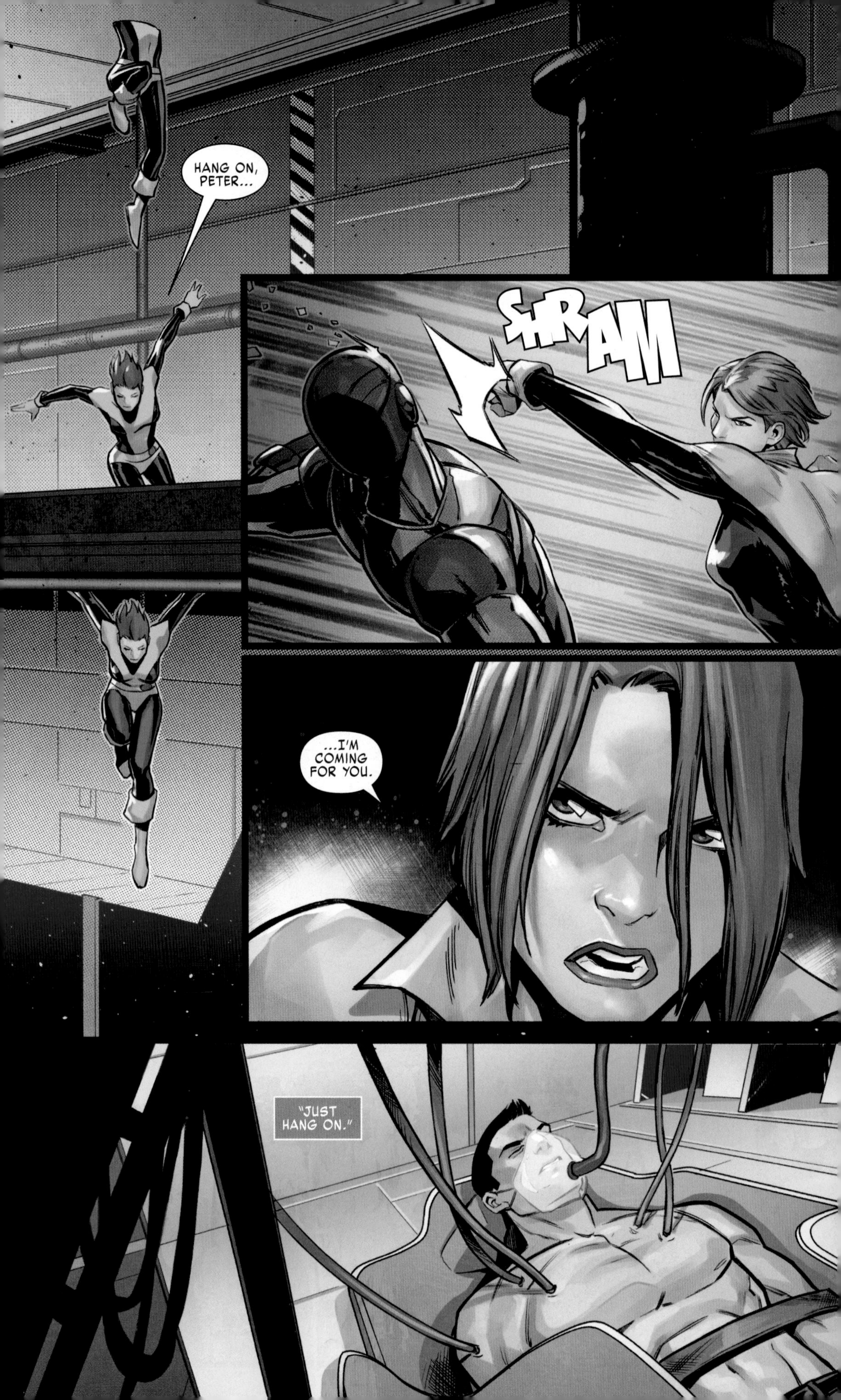
HANG ON, PETER...
SHRAAM
...I'M COMING FOR YOU.
"JUST HANG ON."

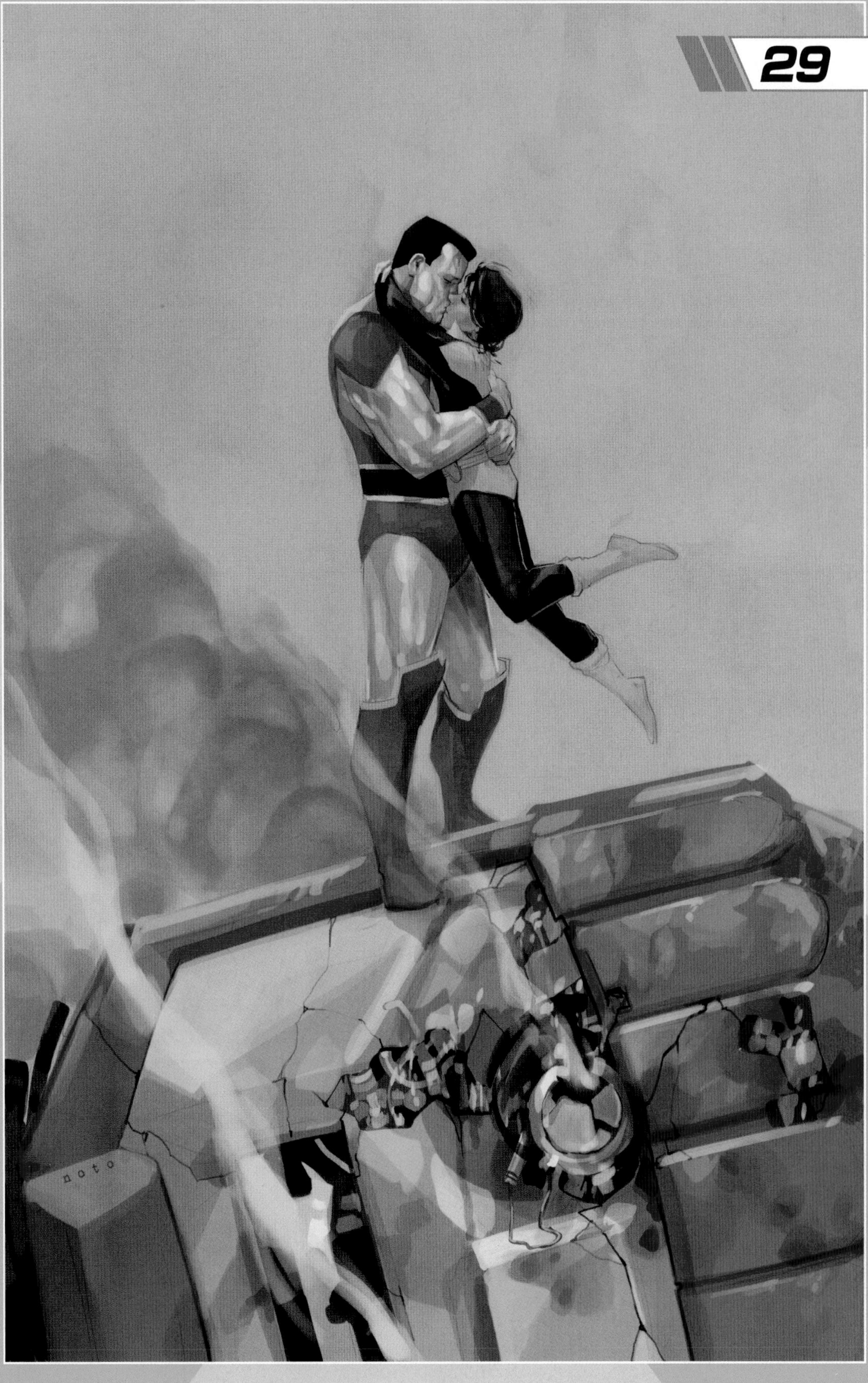
29
noto

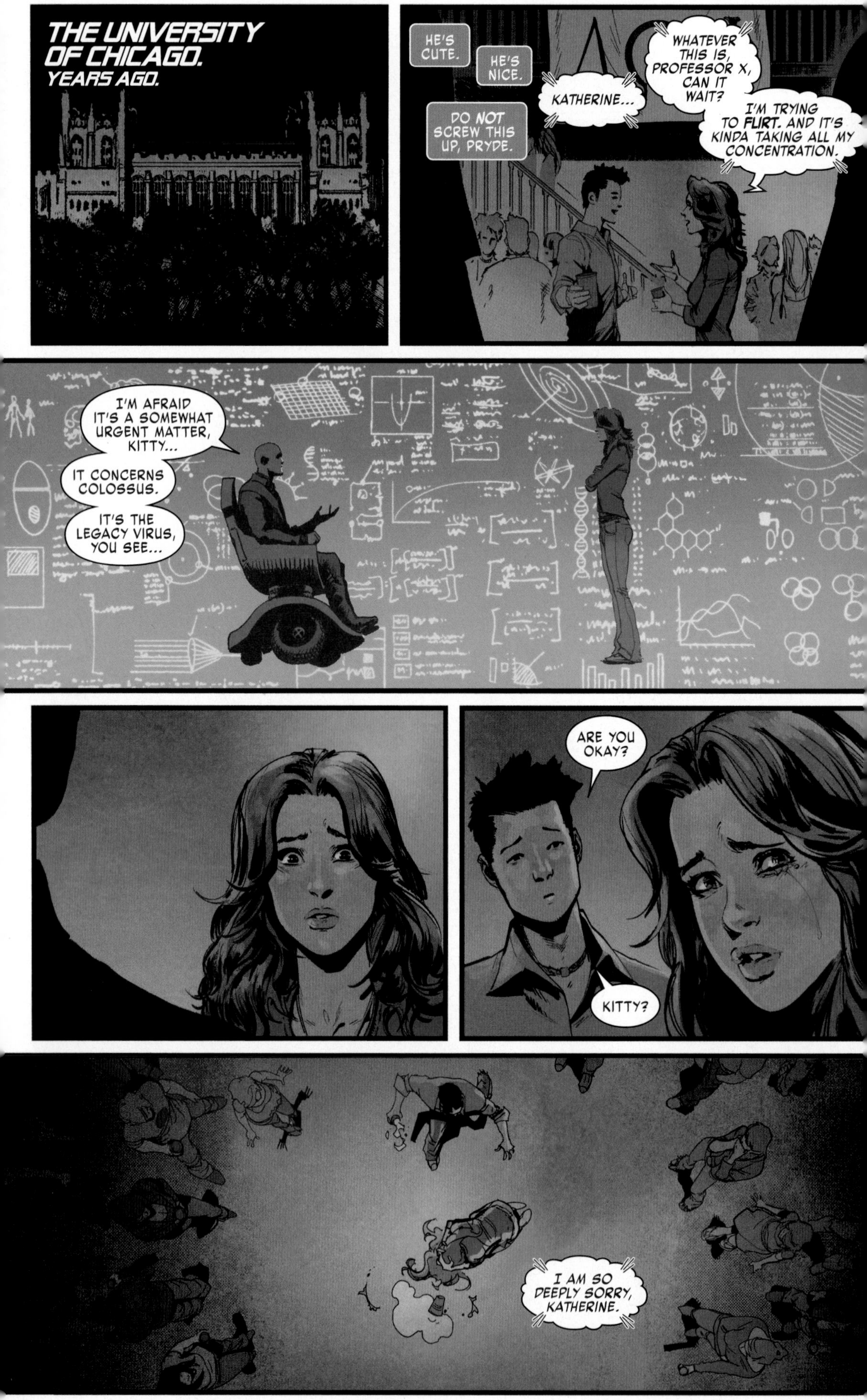
THE UNIVERSITY OF CHICAGO.
YEARS AGO.
HE'S CUTE.
HE'S NICE.
DO NOT SCREW THIS UP, PRYDE.
KATHERINE...
WHATEVER THIS IS, PROFESSOR X, CAN IT WAIT?
I'M TRYING TO FLIRT. AND IT'S KINDA TAKING ALL MY CONCENTRATION.
I'M AFRAID IT'S A SOMEWHAT URGENT MATTER, KITTY...
IT CONCERNS COLOSSUS.
IT'S THE LEGACY VIRUS, YOU SEE...
ARE YOU OKAY?
KITTY?
I AM SO DEEPLY SORRY, KATHERINE.

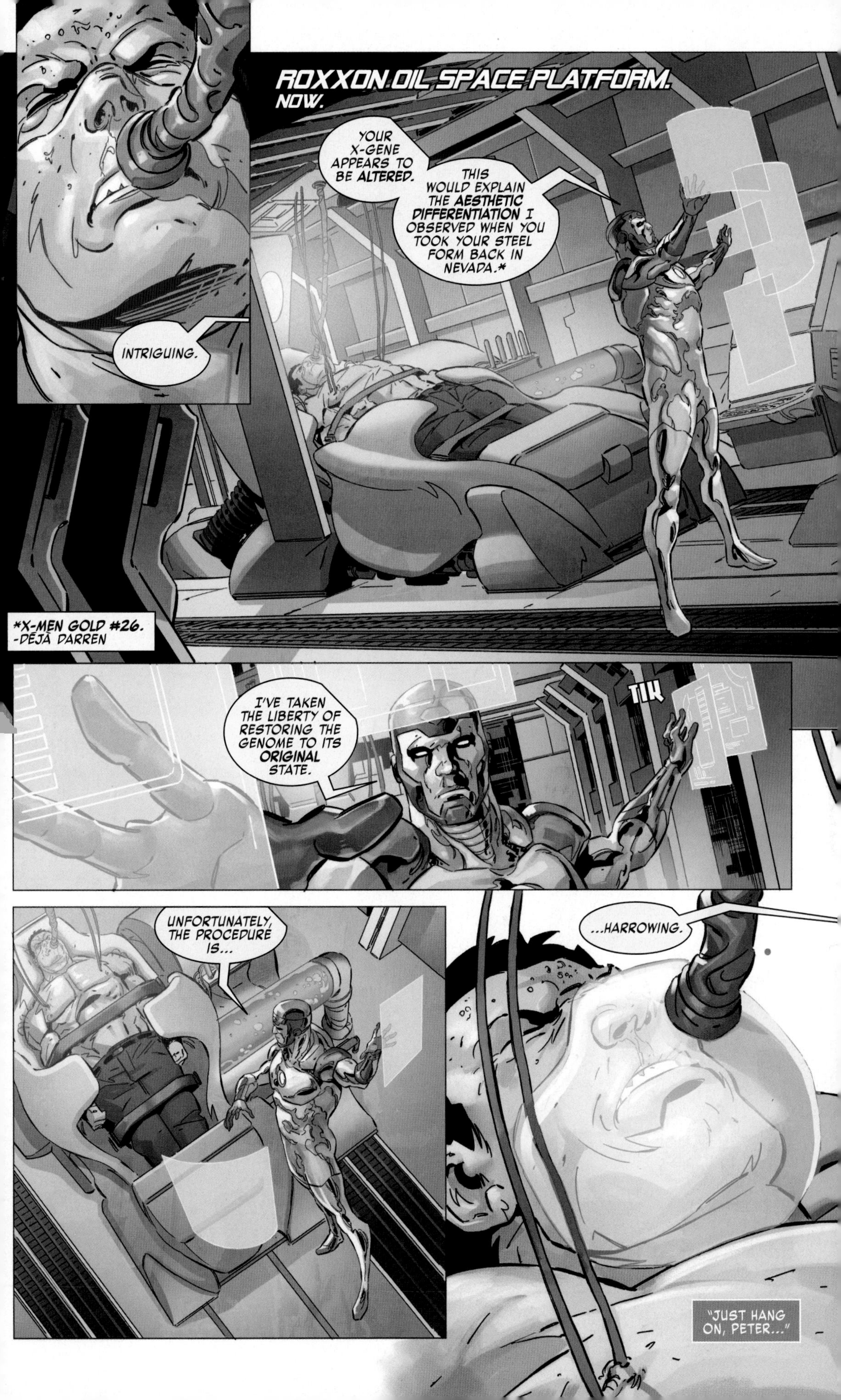
ROXXON OIL SPACE PLATFORM.
NOW.
YOUR X-GENE APPEARS TO BE ALTERED.
THIS WOULD EXPLAIN THE AESTHETIC DIFFERENTIATION I OBSERVED WHEN YOU TOOK YOUR STEEL FORM BACK IN NEVADA.*
INTRIGUING.
*X-MEN GOLD #26. -DÉJÀ DARREN
I'VE TAKEN THE LIBERTY OF RESTORING THE GENOME TO ITS ORIGINAL STATE.
TIK
UNFORTUNATELY, THE PROCEDURE IS...
...HARROWING.
"JUST HANG ON, PETER..."

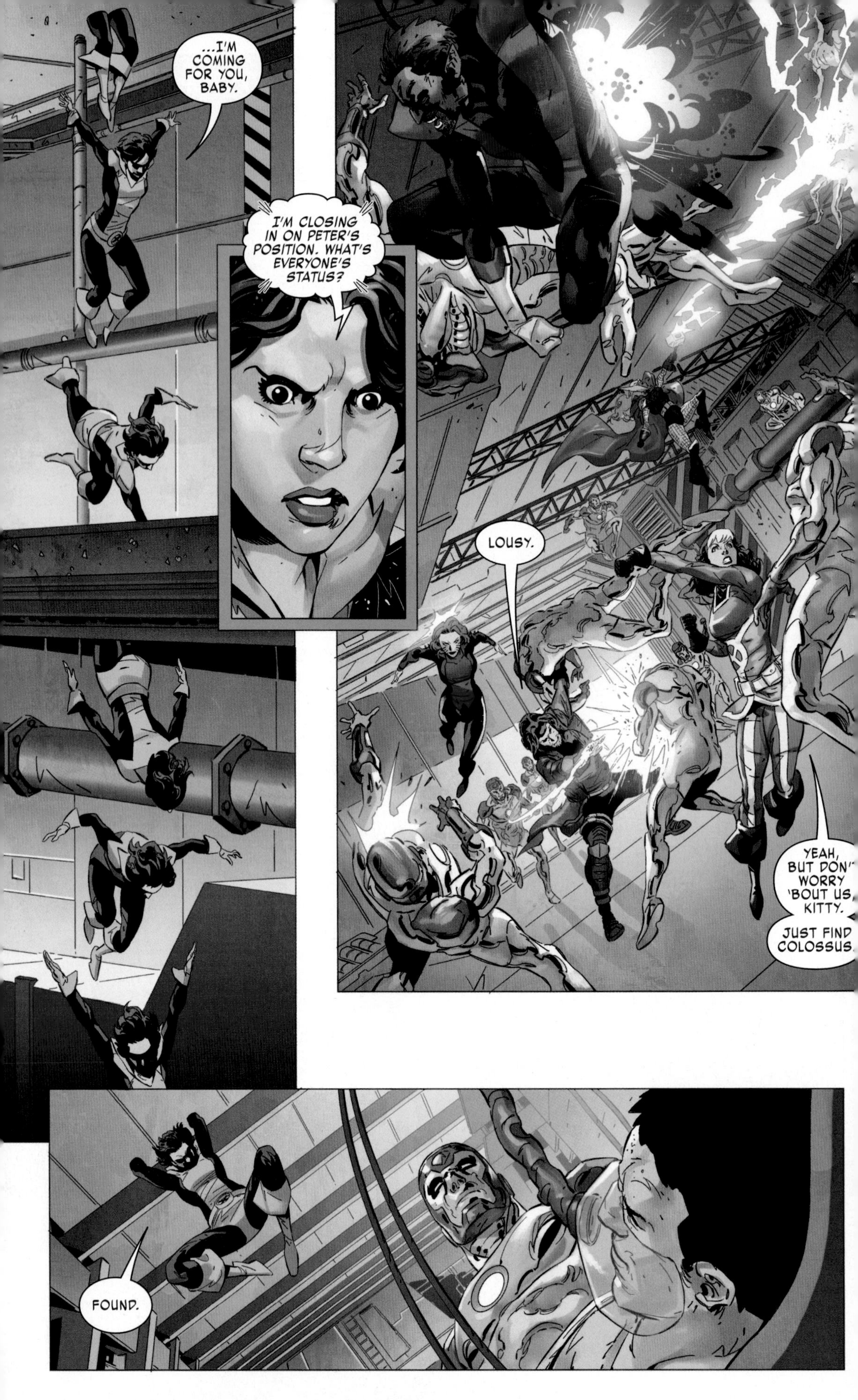
...I'M COMING FOR YOU, BABY.
I'M CLOSING IN ON PETER'S POSITION. WHAT'S EVERYONE'S STATUS?
LOUSY.
YEAH, BUT DON'T WORRY 'BOUT US, KITTY.
JUST FIND COLOSSUS.
FOUND.

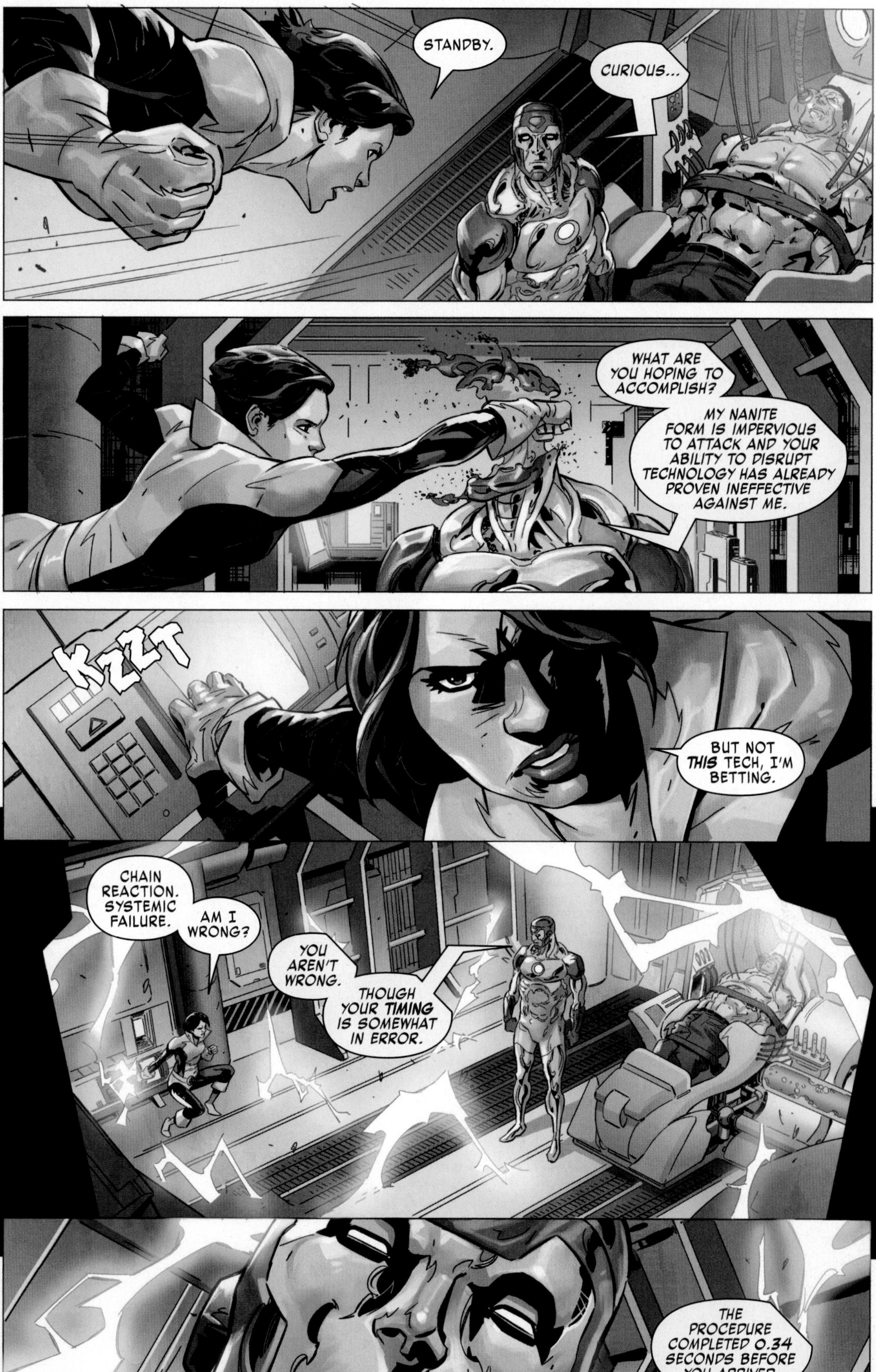
STANDBY.
CURIOUS...
WHAT ARE YOU HOPING TO ACCOMPLISH?
MY NANITE FORM IS IMPERVIOUS TO ATTACK AND YOUR ABILITY TO DISRUPT TECHNOLOGY HAS ALREADY PROVEN INEFFECTIVE AGAINST ME.
KZZT
BUT NOT THIS TECH, I'M BETTING.
CHAIN REACTION. SYSTEMIC FAILURE.
AM I WRONG?
YOU AREN'T WRONG.
THOUGH YOUR TIMING IS SOMEWHAT IN ERROR.
THE PROCEDURE COMPLETED 0.34 SECONDS BEFORE YOU ARRIVED.

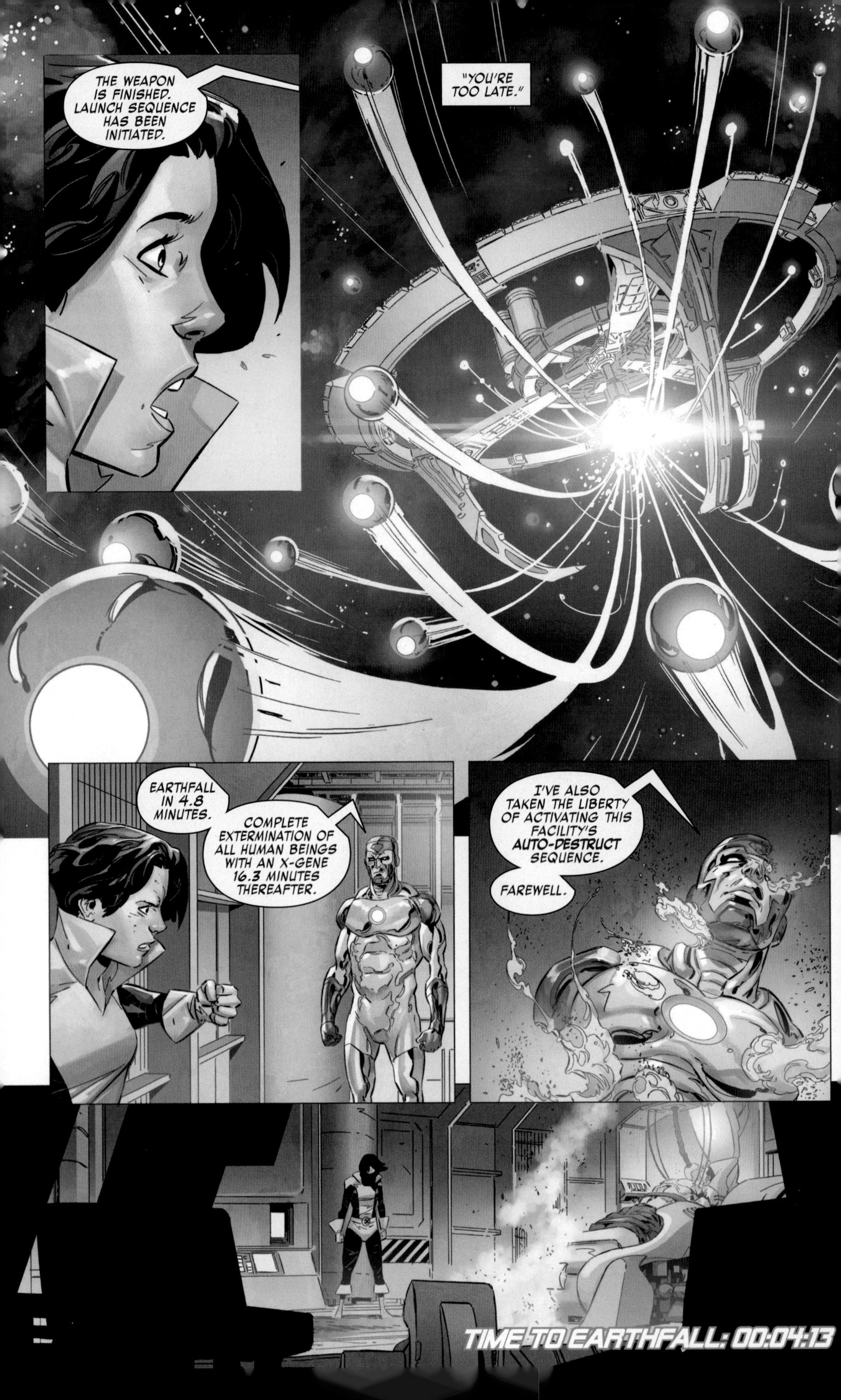

THE WEAPON IS FINISHED. LAUNCH SEQUENCE HAS BEEN INITIATED.
"YOU'RE TOO LATE."
EARTHFALL IN 4.8 MINUTES.
COMPLETE EXTERMINATION OF ALL HUMAN BEINGS WITH AN X-GENE 16.3 MINUTES THEREAFTER.
I'VE ALSO TAKEN THE LIBERTY OF ACTIVATING THIS FACILITY'S **AUTO-DESTRUCT** SEQUENCE.
FAREWELL.
TIME TO EARTHFALL: 00:04:13

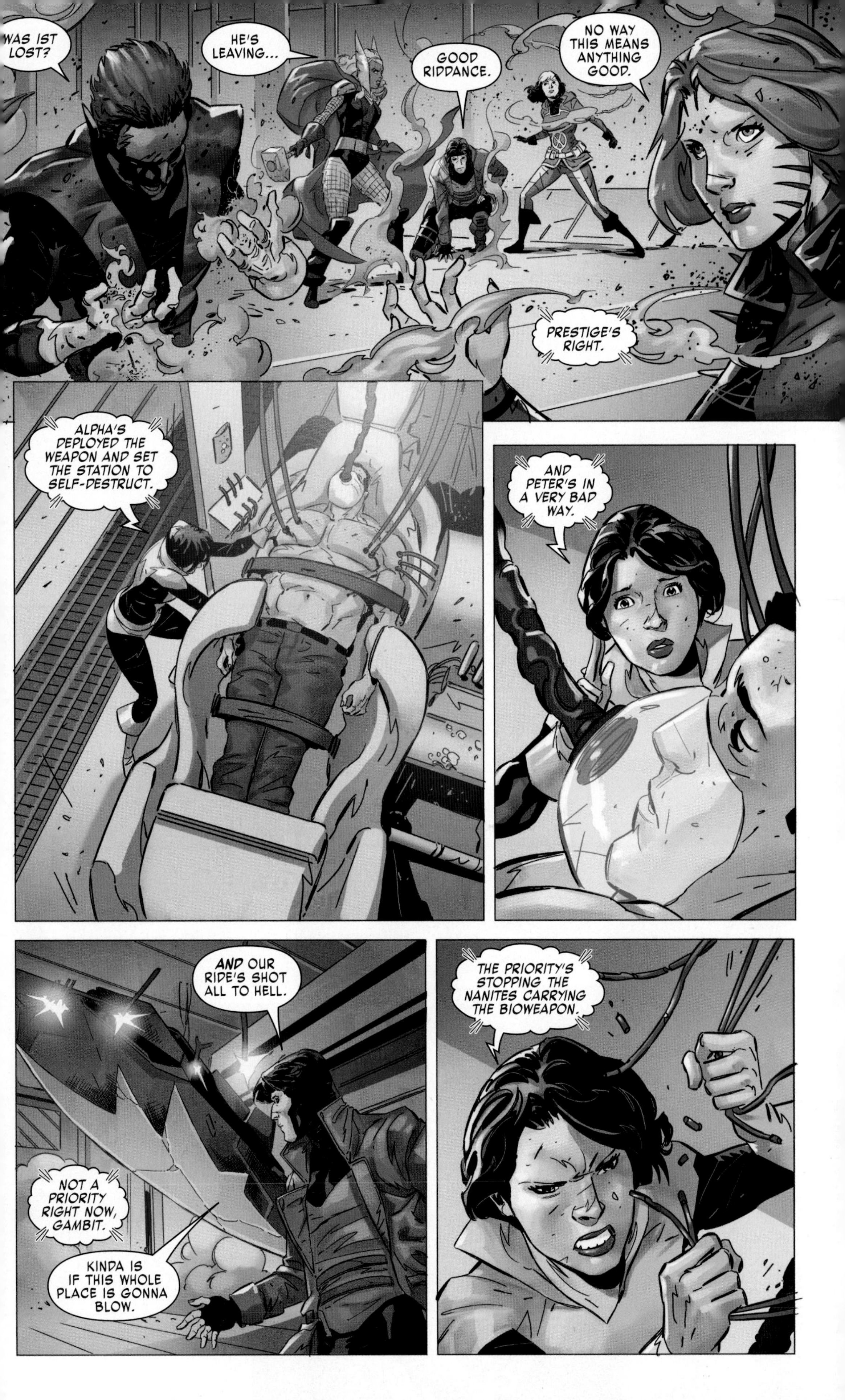
WAS IST LOST?
HE'S LEAVING...
GOOD RIDDANCE.
NO WAY THIS MEANS ANYTHING GOOD.
PRESTIGE'S RIGHT.
ALPHA'S DEPLOYED THE WEAPON AND SET THE STATION TO SELF-DESTRUCT.
AND PETER'S IN A VERY BAD WAY.
AND OUR RIDE'S SHOT ALL TO HELL.
NOT A PRIORITY RIGHT NOW, GAMBIT.
KINDA IS IF THIS WHOLE PLACE IS GONNA BLOW.
THE PRIORITY'S STOPPING THE NANITES CARRYING THE BIOWEAPON.

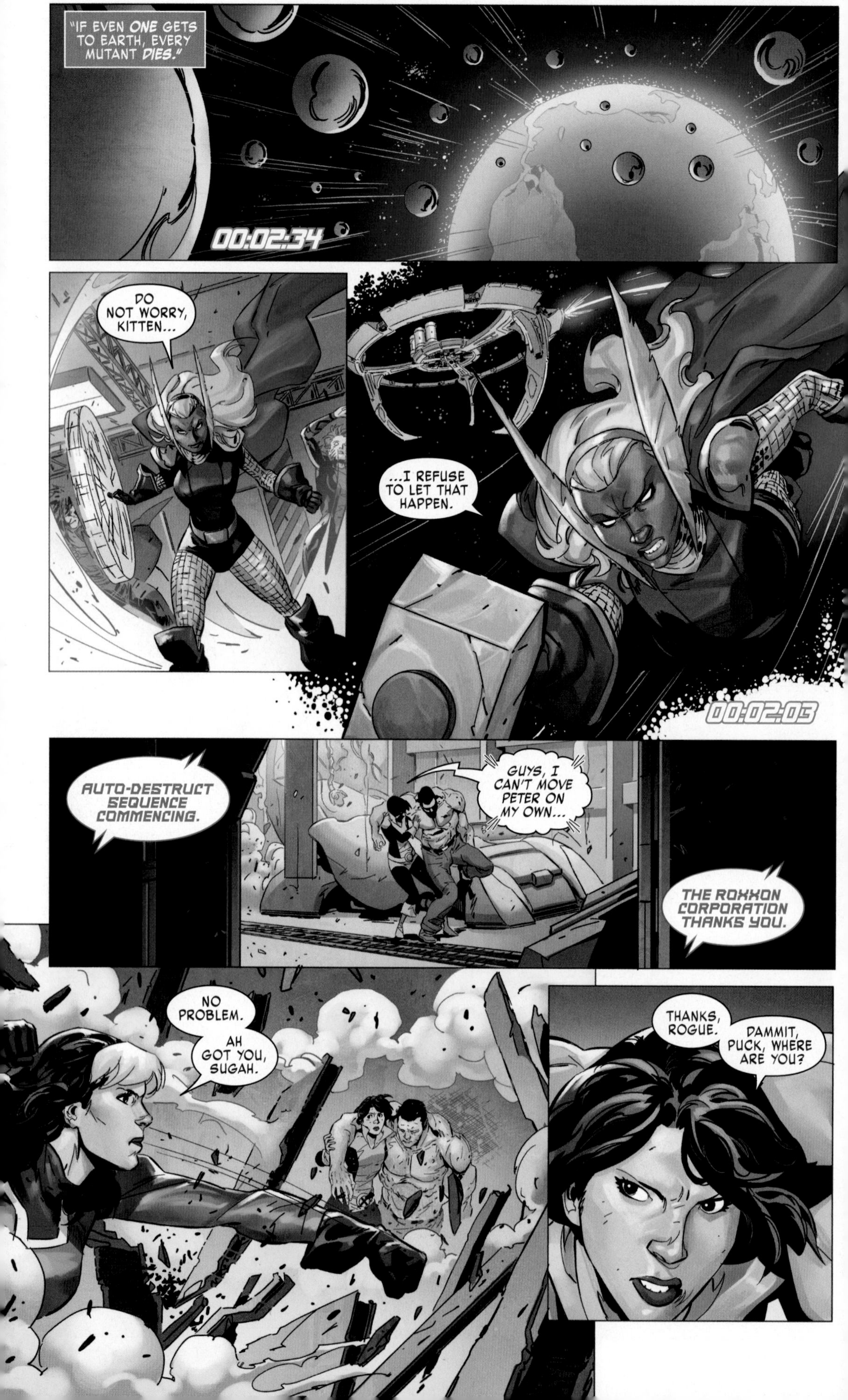
"IF EVEN ONE GETS TO EARTH, EVERY MUTANT DIES."
00:02:34
DO NOT WORRY, KITTEN...
...I REFUSE TO LET THAT HAPPEN.
00:02:03
AUTO-DESTRUCT SEQUENCE COMMENCING.
GUYS, I CAN'T MOVE PETER ON MY OWN...
THE ROXXON CORPORATION THANKS YOU.
NO PROBLEM.
AH GOT YOU, SUGAH.
THANKS, ROGUE.
DAMMIT, PUCK, WHERE ARE YOU?

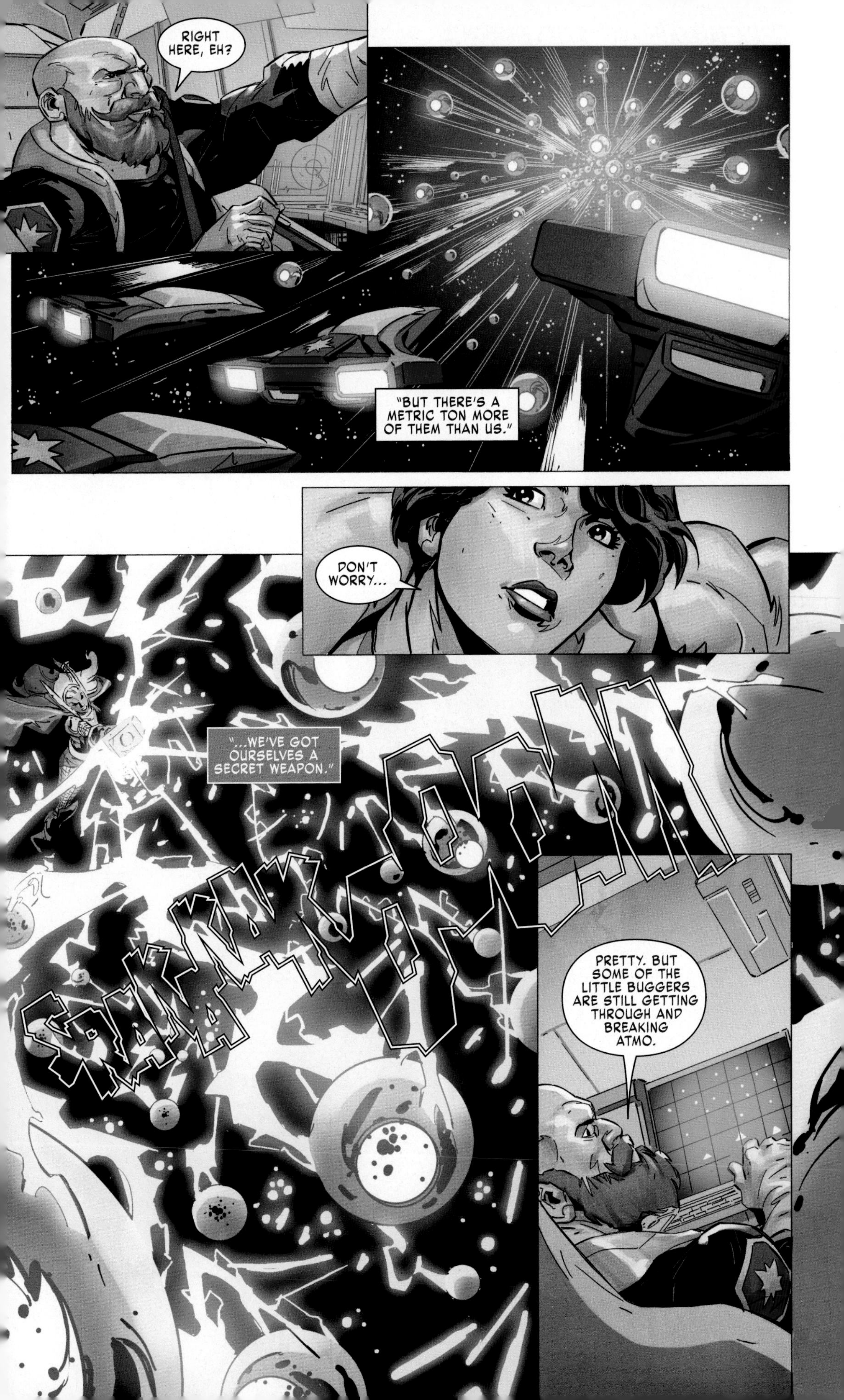
RIGHT HERE, EH?
"BUT THERE'S A METRIC TON MORE OF THEM THAN US."
DON'T WORRY...
"...WE'VE GOT OURSELVES A SECRET WEAPON."
PRETTY. BUT SOME OF THE LITTLE BUGGERS ARE STILL GETTING THROUGH AND BREAKING ATMO.

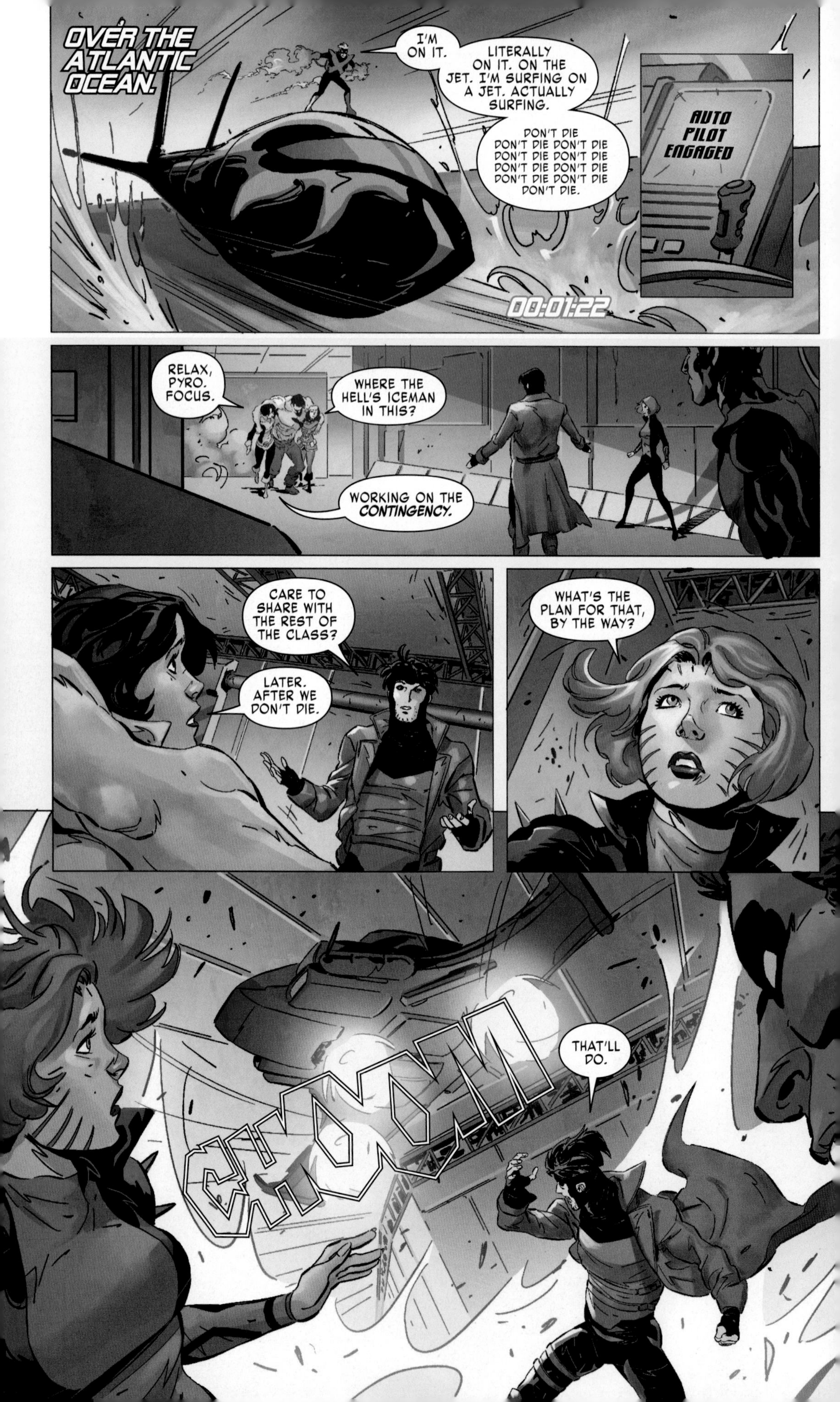
OVER THE ATLANTIC OCEAN.
I'M ON IT.
LITERALLY ON IT. ON THE JET. I'M SURFING ON A JET. ACTUALLY SURFING.
DON'T DIE DON'T DIE DON'T DIE DON'T DIE DON'T DIE DON'T DIE DON'T DIE DON'T DIE DON'T DIE DON'T DIE.
AUTO PILOT ENGAGED
00:01:22
RELAX, PYRO. FOCUS.
WHERE THE HELL'S ICEMAN IN THIS?
WORKING ON THE CONTINGENCY.
CARE TO SHARE WITH THE REST OF THE CLASS?
LATER. AFTER WE DON'T DIE.
WHAT'S THE PLAN FOR THAT, BY THE WAY?
CHOOM
THAT'LL DO.

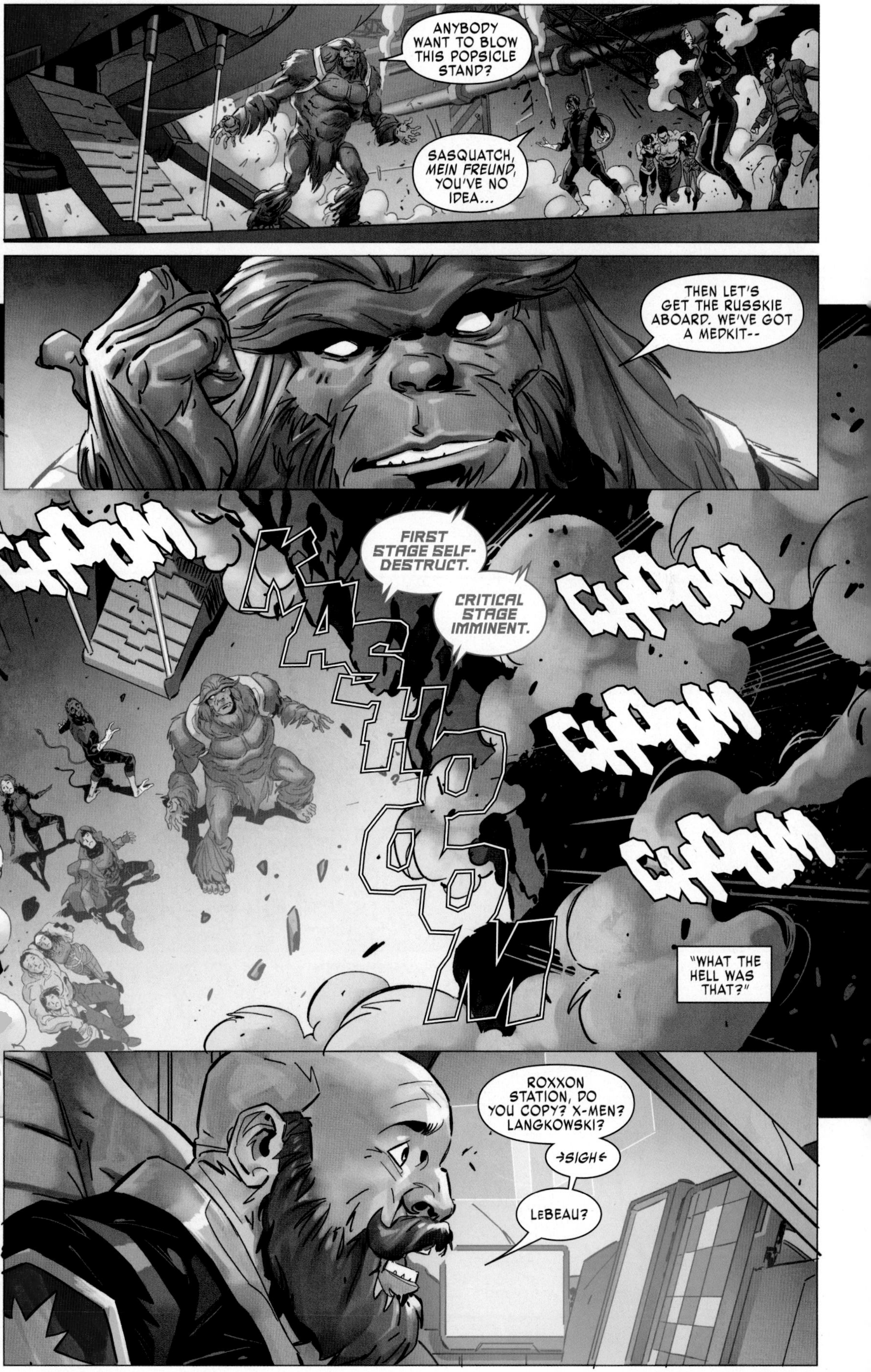
ANYBODY WANT TO BLOW THIS POPSICLE STAND?
SASQUATCH, MEIN FREUND, YOU'VE NO IDEA...
THEN LET'S GET THE RUSSKIE ABOARD. WE'VE GOT A MEDKIT--
FIRST STAGE SELF-DESTRUCT.
CRITICAL STAGE IMMINENT.
"WHAT THE HELL WAS THAT?"
ROXXON STATION, DO YOU COPY? X-MEN? LANGKOWSKI?
→SIGH←
LEBEAU?

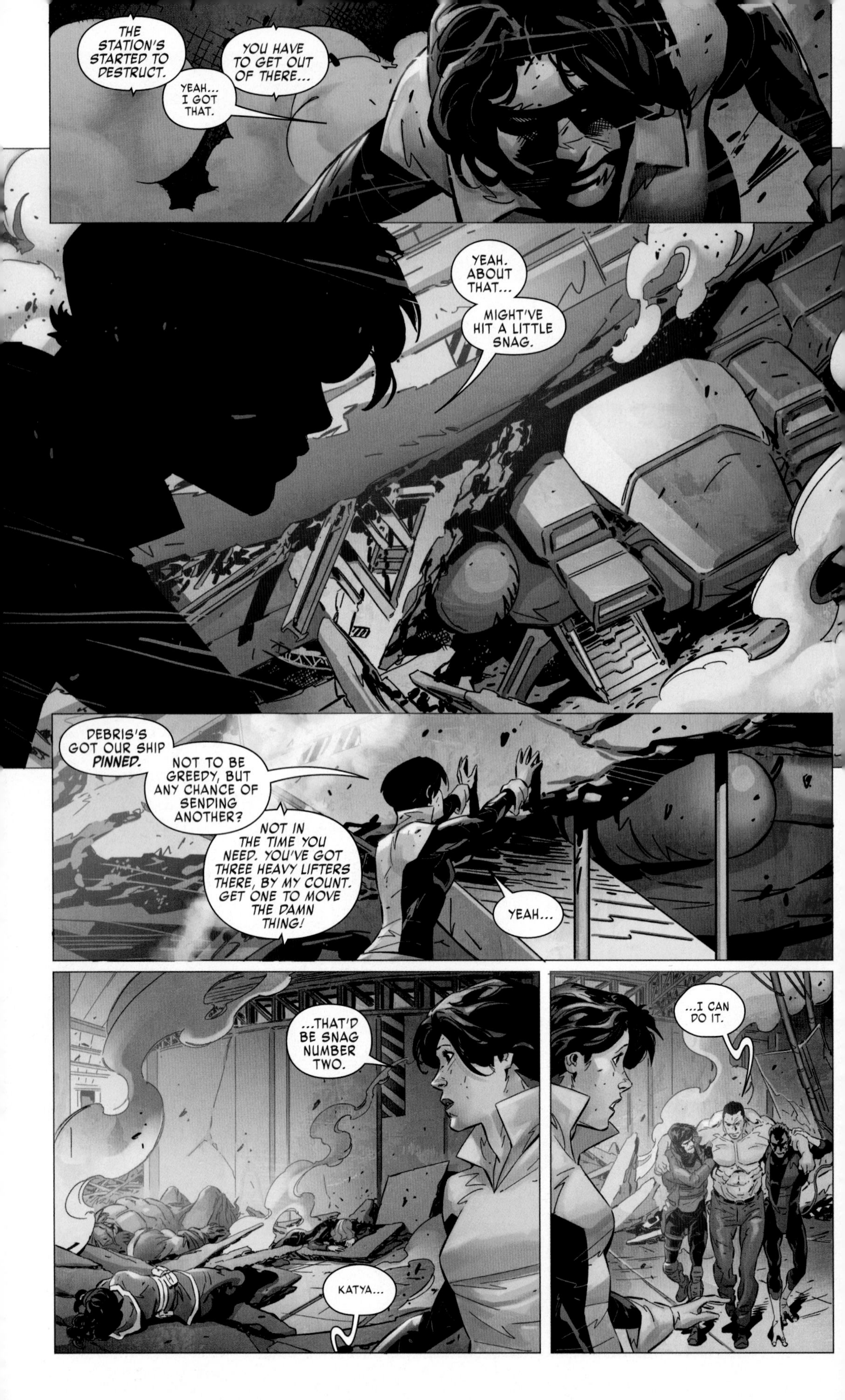
THE STATION'S STARTED TO DESTRUCT.
YOU HAVE TO GET OUT OF THERE...
YEAH... I GOT THAT.
YEAH. ABOUT THAT...
MIGHT'VE HIT A LITTLE SNAG.
DEBRIS'S GOT OUR SHIP PINNED.
NOT TO BE GREEDY, BUT ANY CHANCE OF SENDING ANOTHER?
NOT IN THE TIME YOU NEED. YOU'VE GOT THREE HEAVY LIFTERS THERE, BY MY COUNT. GET ONE TO MOVE THE DAMN THING!
YEAH...
...THAT'D BE SNAG NUMBER TWO.
KATYA...
...I CAN DO IT.

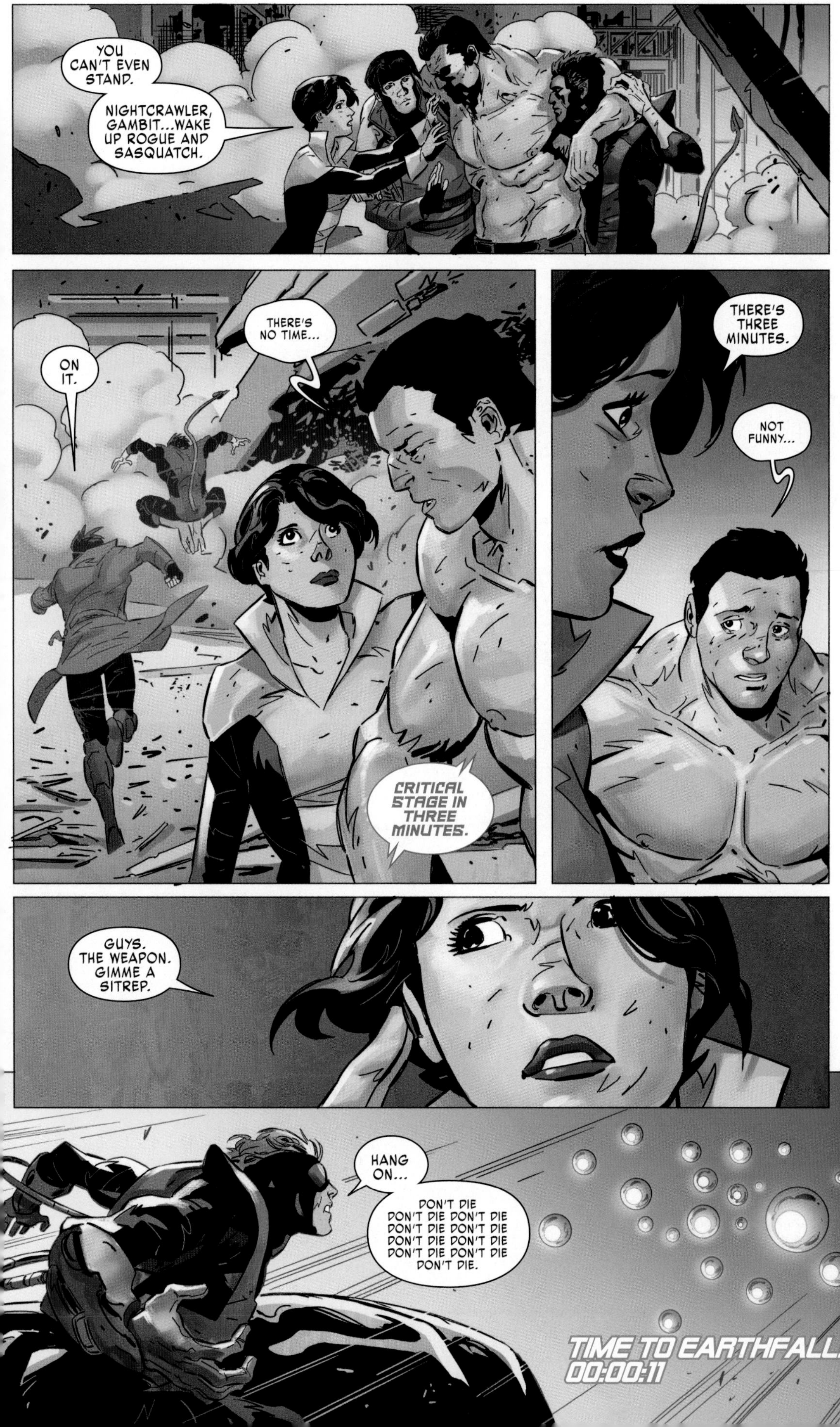

YOU CAN'T EVEN STAND.
NIGHTCRAWLER, GAMBIT...WAKE UP ROGUE AND SASQUATCH.
ON IT.
THERE'S NO TIME...
CRITICAL STAGE IN THREE MINUTES.
THERE'S THREE MINUTES.
NOT FUNNY...
GUYS. THE WEAPON. GIMME A SITREP.
HANG ON...
DON'T DIE DON'T DIE DON'T DIE DON'T DIE DON'T DIE DON'T DIE DON'T DIE DON'T DIE DON'T DIE DON'T DIE.
TIME TO EARTHFALL: 00:00:11

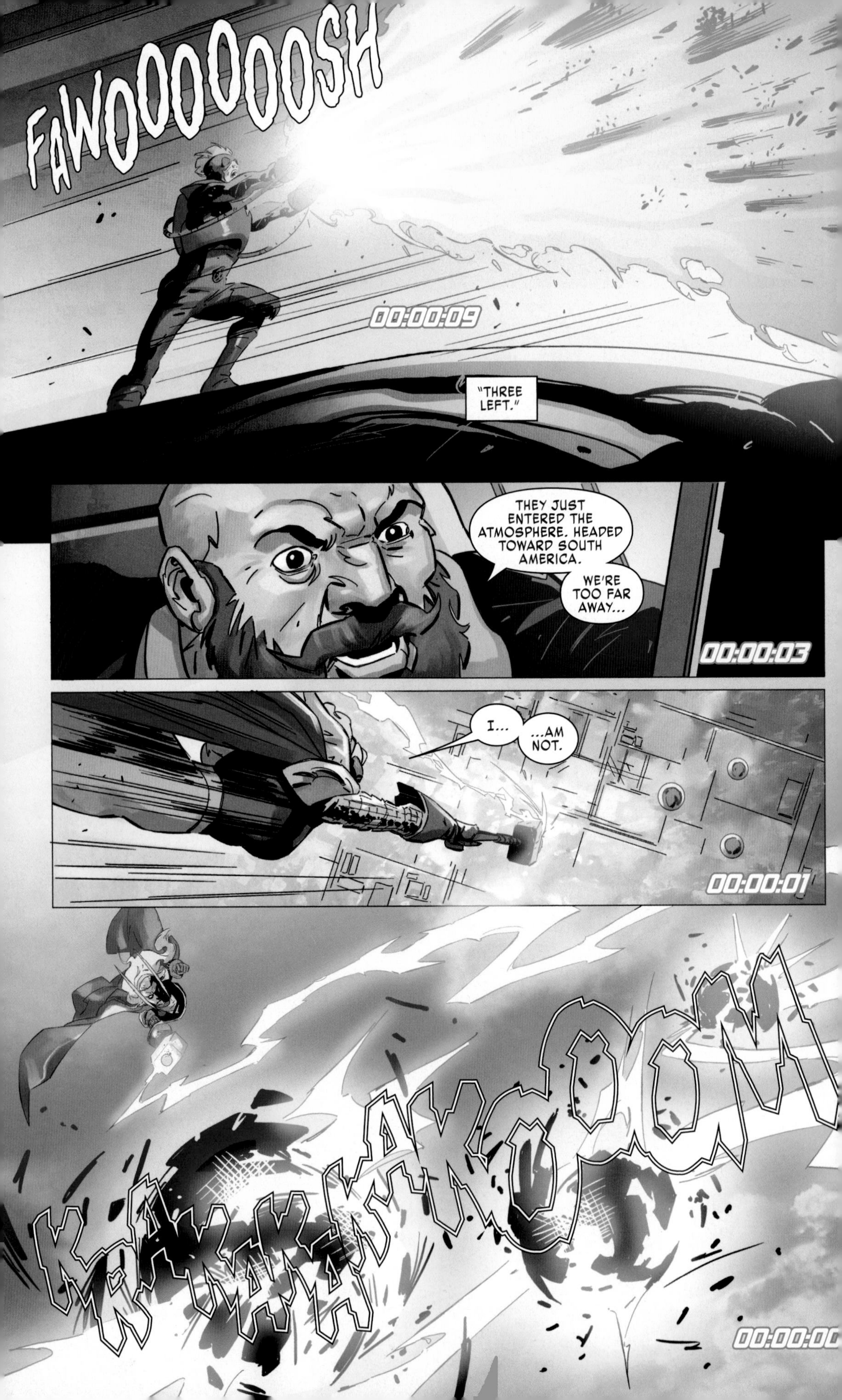
FAWOOOOOOSH
00:00:09
"THREE LEFT."
THEY JUST ENTERED THE ATMOSPHERE. HEADED TOWARD SOUTH AMERICA.
WE'RE TOO FAR AWAY...
00:00:03
I...
...AM NOT.
00:00:01
KRAKAKAKAKOOOM
00:00:00

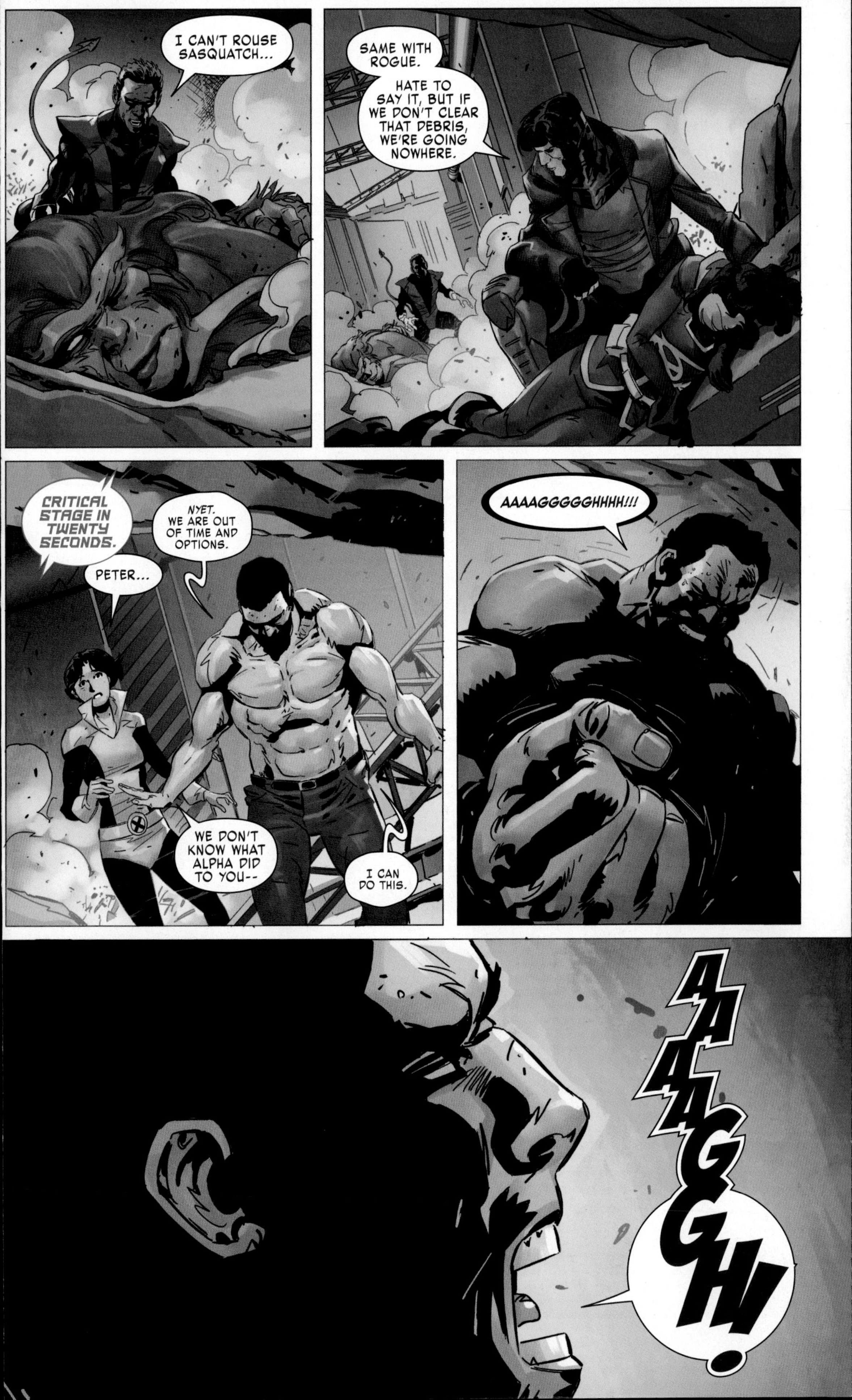
I CAN'T ROUSE SASQUATCH...
SAME WITH ROGUE.
HATE TO SAY IT, BUT IF WE DON'T CLEAR THAT DEBRIS, WE'RE GOING NOWHERE.
CRITICAL STAGE IN TWENTY SECONDS.
PETER...
NYET. WE ARE OUT OF TIME AND OPTIONS.
WE DON'T KNOW WHAT ALPHA DID TO YOU--
I CAN DO THIS.
AAAAGGGGGHHHH!!!
AAAAGGH!

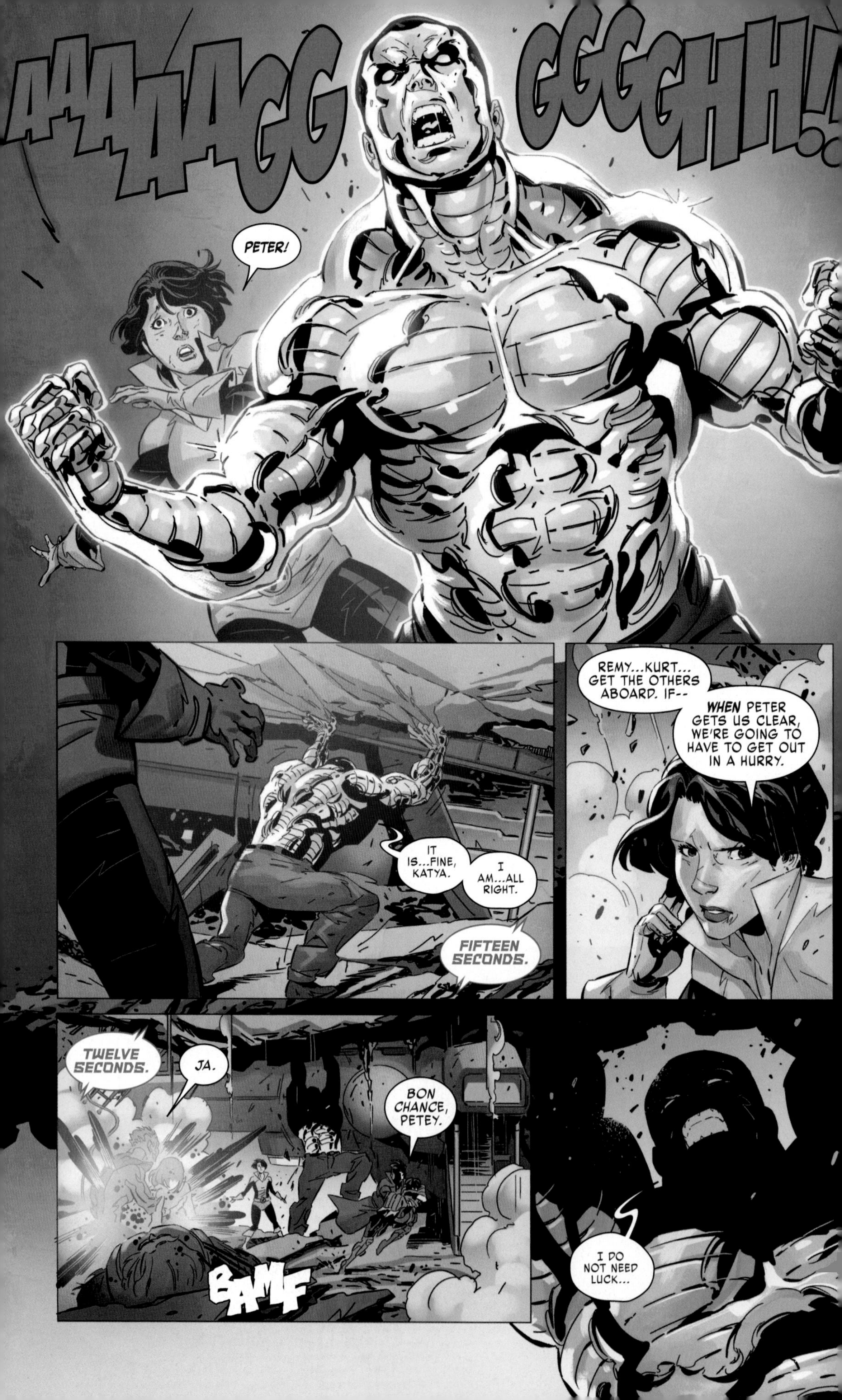
AAAAAAGG GGGGHH!!
PETER!
IT IS...FINE, KATYA.
I AM...ALL RIGHT.
FIFTEEN SECONDS.
REMY...KURT... GET THE OTHERS ABOARD. IF--
WHEN PETER GETS US CLEAR, WE'RE GOING TO HAVE TO GET OUT IN A HURRY.
TWELVE SECONDS.
JA.
BON CHANCE, PETEY.
BAMF
I DO NOT NEED LUCK...

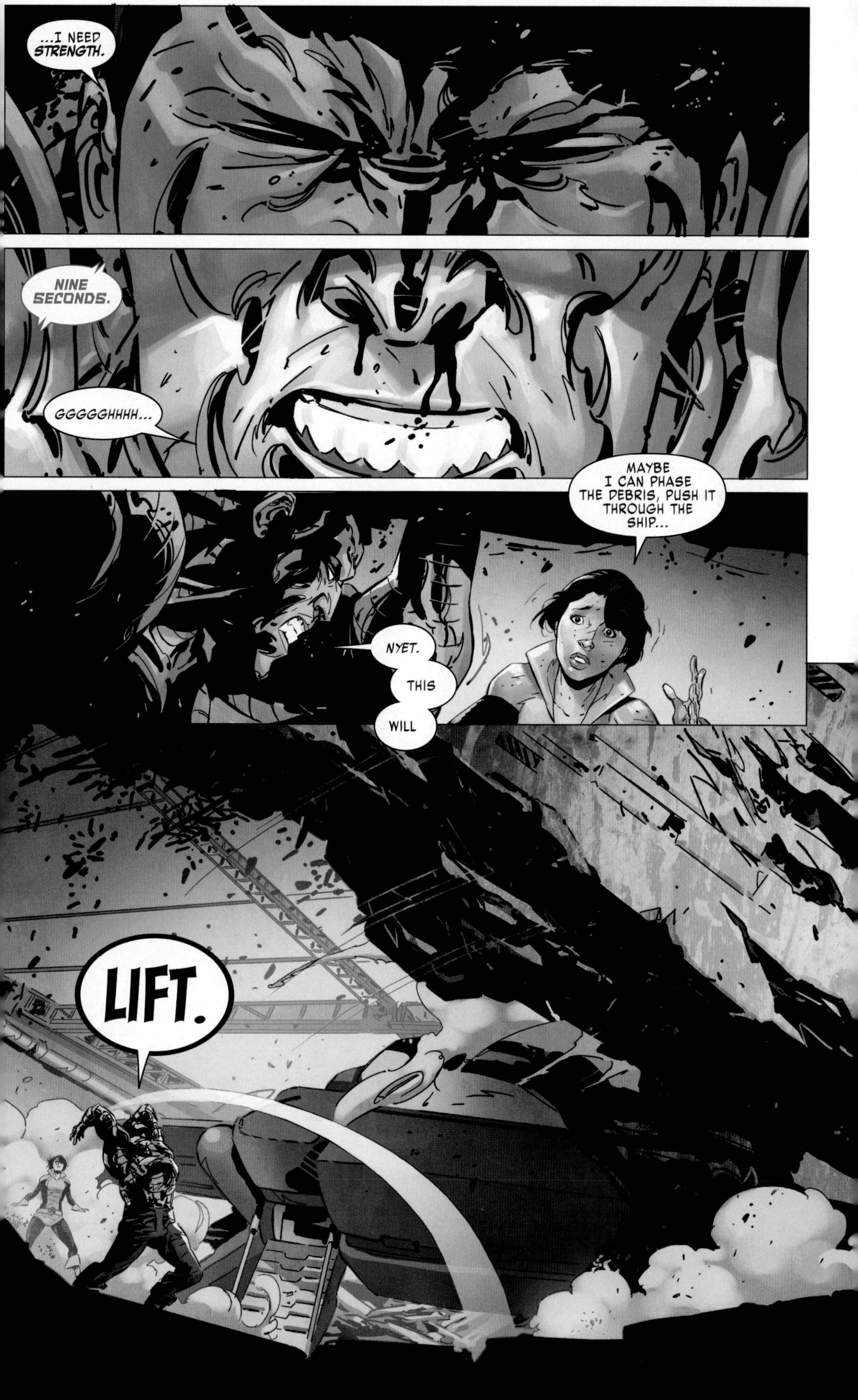
...I NEED STRENGTH.
NINE SECONDS.
GGGGGHHHH...
MAYBE I CAN PHASE THE DEBRIS, PUSH IT THROUGH THE SHIP...
NYET.
THIS
WILL
LIFT.

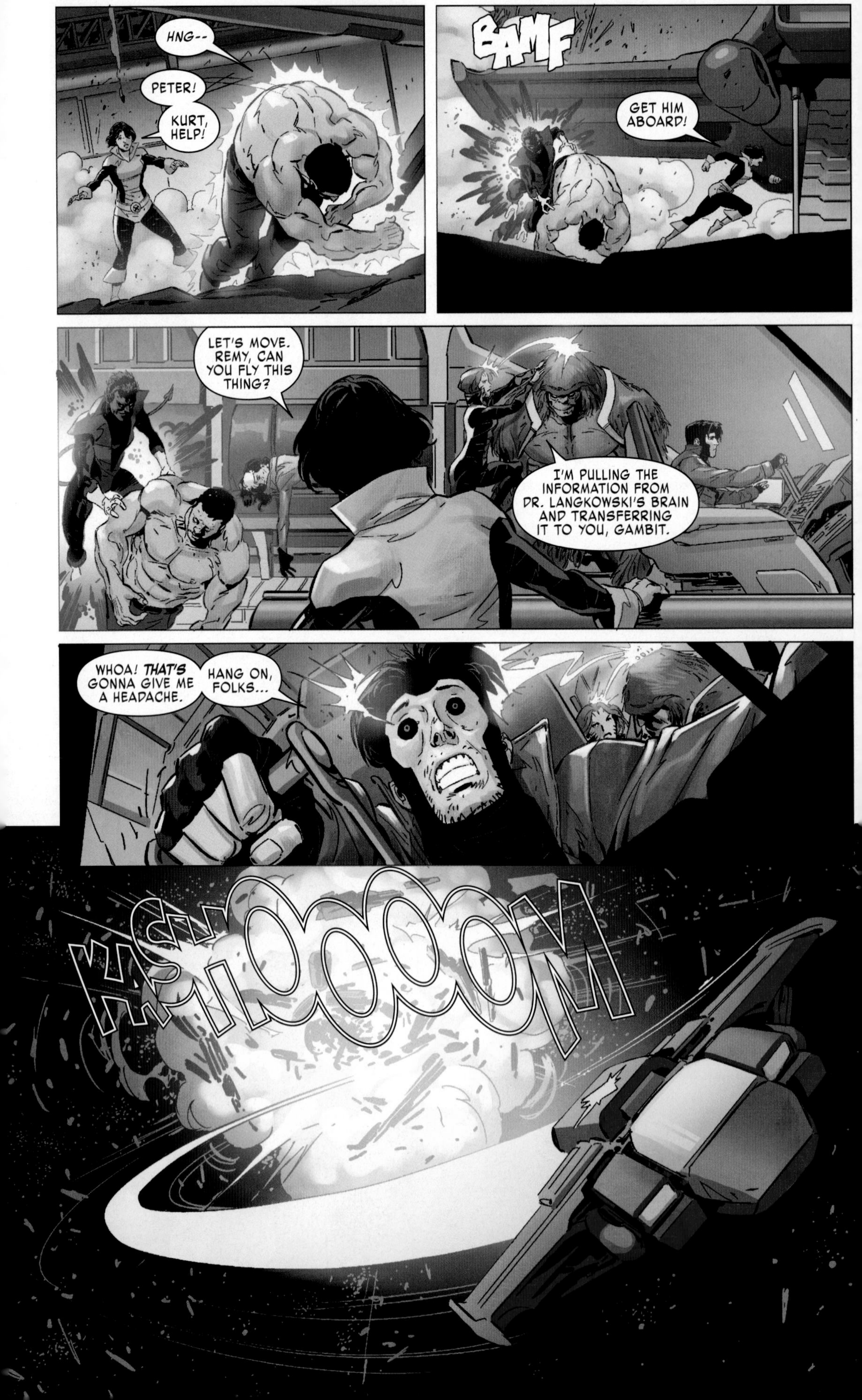
HNG--
PETER!
KURT, HELP!
BAMF
GET HIM ABOARD!
LET'S MOVE. REMY, CAN YOU FLY THIS THING?
I'M PULLING THE INFORMATION FROM DR. LANGKOWSKI'S BRAIN AND TRANSFERRING IT TO YOU, GAMBIT.
WHOA! THAT'S GONNA GIVE ME A HEADACHE.
HANG ON, FOLKS...
KASHOOOOOM

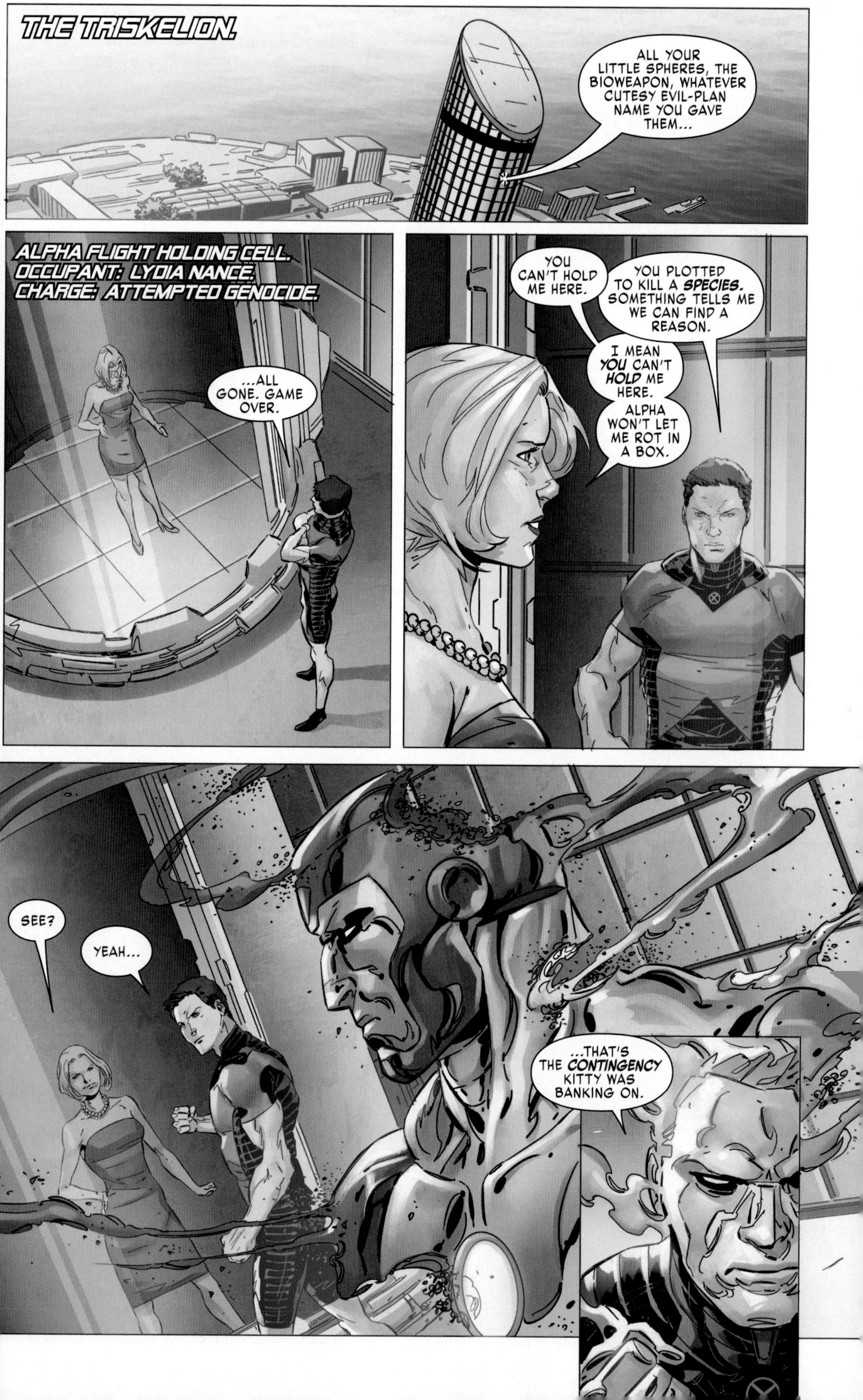

THE TRISKELION.
ALL YOUR LITTLE SPHERES, THE BIOWEAPON, WHATEVER CUTESY EVIL-PLAN NAME YOU GAVE THEM...
ALPHA FLIGHT HOLDING CELL. OCCUPANT: LYDIA NANCE. CHARGE: ATTEMPTED GENOCIDE.
...ALL GONE. GAME OVER.
YOU CAN'T HOLD ME HERE.
YOU PLOTTED TO KILL A SPECIES. SOMETHING TELLS ME WE CAN FIND A REASON.
I MEAN YOU CAN'T HOLD ME HERE.
ALPHA WON'T LET ME ROT IN A BOX.
SEE?
YEAH...
...THAT'S THE CONTINGENCY KITTY WAS BANKING ON.

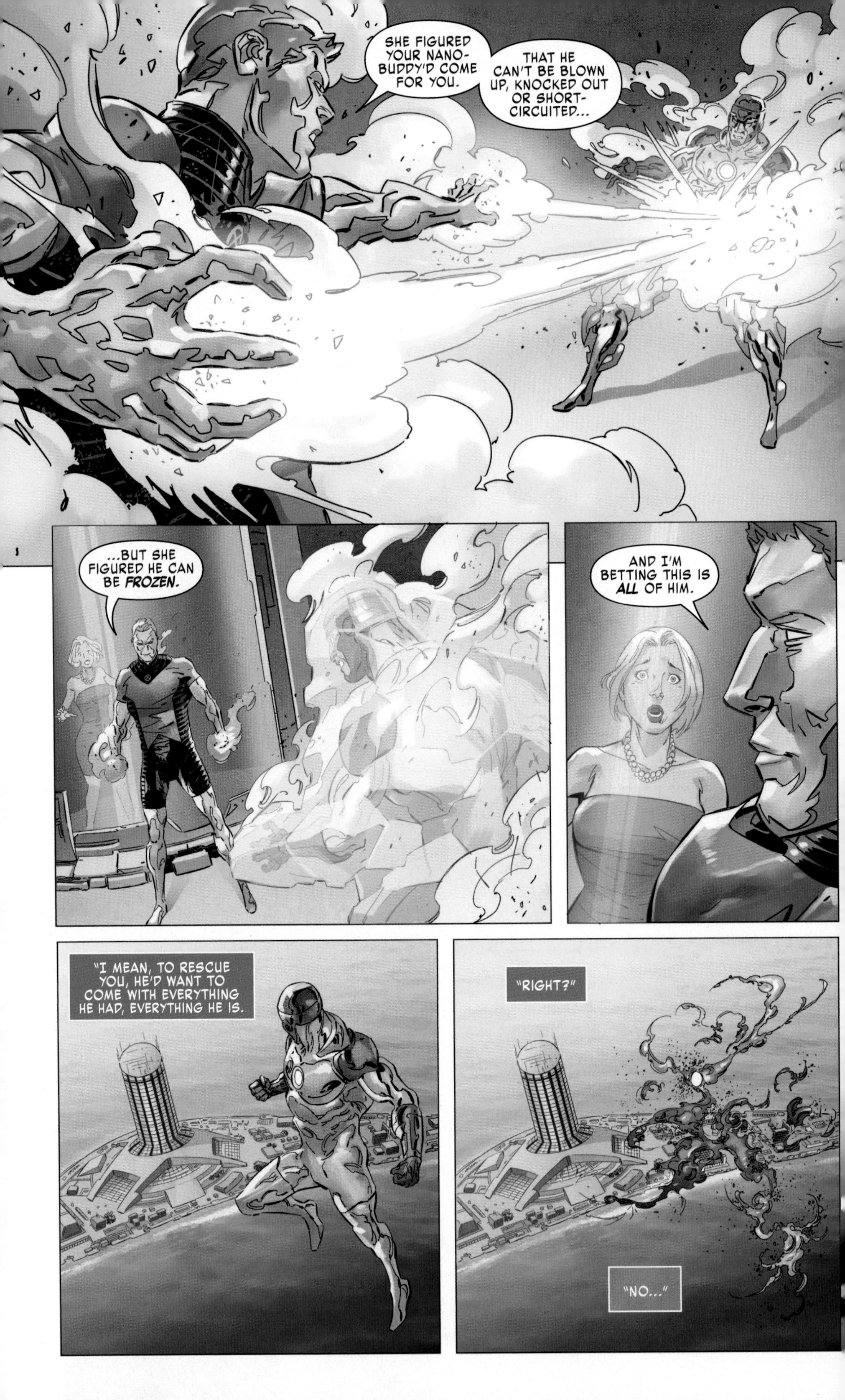
SHE FIGURED YOUR NANO-BUDDY'D COME FOR YOU.
THAT HE CAN'T BE BLOWN UP, KNOCKED OUT OR SHORT-CIRCUITED...
...BUT SHE FIGURED HE CAN BE FROZEN.
AND I'M BETTING THIS IS ALL OF HIM.
"I MEAN, TO RESCUE YOU, HE'D WANT TO COME WITH EVERYTHING HE HAD, EVERYTHING HE IS.
"RIGHT?"
"NO..."

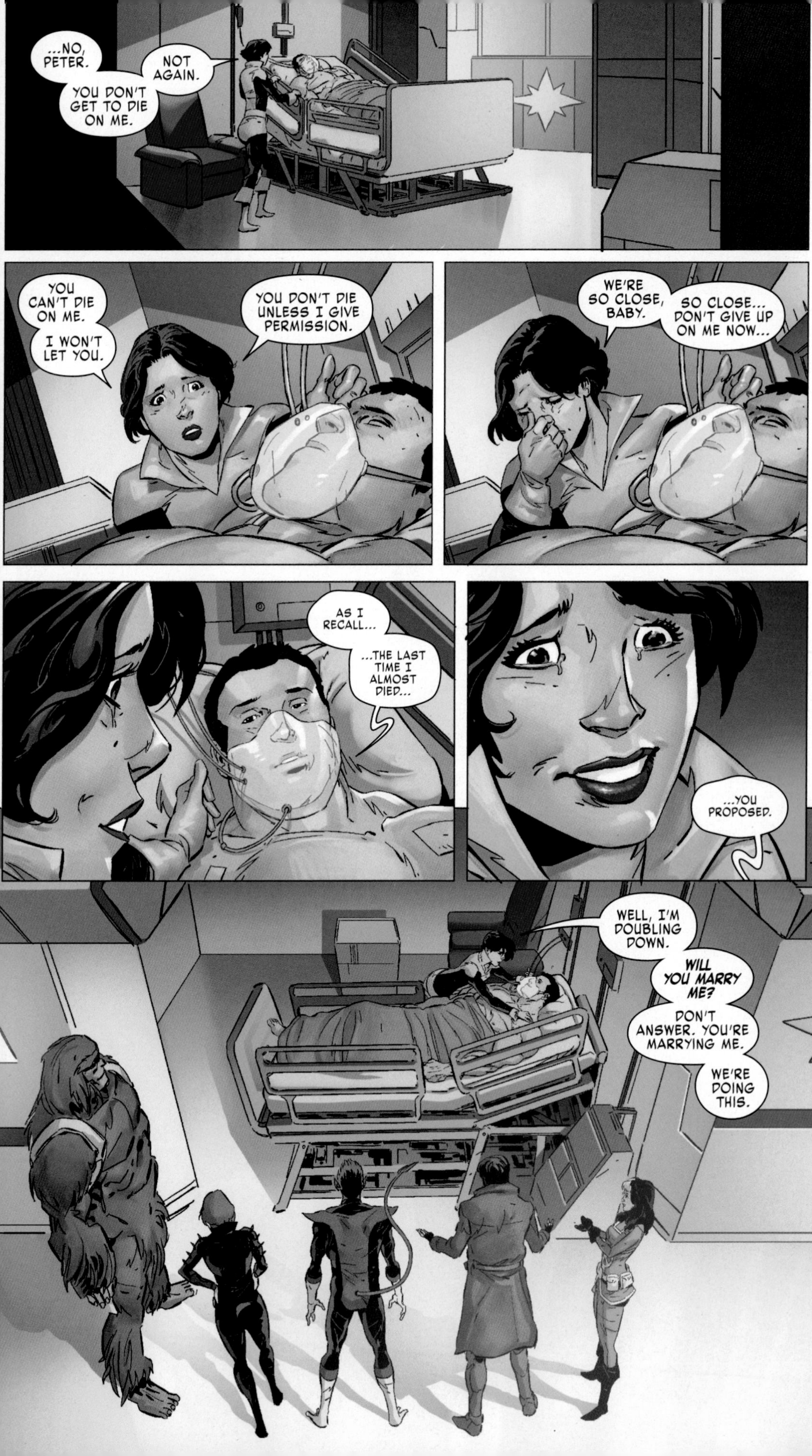
...NO, PETER.
YOU DON'T GET TO DIE ON ME.
NOT AGAIN.
YOU CAN'T DIE ON ME.
I WON'T LET YOU.
YOU DON'T DIE UNLESS I GIVE PERMISSION.
WE'RE SO CLOSE, BABY.
SO CLOSE... DON'T GIVE UP ON ME NOW...
AS I RECALL...
...THE LAST TIME I ALMOST DIED...
...YOU PROPOSED.
WELL, I'M DOUBLING DOWN.
WILL YOU MARRY ME?
DON'T ANSWER. YOU'RE MARRYING ME.
WE'RE DOING THIS.

30

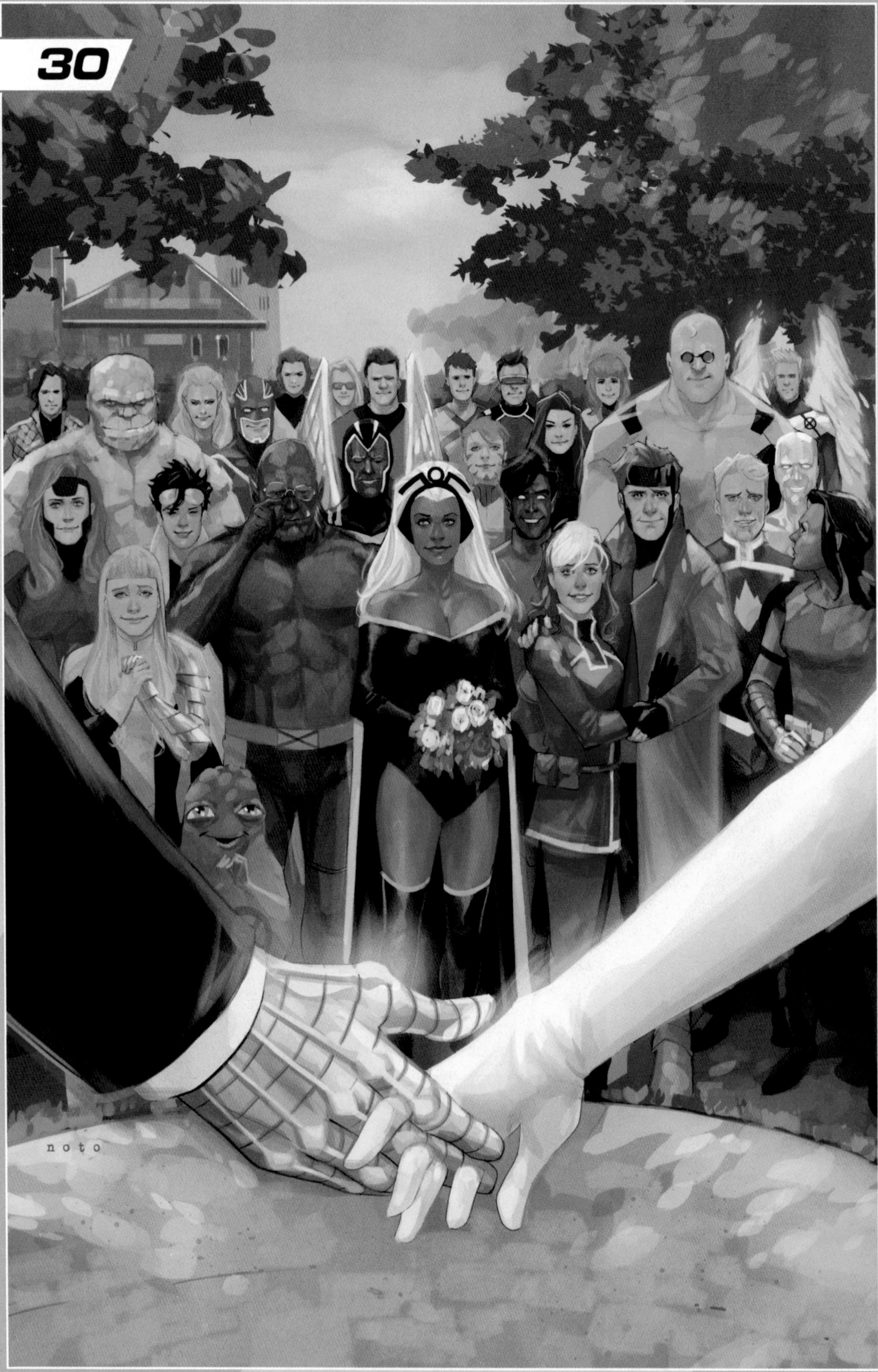
noto

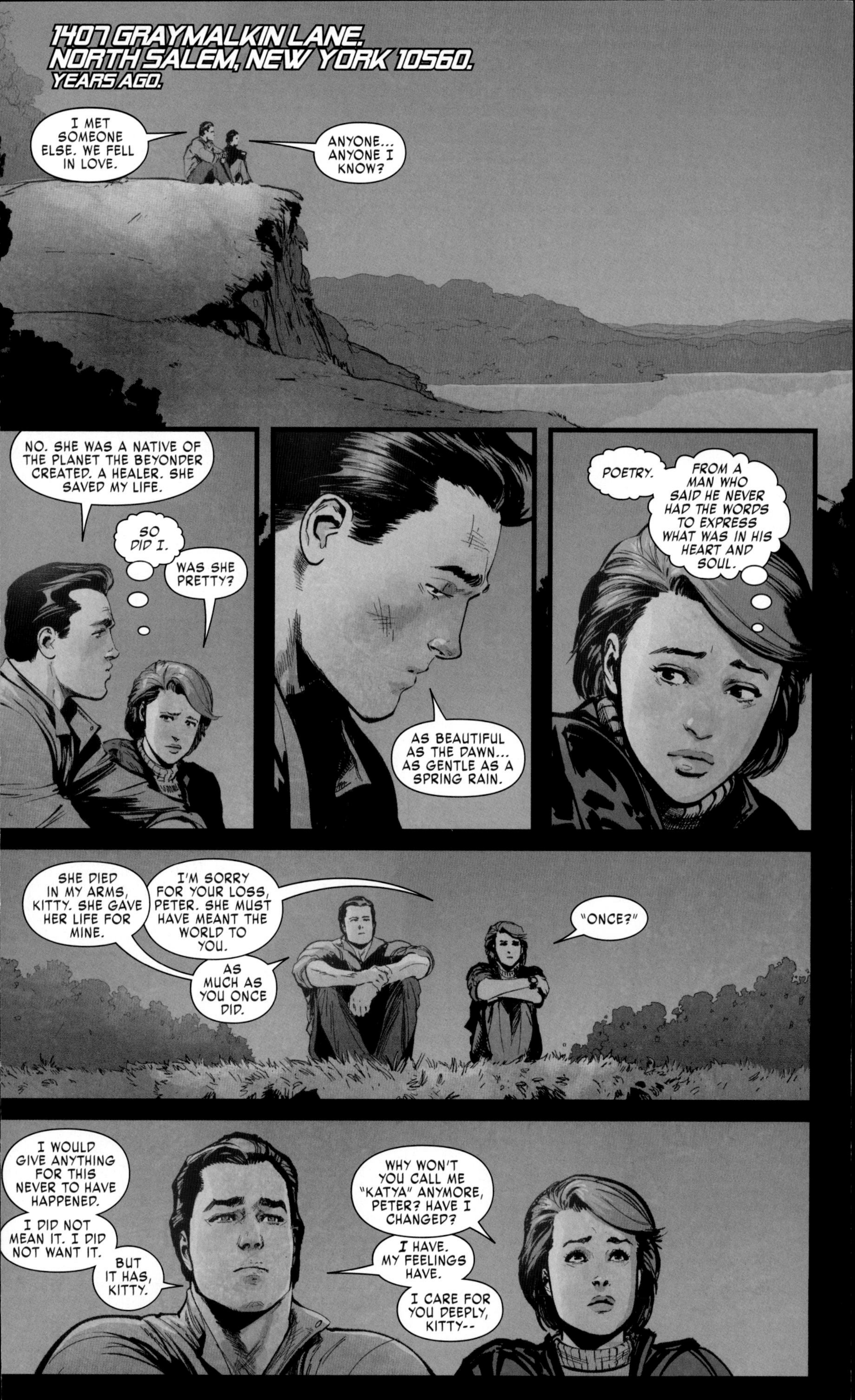
1407 GRAYMALKIN LANE.
NORTH SALEM, NEW YORK 10560.
YEARS AGO.
I MET SOMEONE ELSE. WE FELL IN LOVE.
ANYONE... ANYONE I KNOW?
NO. SHE WAS A NATIVE OF THE PLANET THE BEYONDER CREATED. A HEALER. SHE SAVED MY LIFE.
SO DID I.
WAS SHE PRETTY?
AS BEAUTIFUL AS THE DAWN... AS GENTLE AS A SPRING RAIN.
POETRY.
FROM A MAN WHO SAID HE NEVER HAD THE WORDS TO EXPRESS WHAT WAS IN HIS HEART AND SOUL.
SHE DIED IN MY ARMS, KITTY. SHE GAVE HER LIFE FOR MINE.
I'M SORRY FOR YOUR LOSS, PETER. SHE MUST HAVE MEANT THE WORLD TO YOU.
AS MUCH AS YOU ONCE DID.
"ONCE?"
I WOULD GIVE ANYTHING FOR THIS NEVER TO HAVE HAPPENED.
I DID NOT MEAN IT. I DID NOT WANT IT.
WHY WON'T YOU CALL ME "KATYA" ANYMORE, PETER? HAVE I CHANGED?
BUT IT HAS, KITTY.
I HAVE. MY FEELINGS HAVE.
I CARE FOR YOU DEEPLY, KITTY--

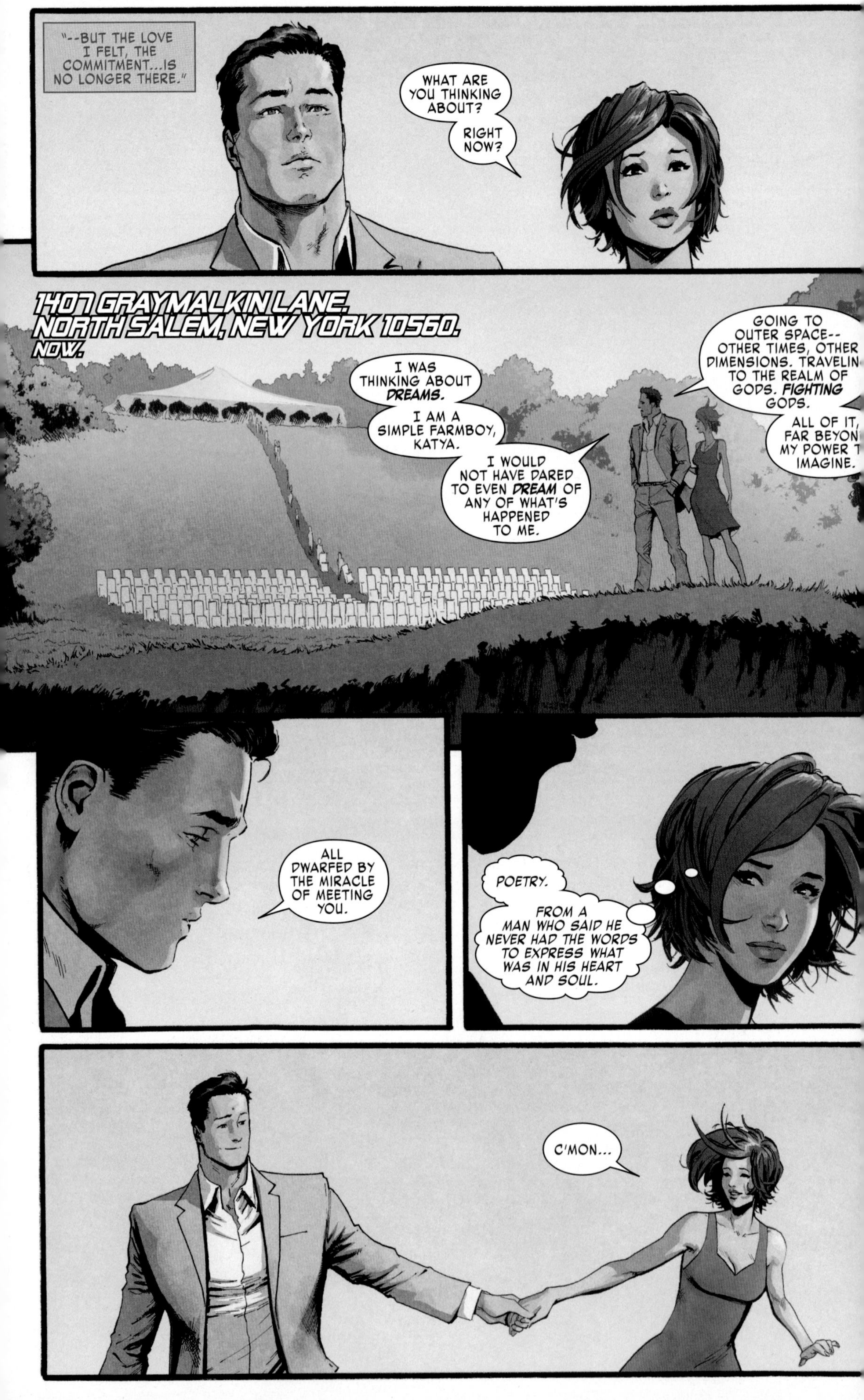
"--BUT THE LOVE I FELT, THE COMMITMENT...IS NO LONGER THERE."
WHAT ARE YOU THINKING ABOUT?
RIGHT NOW?
1407 GRAYMALKIN LANE. NORTH SALEM, NEW YORK 10560. NOW.
I WAS THINKING ABOUT DREAMS.
I AM A SIMPLE FARMBOY, KATYA.
I WOULD NOT HAVE DARED TO EVEN DREAM OF ANY OF WHAT'S HAPPENED TO ME.
GOING TO OUTER SPACE-- OTHER TIMES, OTHER DIMENSIONS. TRAVELIN TO THE REALM OF GODS. FIGHTING GODS.
ALL OF IT, FAR BEYON MY POWER T IMAGINE.
ALL DWARFED BY THE MIRACLE OF MEETING YOU.
POETRY.
FROM A MAN WHO SAID HE NEVER HAD THE WORDS TO EXPRESS WHAT WAS IN HIS HEART AND SOUL.
C'MON...

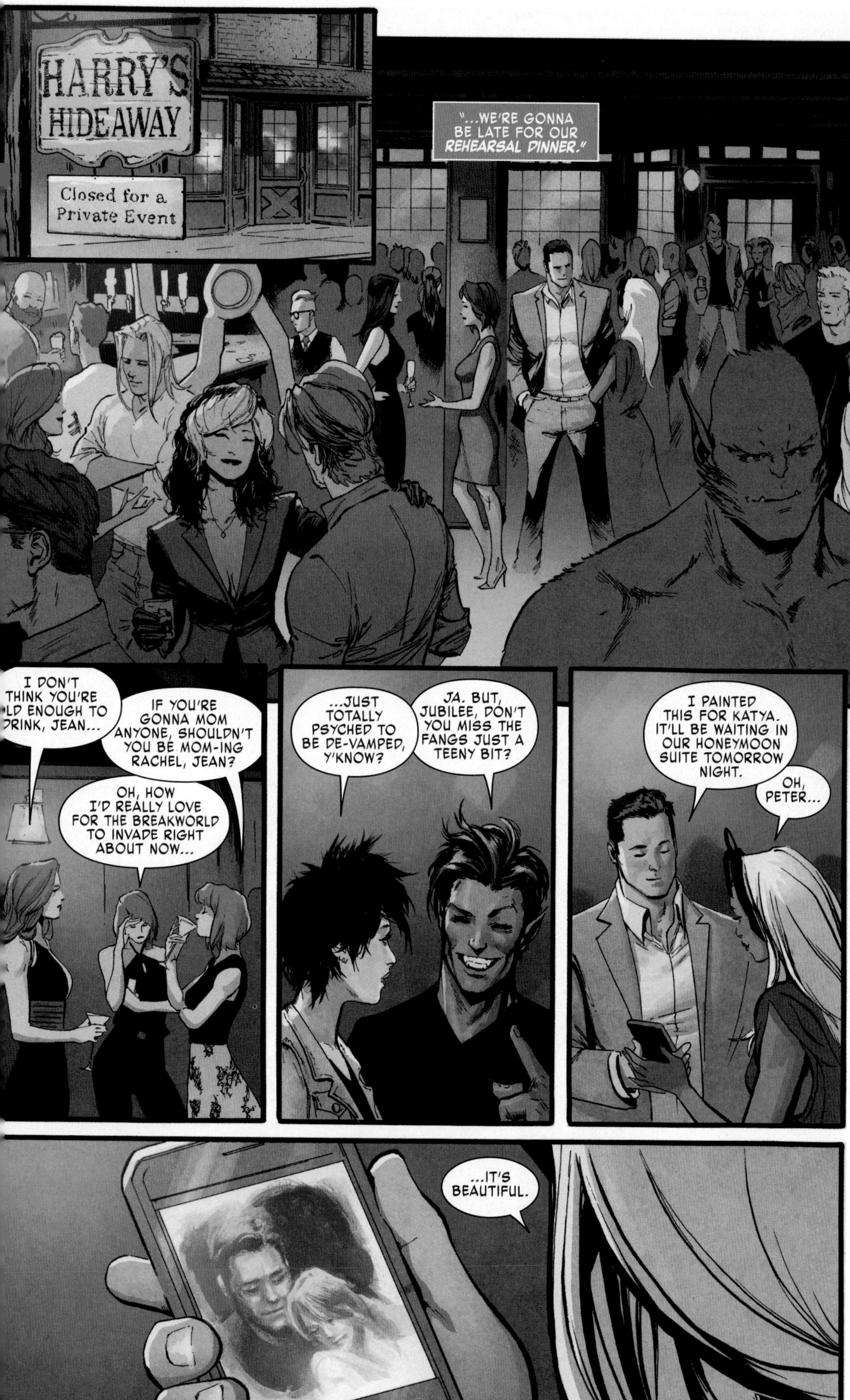

HARRY'S HIDEAWAY
Closed for a Private Event
"...WE'RE GONNA BE LATE FOR OUR REHEARSAL DINNER."
I DON'T THINK YOU'RE OLD ENOUGH TO DRINK, JEAN...
IF YOU'RE GONNA MOM ANYONE, SHOULDN'T YOU BE MOM-ING RACHEL, JEAN?
OH, HOW I'D REALLY LOVE FOR THE BREAKWORLD TO INVADE RIGHT ABOUT NOW...
...JUST TOTALLY PSYCHED TO BE DE-VAMPED, Y'KNOW?
JA. BUT, JUBILEE, DON'T YOU MISS THE FANGS JUST A TEENY BIT?
I PAINTED THIS FOR KATYA. IT'LL BE WAITING IN OUR HONEYMOON SUITE TOMORROW NIGHT.
OH, PETER...
...IT'S BEAUTIFUL.

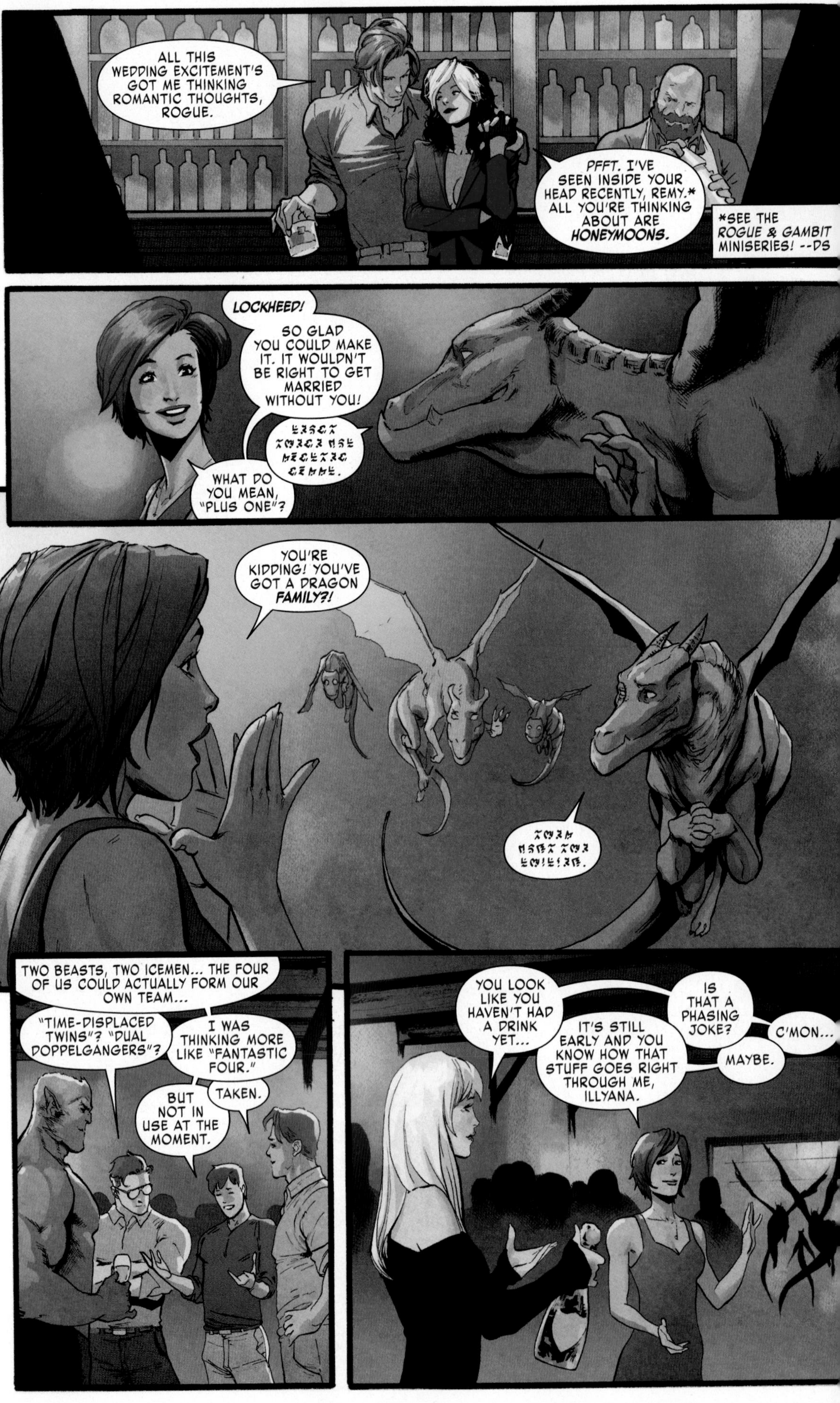

ALL THIS WEDDING EXCITEMENT'S GOT ME THINKING ROMANTIC THOUGHTS, ROGUE.
PFFT. I'VE SEEN INSIDE YOUR HEAD RECENTLY, REMY.* ALL YOU'RE THINKING ABOUT ARE HONEYMOONS.
*SEE THE ROGUE & GAMBIT MINISERIES! --DS
LOCKHEED!
SO GLAD YOU COULD MAKE IT. IT WOULDN'T BE RIGHT TO GET MARRIED WITHOUT YOU!
WHAT DO YOU MEAN, "PLUS ONE"?
YOU'RE KIDDING! YOU'VE GOT A DRAGON FAMILY?!
TWO BEASTS, TWO ICEMEN... THE FOUR OF US COULD ACTUALLY FORM OUR OWN TEAM...
"TIME-DISPLACED TWINS"? "DUAL DOPPELGANGERS"?
I WAS THINKING MORE LIKE "FANTASTIC FOUR."
TAKEN.
BUT NOT IN USE AT THE MOMENT.
YOU LOOK LIKE YOU HAVEN'T HAD A DRINK YET...
IT'S STILL EARLY AND YOU KNOW HOW THAT STUFF GOES RIGHT THROUGH ME, ILLYANA.
IS THAT A PHASING JOKE?
MAYBE.
C'MON...

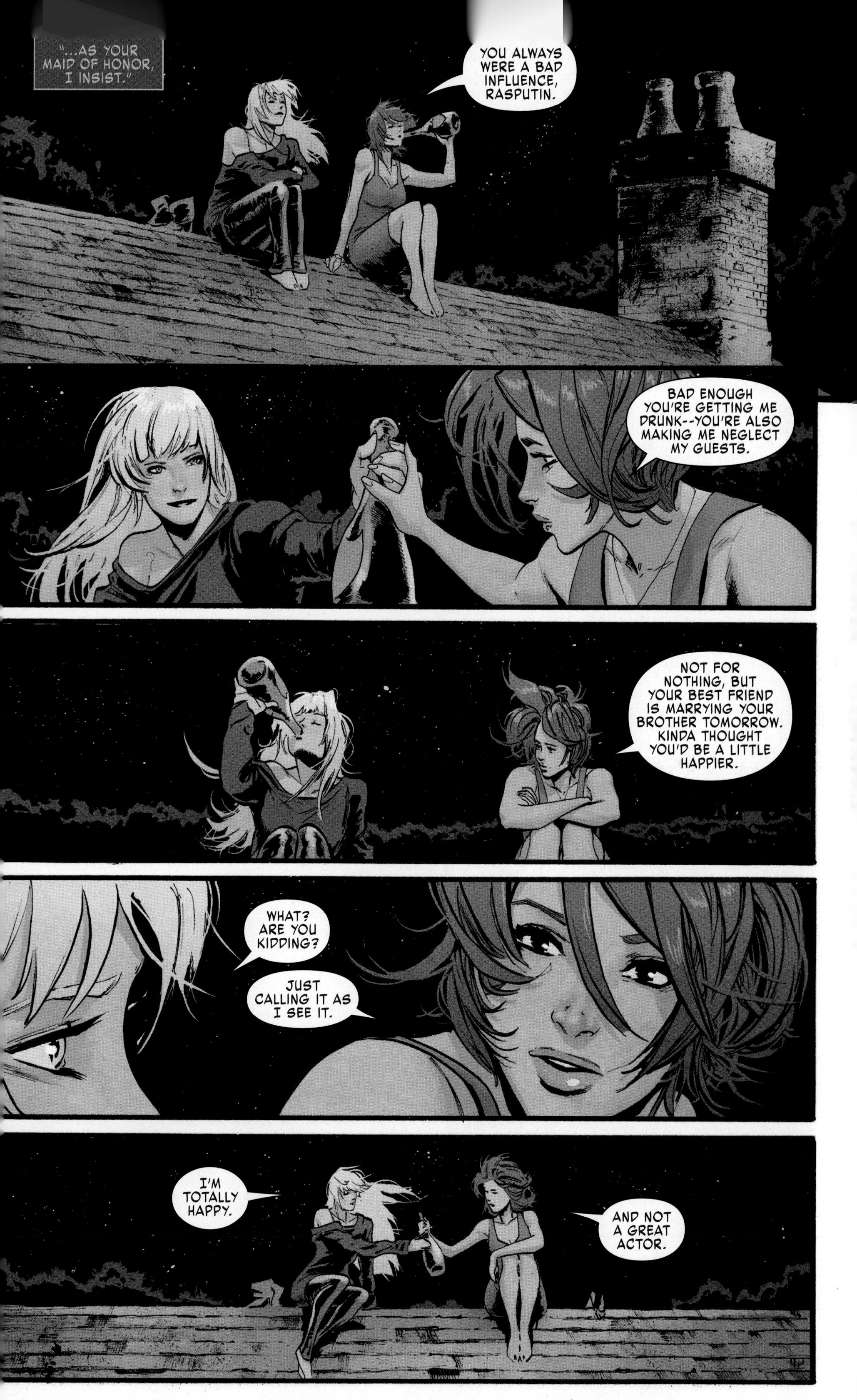
"...AS YOUR MAID OF HONOR, I INSIST."
YOU ALWAYS WERE A BAD INFLUENCE, RASPUTIN.
BAD ENOUGH YOU'RE GETTING ME DRUNK--YOU'RE ALSO MAKING ME NEGLECT MY GUESTS.
NOT FOR NOTHING, BUT YOUR BEST FRIEND IS MARRYING YOUR BROTHER TOMORROW. KINDA THOUGHT YOU'D BE A LITTLE HAPPIER.
WHAT? ARE YOU KIDDING?
JUST CALLING IT AS I SEE IT.
I'M TOTALLY HAPPY.
AND NOT A GREAT ACTOR.

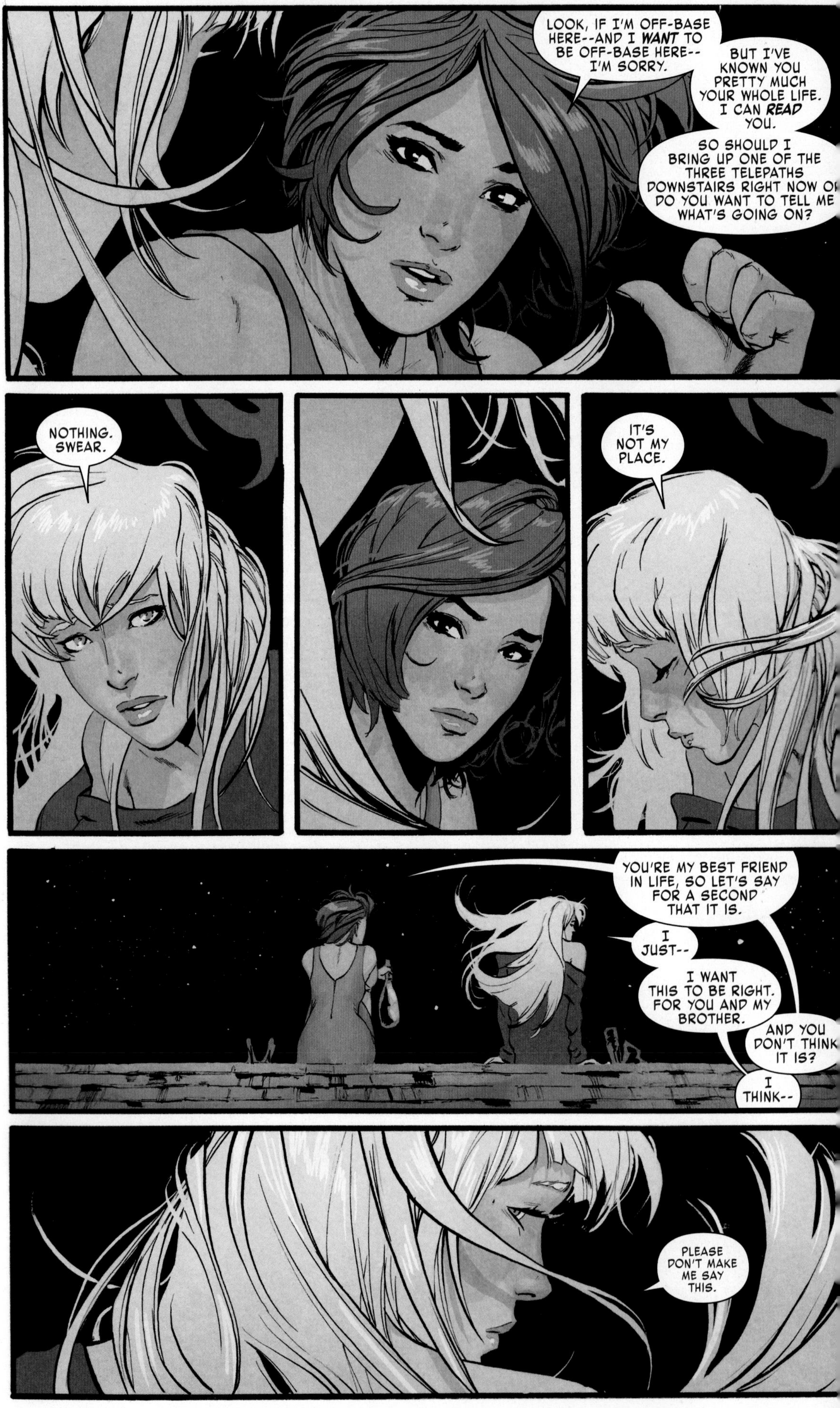
LOOK, IF I'M OFF-BASE HERE--AND I WANT TO BE OFF-BASE HERE--I'M SORRY.
BUT I'VE KNOWN YOU PRETTY MUCH YOUR WHOLE LIFE. I CAN READ YOU.
SO SHOULD I BRING UP ONE OF THE THREE TELEPATHS DOWNSTAIRS RIGHT NOW OR DO YOU WANT TO TELL ME WHAT'S GOING ON?
NOTHING. SWEAR.
IT'S NOT MY PLACE.
YOU'RE MY BEST FRIEND IN LIFE, SO LET'S SAY FOR A SECOND THAT IT IS.
I JUST--
I WANT THIS TO BE RIGHT. FOR YOU AND MY BROTHER.
AND YOU DON'T THINK IT IS?
I THINK--
PLEASE DON'T MAKE ME SAY THIS.

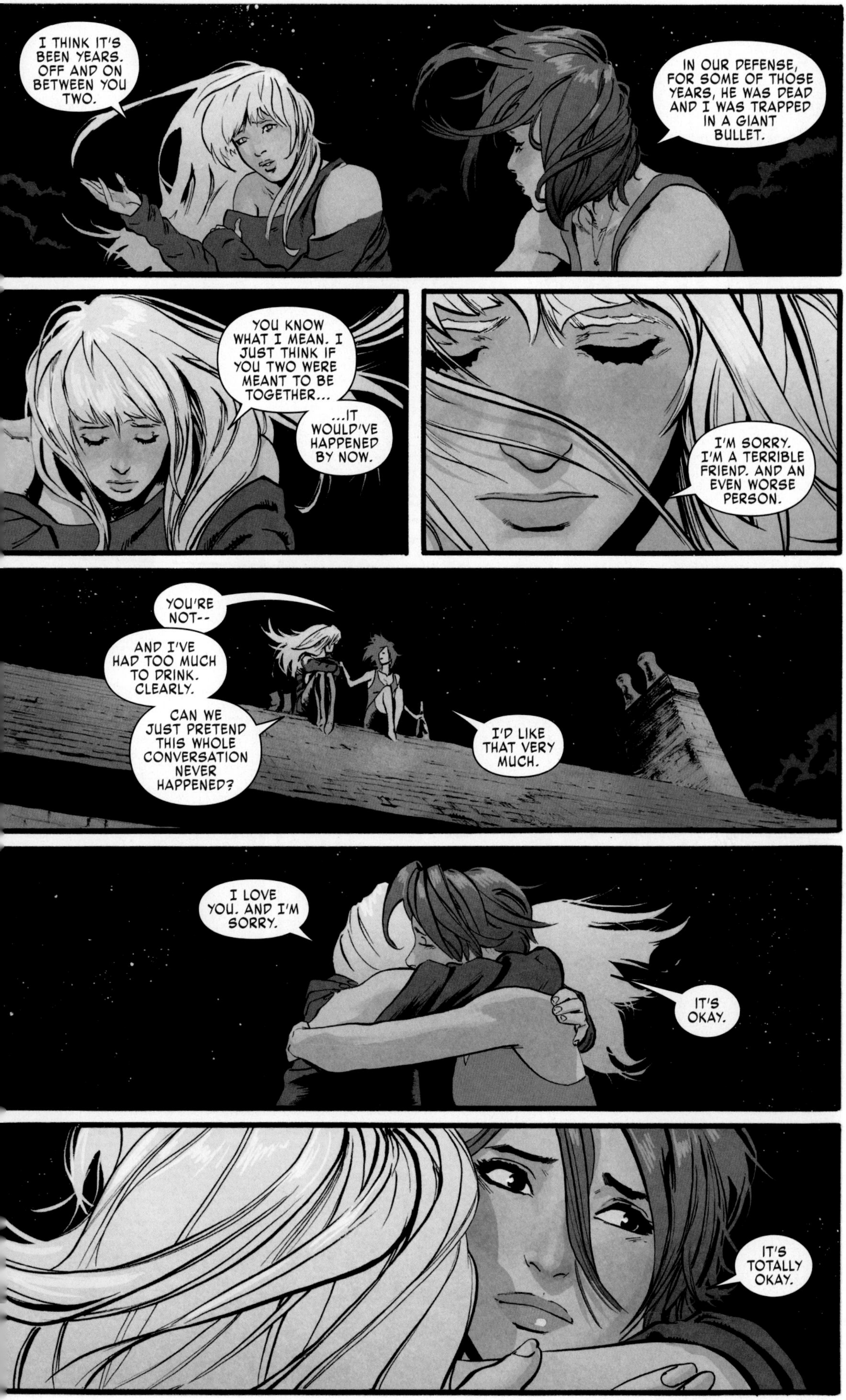
I THINK IT'S BEEN YEARS. OFF AND ON BETWEEN YOU TWO.
IN OUR DEFENSE, FOR SOME OF THOSE YEARS, HE WAS DEAD AND I WAS TRAPPED IN A GIANT BULLET.
YOU KNOW WHAT I MEAN. I JUST THINK IF YOU TWO WERE MEANT TO BE TOGETHER...
...IT WOULD'VE HAPPENED BY NOW.
I'M SORRY. I'M A TERRIBLE FRIEND. AND AN EVEN WORSE PERSON.
YOU'RE NOT--
AND I'VE HAD TOO MUCH TO DRINK. CLEARLY.
CAN WE JUST PRETEND THIS WHOLE CONVERSATION NEVER HAPPENED?
I'D LIKE THAT VERY MUCH.
I LOVE YOU. AND I'M SORRY.
IT'S OKAY.
IT'S TOTALLY OKAY.

THE BIG DAY.

QUIT SQUIRMING...

KLYANUS, BOW TIES ARE AN EVEN MORE EVIL INVENTION THAN SENTINELS...

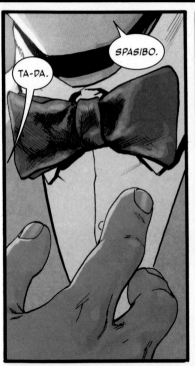

TA-DA.

SPASIBO.

WITH LUCK, ONE DAY YOU'LL DO THE SAME FOR ME.

I WASN'T AWARE THINGS WITH YOU AND RACHEL HAD...

PROGRESSED THAT FAR?

DA.

I LOVE HER, MEIN FREUND.

IN FACT, ONCE WE'RE FINISHED WITH YOUR WEDDING...

...I'M GOING TO PROPOSE TO HER.

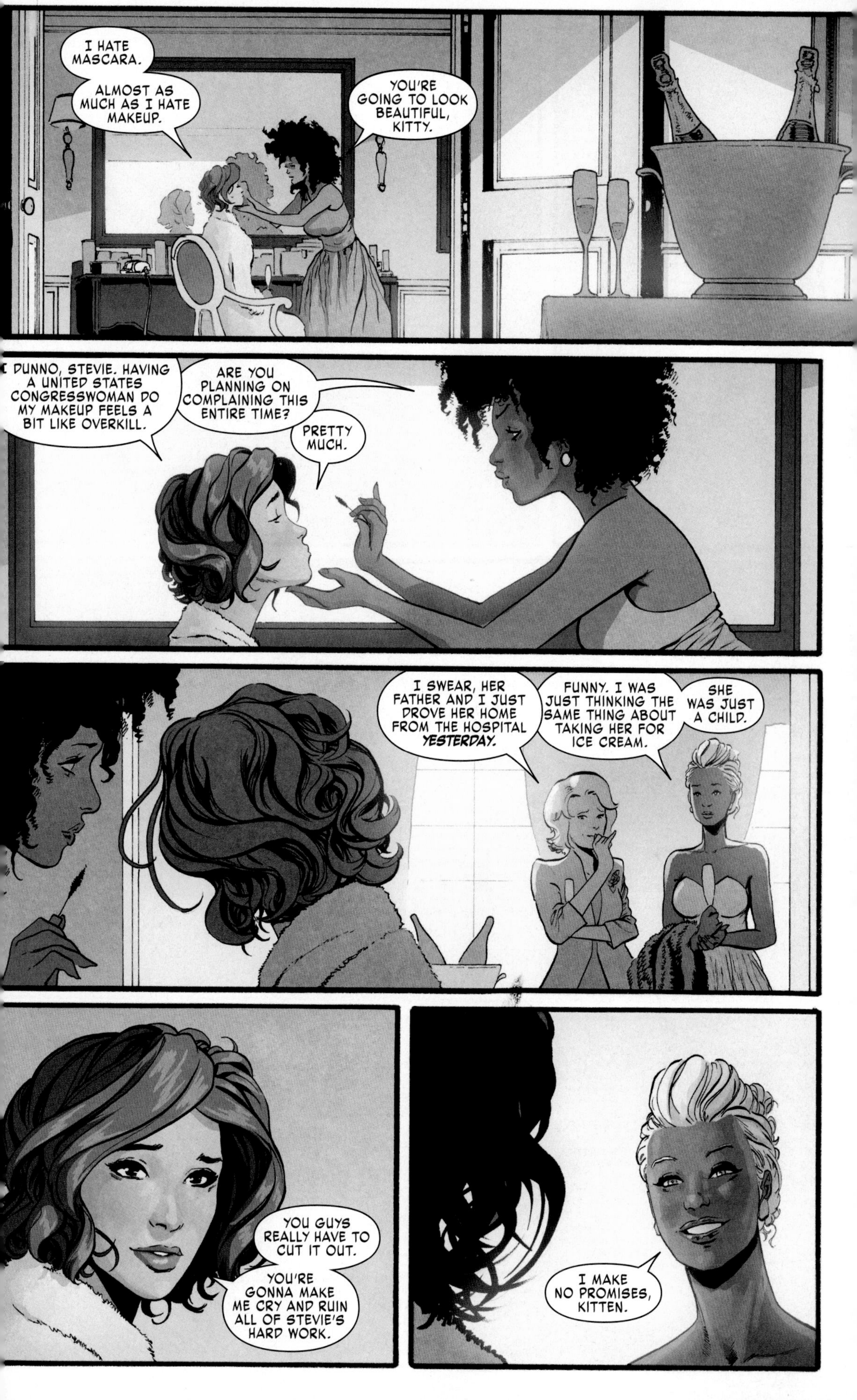
I HATE MASCARA.
ALMOST AS MUCH AS I HATE MAKEUP.
YOU'RE GOING TO LOOK BEAUTIFUL, KITTY.
I DUNNO, STEVIE. HAVING A UNITED STATES CONGRESSWOMAN DO MY MAKEUP FEELS A BIT LIKE OVERKILL.
ARE YOU PLANNING ON COMPLAINING THIS ENTIRE TIME?
PRETTY MUCH.
I SWEAR, HER FATHER AND I JUST DROVE HER HOME FROM THE HOSPITAL *YESTERDAY.*
FUNNY. I WAS JUST THINKING THE SAME THING ABOUT TAKING HER FOR ICE CREAM.
SHE WAS JUST A CHILD.
YOU GUYS REALLY HAVE TO CUT IT OUT.
YOU'RE GONNA MAKE ME CRY AND RUIN ALL OF STEVIE'S HARD WORK.
I MAKE NO PROMISES, KITTEN.

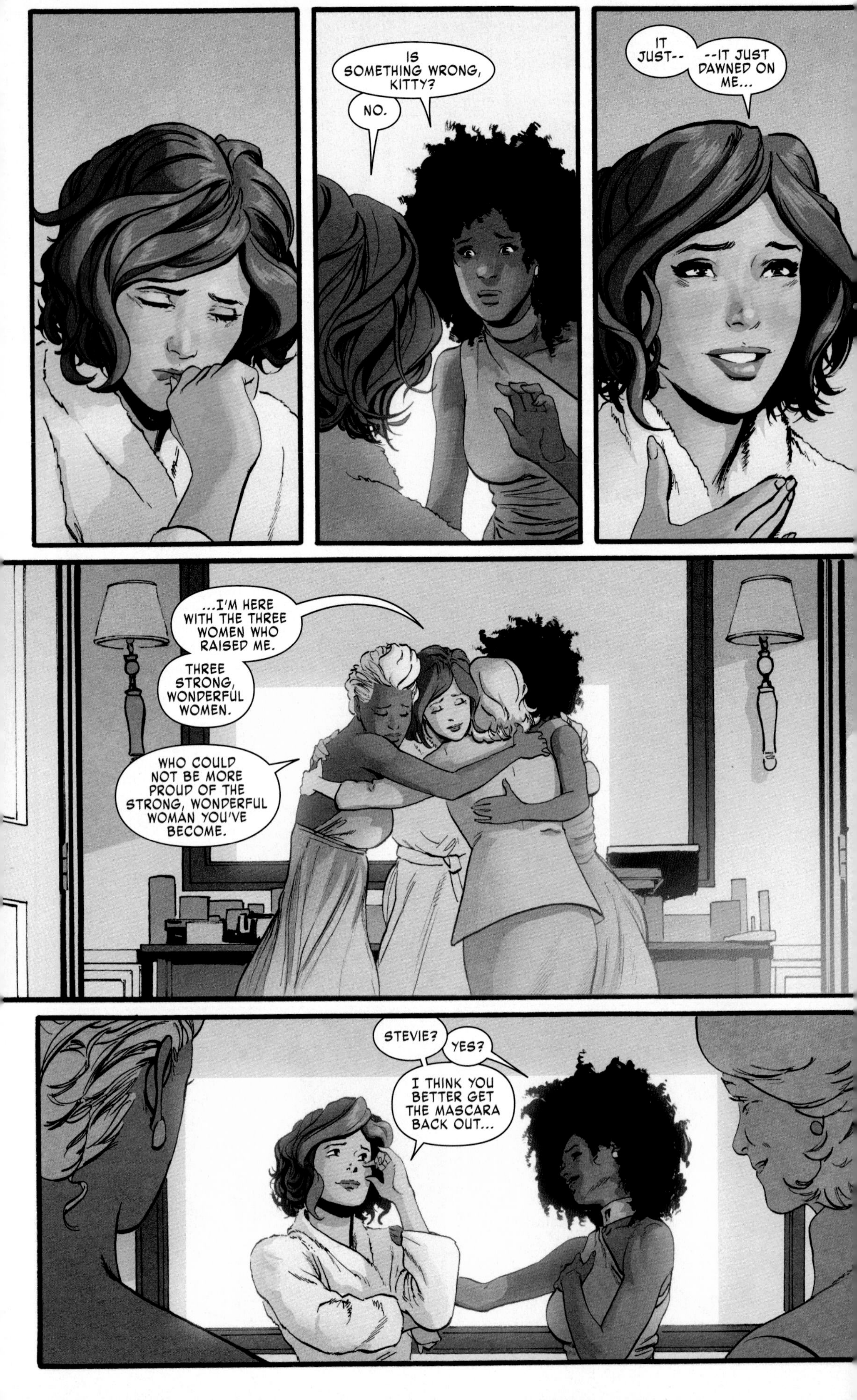
IS SOMETHING WRONG, KITTY?
NO.
IT JUST--
--IT JUST DAWNED ON ME...
...I'M HERE WITH THE THREE WOMEN WHO RAISED ME.
THREE STRONG, WONDERFUL WOMEN.
WHO COULD NOT BE MORE PROUD OF THE STRONG, WONDERFUL WOMAN YOU'VE BECOME.
STEVIE?
YES?
I THINK YOU BETTER GET THE MASCARA BACK OUT...

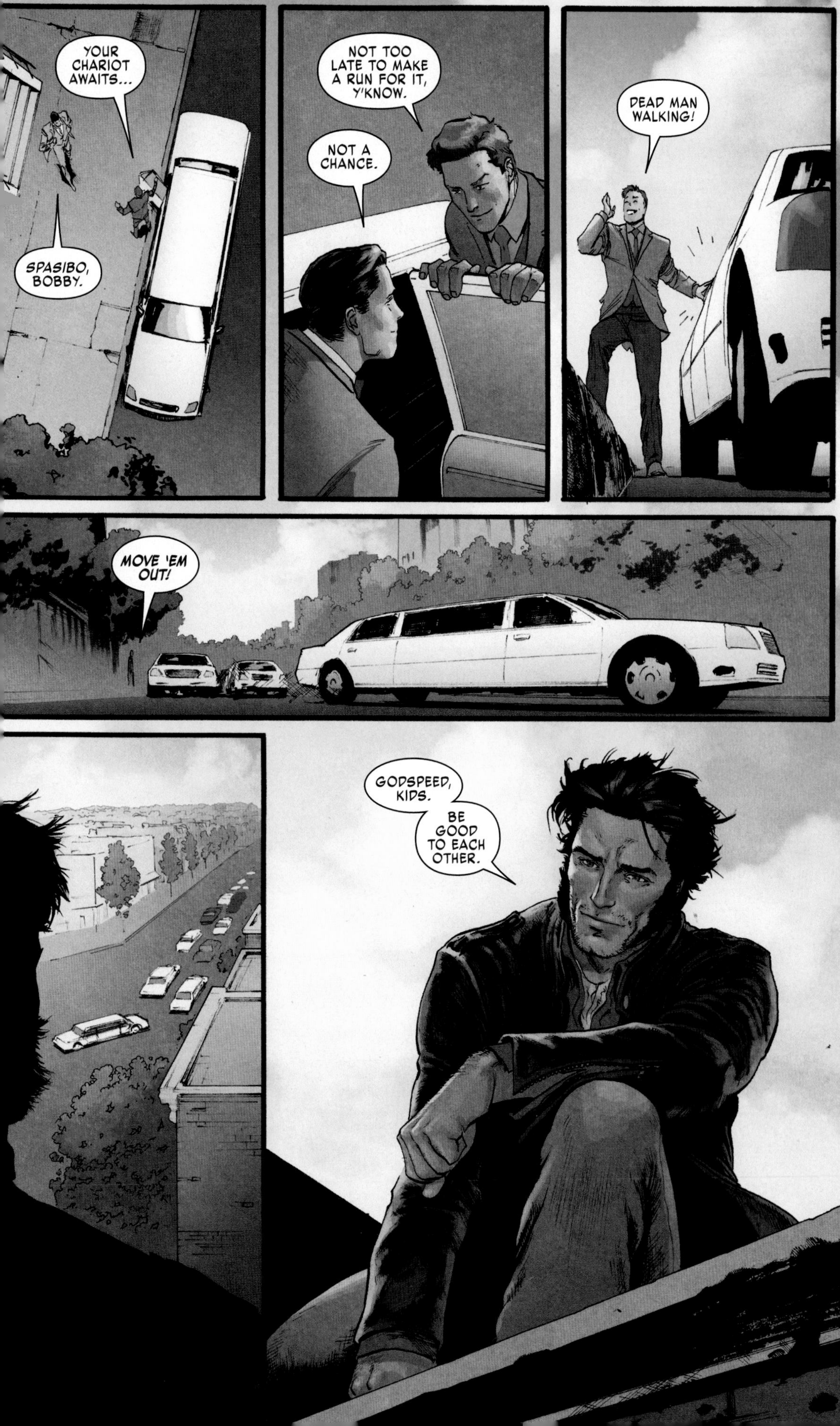
YOUR CHARIOT AWAITS...
SPASIBO, BOBBY.
NOT TOO LATE TO MAKE A RUN FOR IT, Y'KNOW.
NOT A CHANCE.
DEAD MAN WALKING!
MOVE 'EM OUT!
GODSPEED, KIDS.
BE GOOD TO EACH OTHER.

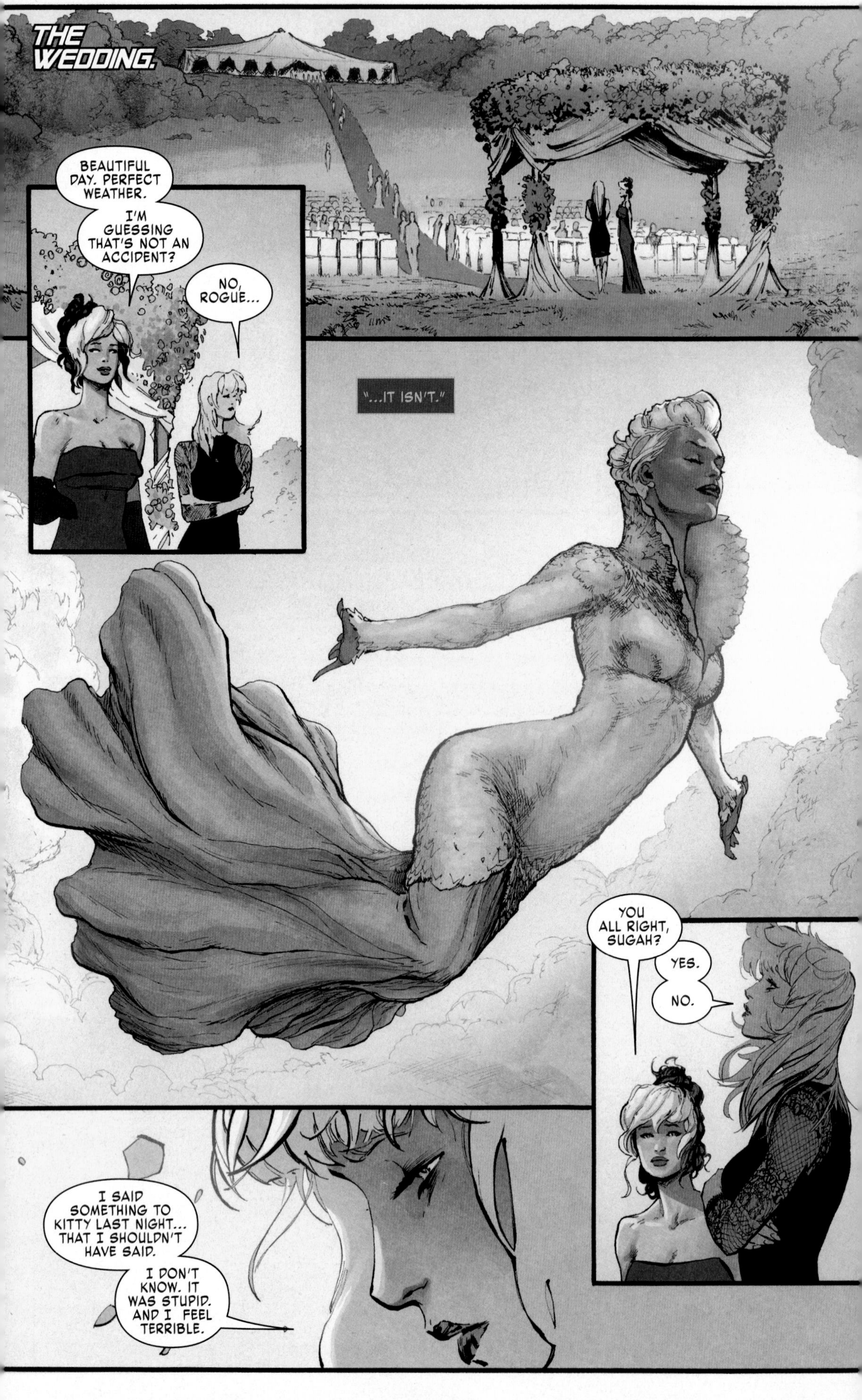
THE WEDDING.
BEAUTIFUL DAY. PERFECT WEATHER.
I'M GUESSING THAT'S NOT AN ACCIDENT?
NO, ROGUE...
"...IT ISN'T."
YOU ALL RIGHT, SUGAH?
YES.
NO.
I SAID SOMETHING TO KITTY LAST NIGHT... THAT I SHOULDN'T HAVE SAID.
I DON'T KNOW. IT WAS STUPID. AND I FEEL TERRIBLE.

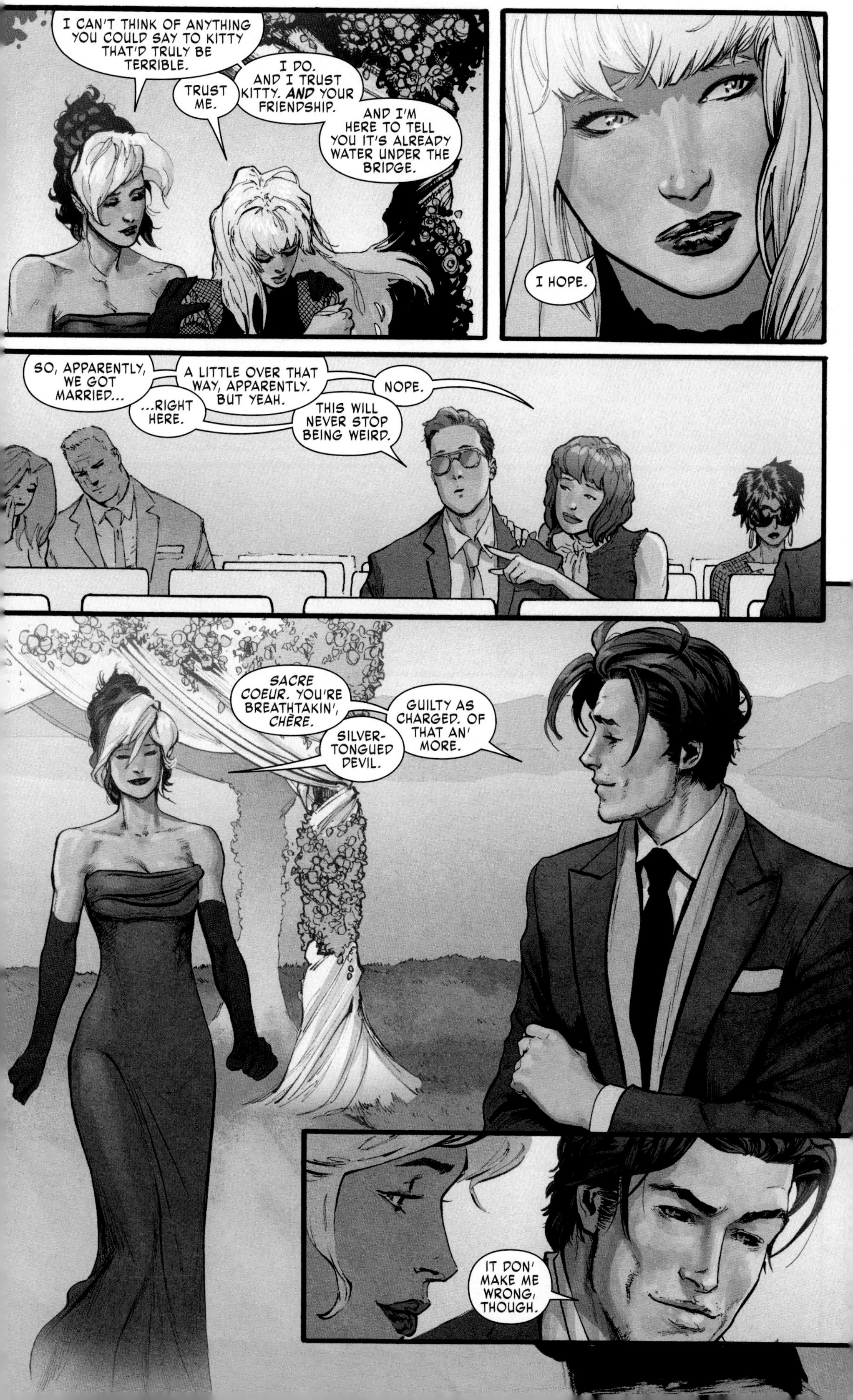
I CAN'T THINK OF ANYTHING YOU COULD SAY TO KITTY THAT'D TRULY BE TERRIBLE.
TRUST ME.
I DO. AND I TRUST KITTY. AND YOUR FRIENDSHIP.
AND I'M HERE TO TELL YOU IT'S ALREADY WATER UNDER THE BRIDGE.
I HOPE.
SO, APPARENTLY, WE GOT MARRIED...
...RIGHT HERE.
A LITTLE OVER THAT WAY, APPARENTLY. BUT YEAH.
THIS WILL NEVER STOP BEING WEIRD.
NOPE.
SACRE COEUR. YOU'RE BREATHTAKIN', CHÈRE.
SILVER-TONGUED DEVIL.
GUILTY AS CHARGED. OF THAT AN' MORE.
IT DON' MAKE ME WRONG, THOUGH.

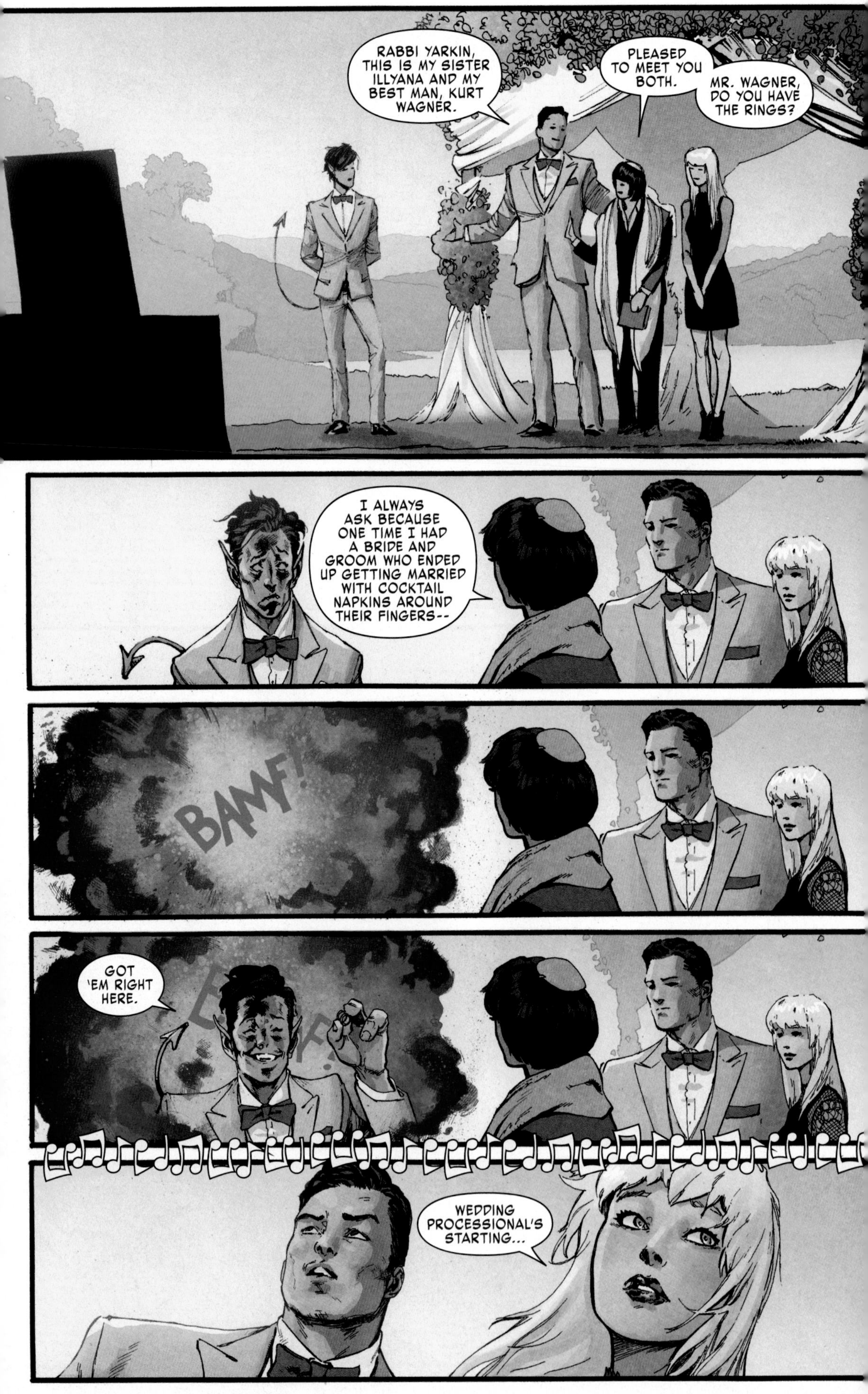
RABBI YARKIN, THIS IS MY SISTER ILLYANA AND MY BEST MAN, KURT WAGNER.
PLEASED TO MEET YOU BOTH.
MR. WAGNER, DO YOU HAVE THE RINGS?
I ALWAYS ASK BECAUSE ONE TIME I HAD A BRIDE AND GROOM WHO ENDED UP GETTING MARRIED WITH COCKTAIL NAPKINS AROUND THEIR FINGERS--
BAMF!
GOT 'EM RIGHT HERE.
WEDDING PROCESSIONAL'S STARTING...

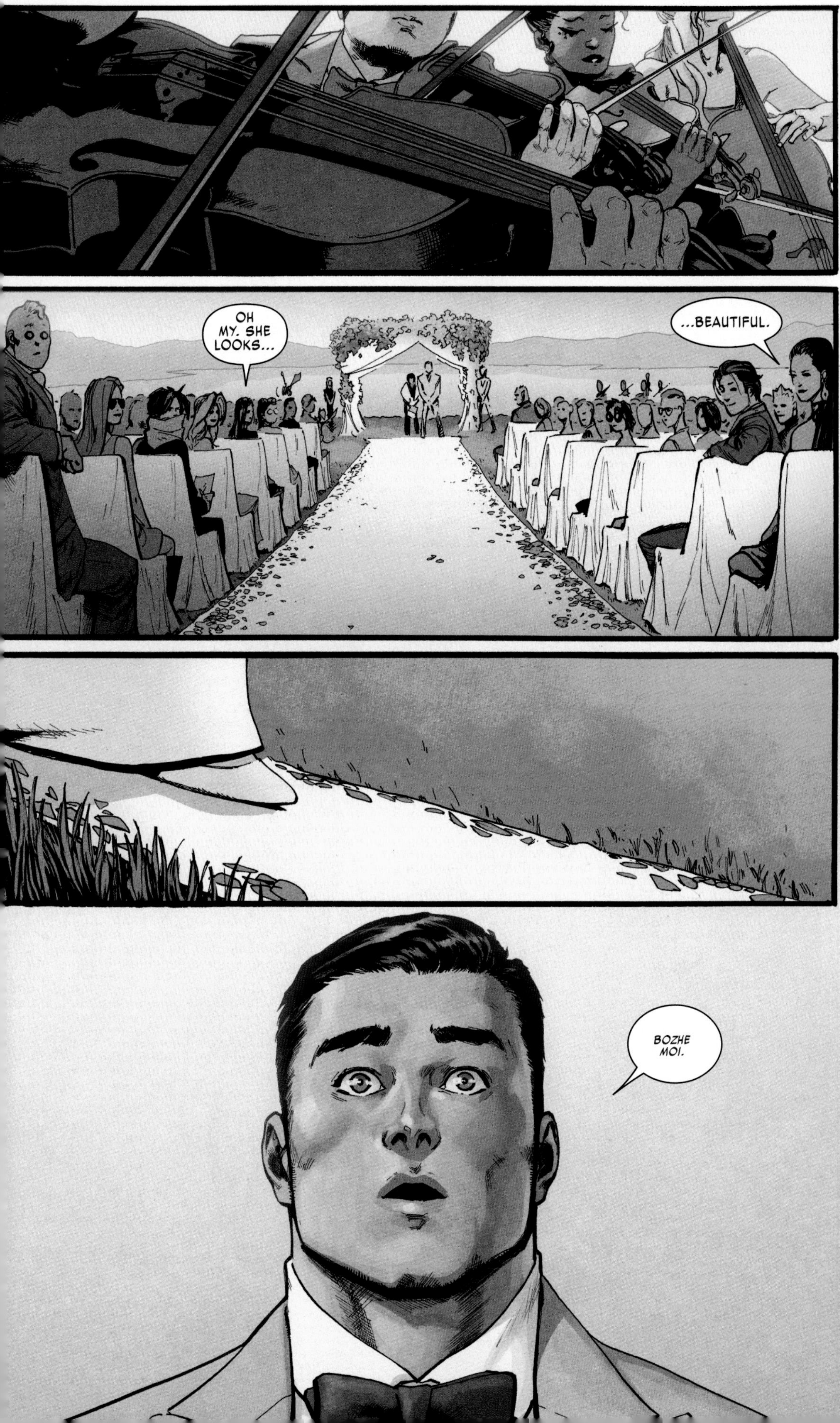
OH MY. SHE LOOKS...
...BEAUTIFUL.
BOZHE MOI.

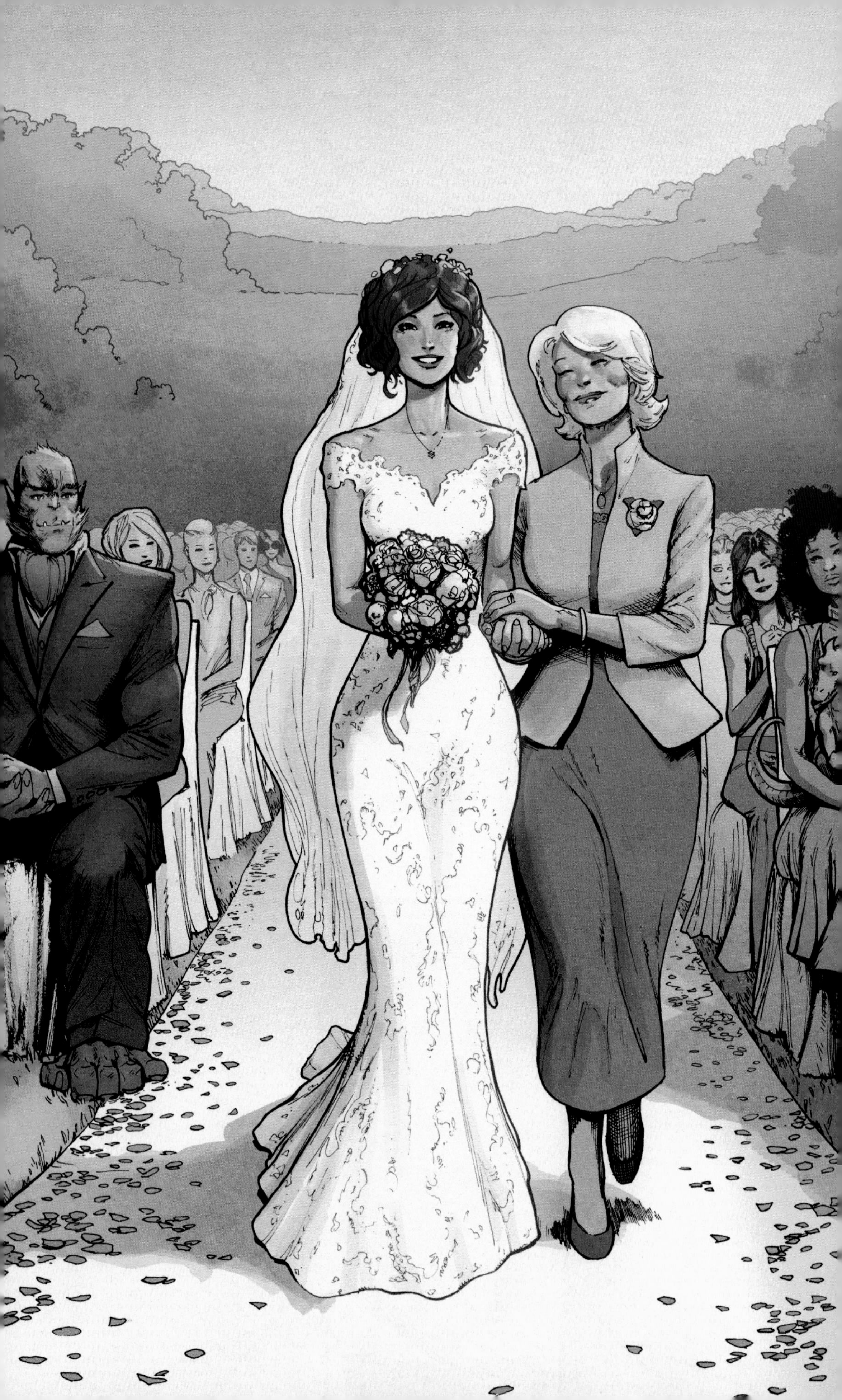

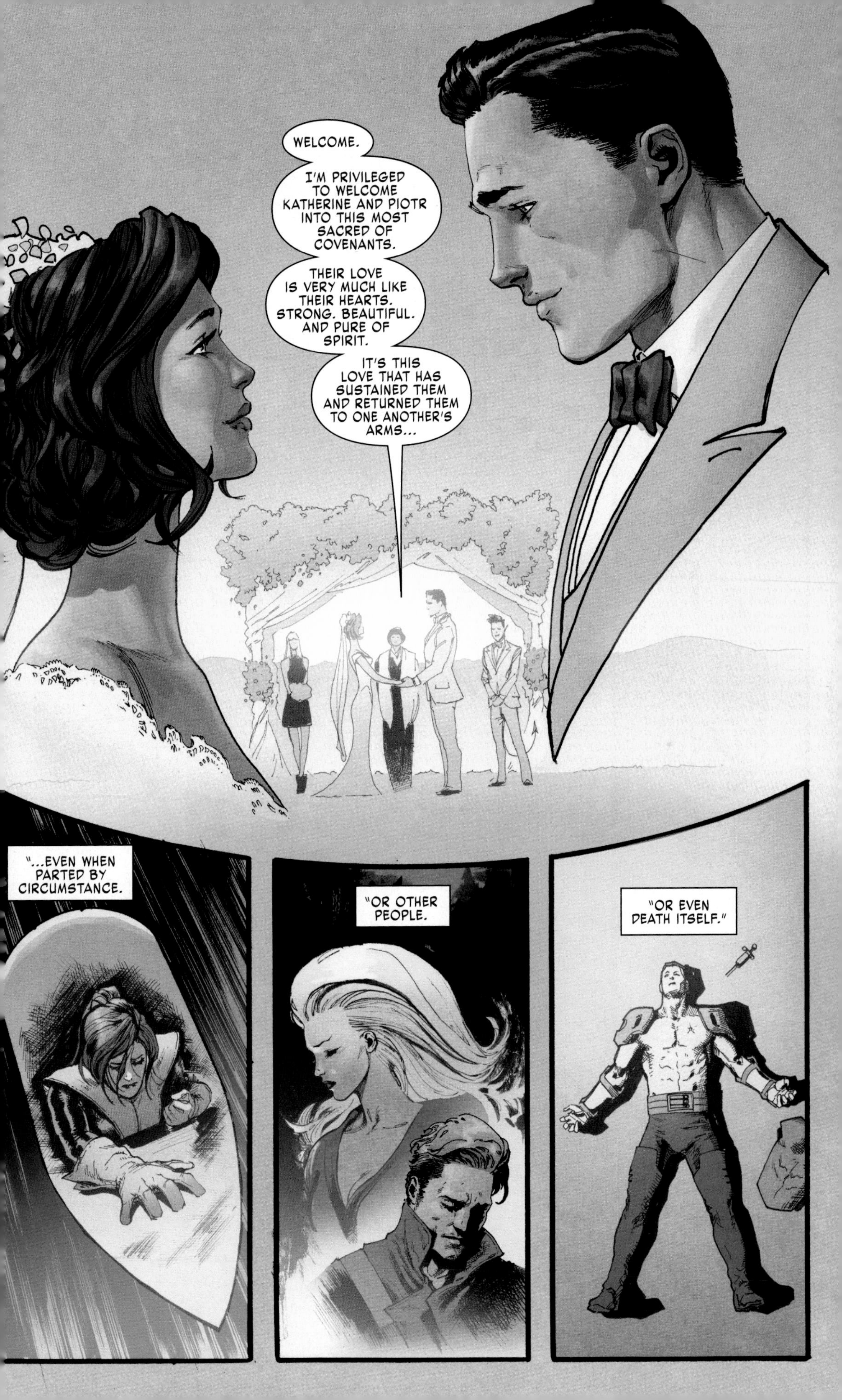

WELCOME.
I'M PRIVILEGED TO WELCOME KATHERINE AND PIOTR INTO THIS MOST SACRED OF COVENANTS.
THEIR LOVE IS VERY MUCH LIKE THEIR HEARTS. STRONG. BEAUTIFUL. AND PURE OF SPIRIT.
IT'S THIS LOVE THAT HAS SUSTAINED THEM AND RETURNED THEM TO ONE ANOTHER'S ARMS...
"...EVEN WHEN PARTED BY CIRCUMSTANCE.
"OR OTHER PEOPLE.
"OR EVEN DEATH ITSELF."

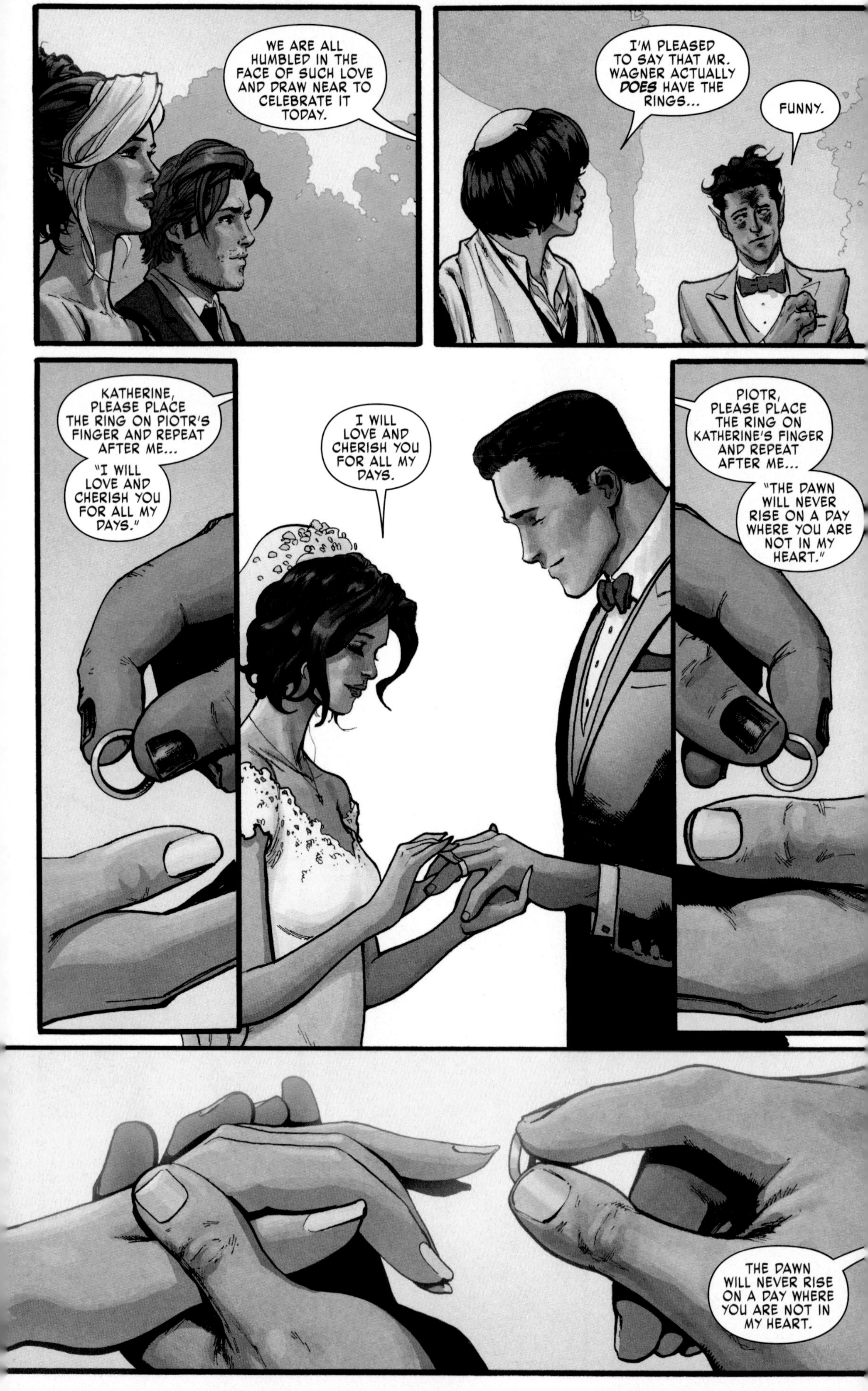
WE ARE ALL HUMBLED IN THE FACE OF SUCH LOVE AND DRAW NEAR TO CELEBRATE IT TODAY.
I'M PLEASED TO SAY THAT MR. WAGNER ACTUALLY *DOES* HAVE THE RINGS...
FUNNY.
KATHERINE, PLEASE PLACE THE RING ON PIOTR'S FINGER AND REPEAT AFTER ME...
"I WILL LOVE AND CHERISH YOU FOR ALL MY DAYS."
I WILL LOVE AND CHERISH YOU FOR ALL MY DAYS.
PIOTR, PLEASE PLACE THE RING ON KATHERINE'S FINGER AND REPEAT AFTER ME...
"THE DAWN WILL NEVER RISE ON A DAY WHERE YOU ARE NOT IN MY HEART."
THE DAWN WILL NEVER RISE ON A DAY WHERE YOU ARE NOT IN MY HEART.

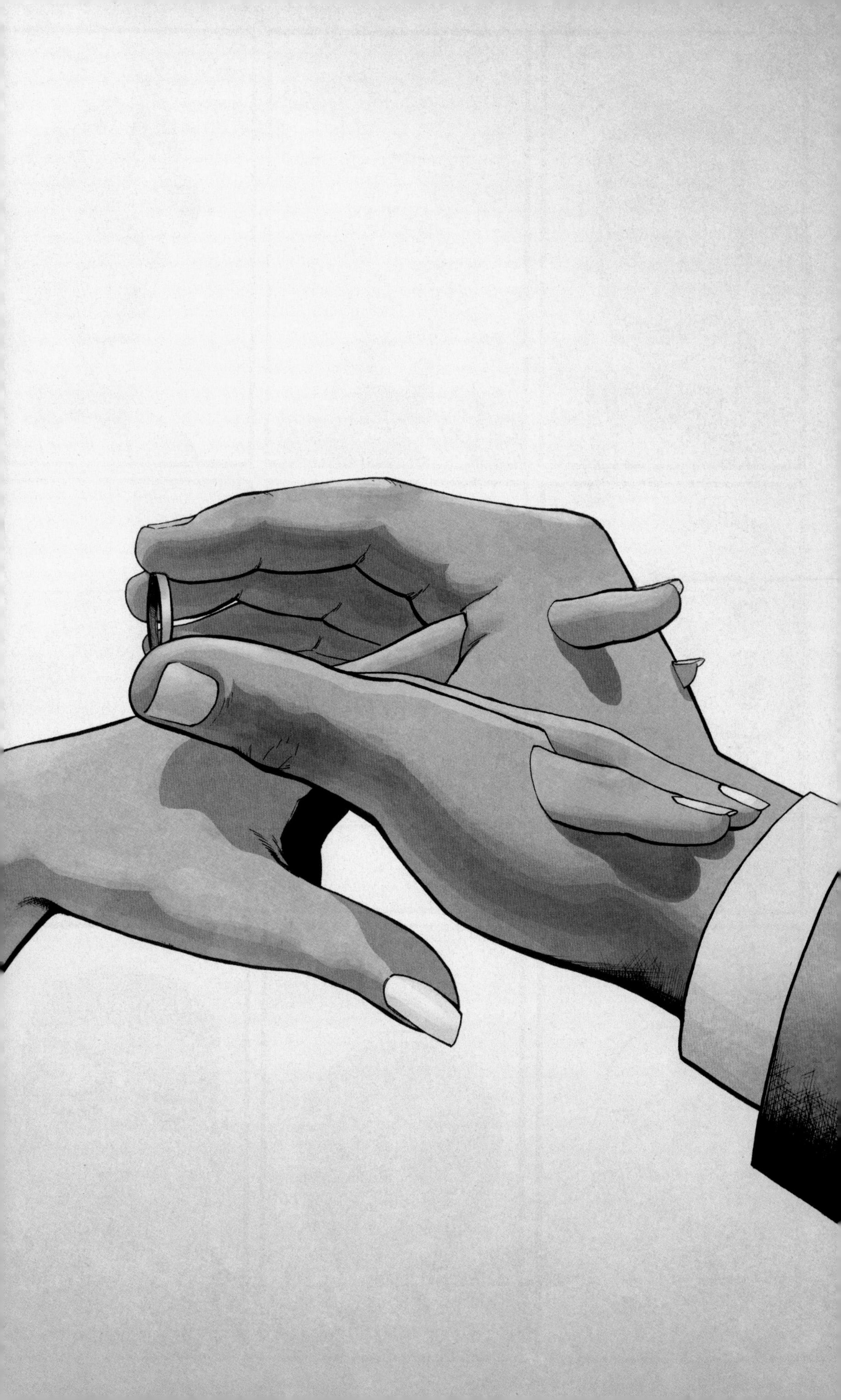

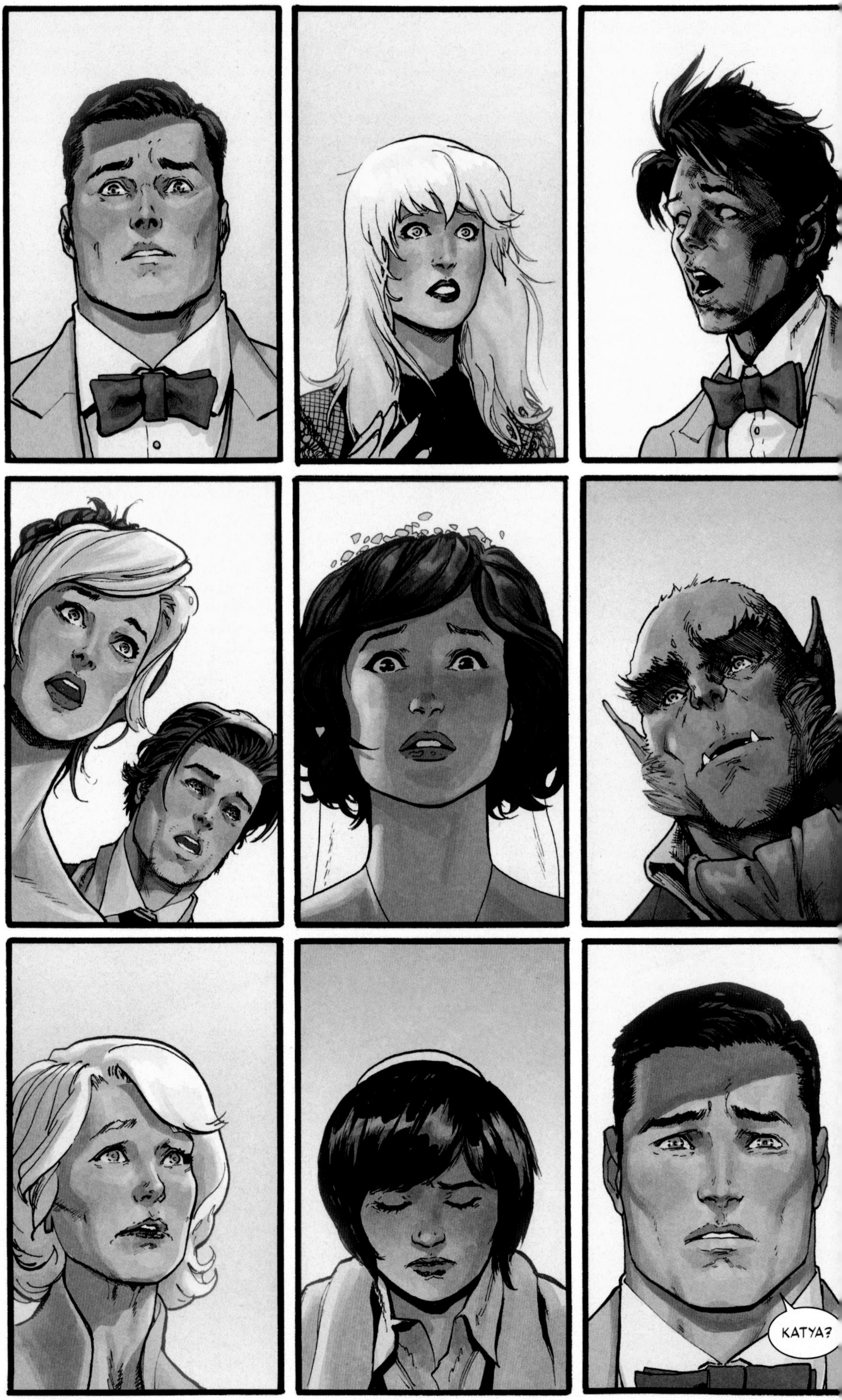
KATYA?

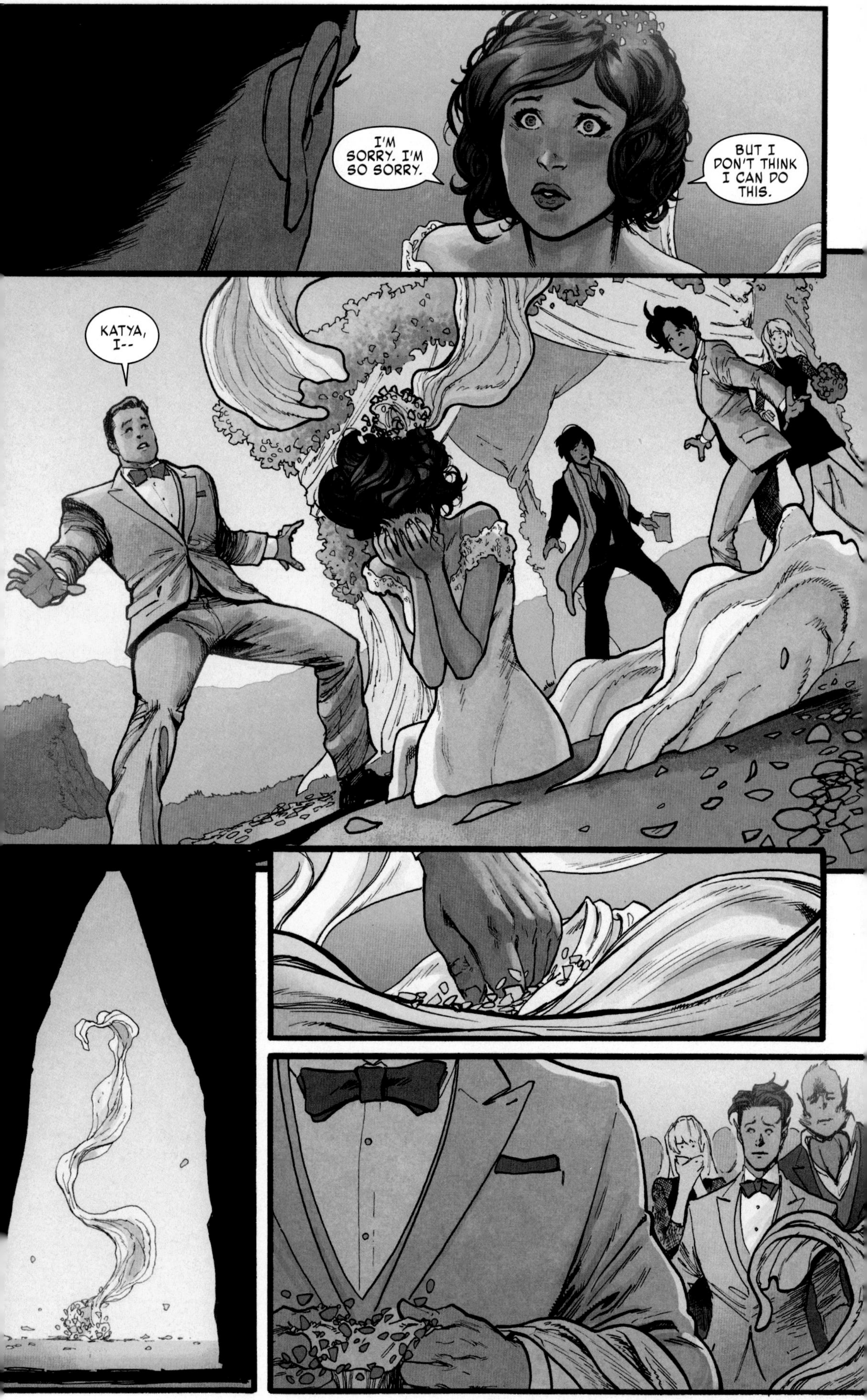
I'M SORRY. I'M SO SORRY.
BUT I DON'T THINK I CAN DO THIS.
KATYA, I--

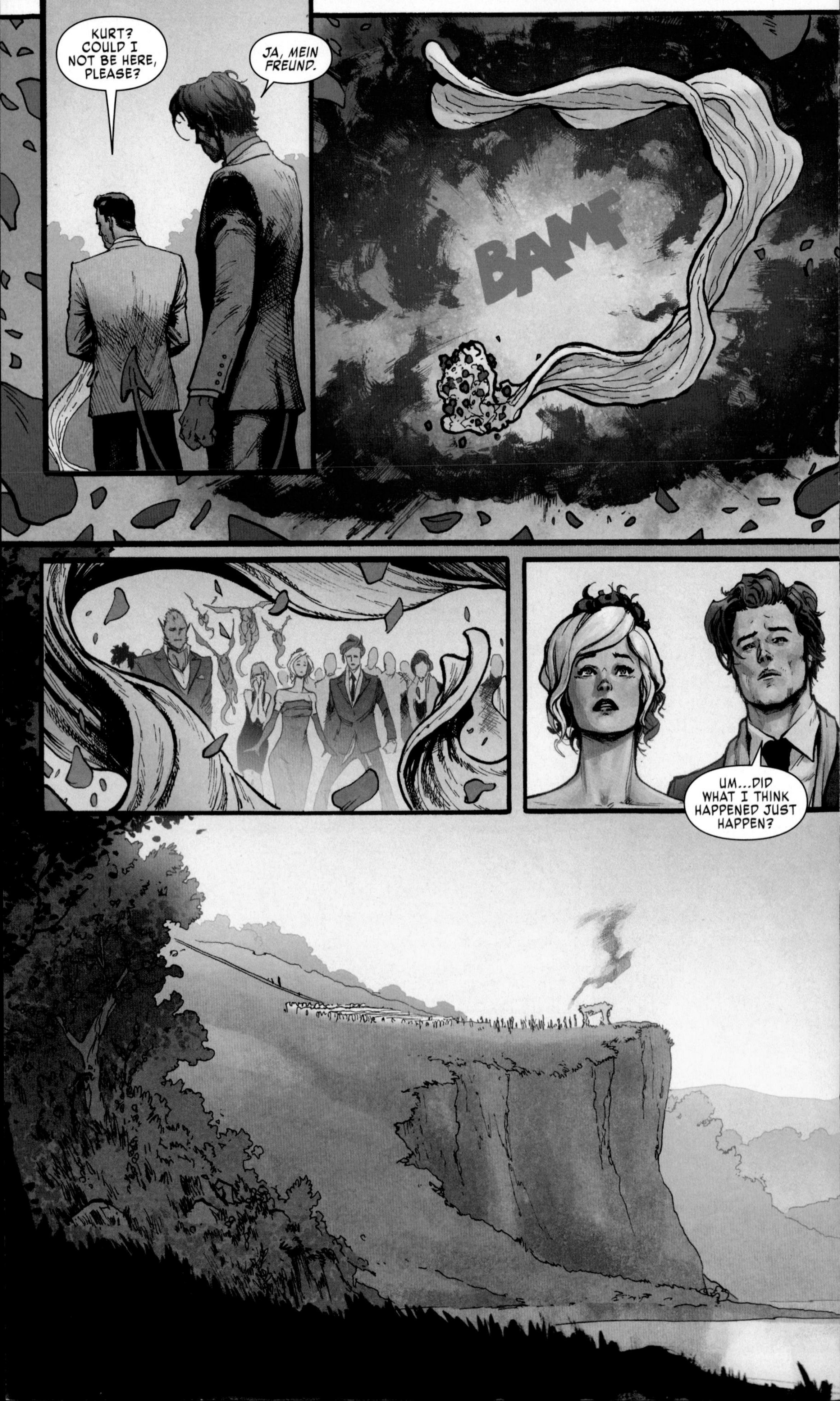
KURT? COULD I NOT BE HERE, PLEASE?
JA, MEIN FREUND.
BAMF
UM...DID WHAT I THINK HAPPENED JUST HAPPEN?

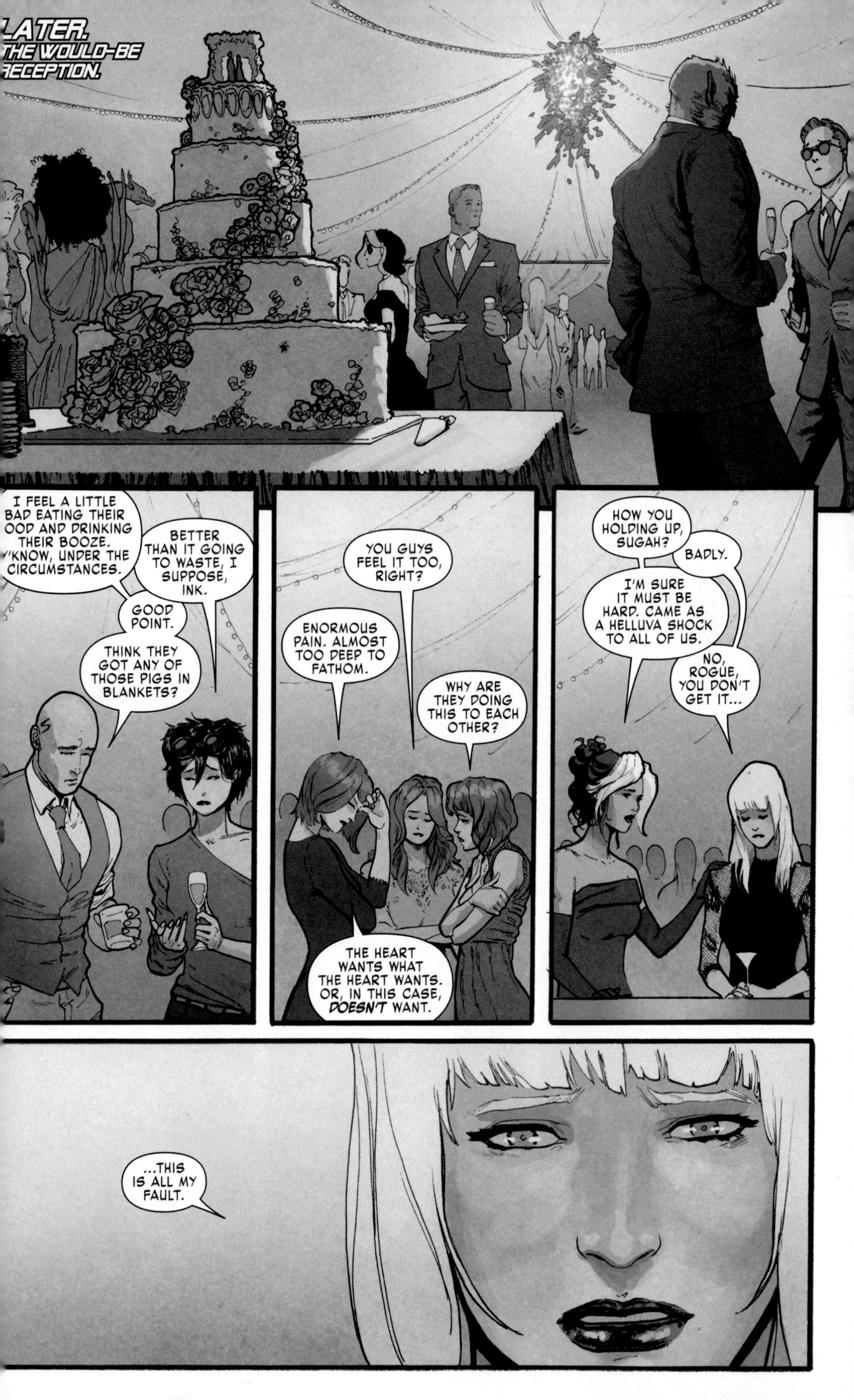
LATER. THE WOULD-BE RECEPTION.
I FEEL A LITTLE BAD EATING THEIR FOOD AND DRINKING THEIR BOOZE. Y'KNOW, UNDER THE CIRCUMSTANCES.
BETTER THAN IT GOING TO WASTE, I SUPPOSE, INK.
GOOD POINT.
THINK THEY GOT ANY OF THOSE PIGS IN BLANKETS?
YOU GUYS FEEL IT TOO, RIGHT?
ENORMOUS PAIN. ALMOST TOO DEEP TO FATHOM.
WHY ARE THEY DOING THIS TO EACH OTHER?
THE HEART WANTS WHAT THE HEART WANTS. OR, IN THIS CASE, DOESN'T WANT.
HOW YOU HOLDING UP, SUGAH?
BADLY.
I'M SURE IT MUST BE HARD. CAME AS A HELLUVA SHOCK TO ALL OF US.
NO, ROGUE, YOU DON'T GET IT...
...THIS IS ALL MY FAULT.

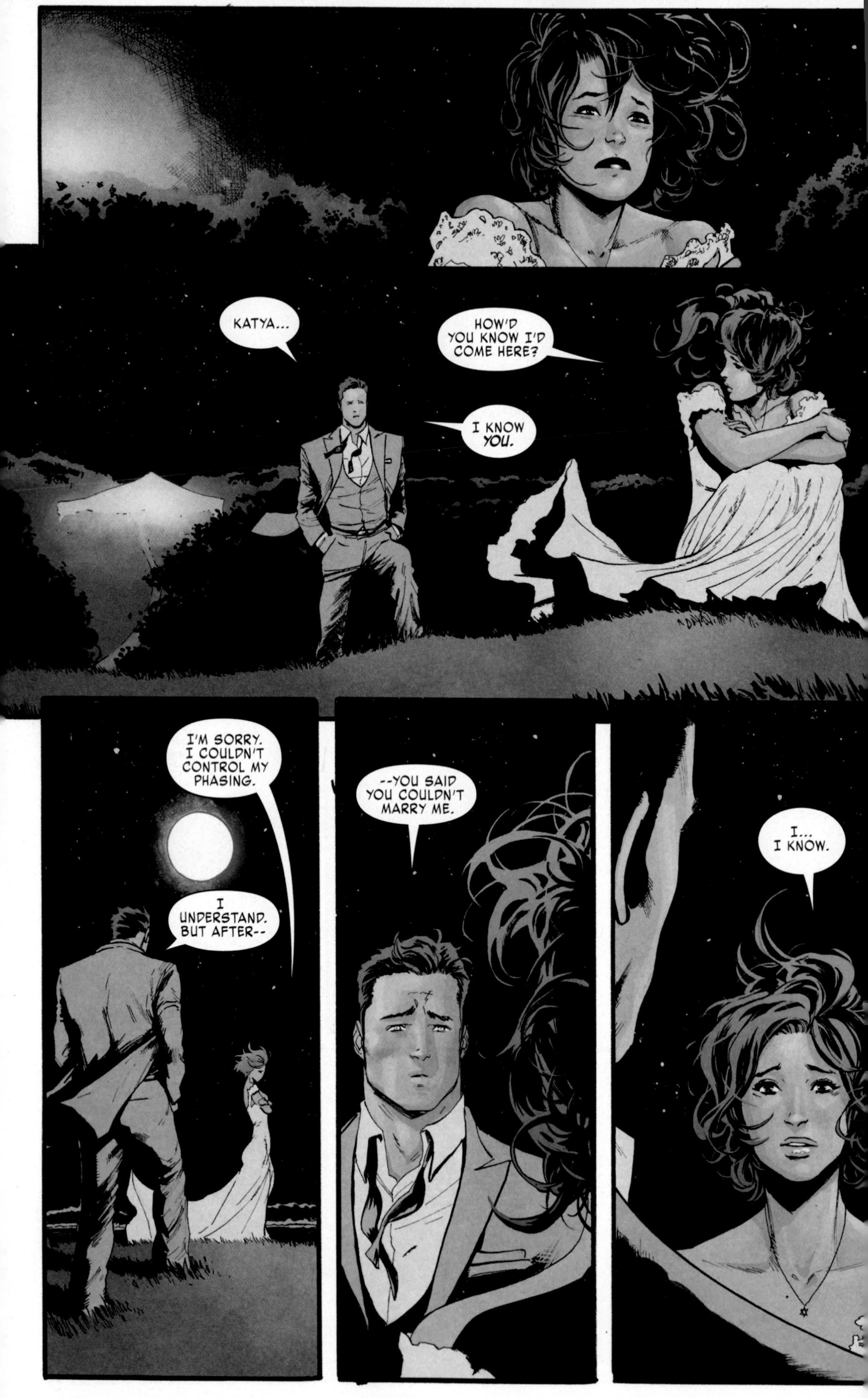
KATYA...
HOW'D YOU KNOW I'D COME HERE?
I KNOW YOU.
I'M SORRY. I COULDN'T CONTROL MY PHASING.
I UNDERSTAND. BUT AFTER--
--YOU SAID YOU COULDN'T MARRY ME.
I... I KNOW.

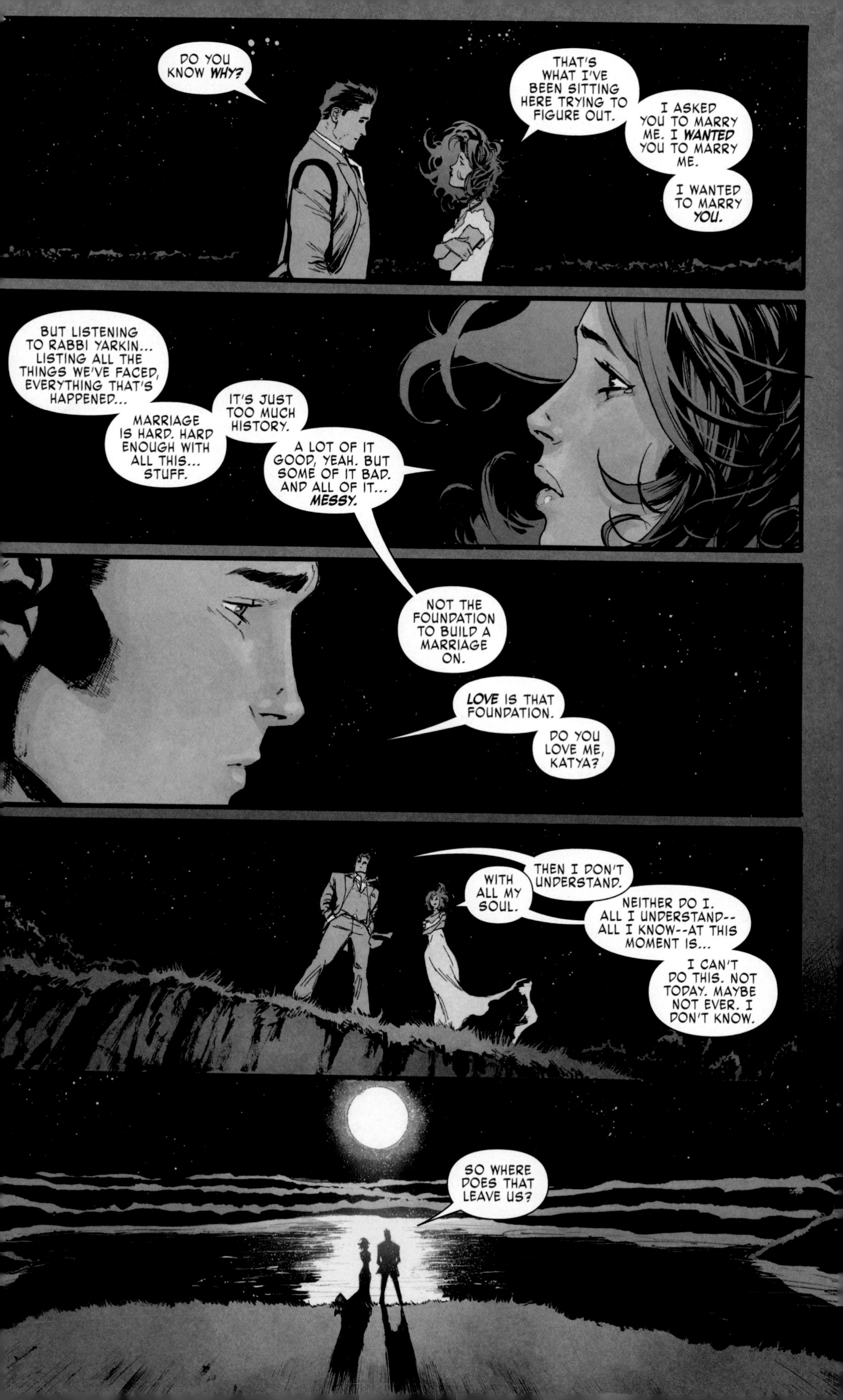
DO YOU KNOW WHY?
THAT'S WHAT I'VE BEEN SITTING HERE TRYING TO FIGURE OUT.
I ASKED YOU TO MARRY ME. I WANTED YOU TO MARRY ME.
I WANTED TO MARRY YOU.
BUT LISTENING TO RABBI YARKIN... LISTING ALL THE THINGS WE'VE FACED, EVERYTHING THAT'S HAPPENED...
MARRIAGE IS HARD. HARD ENOUGH WITH ALL THIS... STUFF.
IT'S JUST TOO MUCH HISTORY.
A LOT OF IT GOOD, YEAH. BUT SOME OF IT BAD. AND ALL OF IT... MESSY.
NOT THE FOUNDATION TO BUILD A MARRIAGE ON.
LOVE IS THAT FOUNDATION.
DO YOU LOVE ME, KATYA?
WITH ALL MY SOUL.
THEN I DON'T UNDERSTAND.
NEITHER DO I. ALL I UNDERSTAND-- ALL I KNOW--AT THIS MOMENT IS...
I CAN'T DO THIS. NOT TODAY. MAYBE NOT EVER. I DON'T KNOW.
SO WHERE DOES THAT LEAVE US?

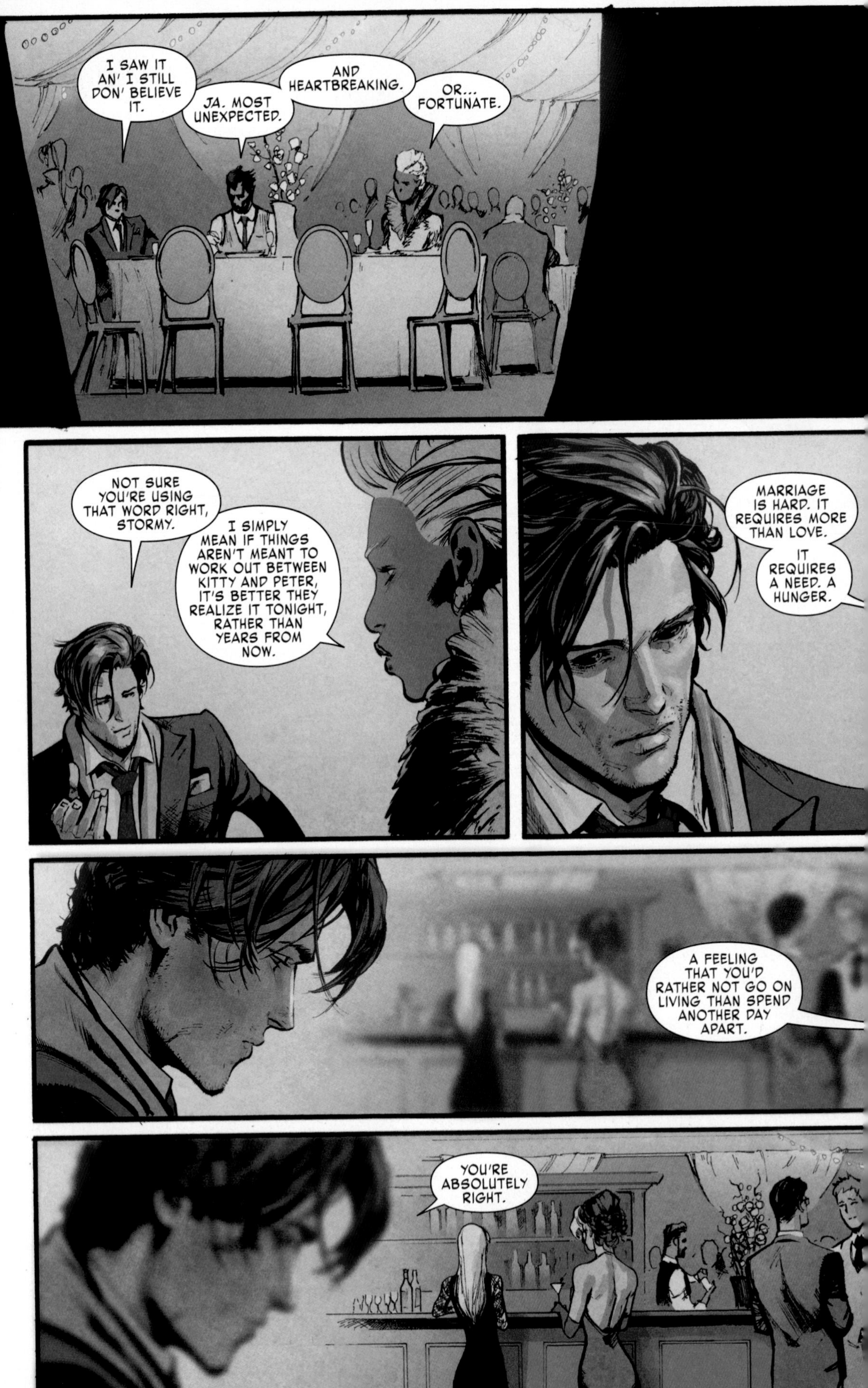
I SAW IT AN' I STILL DON' BELIEVE IT.
JA. MOST UNEXPECTED.
AND HEARTBREAKING.
OR... FORTUNATE.
NOT SURE YOU'RE USING THAT WORD RIGHT, STORMY.
I SIMPLY MEAN IF THINGS AREN'T MEANT TO WORK OUT BETWEEN KITTY AND PETER, IT'S BETTER THEY REALIZE IT TONIGHT, RATHER THAN YEARS FROM NOW.
MARRIAGE IS HARD. IT REQUIRES MORE THAN LOVE.
IT REQUIRES A NEED. A HUNGER.
A FEELING THAT YOU'D RATHER NOT GO ON LIVING THAN SPEND ANOTHER DAY APART.
YOU'RE ABSOLUTELY RIGHT.

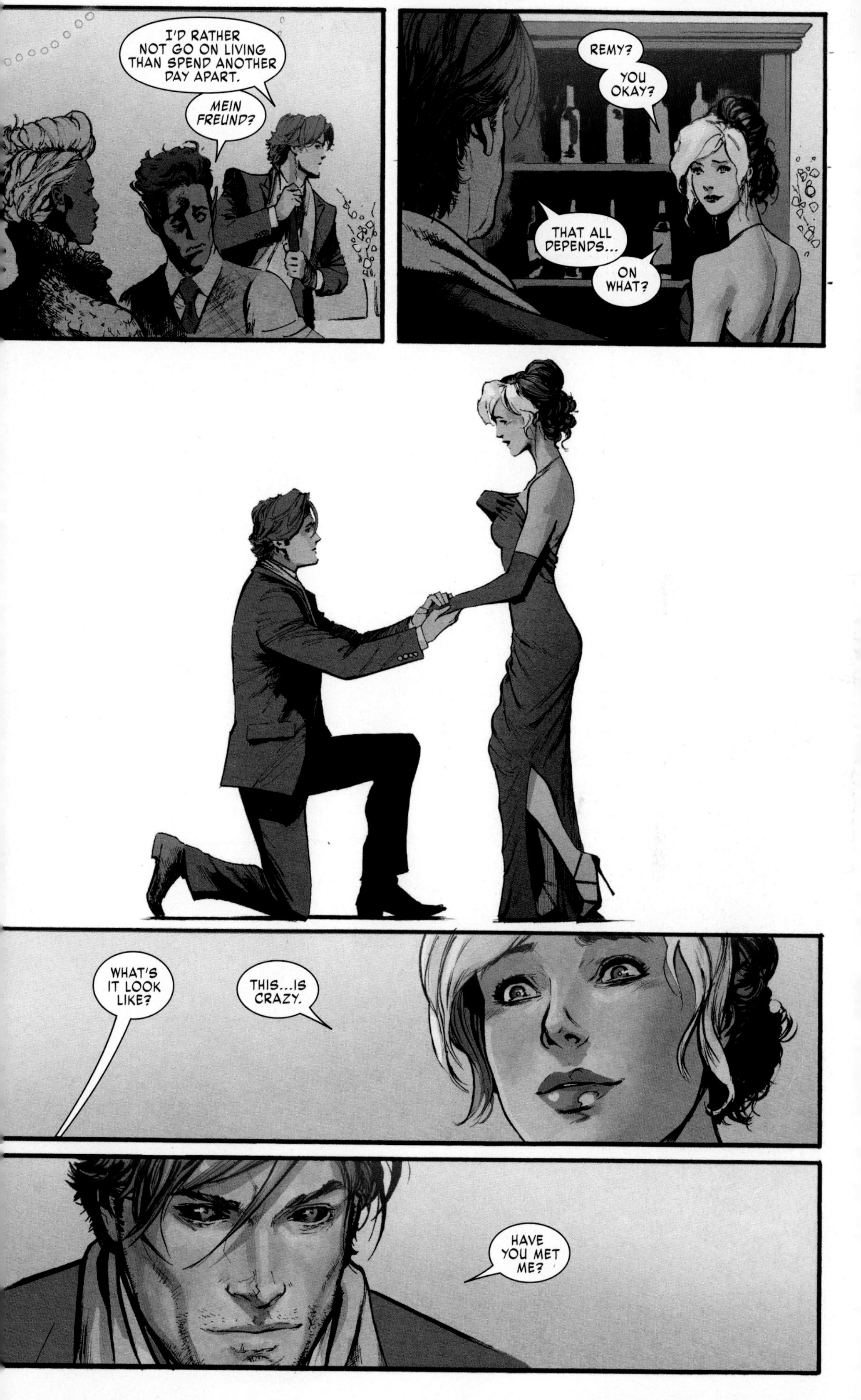

I'D RATHER NOT GO ON LIVING THAN SPEND ANOTHER DAY APART.
MEIN FREUND?
REMY?
YOU OKAY?
THAT ALL DEPENDS...
ON WHAT?
WHAT'S IT LOOK LIKE?
THIS...IS CRAZY.
HAVE YOU MET ME?

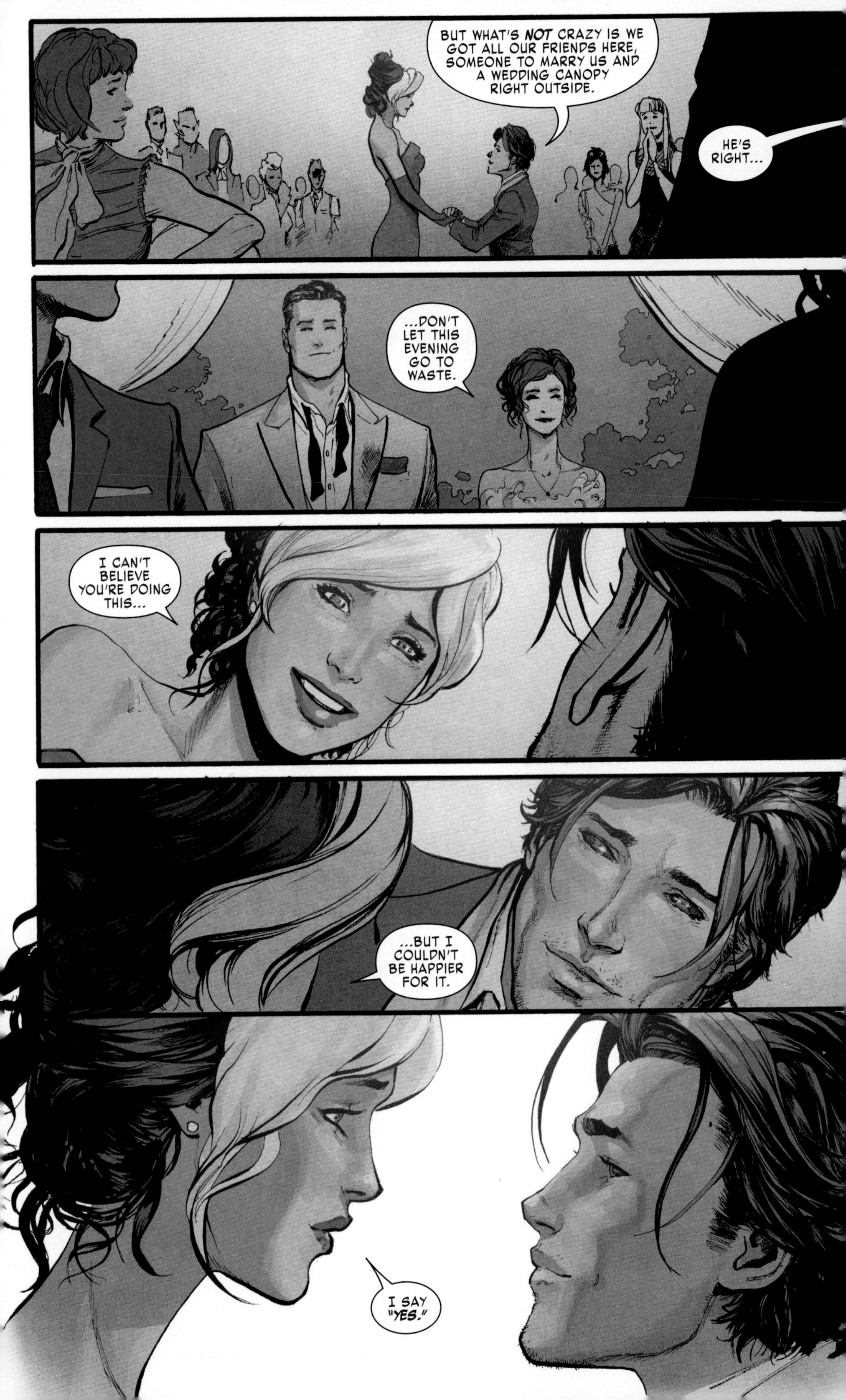
BUT WHAT'S *NOT* CRAZY IS WE GOT ALL OUR FRIENDS HERE, SOMEONE TO MARRY US AND A WEDDING CANOPY RIGHT OUTSIDE.
HE'S RIGHT...
...DON'T LET THIS EVENING GO TO WASTE.
I CAN'T BELIEVE YOU'RE DOING THIS...
...BUT I COULDN'T BE HAPPIER FOR IT.
I SAY "*YES.*"

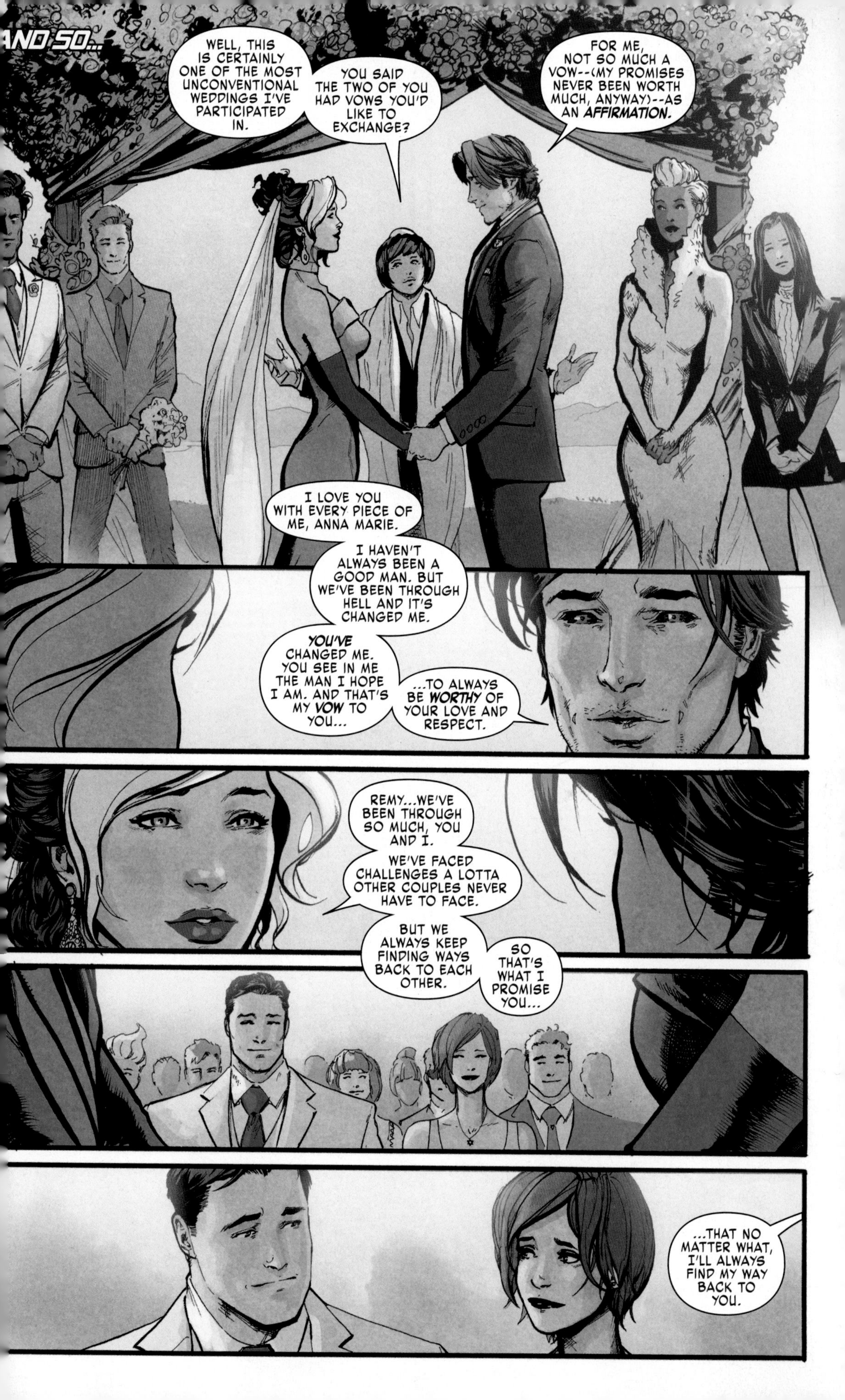
AND SO...
WELL, THIS IS CERTAINLY ONE OF THE MOST UNCONVENTIONAL WEDDINGS I'VE PARTICIPATED IN.
YOU SAID THE TWO OF YOU HAD VOWS YOU'D LIKE TO EXCHANGE?
FOR ME, NOT SO MUCH A VOW--(MY PROMISES NEVER BEEN WORTH MUCH, ANYWAY)--AS AN AFFIRMATION.
I LOVE YOU WITH EVERY PIECE OF ME, ANNA MARIE.
I HAVEN'T ALWAYS BEEN A GOOD MAN. BUT WE'VE BEEN THROUGH HELL AND IT'S CHANGED ME.
YOU'VE CHANGED ME. YOU SEE IN ME THE MAN I HOPE I AM. AND THAT'S MY VOW TO YOU...
...TO ALWAYS BE WORTHY OF YOUR LOVE AND RESPECT.
REMY...WE'VE BEEN THROUGH SO MUCH, YOU AND I.
WE'VE FACED CHALLENGES A LOTTA OTHER COUPLES NEVER HAVE TO FACE.
BUT WE ALWAYS KEEP FINDING WAYS BACK TO EACH OTHER.
SO THAT'S WHAT I PROMISE YOU...
...THAT NO MATTER WHAT, I'LL ALWAYS FIND MY WAY BACK TO YOU.

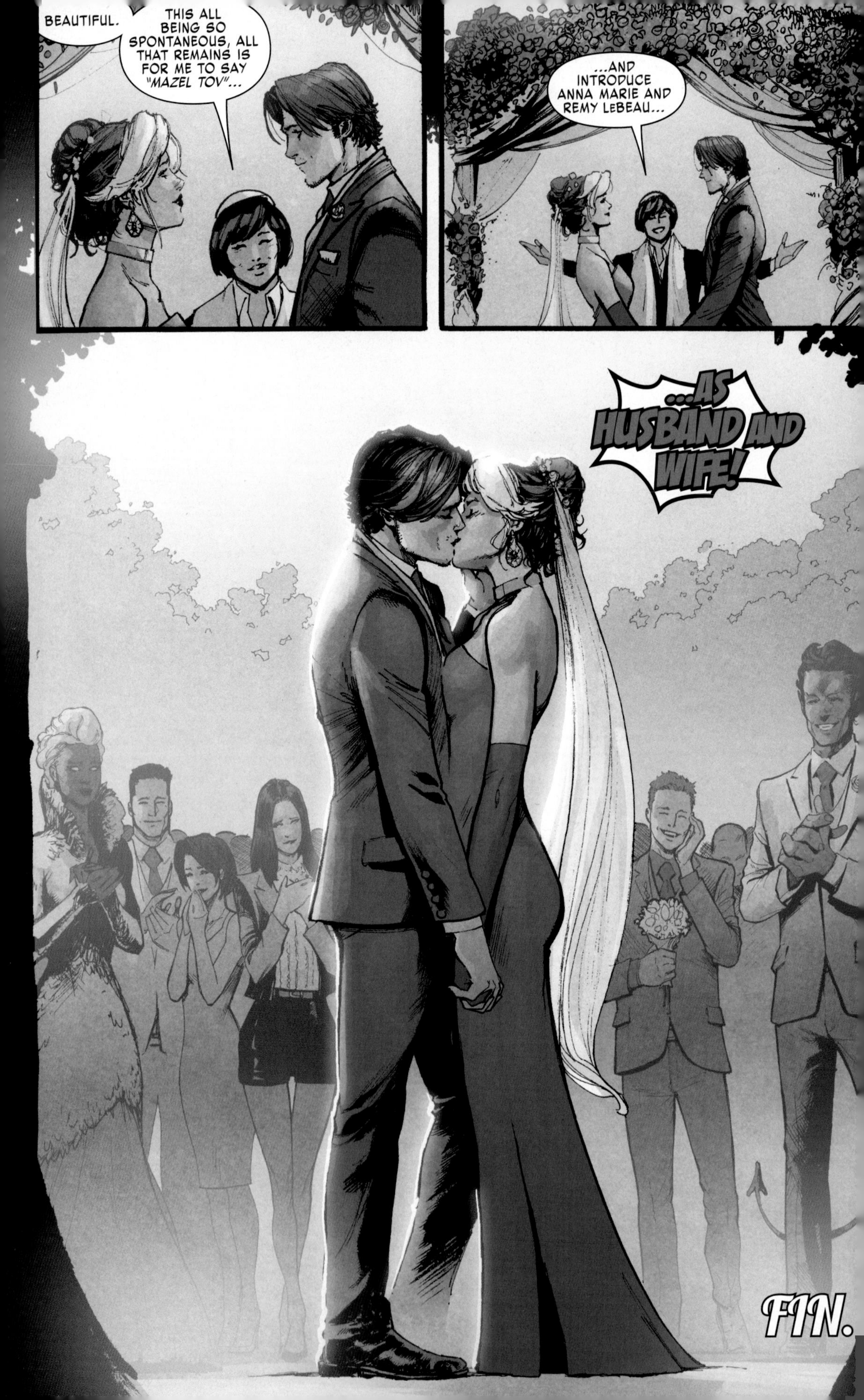
BEAUTIFUL.
THIS ALL BEING SO SPONTANEOUS, ALL THAT REMAINS IS FOR ME TO SAY "MAZEL TOV"...
...AND INTRODUCE ANNA MARIE AND REMY LeBEAU...
...AS HUSBAND AND WIFE!
FIN.

X-MEN: THE WEDDING SPECIAL #1

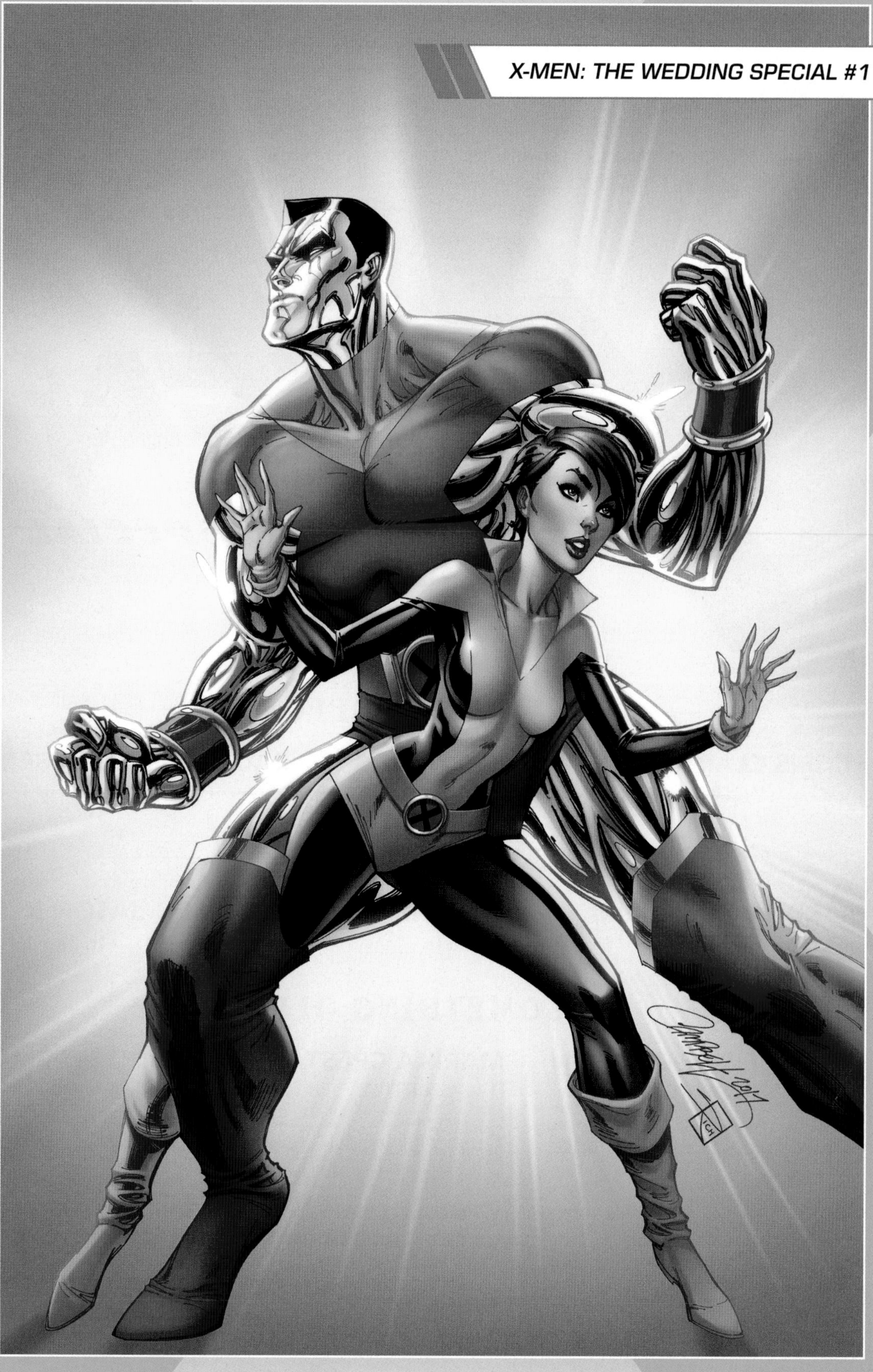

GENETICALLY GIFTED WITH UNCANNY ABILITIES, MUTANTS ARE BELIEVED TO BE THE NEXT STAGE OF HUMAN EVOLUTION. WHILE THE WORLD HATES AND FEARS THEM, KITTY PRYDE HAS RE-FORMED THE TEAM OF MUTANT HEROES KNOWN AS THE X-MEN TO USE THEIR POWERS FOR GOOD AND SPREAD A POSITIVE IMAGE OF MUTANTKIND.

WHEN KITTY PRYDE RECONNECTED WITH THE X-MEN, SHE ALSO RECONNECTED WITH FORMER LOVER PIOTR RASPUTIN, A.K.A. THE METALLIC MUTANT NAMED COLOSSUS! THEIR REVIVED ROMANCE QUICKLY BLOSSOMED INTO AN ENGAGEMENT. BUT WHAT'S A WEDDING WITHOUT THE RESPECTIVE BACHELOR AND BACHELORETTE PARTIES…

X-MEN
THE WEDDING SPECIAL

THE DREAM BEFORE

CHRIS CLAREMONT
WRITER

TODD NAUCK
ARTIST

RACHELLE ROSENBERG
COLOR ARTIST

BOYS' NIGHT OUT

MARC GUGGENHEIM
WRITER

GREG LAND
ARTIST

JAY LEISTEN
INKER

JASON KEITH
COLOR ARTIST

SOMETHING OLD

KELLY THOMPSON
WRITER

MARIKA CRESTA
ARTIST

FEDERICO BLEE
COLOR ARTIST

• • • • • • •

LETTERER **VC's COLONEL CLAYTON COWLES**   ASSISTANT EDITOR **ANNALISE BISSA**
COVER **J. SCOTT CAMPBELL WITH SABINE RICH**   EDITORS **DARREN SHAN with MARK PANICCIA**
VARIANT COVER **TERRY DODSON & RACHEL DODSON**   X-MEN GROUP EDITOR **JORDAN D. WHITE**

X-MEN CREATED BY **STAN LEE AND JACK KIRBY**

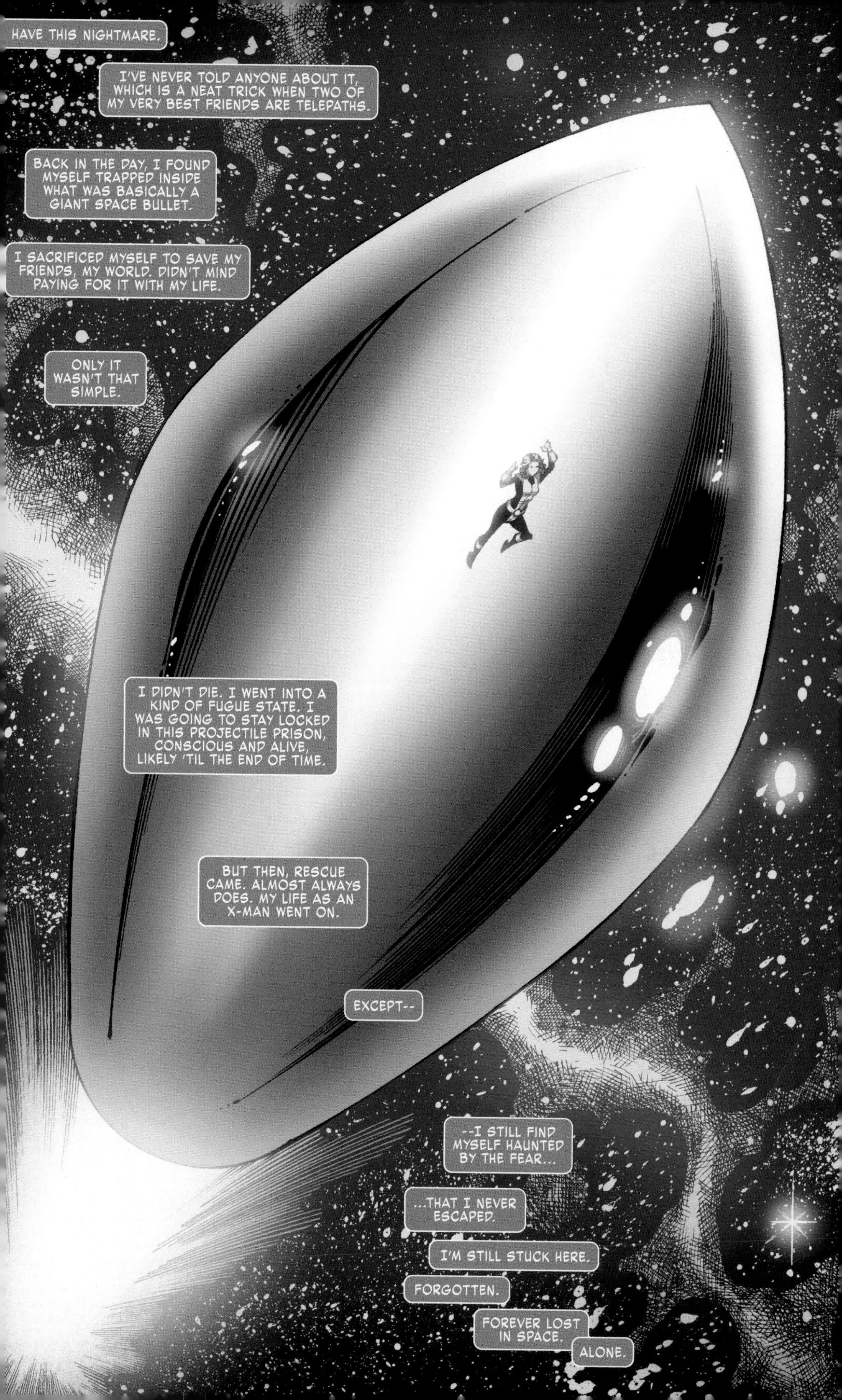
HAVE THIS NIGHTMARE.
I'VE NEVER TOLD ANYONE ABOUT IT, WHICH IS A NEAT TRICK WHEN TWO OF MY VERY BEST FRIENDS ARE TELEPATHS.
BACK IN THE DAY, I FOUND MYSELF TRAPPED INSIDE WHAT WAS BASICALLY A GIANT SPACE BULLET.
I SACRIFICED MYSELF TO SAVE MY FRIENDS, MY WORLD. DIDN'T MIND PAYING FOR IT WITH MY LIFE.
ONLY IT WASN'T THAT SIMPLE.
I DIDN'T DIE. I WENT INTO A KIND OF FUGUE STATE. I WAS GOING TO STAY LOCKED IN THIS PROJECTILE PRISON, CONSCIOUS AND ALIVE, LIKELY 'TIL THE END OF TIME.
BUT THEN, RESCUE CAME. ALMOST ALWAYS DOES. MY LIFE AS AN X-MAN WENT ON.
EXCEPT--
--I STILL FIND MYSELF HAUNTED BY THE FEAR...
...THAT I NEVER ESCAPED.
I'M STILL STUCK HERE.
FORGOTTEN.
FOREVER LOST IN SPACE.
ALONE.

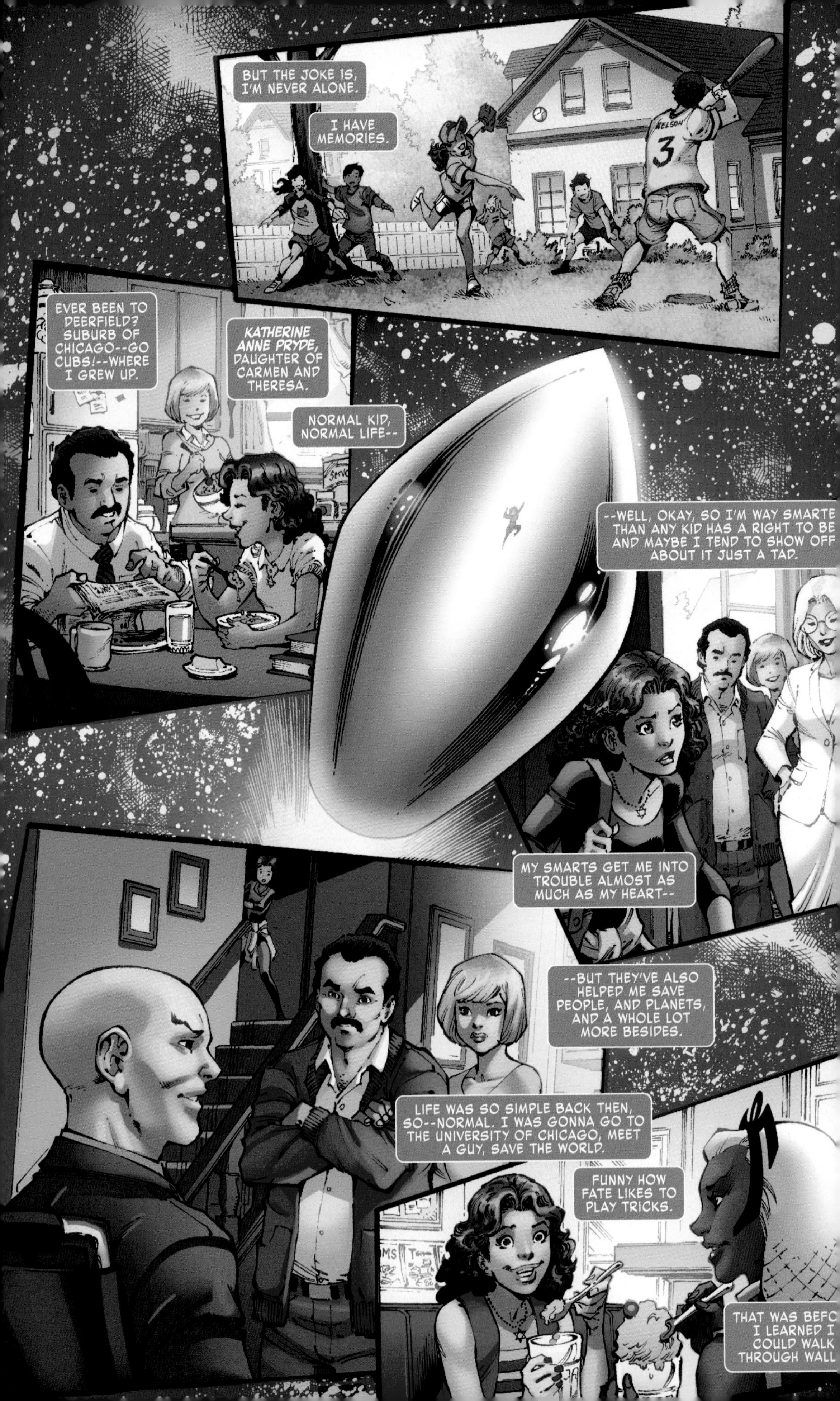

BUT THE JOKE IS, I'M NEVER ALONE.
I HAVE MEMORIES.
NELSON
3
EVER BEEN TO DEERFIELD? SUBURB OF CHICAGO--GO CUBS!--WHERE I GREW UP.
KATHERINE ANNE PRYDE, DAUGHTER OF CARMEN AND THERESA.
NORMAL KID, NORMAL LIFE--
--WELL, OKAY, SO I'M WAY SMARTE THAN ANY KID HAS A RIGHT TO BE AND MAYBE I TEND TO SHOW OFF ABOUT IT JUST A TAD.
MY SMARTS GET ME INTO TROUBLE ALMOST AS MUCH AS MY HEART--
--BUT THEY'VE ALSO HELPED ME SAVE PEOPLE, AND PLANETS, AND A WHOLE LOT MORE BESIDES.
LIFE WAS SO SIMPLE BACK THEN, SO--NORMAL. I WAS GONNA GO TO THE UNIVERSITY OF CHICAGO, MEET A GUY, SAVE THE WORLD.
FUNNY HOW FATE LIKES TO PLAY TRICKS.
THAT WAS BEFO I LEARNED I COULD WALK THROUGH WALL

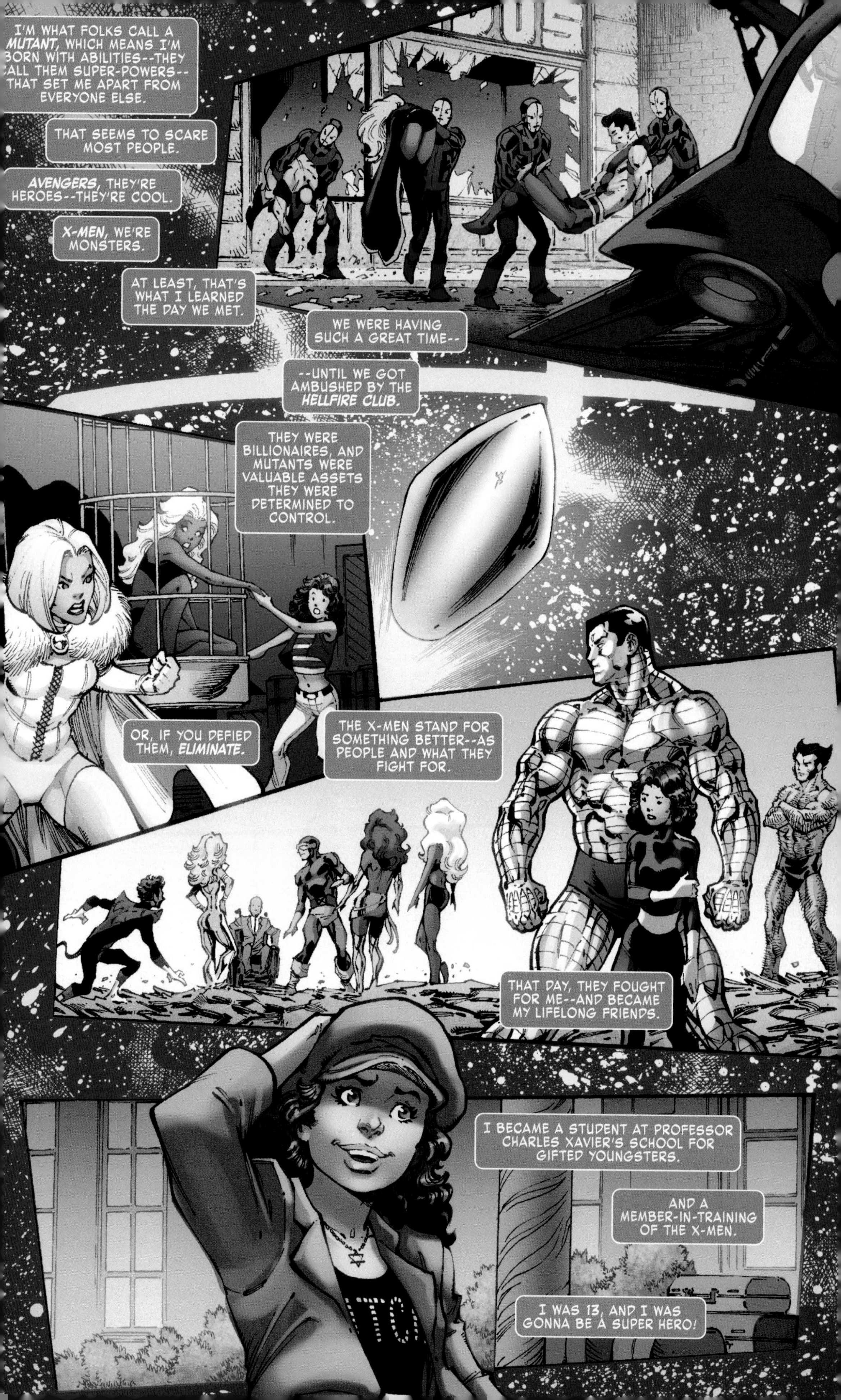

I'M WHAT FOLKS CALL A *MUTANT*, WHICH MEANS I'M BORN WITH ABILITIES--THEY CALL THEM SUPER-POWERS--THAT SET ME APART FROM EVERYONE ELSE.
THAT SEEMS TO SCARE MOST PEOPLE.
AVENGERS, THEY'RE HEROES--THEY'RE COOL.
X-MEN, WE'RE MONSTERS.
AT LEAST, THAT'S WHAT I LEARNED THE DAY WE MET.
WE WERE HAVING SUCH A GREAT TIME--
--UNTIL WE GOT AMBUSHED BY THE *HELLFIRE CLUB.*
THEY WERE BILLIONAIRES, AND MUTANTS WERE VALUABLE ASSETS THEY WERE DETERMINED TO CONTROL.
OR, IF YOU DEFIED THEM, *ELIMINATE.*
THE X-MEN STAND FOR SOMETHING BETTER--AS PEOPLE AND WHAT THEY FIGHT FOR.
THAT DAY, THEY FOUGHT FOR ME--AND BECAME MY LIFELONG FRIENDS.
I BECAME A STUDENT AT PROFESSOR CHARLES XAVIER'S SCHOOL FOR GIFTED YOUNGSTERS.
AND A MEMBER-IN-TRAINING OF THE X-MEN.
I WAS 13, AND I WAS GONNA BE A SUPER HERO!

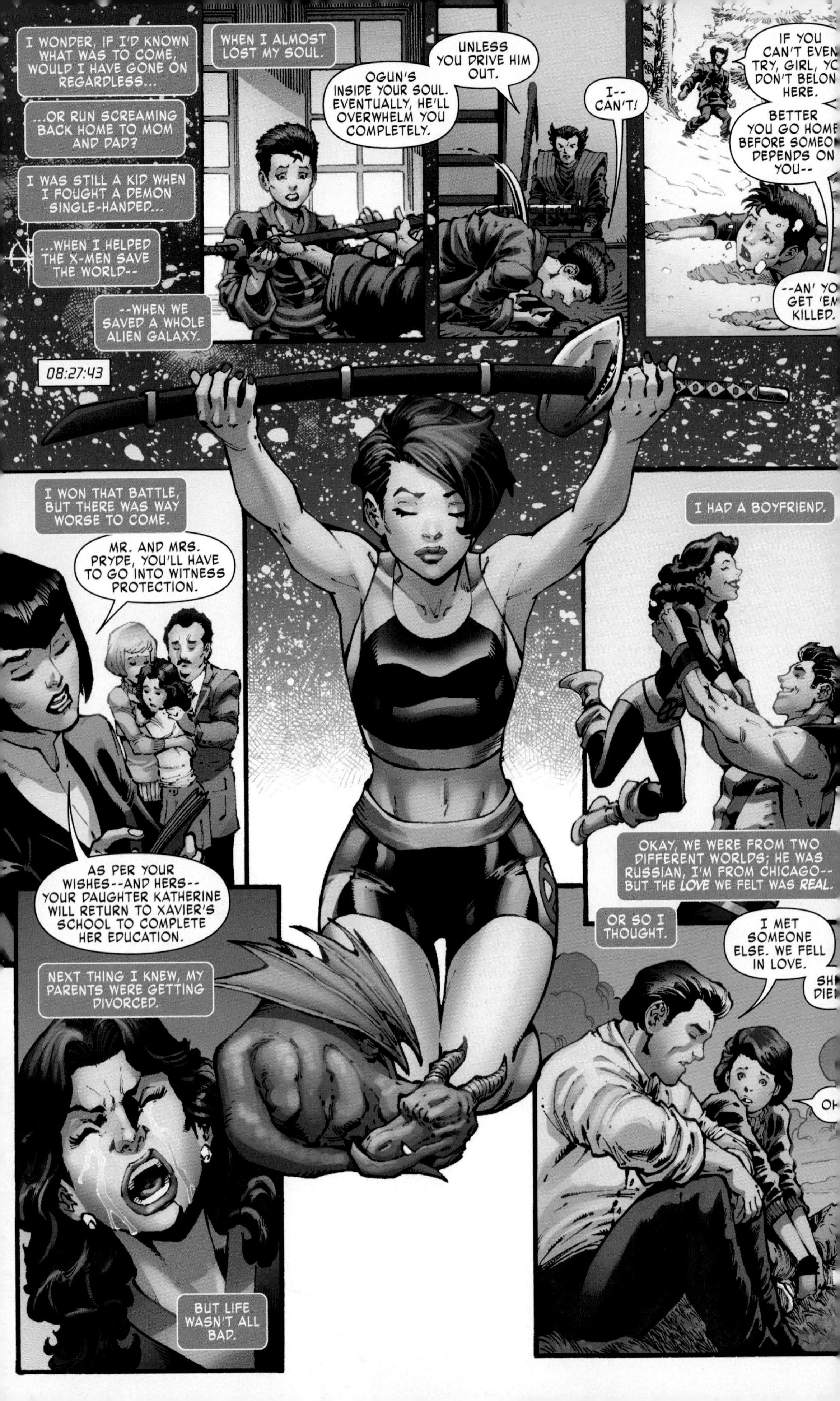
I WONDER, IF I'D KNOWN WHAT WAS TO COME, WOULD I HAVE GONE ON REGARDLESS...
...OR RUN SCREAMING BACK HOME TO MOM AND DAD?
I WAS STILL A KID WHEN I FOUGHT A DEMON SINGLE-HANDED...
...WHEN I HELPED THE X-MEN SAVE THE WORLD--
--WHEN WE SAVED A WHOLE ALIEN GALAXY.
WHEN I ALMOST LOST MY SOUL.
OGUN'S INSIDE YOUR SOUL. EVENTUALLY, HE'LL OVERWHELM YOU COMPLETELY.
UNLESS YOU DRIVE HIM OUT.
I-- CAN'T!
IF YOU CAN'T EVEN TRY, GIRL, YO DON'T BELON HERE.
BETTER YOU GO HOME BEFORE SOMEO DEPENDS ON YOU--
--AN' YO GET 'EM KILLED.
08:27:43
I WON THAT BATTLE, BUT THERE WAS WAY WORSE TO COME.
MR. AND MRS. PRYDE, YOU'LL HAVE TO GO INTO WITNESS PROTECTION.
AS PER YOUR WISHES--AND HERS--YOUR DAUGHTER KATHERINE WILL RETURN TO XAVIER'S SCHOOL TO COMPLETE HER EDUCATION.
NEXT THING I KNEW, MY PARENTS WERE GETTING DIVORCED.
BUT LIFE WASN'T ALL BAD.
I HAD A BOYFRIEND.
OKAY, WE WERE FROM TWO DIFFERENT WORLDS; HE WAS RUSSIAN, I'M FROM CHICAGO--BUT THE LOVE WE FELT WAS REAL.
OR SO I THOUGHT.
I MET SOMEONE ELSE. WE FELL IN LOVE.
SH DIE
OH

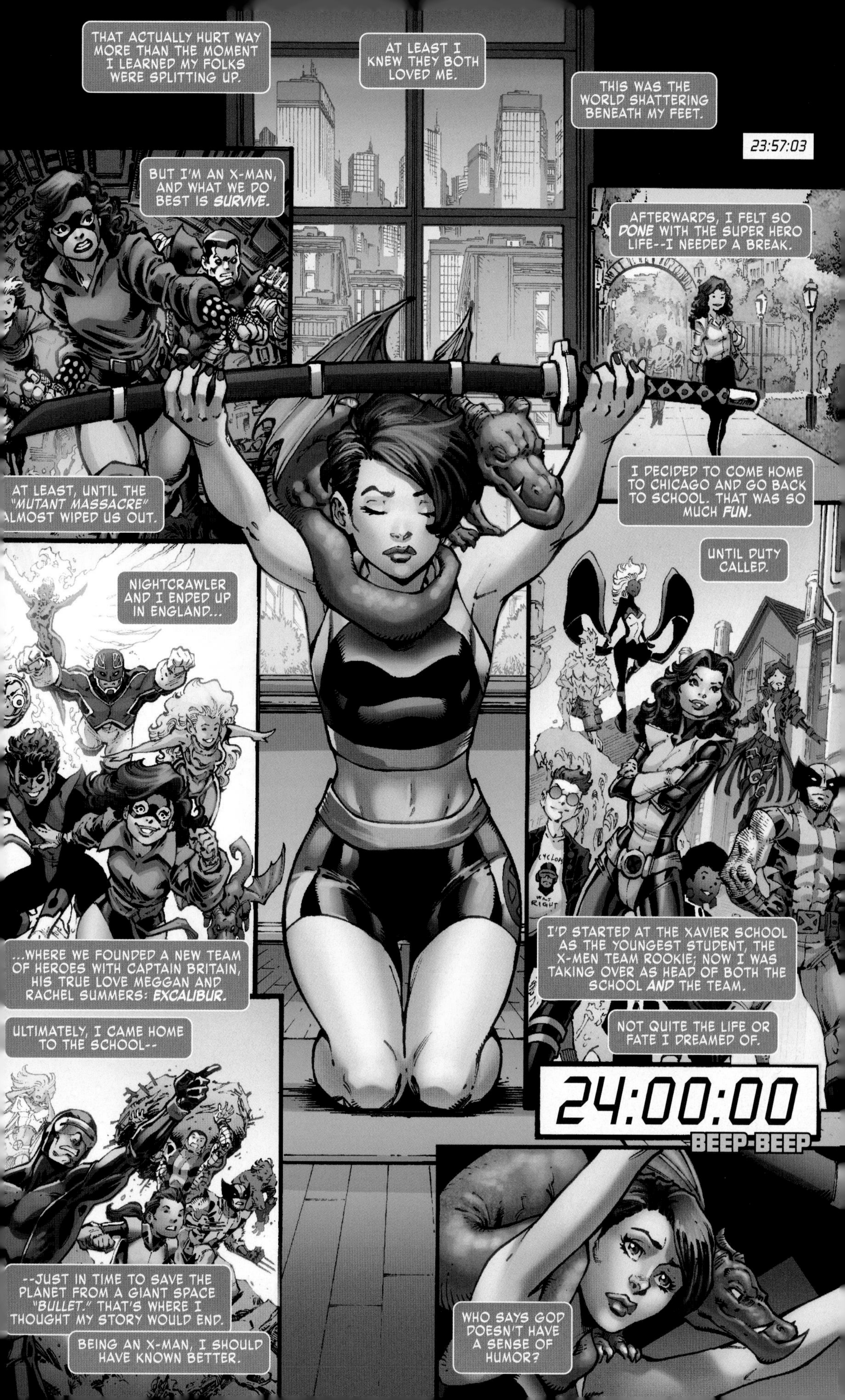
THAT ACTUALLY HURT WAY MORE THAN THE MOMENT I LEARNED MY FOLKS WERE SPLITTING UP.
AT LEAST I KNEW THEY BOTH LOVED ME.
THIS WAS THE WORLD SHATTERING BENEATH MY FEET.
23:57:03
BUT I'M AN X-MAN, AND WHAT WE DO BEST IS SURVIVE.
AT LEAST, UNTIL THE "MUTANT MASSACRE" ALMOST WIPED US OUT.
AFTERWARDS, I FELT SO DONE WITH THE SUPER HERO LIFE--I NEEDED A BREAK.
I DECIDED TO COME HOME TO CHICAGO AND GO BACK TO SCHOOL. THAT WAS SO MUCH FUN.
UNTIL DUTY CALLED.
NIGHTCRAWLER AND I ENDED UP IN ENGLAND...
...WHERE WE FOUNDED A NEW TEAM OF HEROES WITH CAPTAIN BRITAIN, HIS TRUE LOVE MEGGAN AND RACHEL SUMMERS: EXCALIBUR.
ULTIMATELY, I CAME HOME TO THE SCHOOL--
--JUST IN TIME TO SAVE THE PLANET FROM A GIANT SPACE "BULLET." THAT'S WHERE I THOUGHT MY STORY WOULD END.
BEING AN X-MAN, I SHOULD HAVE KNOWN BETTER.
I'D STARTED AT THE XAVIER SCHOOL AS THE YOUNGEST STUDENT, THE X-MEN TEAM ROOKIE; NOW I WAS TAKING OVER AS HEAD OF BOTH THE SCHOOL AND THE TEAM.
NOT QUITE THE LIFE OR FATE I DREAMED OF.
24:00:00
BEEP-BEEP
WHO SAYS GOD DOESN'T HAVE A SENSE OF HUMOR?

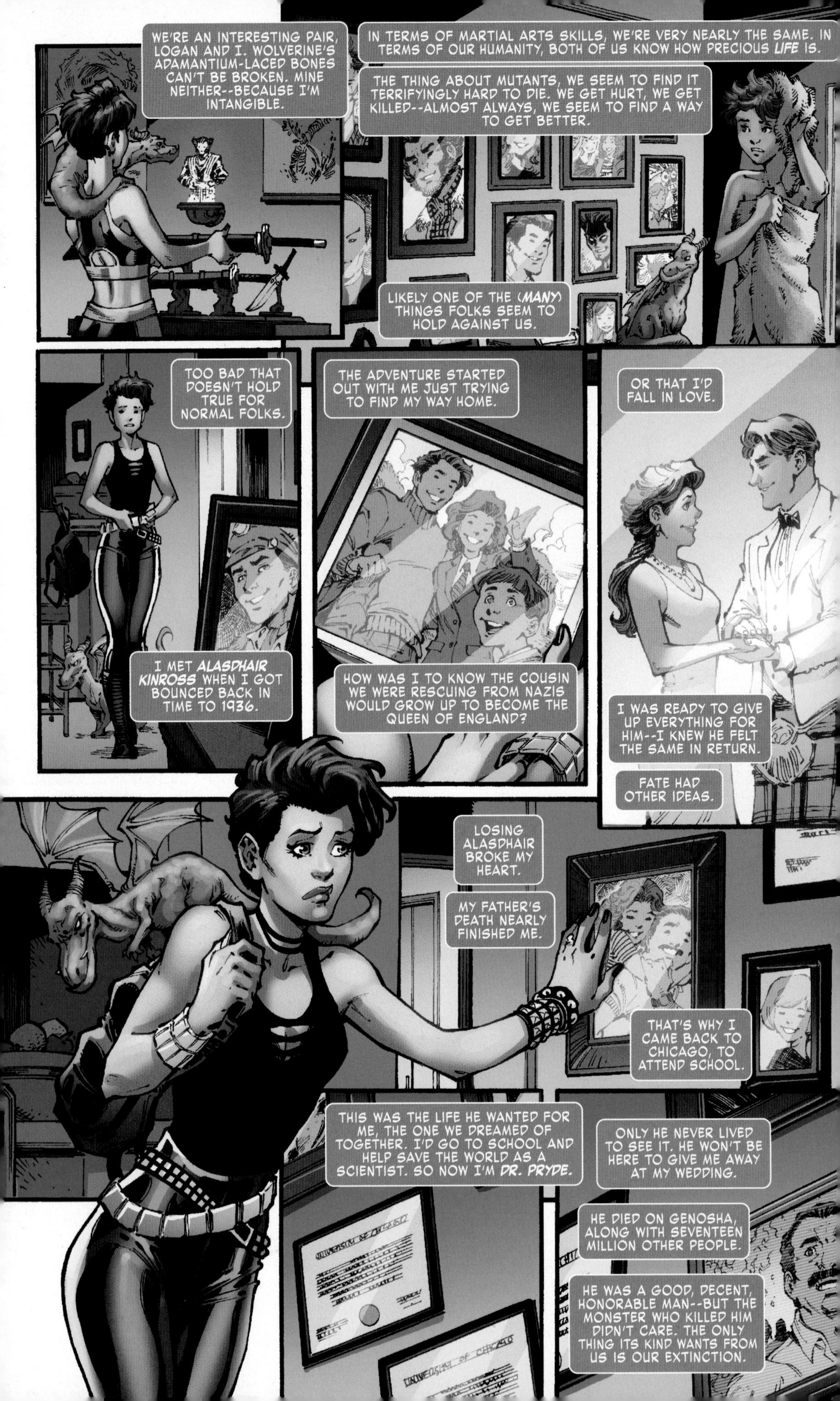
WE'RE AN INTERESTING PAIR, LOGAN AND I. WOLVERINE'S ADAMANTIUM-LACED BONES CAN'T BE BROKEN. MINE NEITHER--BECAUSE I'M INTANGIBLE.
IN TERMS OF MARTIAL ARTS SKILLS, WE'RE VERY NEARLY THE SAME. IN TERMS OF OUR HUMANITY, BOTH OF US KNOW HOW PRECIOUS *LIFE* IS.
THE THING ABOUT MUTANTS, WE SEEM TO FIND IT TERRIFYINGLY HARD TO DIE. WE GET HURT, WE GET KILLED--ALMOST ALWAYS, WE SEEM TO FIND A WAY TO GET BETTER.
LIKELY ONE OF THE (*MANY*) THINGS FOLKS SEEM TO HOLD AGAINST US.
TOO BAD THAT DOESN'T HOLD TRUE FOR NORMAL FOLKS.
I MET *ALASDHAIR KINROSS* WHEN I GOT BOUNCED BACK IN TIME TO 1936.
THE ADVENTURE STARTED OUT WITH ME JUST TRYING TO FIND MY WAY HOME.
HOW WAS I TO KNOW THE COUSIN WE WERE RESCUING FROM NAZIS WOULD GROW UP TO BECOME THE QUEEN OF ENGLAND?
OR THAT I'D FALL IN LOVE.
I WAS READY TO GIVE UP EVERYTHING FOR HIM--I KNEW HE FELT THE SAME IN RETURN.
FATE HAD OTHER IDEAS.
LOSING ALASDHAIR BROKE MY HEART.
MY FATHER'S DEATH NEARLY FINISHED ME.
THAT'S WHY I CAME BACK TO CHICAGO, TO ATTEND SCHOOL.
THIS WAS THE LIFE HE WANTED FOR ME, THE ONE WE DREAMED OF TOGETHER. I'D GO TO SCHOOL AND HELP SAVE THE WORLD AS A SCIENTIST. SO NOW I'M *DR. PRYDE*.
ONLY HE NEVER LIVED TO SEE IT. HE WON'T BE HERE TO GIVE ME AWAY AT MY WEDDING.
HE DIED ON GENOSHA, ALONG WITH SEVENTEEN MILLION OTHER PEOPLE.
HE WAS A GOOD, DECENT, HONORABLE MAN--BUT THE MONSTER WHO KILLED HIM DIDN'T CARE. THE ONLY THING ITS KIND WANTS FROM US IS OUR EXTINCTION.

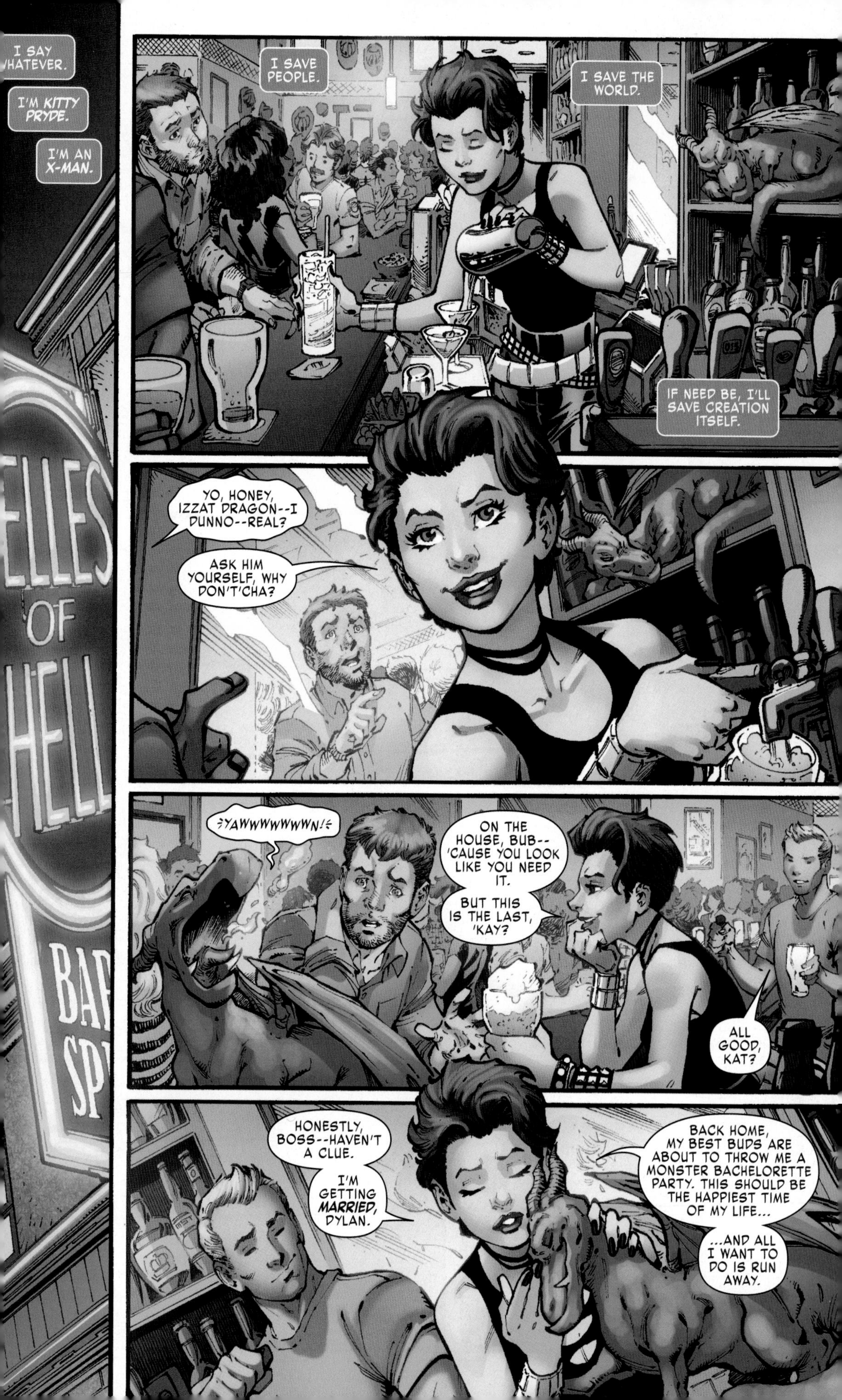
I SAY WHATEVER.
I'M KITTY PRYDE.
I'M AN X-MAN.
I SAVE PEOPLE.
I SAVE THE WORLD.
IF NEED BE, I'LL SAVE CREATION ITSELF.
YO, HONEY, IZZAT DRAGON--I DUNNO--REAL?
ASK HIM YOURSELF, WHY DON'T'CHA?
ELLES OF HELL
BAR
SP
YAWWWWWWWN!
ON THE HOUSE, BUB-- 'CAUSE YOU LOOK LIKE YOU NEED IT.
BUT THIS IS THE LAST, 'KAY?
ALL GOOD, KAT?
HONESTLY, BOSS--HAVEN'T A CLUE.
I'M GETTING MARRIED, DYLAN.
BACK HOME, MY BEST BUDS ARE ABOUT TO THROW ME A MONSTER BACHELORETTE PARTY. THIS SHOULD BE THE HAPPIEST TIME OF MY LIFE...
...AND ALL I WANT TO DO IS RUN AWAY.

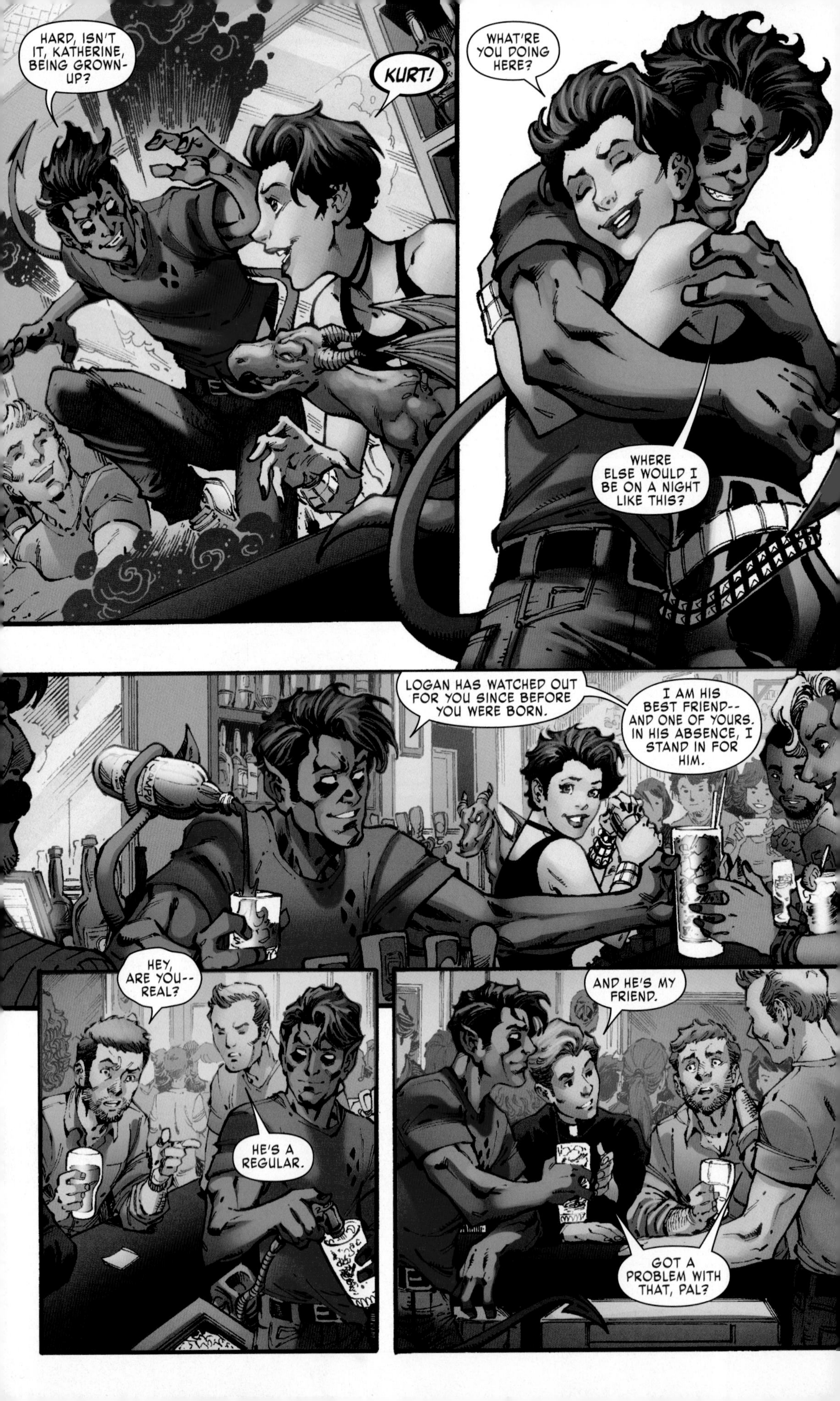
HARD, ISN'T IT, KATHERINE, BEING GROWN-UP?
KURT!
WHAT'RE YOU DOING HERE?
WHERE ELSE WOULD I BE ON A NIGHT LIKE THIS?
LOGAN HAS WATCHED OUT FOR YOU SINCE BEFORE YOU WERE BORN.
I AM HIS BEST FRIEND-- AND ONE OF YOURS. IN HIS ABSENCE, I STAND IN FOR HIM.
HEY, ARE YOU-- REAL?
HE'S A REGULAR.
AND HE'S MY FRIEND.
GOT A PROBLEM WITH THAT, PAL?

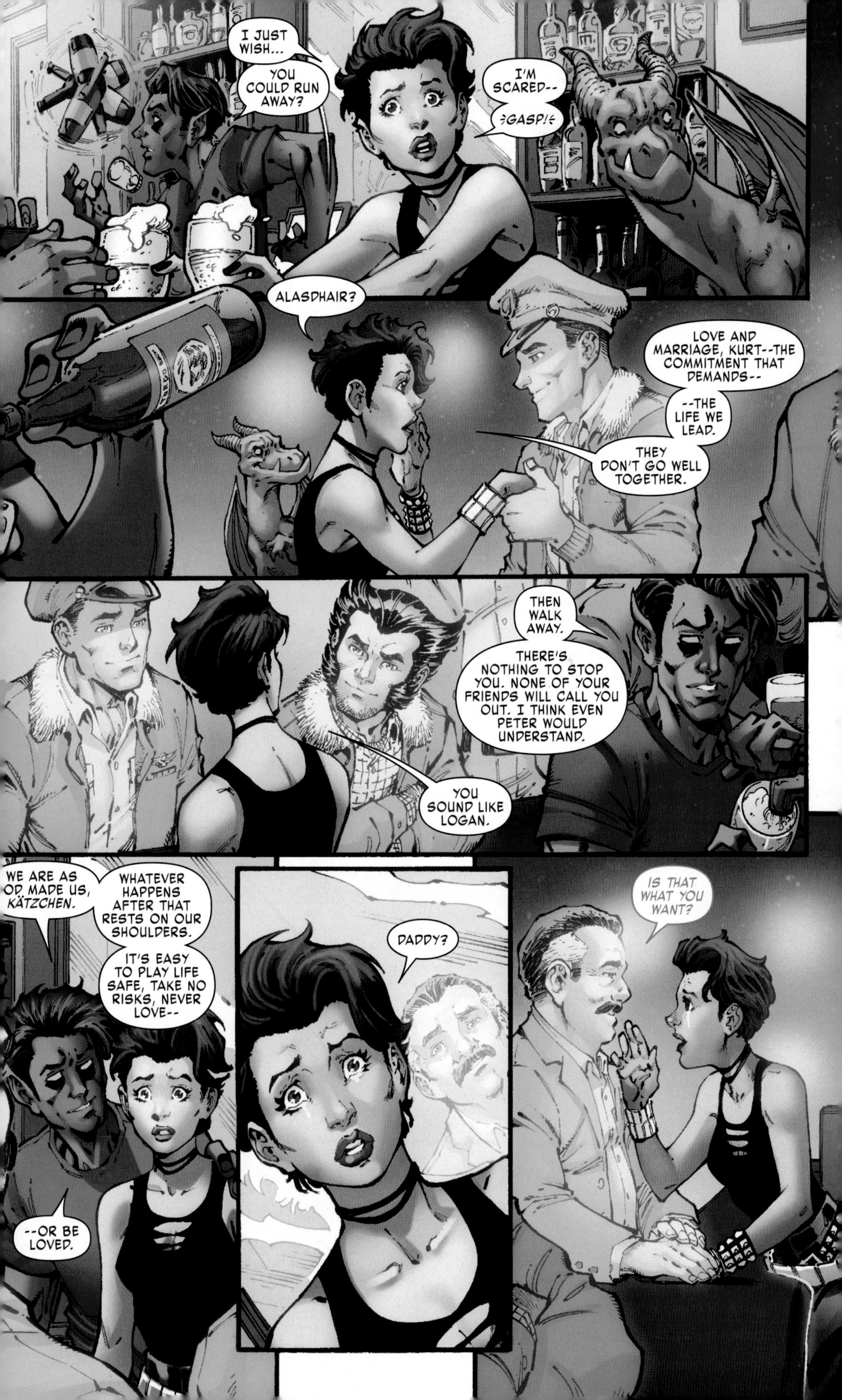
I JUST WISH...
YOU COULD RUN AWAY?
I'M SCARED--
GASP!
ALASDHAIR?
LOVE AND MARRIAGE, KURT--THE COMMITMENT THAT DEMANDS--
--THE LIFE WE LEAD.
THEY DON'T GO WELL TOGETHER.
THEN WALK AWAY.
THERE'S NOTHING TO STOP YOU. NONE OF YOUR FRIENDS WILL CALL YOU OUT. I THINK EVEN PETER WOULD UNDERSTAND.
YOU SOUND LIKE LOGAN.
WE ARE AS OD MADE US, KÄTZCHEN.
WHATEVER HAPPENS AFTER THAT RESTS ON OUR SHOULDERS.
IT'S EASY TO PLAY LIFE SAFE, TAKE NO RISKS, NEVER LOVE--
--OR BE LOVED.
DADDY?
IS THAT WHAT YOU WANT?

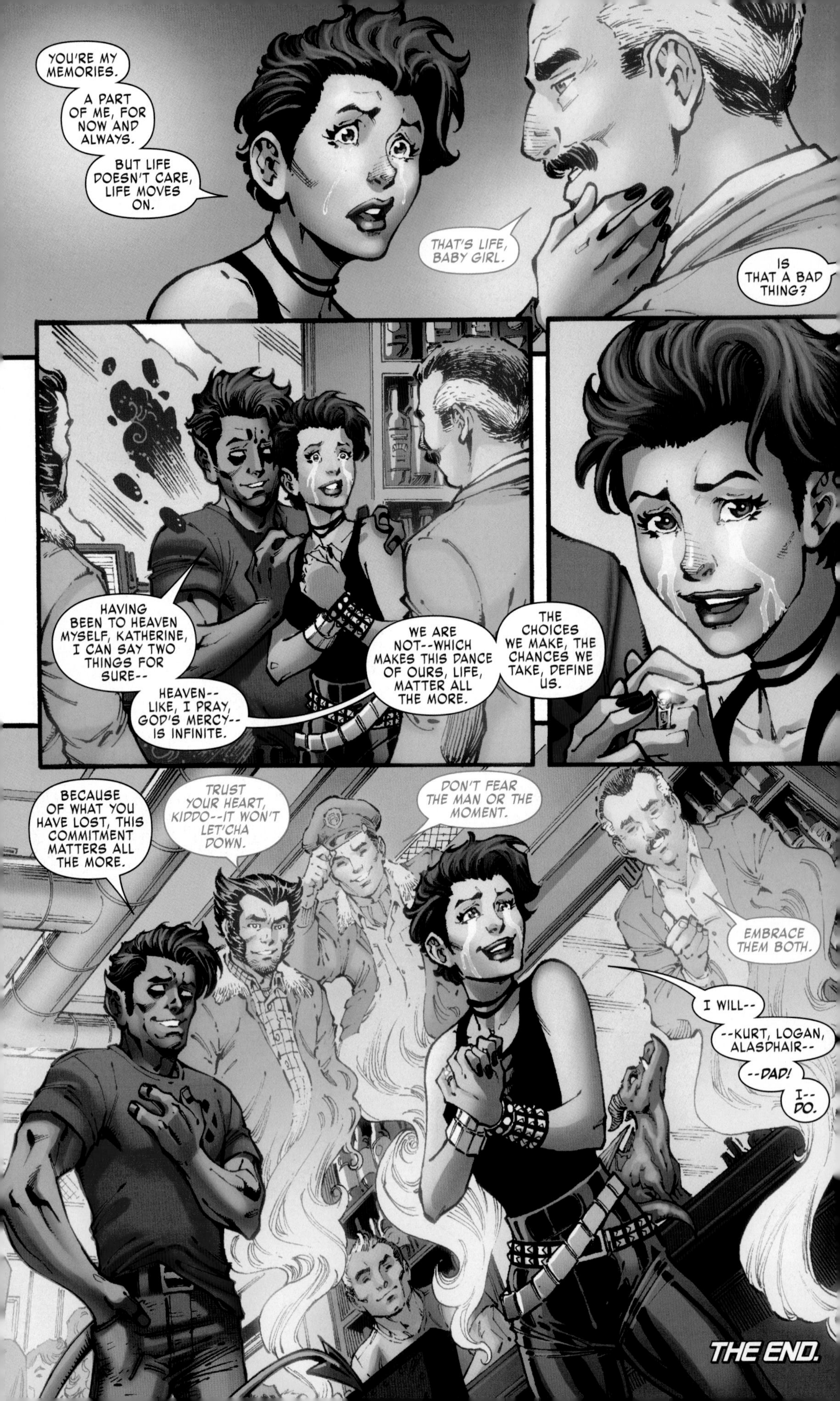
YOU'RE MY MEMORIES.
A PART OF ME, FOR NOW AND ALWAYS.
BUT LIFE DOESN'T CARE, LIFE MOVES ON.
THAT'S LIFE, BABY GIRL.
IS THAT A BAD THING?
HAVING BEEN TO HEAVEN MYSELF, KATHERINE, I CAN SAY TWO THINGS FOR SURE--
HEAVEN--LIKE, I PRAY, GOD'S MERCY--IS INFINITE.
WE ARE NOT--WHICH MAKES THIS DANCE OF OURS, LIFE, MATTER ALL THE MORE.
THE CHOICES WE MAKE, THE CHANCES WE TAKE, DEFINE US.
BECAUSE OF WHAT YOU HAVE LOST, THIS COMMITMENT MATTERS ALL THE MORE.
TRUST YOUR HEART, KIDDO--IT WON'T LET'CHA DOWN.
DON'T FEAR THE MAN OR THE MOMENT.
EMBRACE THEM BOTH.
I WILL--
--KURT, LOGAN, ALASDHAIR--
--DAD!
I--DO.
THE END.

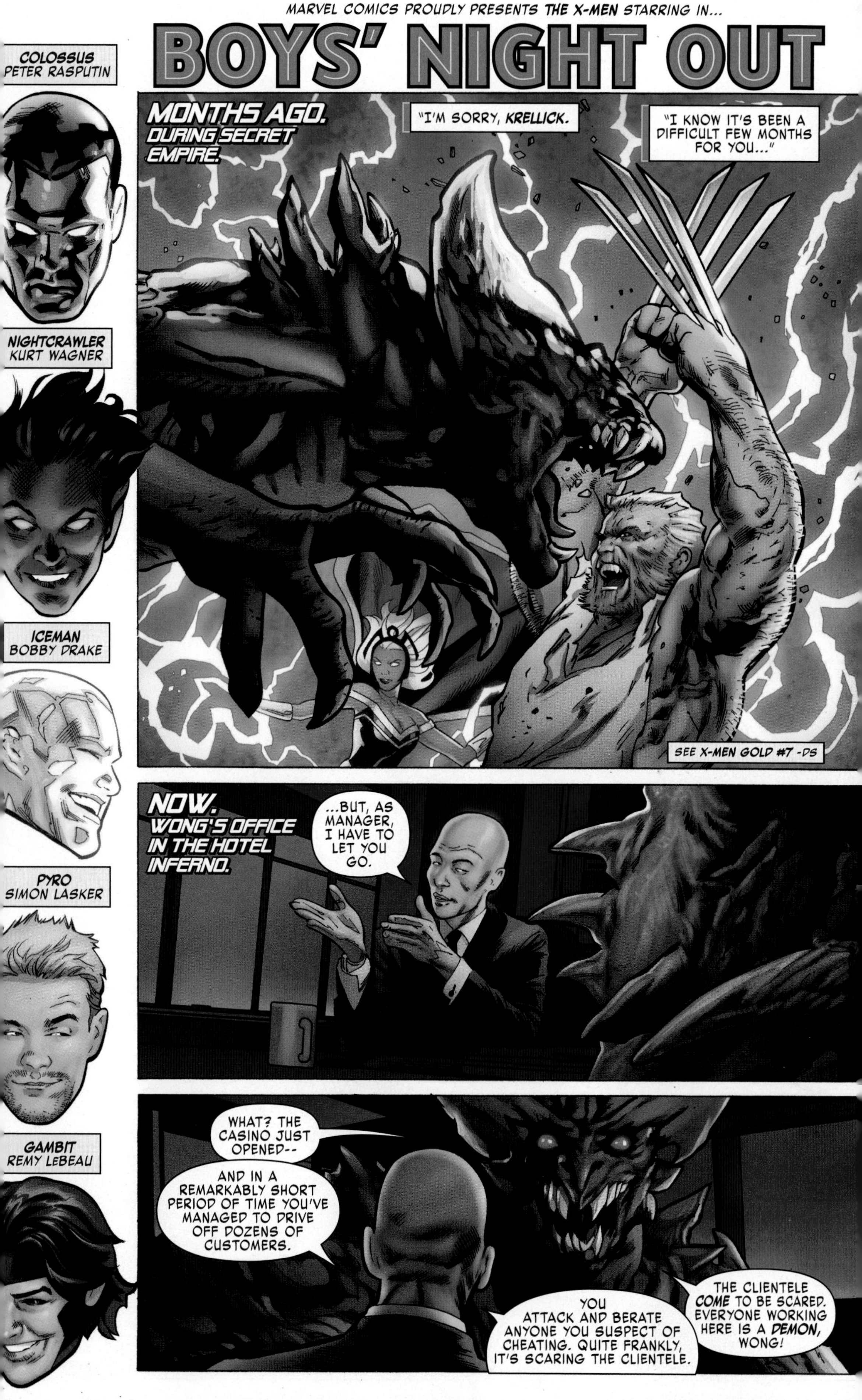

MARVEL COMICS PROUDLY PRESENTS THE X-MEN STARRING IN...
BOYS' NIGHT OUT
COLOSSUS PETER RASPUTIN
NIGHTCRAWLER KURT WAGNER
ICEMAN BOBBY DRAKE
PYRO SIMON LASKER
GAMBIT REMY LEBEAU
MONTHS AGO. DURING SECRET EMPIRE.
"I'M SORRY, KRELLICK.
"I KNOW IT'S BEEN A DIFFICULT FEW MONTHS FOR YOU..."
SEE X-MEN GOLD #7 -DS
NOW. WONG'S OFFICE IN THE HOTEL INFERNO.
...BUT, AS MANAGER, I HAVE TO LET YOU GO.
WHAT? THE CASINO JUST OPENED--
AND IN A REMARKABLY SHORT PERIOD OF TIME YOU'VE MANAGED TO DRIVE OFF DOZENS OF CUSTOMERS.
YOU ATTACK AND BERATE ANYONE YOU SUSPECT OF CHEATING. QUITE FRANKLY, IT'S SCARING THE CLIENTELE.
THE CLIENTELE COME TO BE SCARED. EVERYONE WORKING HERE IS A DEMON, WONG!

AND YET YOU SEEM TO BE THE ONLY ONE *BROADCASTING* YOUR HATRED OF HUMANS.

THEY ARE RUDE AND ENTITLED. NOT TO MENTION *WEAK.*

SEE WHAT I MEAN?

I CAN GIVE YOU ONE MONTH'S SEVERANCE.

AGAIN...

"...I'M VERY SORRY."

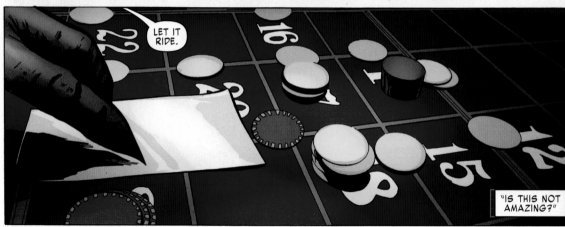

LET IT RIDE.

"IS THIS NOT AMAZING?"

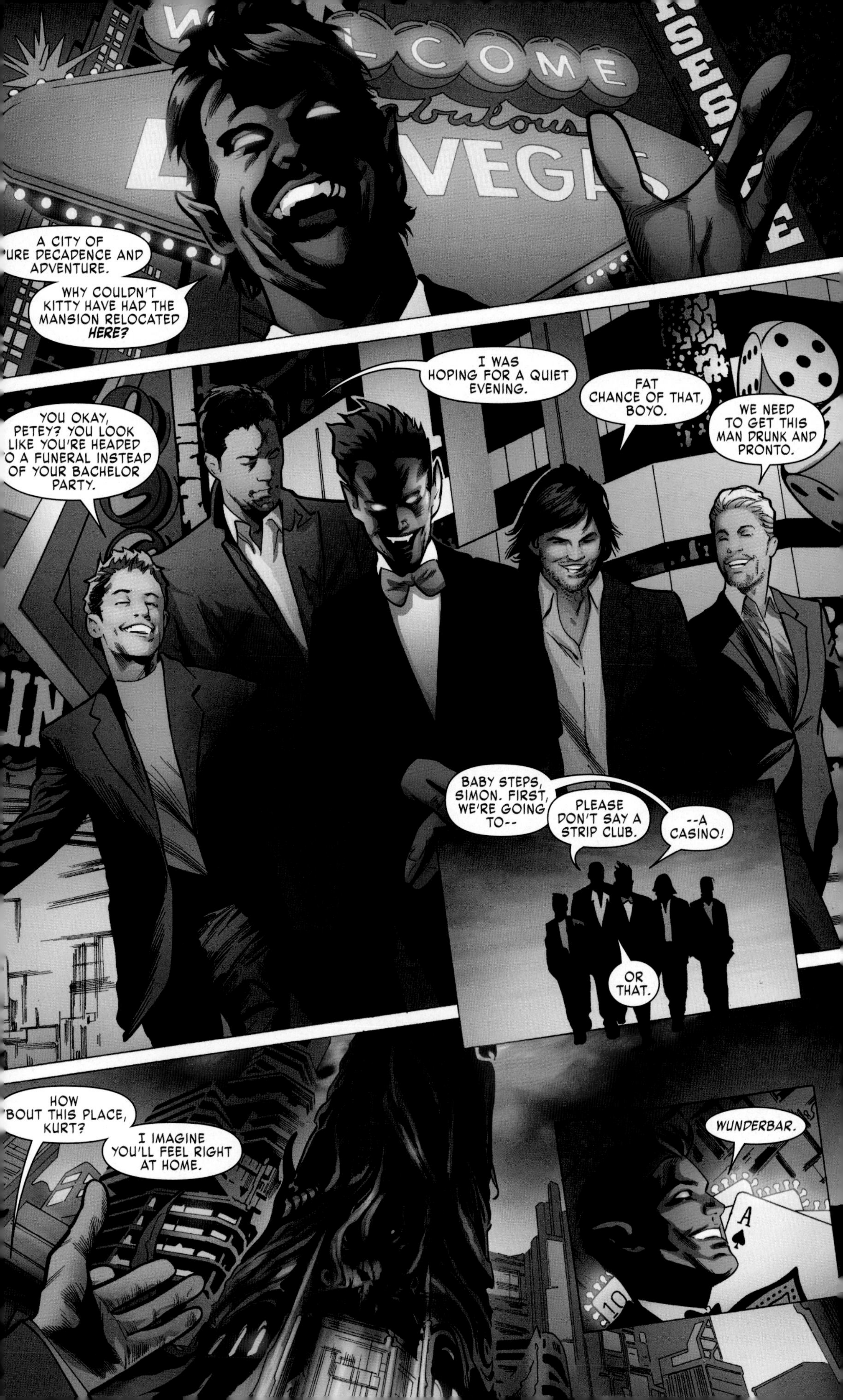

WELCOME
Fabulous
LAS VEGAS
A CITY OF PURE DECADENCE AND ADVENTURE.
WHY COULDN'T KITTY HAVE HAD THE MANSION RELOCATED *HERE?*
YOU OKAY, PETEY? YOU LOOK LIKE YOU'RE HEADED TO A FUNERAL INSTEAD OF YOUR BACHELOR PARTY.
I WAS HOPING FOR A QUIET EVENING.
FAT CHANCE OF THAT, BOYO.
WE NEED TO GET THIS MAN DRUNK AND PRONTO.
BABY STEPS, SIMON. FIRST, WE'RE GOING TO--
PLEASE DON'T SAY A STRIP CLUB.
--A CASINO!
OR THAT.
HOW 'BOUT THIS PLACE, KURT?
I IMAGINE YOU'LL FEEL RIGHT AT HOME.
WUNDERBAR.

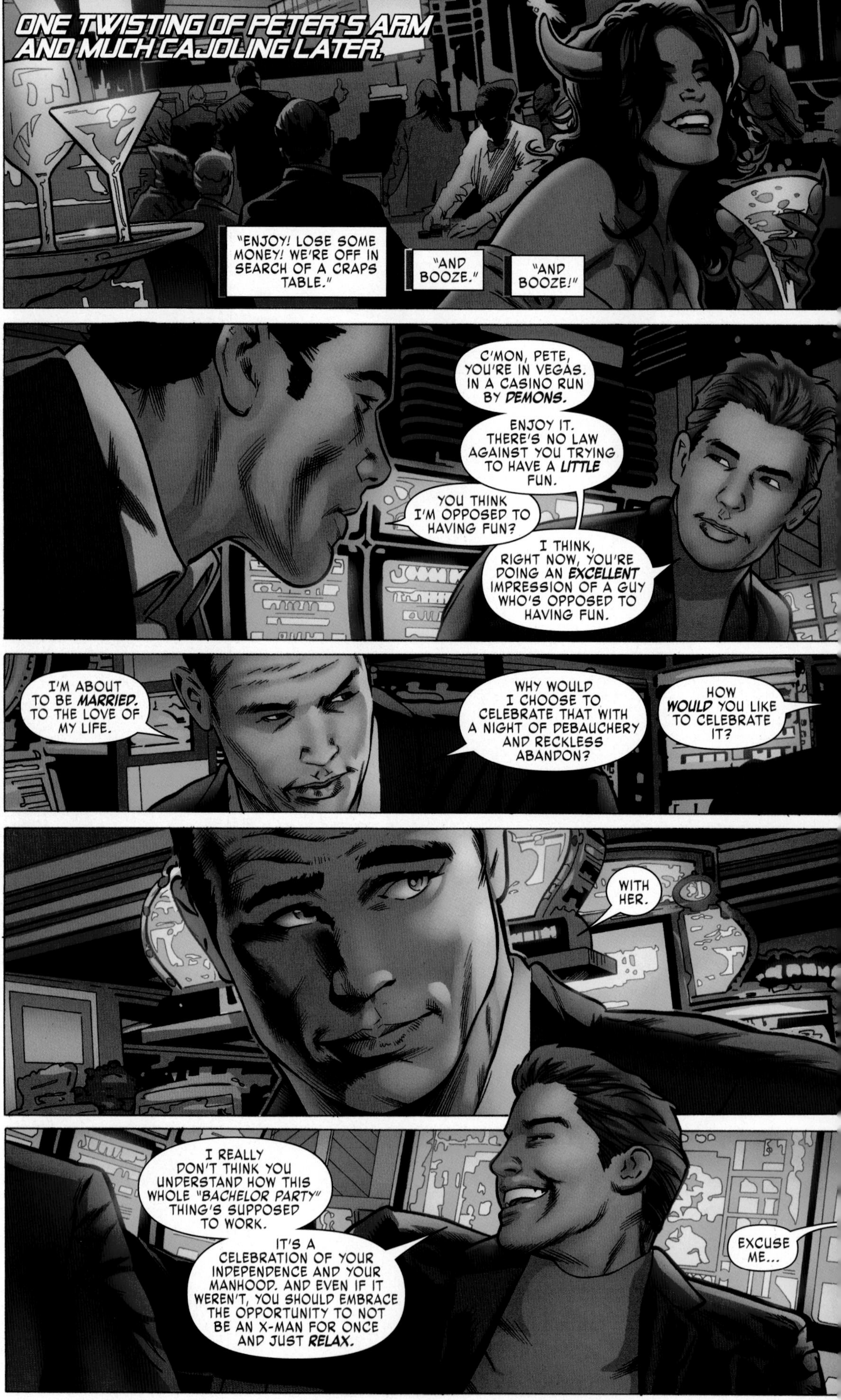

ONE TWISTING OF PETER'S ARM AND MUCH CAJOLING LATER.
"ENJOY! LOSE SOME MONEY! WE'RE OFF IN SEARCH OF A CRAPS TABLE."
"AND BOOZE."
"AND BOOZE!"
C'MON, PETE, YOU'RE IN VEGAS. IN A CASINO RUN BY DEMONS.
ENJOY IT. THERE'S NO LAW AGAINST YOU TRYING TO HAVE A LITTLE FUN.
YOU THINK I'M OPPOSED TO HAVING FUN?
I THINK, RIGHT NOW, YOU'RE DOING AN EXCELLENT IMPRESSION OF A GUY WHO'S OPPOSED TO HAVING FUN.
I'M ABOUT TO BE MARRIED. TO THE LOVE OF MY LIFE.
WHY WOULD I CHOOSE TO CELEBRATE THAT WITH A NIGHT OF DEBAUCHERY AND RECKLESS ABANDON?
HOW WOULD YOU LIKE TO CELEBRATE IT?
WITH HER.
I REALLY DON'T THINK YOU UNDERSTAND HOW THIS WHOLE "BACHELOR PARTY" THING'S SUPPOSED TO WORK.
IT'S A CELEBRATION OF YOUR INDEPENDENCE AND YOUR MANHOOD. AND EVEN IF IT WEREN'T, YOU SHOULD EMBRACE THE OPPORTUNITY TO NOT BE AN X-MAN FOR ONCE AND JUST RELAX.
EXCUSE ME...

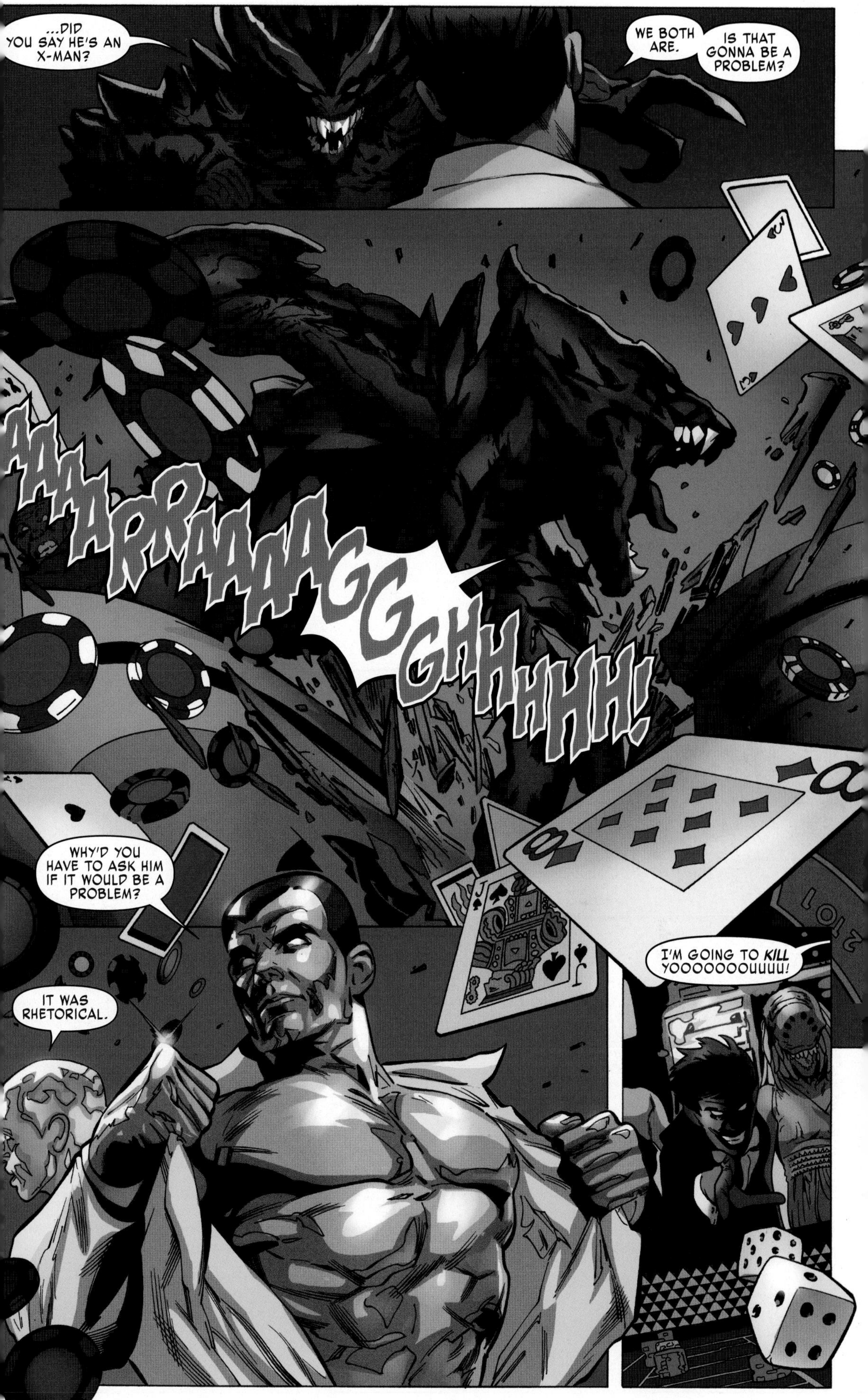
...DID YOU SAY HE'S AN X-MAN?
WE BOTH ARE.
IS THAT GONNA BE A PROBLEM?
AAAARRAAAAGGGHHHHH!
WHY'D YOU HAVE TO ASK HIM IF IT WOULD BE A PROBLEM?
IT WAS RHETORICAL.
I'M GOING TO KILL YOOOOOOOUUUU!

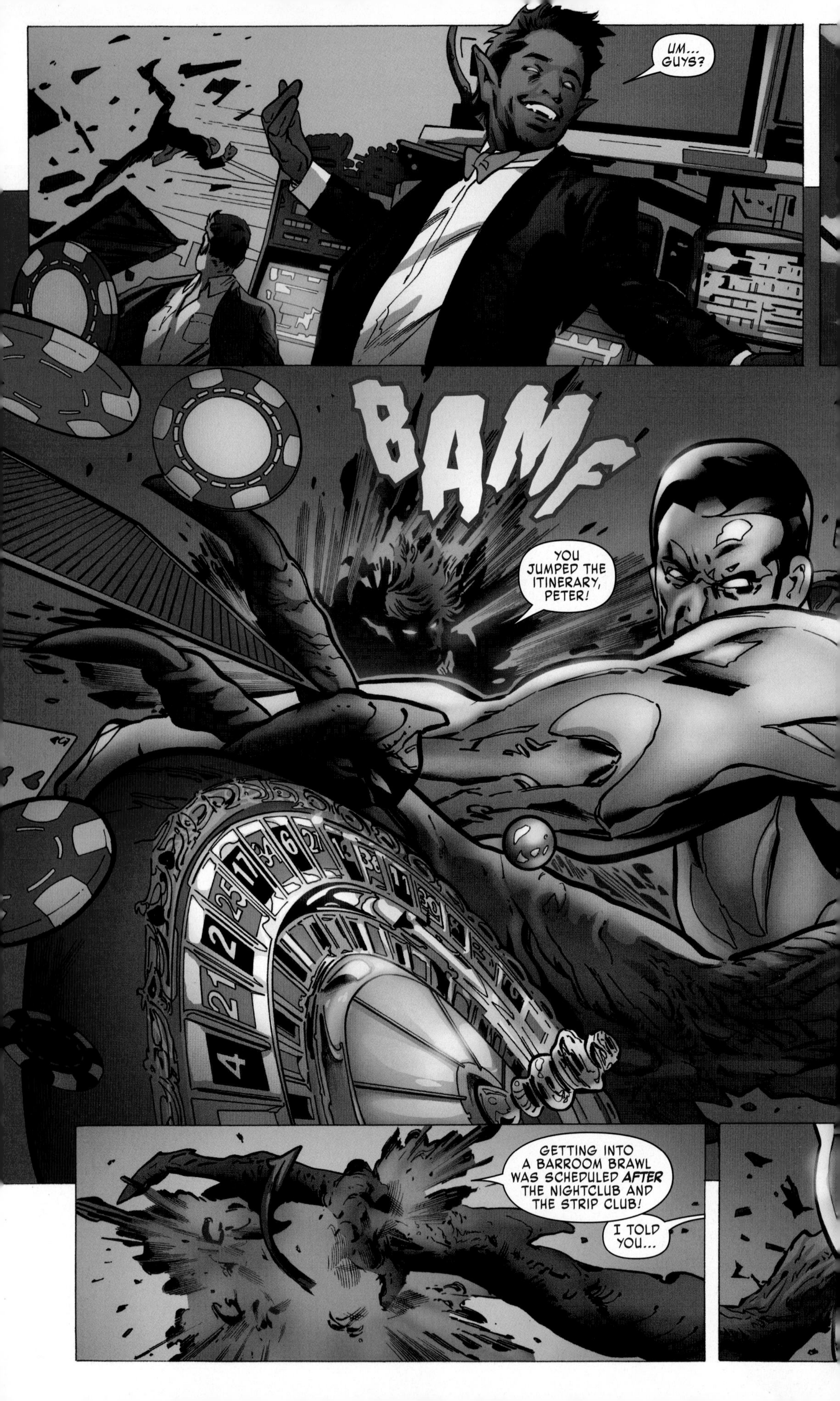
UM... GUYS?
BAMF
YOU JUMPED THE ITINERARY, PETER!
GETTING INTO A BARROOM BRAWL WAS SCHEDULED *AFTER* THE NIGHTCLUB AND THE STRIP CLUB!
I TOLD YOU...

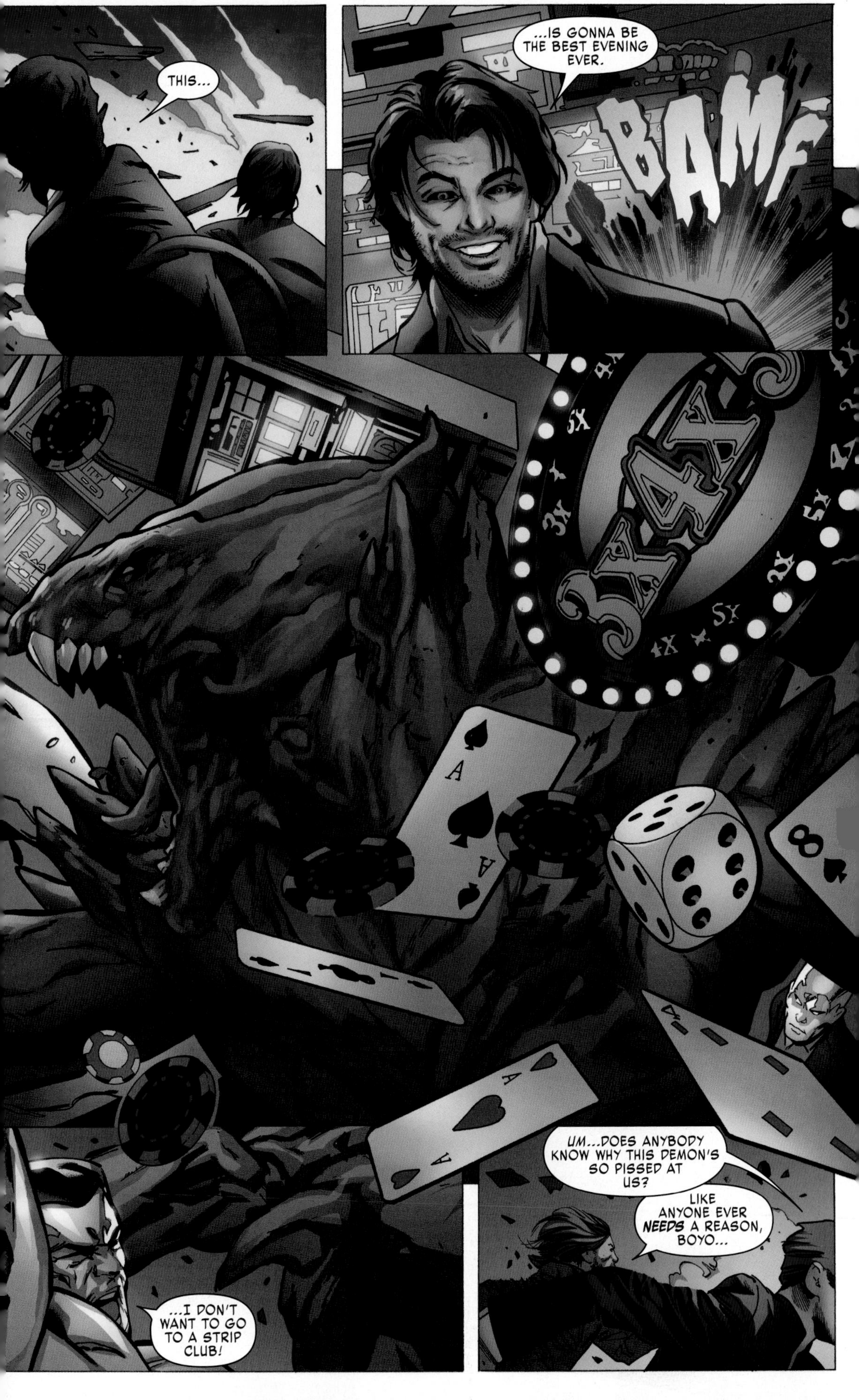
THIS...
...IS GONNA BE THE BEST EVENING EVER.
BAMF
UM...DOES ANYBODY KNOW WHY THIS DEMON'S SO PISSED AT US?
LIKE ANYONE EVER NEEDS A REASON, BOYO...
...I DON'T WANT TO GO TO A STRIP CLUB!

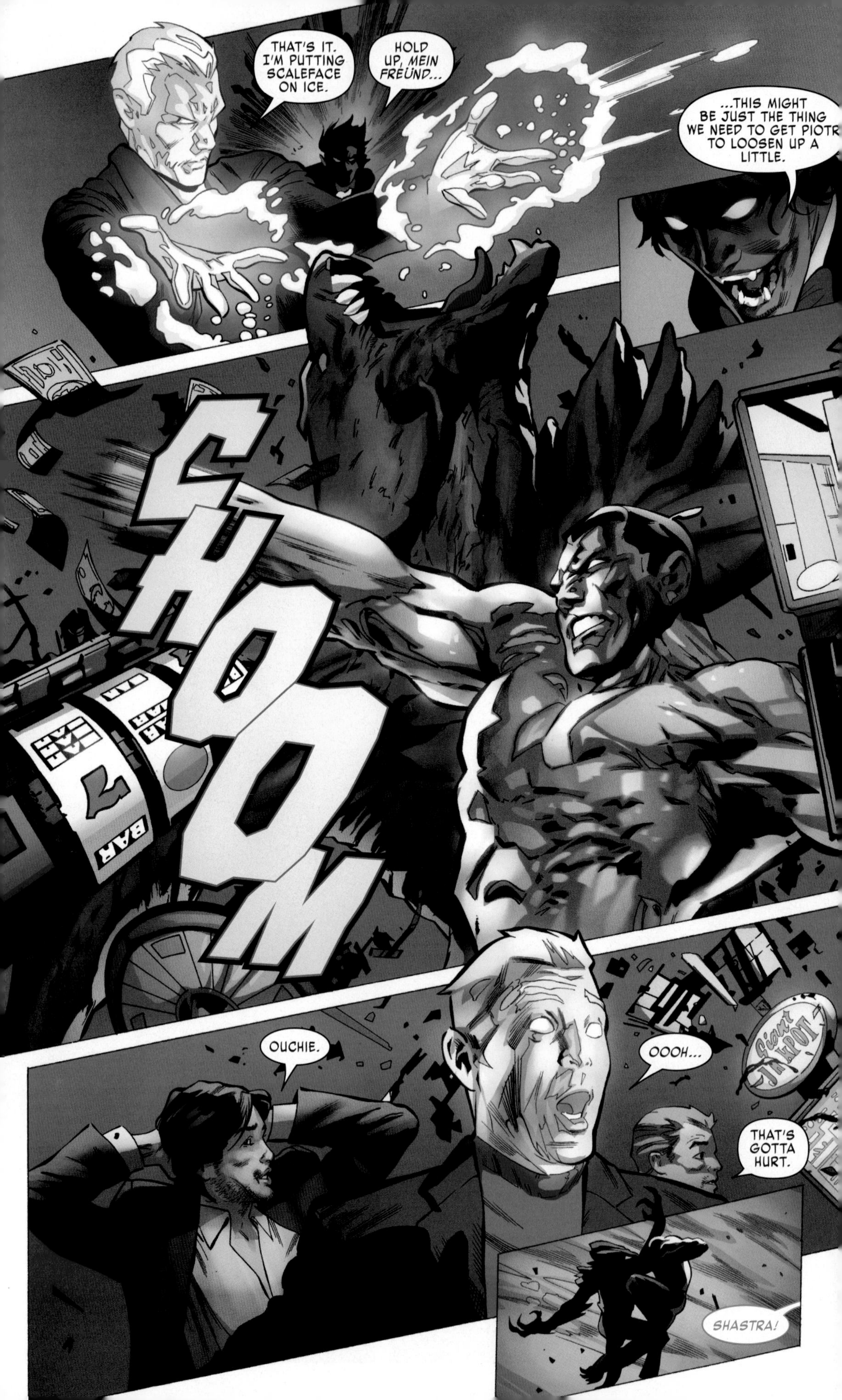
THAT'S IT. I'M PUTTING SCALEFACE ON ICE.
HOLD UP, MEIN FREÜND...
...THIS MIGHT BE JUST THE THING WE NEED TO GET PIOTR TO LOOSEN UP A LITTLE.
CHOOM
BAR
BAR
7
BAR
OUCHIE.
OOOH...
Giant JACKPOT
THAT'S GOTTA HURT.
SHASTRA!

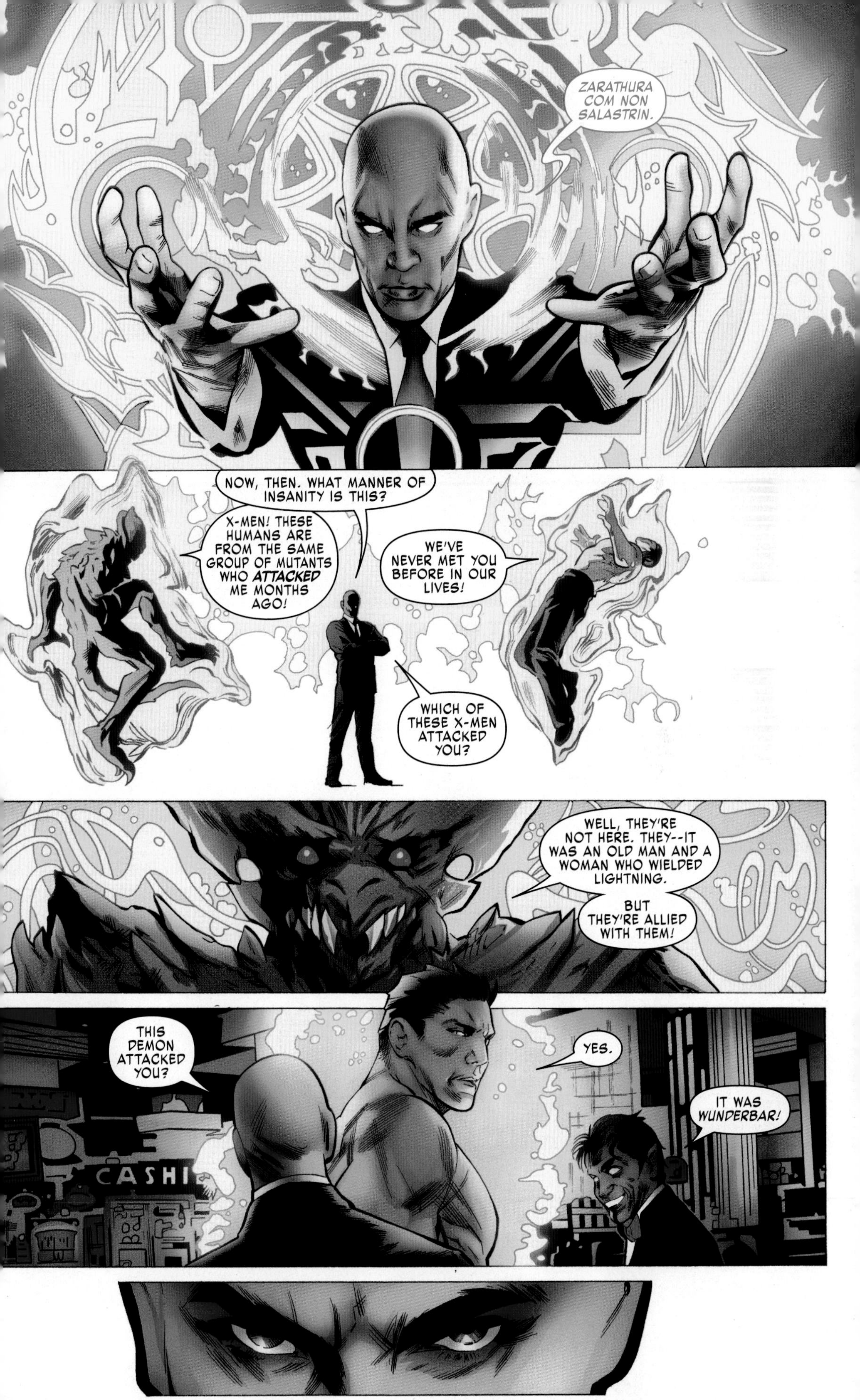
ZARATHURA COM NON SALASTRIN.
NOW, THEN. WHAT MANNER OF INSANITY IS THIS?
X-MEN! THESE HUMANS ARE FROM THE SAME GROUP OF MUTANTS WHO *ATTACKED* ME MONTHS AGO!
WE'VE NEVER MET YOU BEFORE IN OUR LIVES!
WHICH OF THESE X-MEN ATTACKED YOU?
WELL, THEY'RE NOT HERE. THEY--IT WAS AN OLD MAN AND A WOMAN WHO WIELDED LIGHTNING.
BUT THEY'RE ALLIED WITH THEM!
THIS DEMON ATTACKED YOU?
YES.
IT WAS *WUNDERBAR!*
CASHI

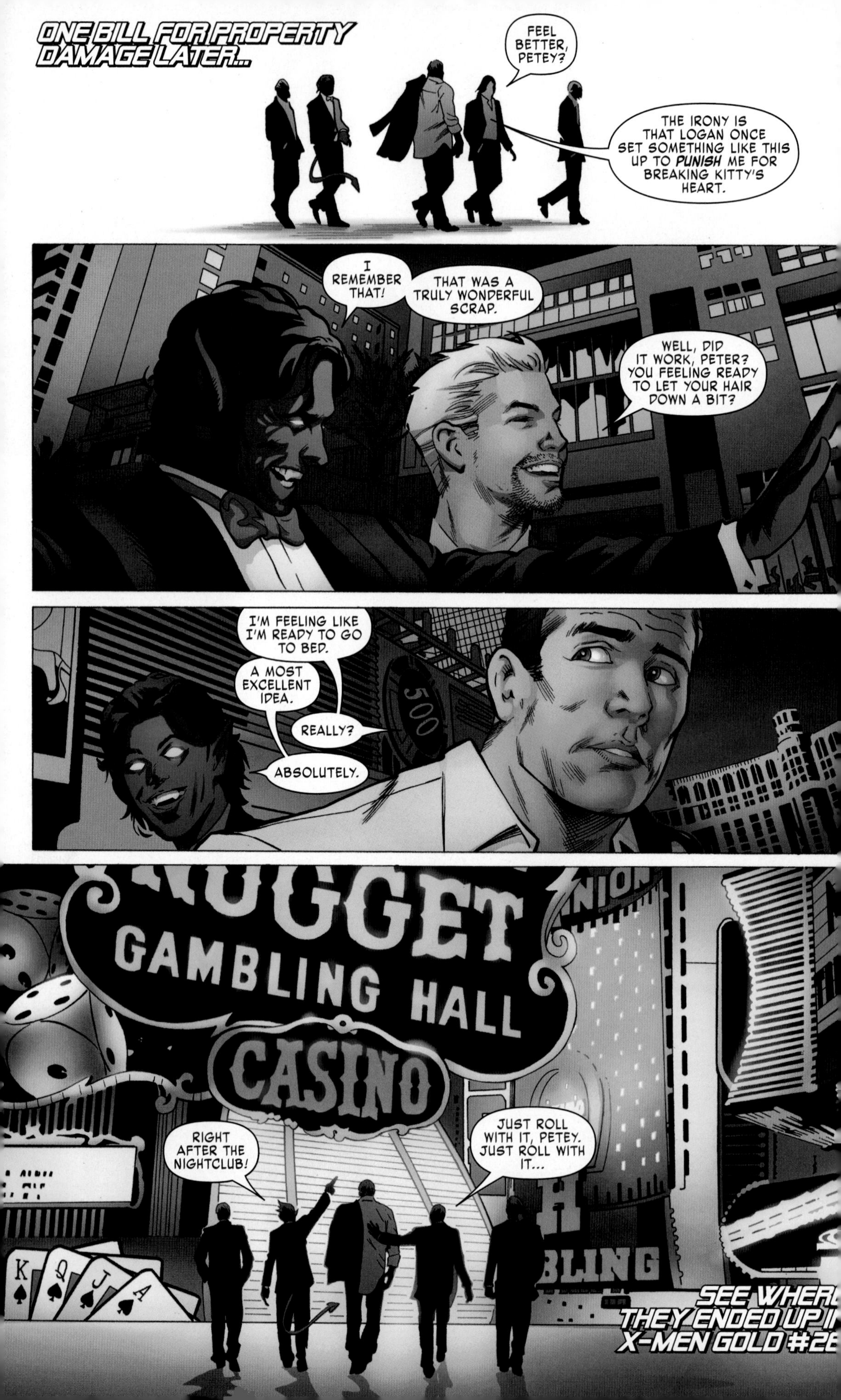
ONE BILL FOR PROPERTY DAMAGE LATER...
FEEL BETTER, PETEY?
THE IRONY IS THAT LOGAN ONCE SET SOMETHING LIKE THIS UP TO PUNISH ME FOR BREAKING KITTY'S HEART.
I REMEMBER THAT!
THAT WAS A TRULY WONDERFUL SCRAP.
WELL, DID IT WORK, PETER? YOU FEELING READY TO LET YOUR HAIR DOWN A BIT?
I'M FEELING LIKE I'M READY TO GO TO BED.
A MOST EXCELLENT IDEA.
REALLY?
ABSOLUTELY.
500
GAMBLING HALL
CASINO
RIGHT AFTER THE NIGHTCLUB!
JUST ROLL WITH IT, PETEY. JUST ROLL WITH IT...
SEE WHER
THEY ENDED UP I
X-MEN GOLD #2

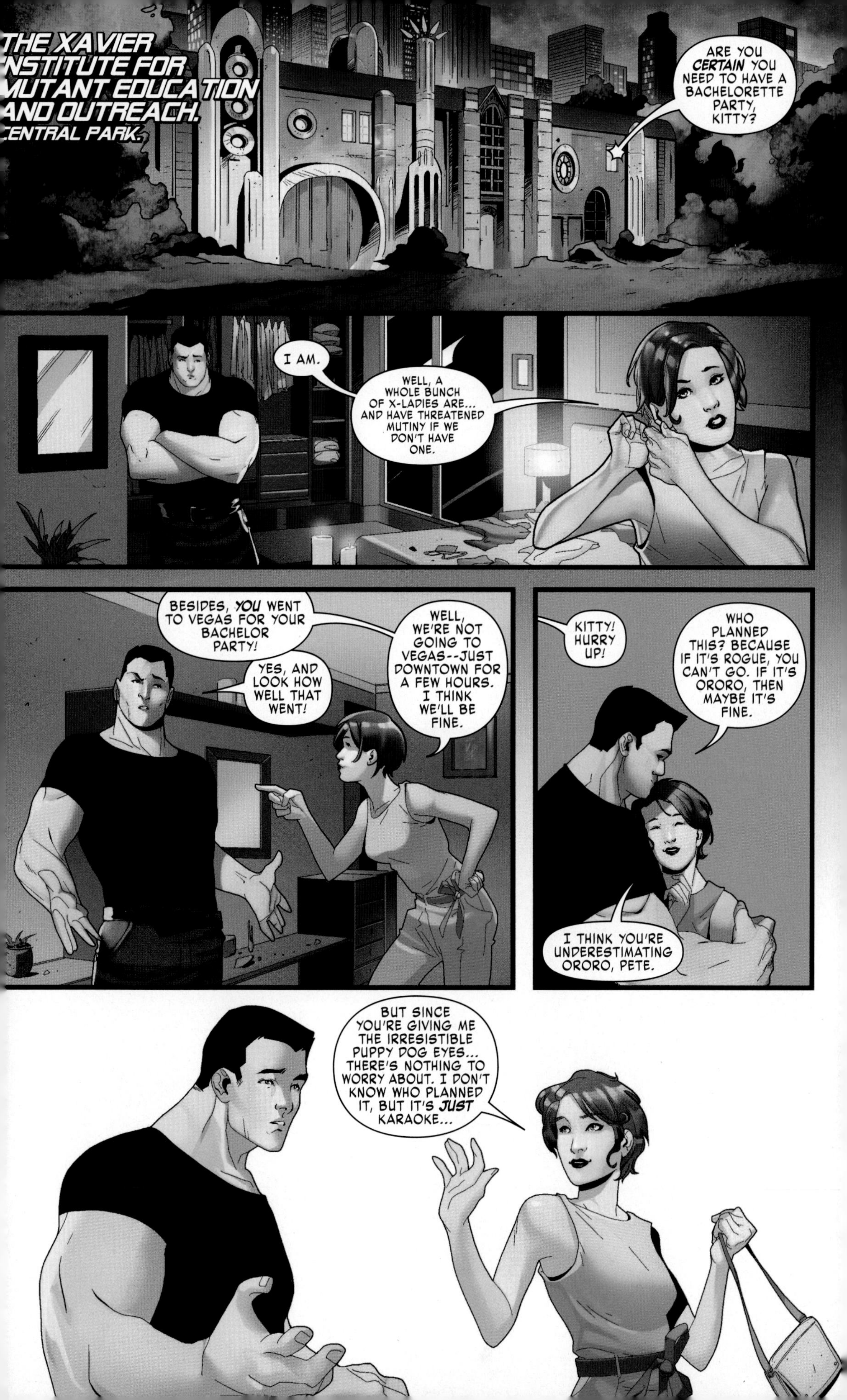
THE XAVIER INSTITUTE FOR MUTANT EDUCATION AND OUTREACH. CENTRAL PARK.
ARE YOU CERTAIN YOU NEED TO HAVE A BACHELORETTE PARTY, KITTY?
I AM.
WELL, A WHOLE BUNCH OF X-LADIES ARE... AND HAVE THREATENED MUTINY IF WE DON'T HAVE ONE.
BESIDES, YOU WENT TO VEGAS FOR YOUR BACHELOR PARTY!
YES, AND LOOK HOW WELL THAT WENT!
WELL, WE'RE NOT GOING TO VEGAS--JUST DOWNTOWN FOR A FEW HOURS. I THINK WE'LL BE FINE.
KITTY! HURRY UP!
WHO PLANNED THIS? BECAUSE IF IT'S ROGUE, YOU CAN'T GO. IF IT'S ORORO, THEN MAYBE IT'S FINE.
I THINK YOU'RE UNDERESTIMATING ORORO, PETE.
BUT SINCE YOU'RE GIVING ME THE IRRESISTIBLE PUPPY DOG EYES... THERE'S NOTHING TO WORRY ABOUT. I DON'T KNOW WHO PLANNED IT, BUT IT'S JUST KARAOKE...

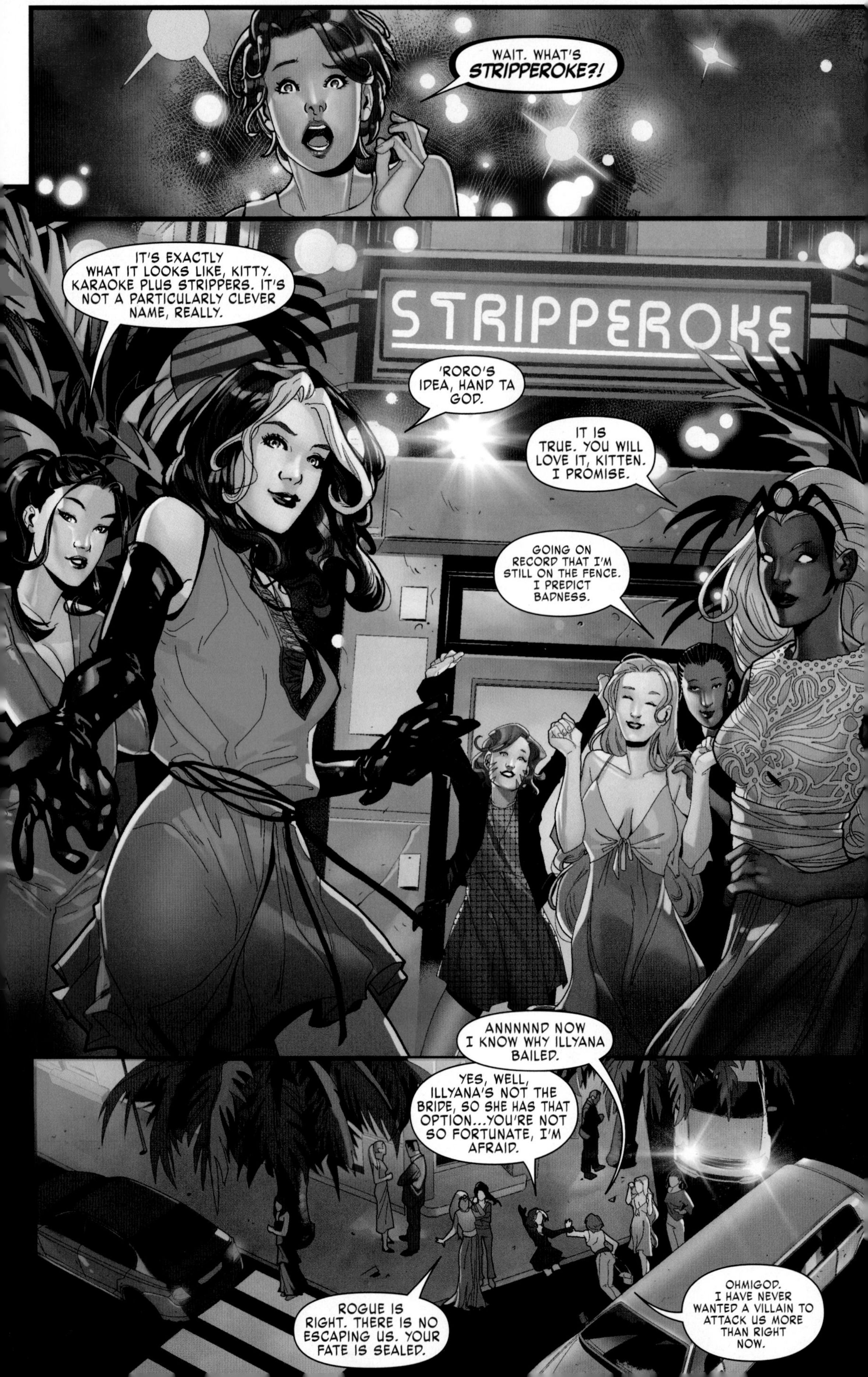
WAIT. WHAT'S STRIPPEROKE?!
IT'S EXACTLY WHAT IT LOOKS LIKE, KITTY. KARAOKE PLUS STRIPPERS. IT'S NOT A PARTICULARLY CLEVER NAME, REALLY.
STRIPPEROKE
'RORO'S IDEA, HAND TA GOD.
IT IS TRUE. YOU WILL LOVE IT, KITTEN. I PROMISE.
GOING ON RECORD THAT I'M STILL ON THE FENCE. I PREDICT BADNESS.
ANNNNND NOW I KNOW WHY ILLYANA BAILED.
YES, WELL, ILLYANA'S NOT THE BRIDE, SO SHE HAS THAT OPTION...YOU'RE NOT SO FORTUNATE, I'M AFRAID.
ROGUE IS RIGHT. THERE IS NO ESCAPING US. YOUR FATE IS SEALED.
OHMIGOD. I HAVE NEVER WANTED A VILLAIN TO ATTACK US MORE THAN RIGHT NOW.

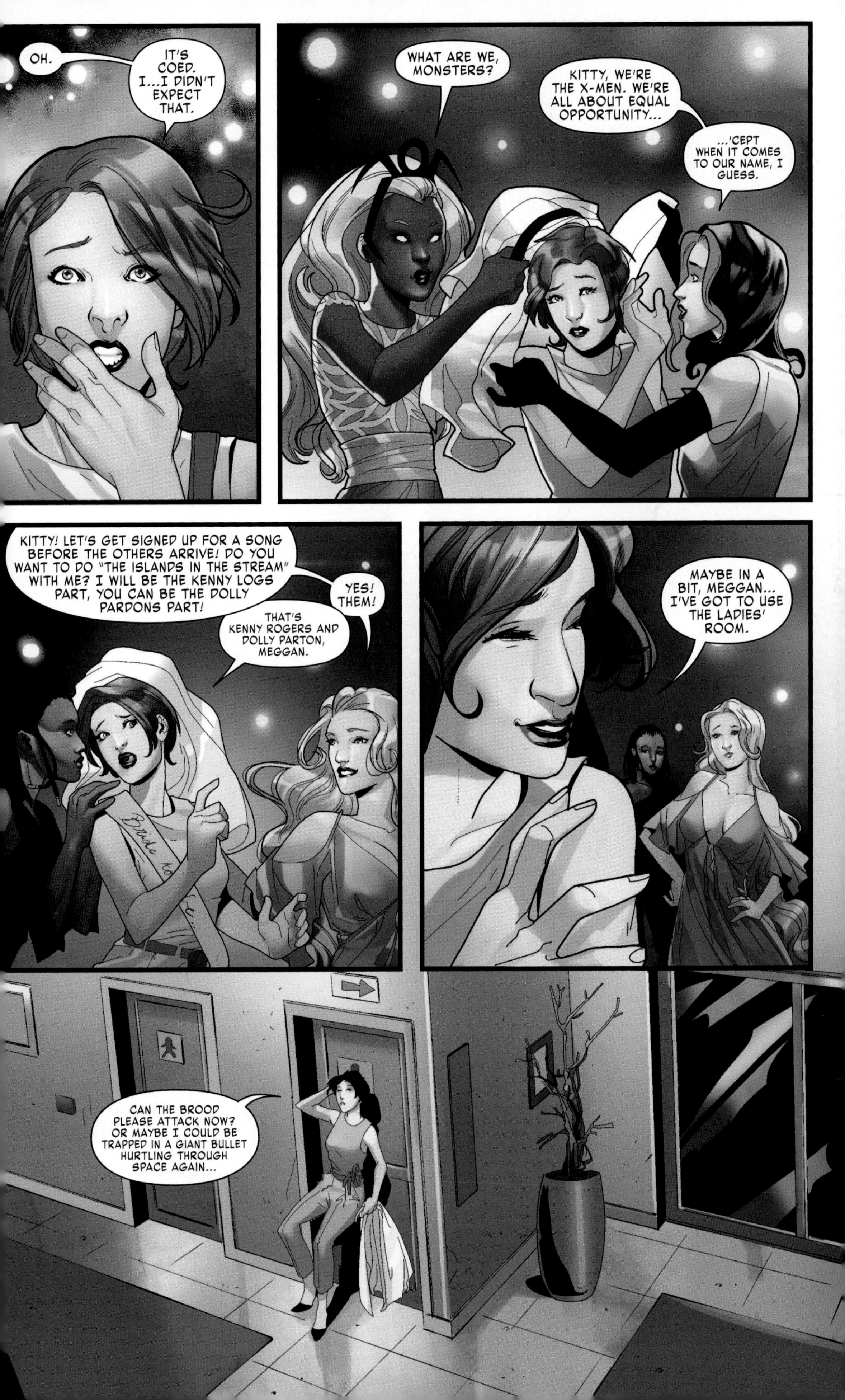
OH.
IT'S COED. I...I DIDN'T EXPECT THAT.
WHAT ARE WE, MONSTERS?
KITTY, WE'RE THE X-MEN. WE'RE ALL ABOUT EQUAL OPPORTUNITY...
...'CEPT WHEN IT COMES TO OUR NAME, I GUESS.
KITTY! LET'S GET SIGNED UP FOR A SONG BEFORE THE OTHERS ARRIVE! DO YOU WANT TO DO "THE ISLANDS IN THE STREAM" WITH ME? I WILL BE THE KENNY LOGS PART, YOU CAN BE THE DOLLY PARDONS PART!
THAT'S KENNY ROGERS AND DOLLY PARTON, MEGGAN.
YES! THEM!
MAYBE IN A BIT, MEGGAN... I'VE GOT TO USE THE LADIES' ROOM.
CAN THE BROOD PLEASE ATTACK NOW? OR MAYBE I COULD BE TRAPPED IN A GIANT BULLET HURTLING THROUGH SPACE AGAIN...

...I'M NOT ASKING FOR MUCH HERE.

WHAT'S THAT, KITTY?

YOU SAY SOMETHING?

JUST... FEELING A LITTLE WARM, THAT'S ALL. EVERYTHING IS KIND OF A LOT RIGHT NOW? NERVES, I GUESS.

I KNOW YOU ALREADY TRIED TO TALK SOME SENSE INTO ME ONCE...BUT A CASE OF COLD FEET IS NORMAL, RIGHT?

ABSOLUTELY, GIRL. THE BIG DAY IS IMMINENT, I'D BE WORRIED ABOUT YA IF YA WEREN'T NERVOUS. IT'S ONLY NATURAL.

TRUE. GOOD POINT. WHAT ABOUT YOU, ROGUE?

YOU LOOK...

...HONESTLY? YOU LOOK INSANELY HAPPY. YOU'RE RADIANT.

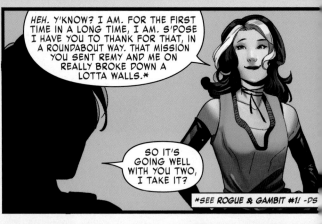

HEH. Y'KNOW? I AM. FOR THE FIRST TIME IN A LONG TIME, I AM. S'POSE I HAVE YOU TO THANK FOR THAT, IN A ROUNDABOUT WAY. THAT MISSION YOU SENT REMY AND ME ON REALLY BROKE DOWN A LOTTA WALLS.*

SO IT'S GOING WELL WITH YOU TWO, I TAKE IT?

*SEE ROGUE & GAMBIT #1! –DS

IT IS. I MEAN, MY POWERS NOT BEING UNDER MY CONTROL IS STILL...A CHALLENGE. BUT WE'RE GOOD. WE'RE MAYBE THE BEST WE'VE EVER BEEN.

IF YOU DON'T MIND MY ASKING...WHAT CHANGED?

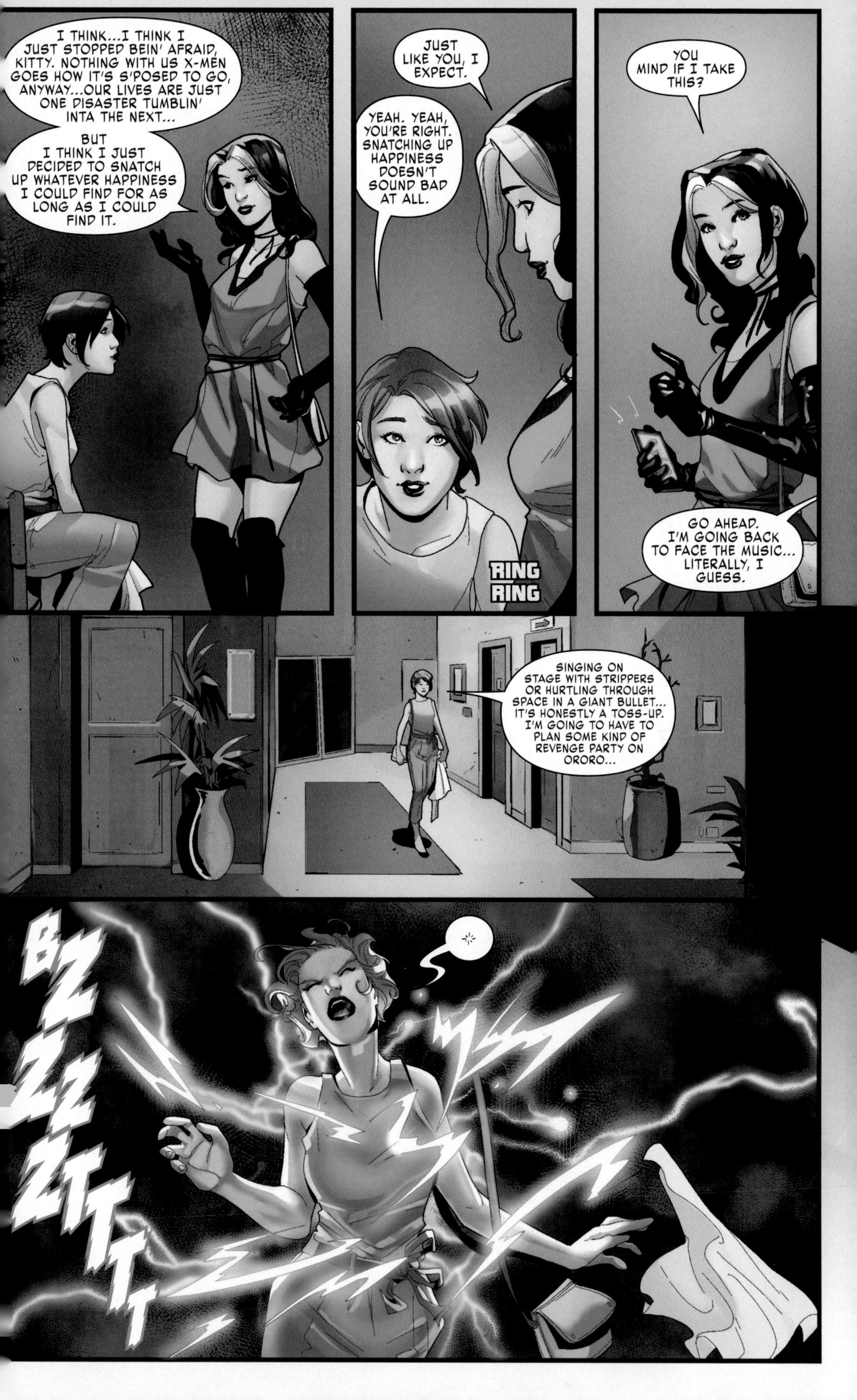
I THINK...I THINK I JUST STOPPED BEIN' AFRAID, KITTY. NOTHING WITH US X-MEN GOES HOW IT'S S'POSED TO GO, ANYWAY...OUR LIVES ARE JUST ONE DISASTER TUMBLIN' INTA THE NEXT...
BUT I THINK I JUST DECIDED TO SNATCH UP WHATEVER HAPPINESS I COULD FIND FOR AS LONG AS I COULD FIND IT.
JUST LIKE YOU, I EXPECT.
YEAH. YEAH, YOU'RE RIGHT. SNATCHING UP HAPPINESS DOESN'T SOUND BAD AT ALL.
RING RING
YOU MIND IF I TAKE THIS?
GO AHEAD. I'M GOING BACK TO FACE THE MUSIC... LITERALLY, I GUESS.
SINGING ON STAGE WITH STRIPPERS OR HURTLING THROUGH SPACE IN A GIANT BULLET... IT'S HONESTLY A TOSS-UP. I'M GOING TO HAVE TO PLAN SOME KIND OF REVENGE PARTY ON ORORO...
BZZZZTTTTT

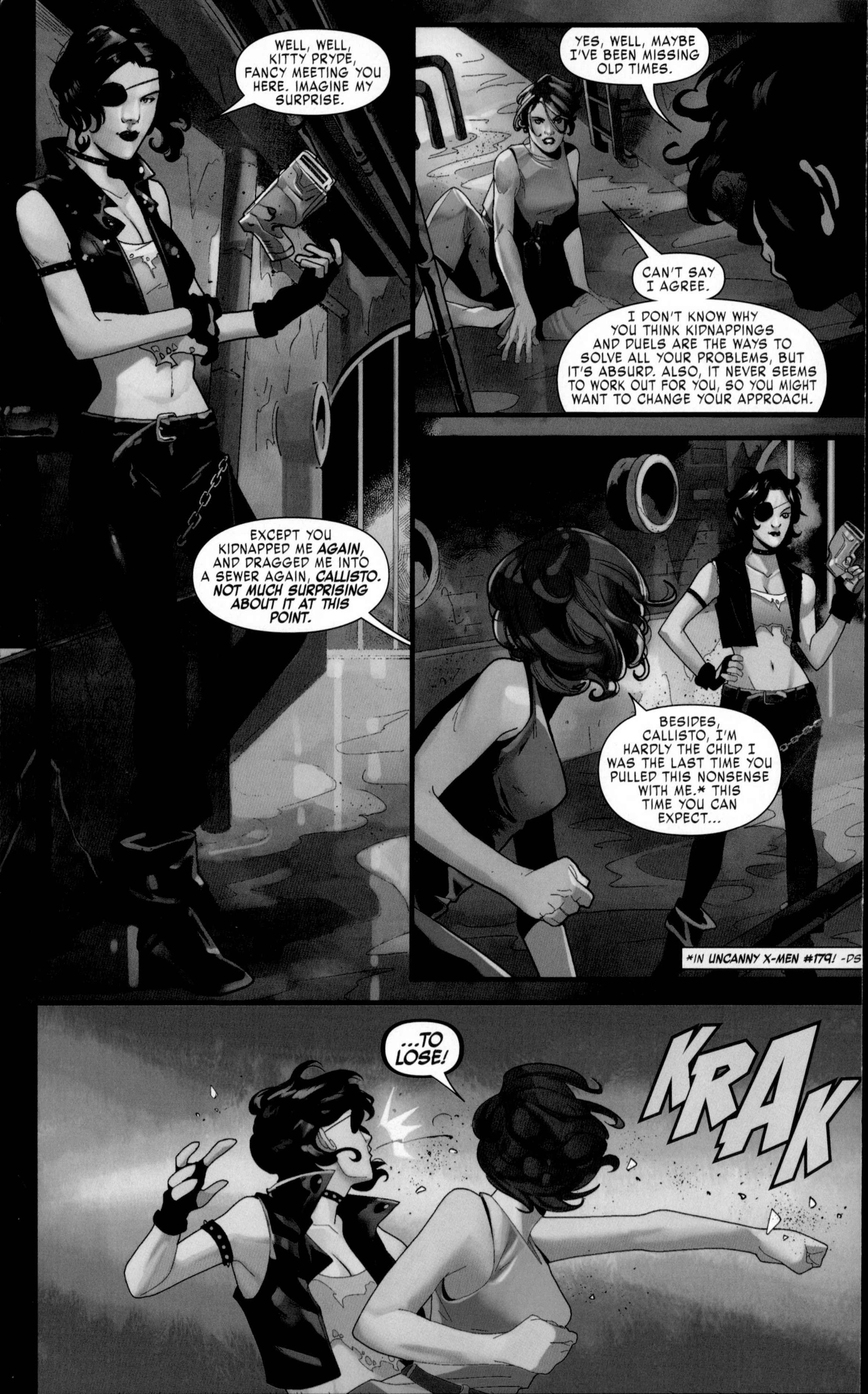
WELL, WELL, KITTY PRYDE, FANCY MEETING YOU HERE. IMAGINE MY SURPRISE.
EXCEPT YOU KIDNAPPED ME AGAIN, AND DRAGGED ME INTO A SEWER AGAIN, CALLISTO. NOT MUCH SURPRISING ABOUT IT AT THIS POINT.
YES, WELL, MAYBE I'VE BEEN MISSING OLD TIMES.
CAN'T SAY I AGREE.
I DON'T KNOW WHY YOU THINK KIDNAPPINGS AND DUELS ARE THE WAYS TO SOLVE ALL YOUR PROBLEMS, BUT IT'S ABSURD. ALSO, IT NEVER SEEMS TO WORK OUT FOR YOU, SO YOU MIGHT WANT TO CHANGE YOUR APPROACH.
BESIDES, CALLISTO, I'M HARDLY THE CHILD I WAS THE LAST TIME YOU PULLED THIS NONSENSE WITH ME.* THIS TIME YOU CAN EXPECT...
*IN UNCANNY X-MEN #179! -DS
...TO LOSE!
KRAK

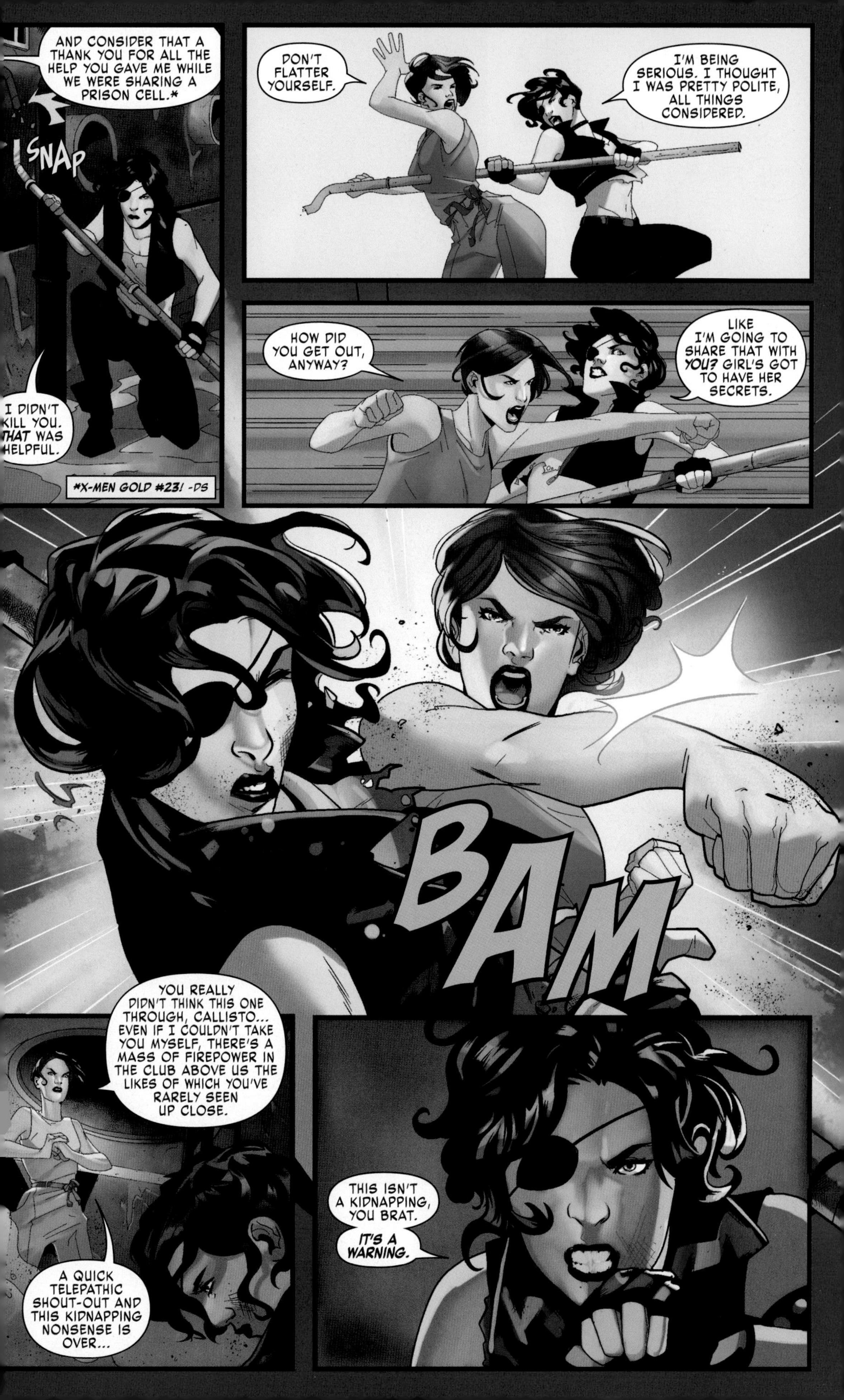
AND CONSIDER THAT A THANK YOU FOR ALL THE HELP YOU GAVE ME WHILE WE WERE SHARING A PRISON CELL.*
SNAP
I DIDN'T KILL YOU. THAT WAS HELPFUL.
*X-MEN GOLD #23! -DS
DON'T FLATTER YOURSELF.
I'M BEING SERIOUS. I THOUGHT I WAS PRETTY POLITE, ALL THINGS CONSIDERED.
HOW DID YOU GET OUT, ANYWAY?
LIKE I'M GOING TO SHARE THAT WITH YOU? GIRL'S GOT TO HAVE HER SECRETS.
BAM
YOU REALLY DIDN'T THINK THIS ONE THROUGH, CALLISTO... EVEN IF I COULDN'T TAKE YOU MYSELF, THERE'S A MASS OF FIREPOWER IN THE CLUB ABOVE US THE LIKES OF WHICH YOU'VE RARELY SEEN UP CLOSE.
A QUICK TELEPATHIC SHOUT-OUT AND THIS KIDNAPPING NONSENSE IS OVER...
THIS ISN'T A KIDNAPPING, YOU BRAT.
IT'S A WARNING.

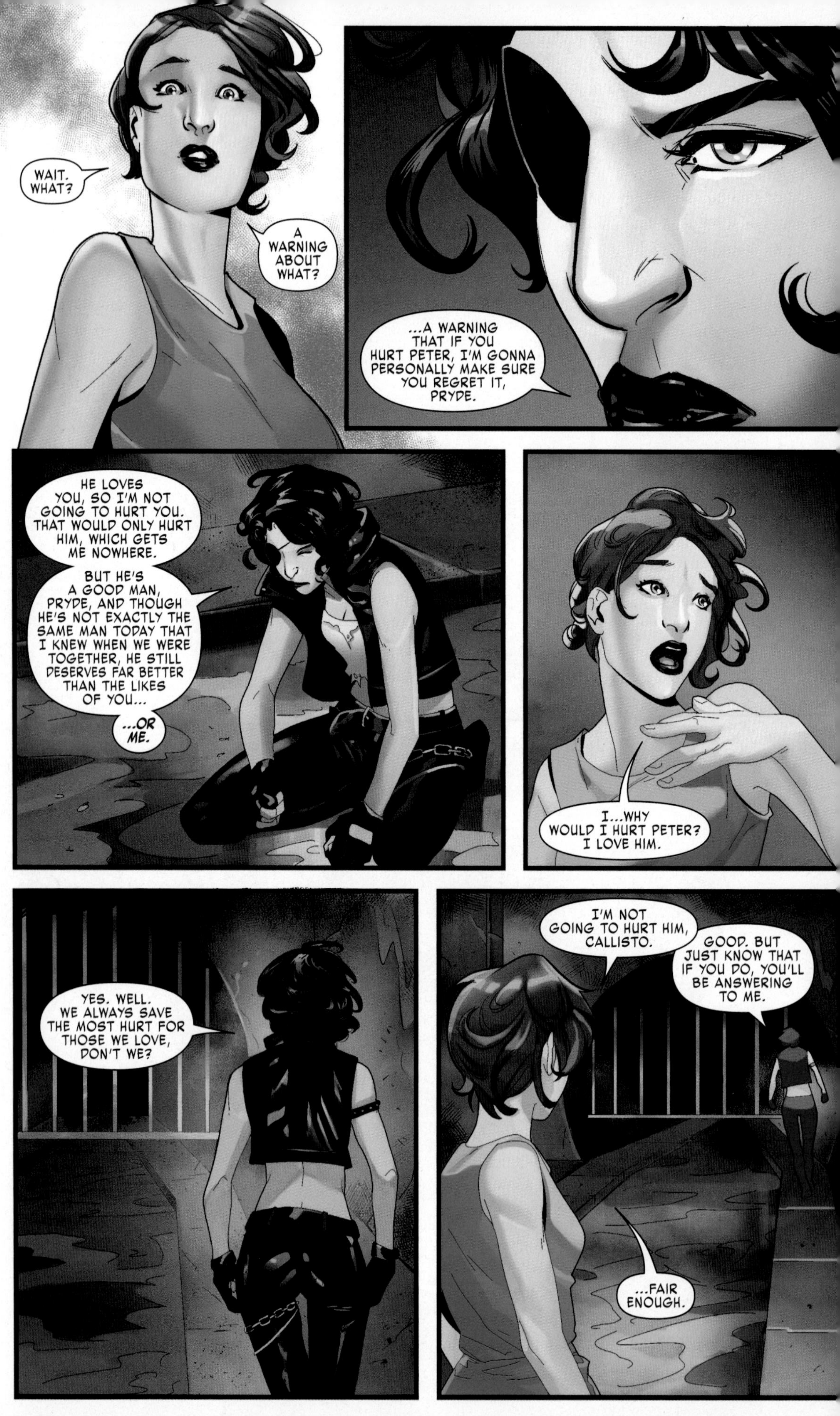
WAIT. WHAT?
A WARNING ABOUT WHAT?
...A WARNING THAT IF YOU HURT PETER, I'M GONNA PERSONALLY MAKE SURE YOU REGRET IT, PRYDE.
HE LOVES YOU, SO I'M NOT GOING TO HURT YOU. THAT WOULD ONLY HURT HIM, WHICH GETS ME NOWHERE.
BUT HE'S A GOOD MAN, PRYDE, AND THOUGH HE'S NOT EXACTLY THE SAME MAN TODAY THAT I KNEW WHEN WE WERE TOGETHER, HE STILL DESERVES FAR BETTER THAN THE LIKES OF YOU...
...OR ME.
I...WHY WOULD I HURT PETER? I LOVE HIM.
YES. WELL. WE ALWAYS SAVE THE MOST HURT FOR THOSE WE LOVE, DON'T WE?
I'M NOT GOING TO HURT HIM, CALLISTO.
GOOD. BUT JUST KNOW THAT IF YOU DO, YOU'LL BE ANSWERING TO ME.
...FAIR ENOUGH.

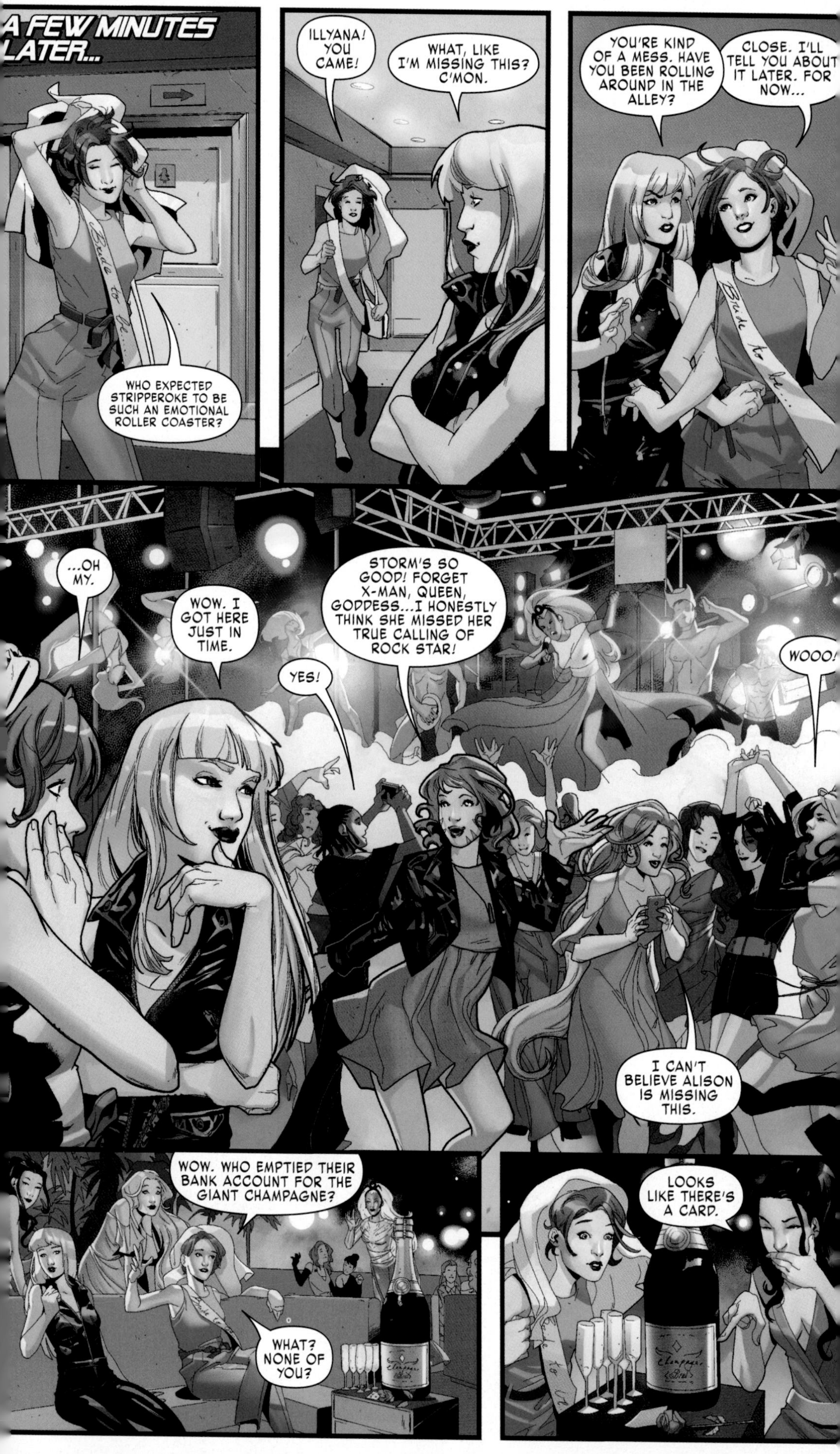
A FEW MINUTES LATER...
WHO EXPECTED STRIPPEROKE TO BE SUCH AN EMOTIONAL ROLLER COASTER?
ILLYANA! YOU CAME!
WHAT, LIKE I'M MISSING THIS? C'MON.
YOU'RE KIND OF A MESS. HAVE YOU BEEN ROLLING AROUND IN THE ALLEY?
CLOSE. I'LL TELL YOU ABOUT IT LATER. FOR NOW...
...OH MY.
WOW. I GOT HERE JUST IN TIME.
STORM'S SO GOOD! FORGET X-MAN, QUEEN, GODDESS...I HONESTLY THINK SHE MISSED HER TRUE CALLING OF ROCK STAR!
YES!
WOOO!
I CAN'T BELIEVE ALISON IS MISSING THIS.
WOW. WHO EMPTIED THEIR BANK ACCOUNT FOR THE GIANT CHAMPAGNE?
WHAT? NONE OF YOU?
LOOKS LIKE THERE'S A CARD.

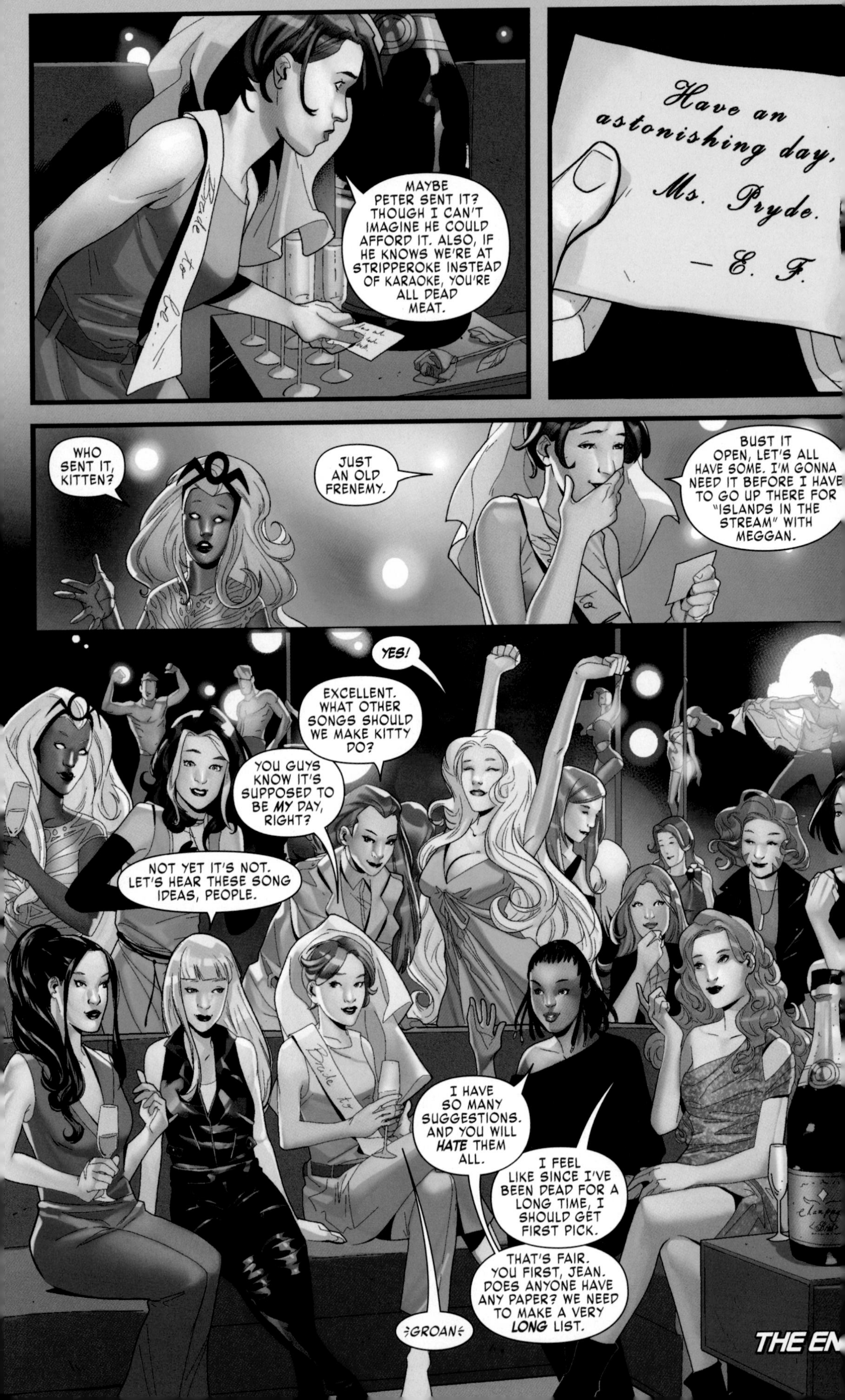

MAYBE PETER SENT IT? THOUGH I CAN'T IMAGINE HE COULD AFFORD IT. ALSO, IF HE KNOWS WE'RE AT STRIPPEROKE INSTEAD OF KARAOKE, YOU'RE ALL DEAD MEAT.
Have an astonishing day, Ms. Pryde.
— E. F.
WHO SENT IT, KITTEN?
JUST AN OLD FRENEMY.
BUST IT OPEN, LET'S ALL HAVE SOME. I'M GONNA NEED IT BEFORE I HAVE TO GO UP THERE FOR "ISLANDS IN THE STREAM" WITH MEGGAN.
YES!
EXCELLENT. WHAT OTHER SONGS SHOULD WE MAKE KITTY DO?
YOU GUYS KNOW IT'S SUPPOSED TO BE MY DAY, RIGHT?
NOT YET IT'S NOT. LET'S HEAR THESE SONG IDEAS, PEOPLE.
I HAVE SO MANY SUGGESTIONS. AND YOU WILL HATE THEM ALL.
I FEEL LIKE SINCE I'VE BEEN DEAD FOR A LONG TIME, I SHOULD GET FIRST PICK.
THAT'S FAIR. YOU FIRST, JEAN. DOES ANYONE HAVE ANY PAPER? WE NEED TO MAKE A VERY LONG LIST.
GROAN
THE EN

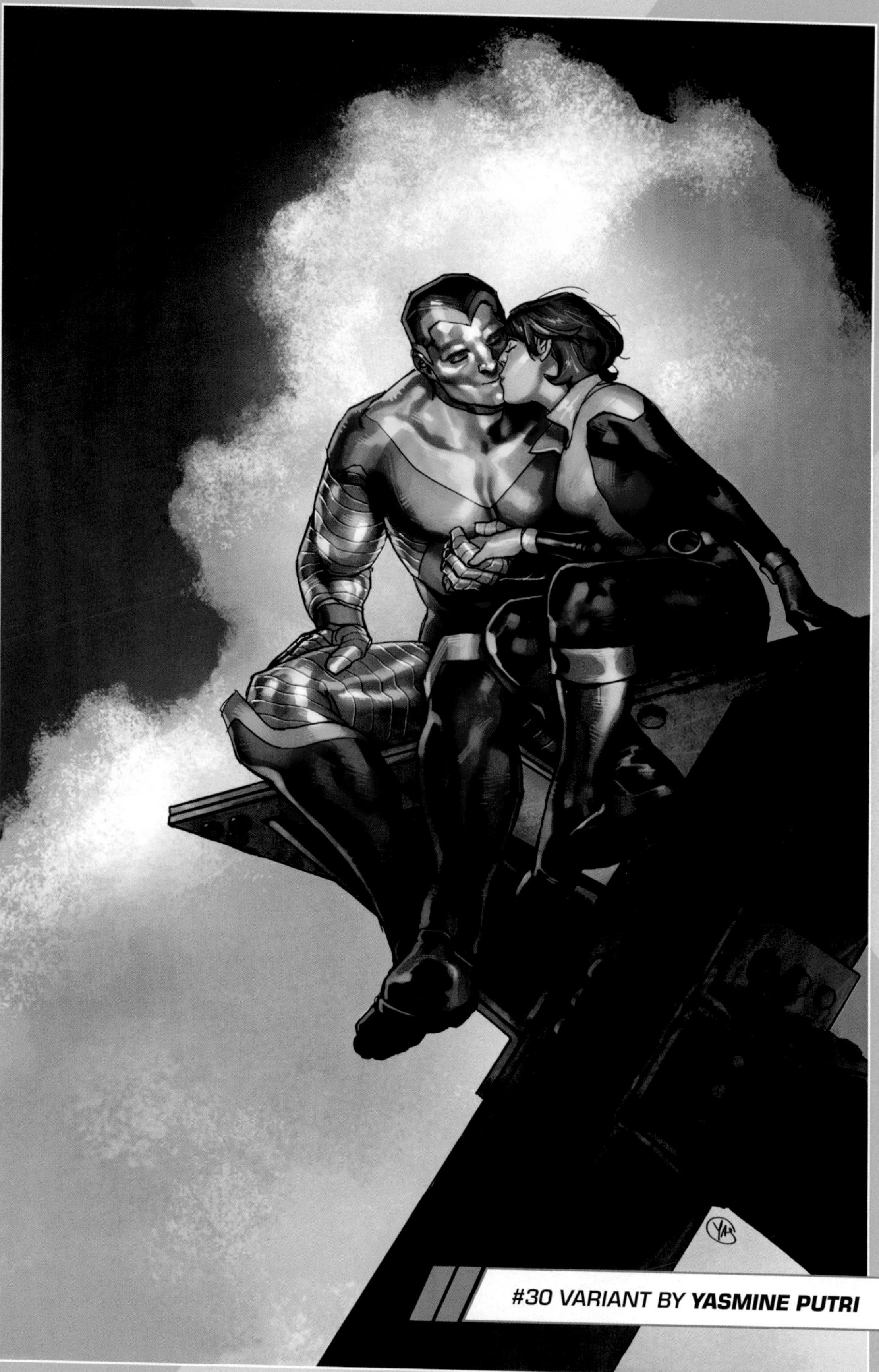

#30 VARIANT BY **YASMINE PUTRI**

#30 VARIANT BY **J. SCOTT CAMPBELL** & **SABINE RICH**

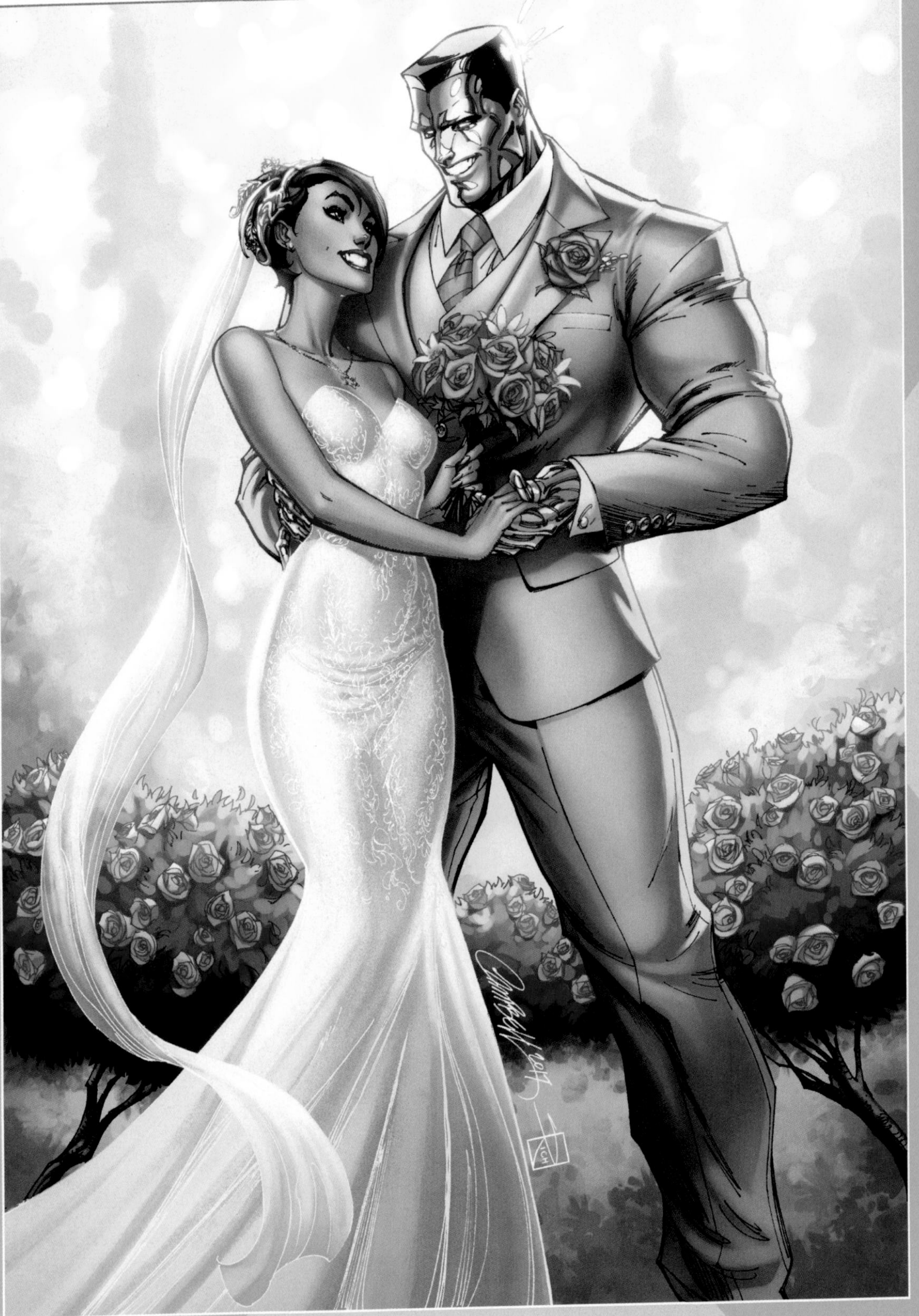

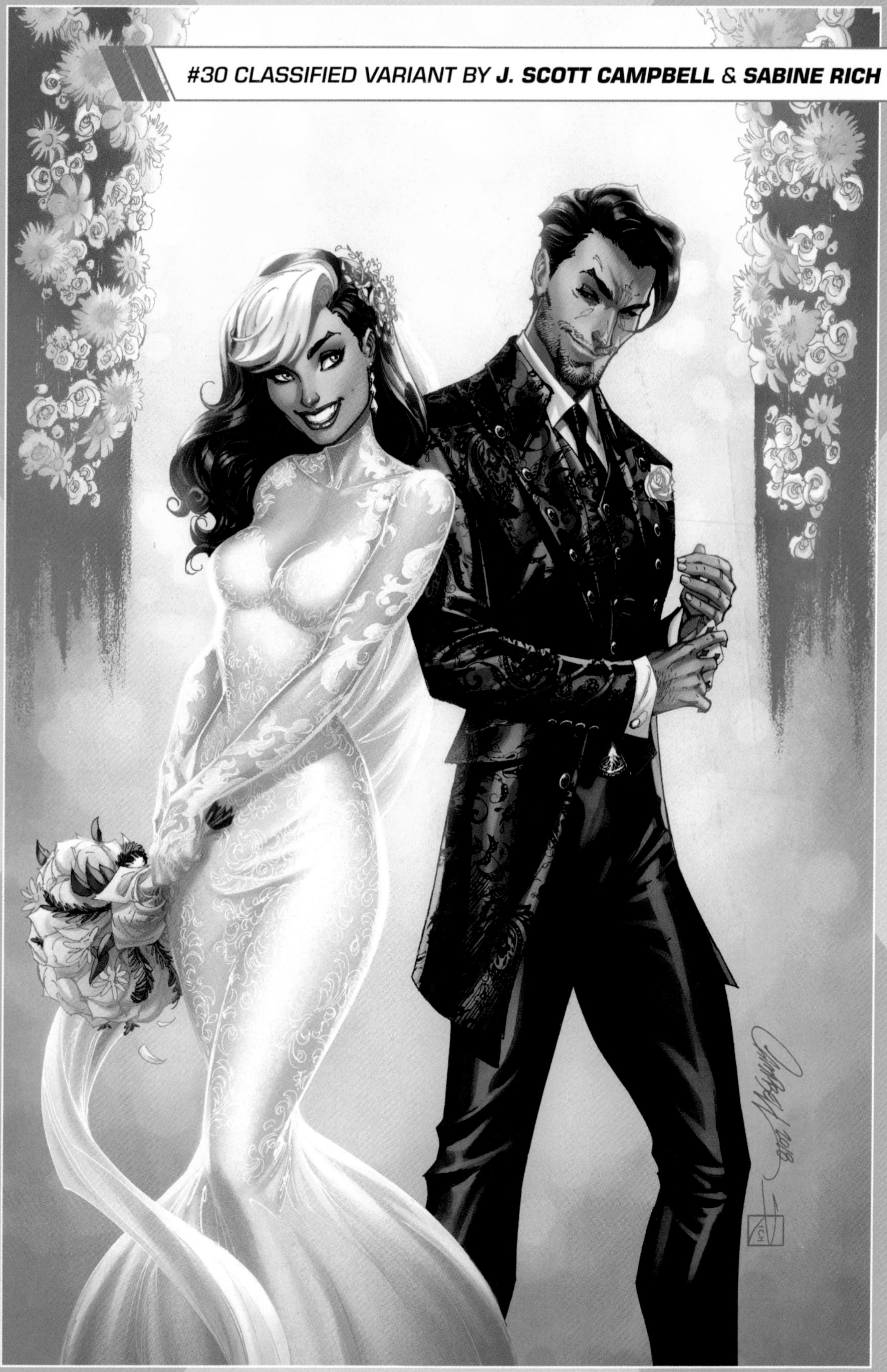

#30 CLASSIFIED VARIANT BY **J. SCOTT CAMPBELL** & **SABINE RICH**

#30 VARIANT BY **TYLER KIRKHAM** & **ARIF PRIANTO**

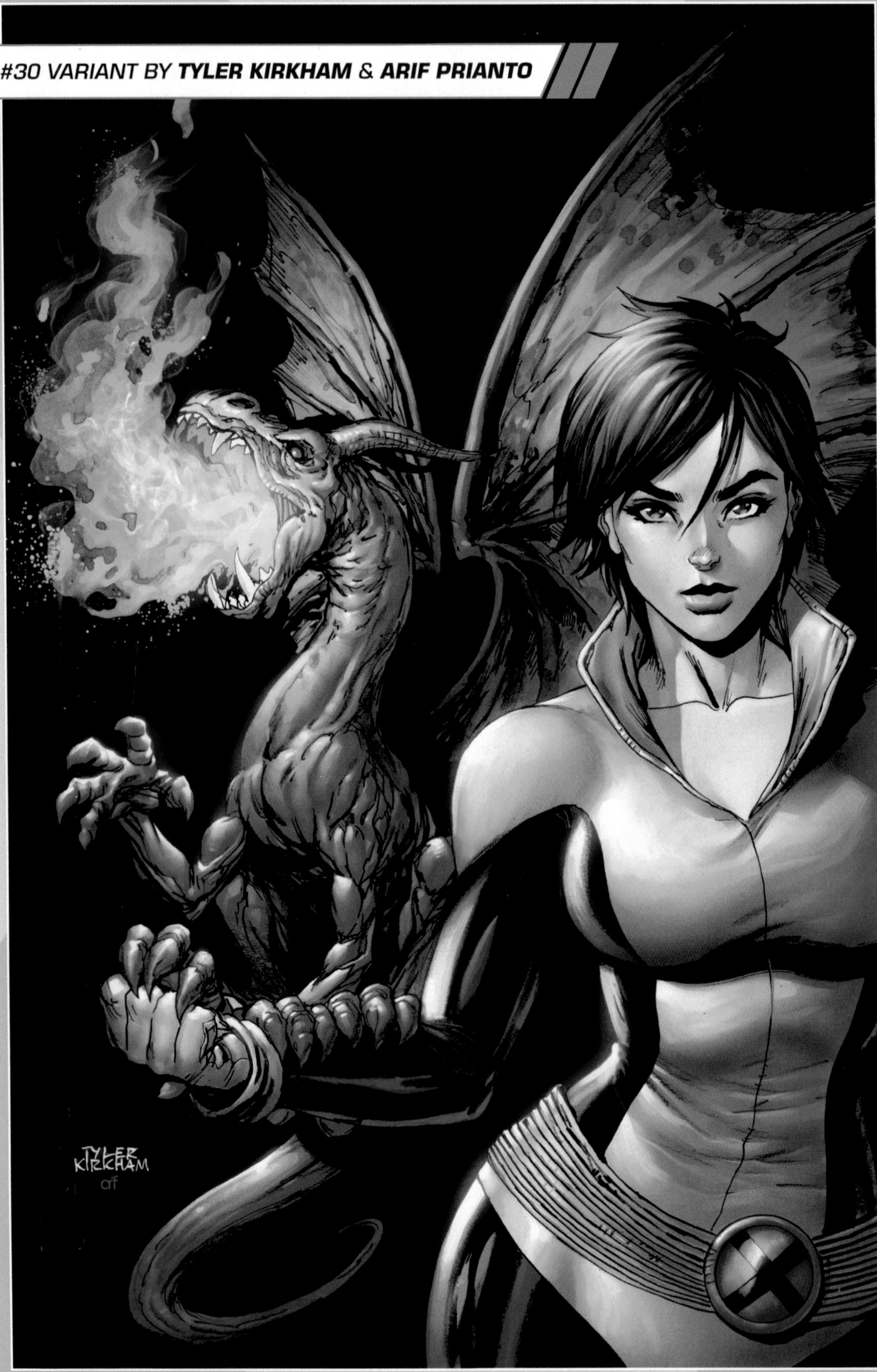
TYLER KIRKHAM
arif

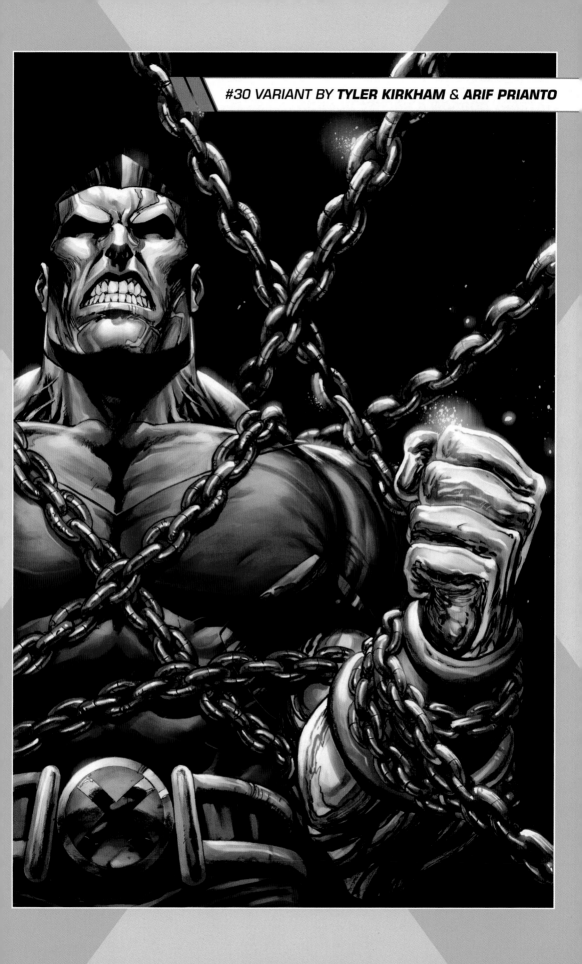

#30 VARIANT BY **TYLER KIRKHAM** & **ARIF PRIANTO**

X-MEN: THE WEDDING SPECIAL #1 VARIANT
*BY **TERRY DODSON** & **RACHEL DODSON***

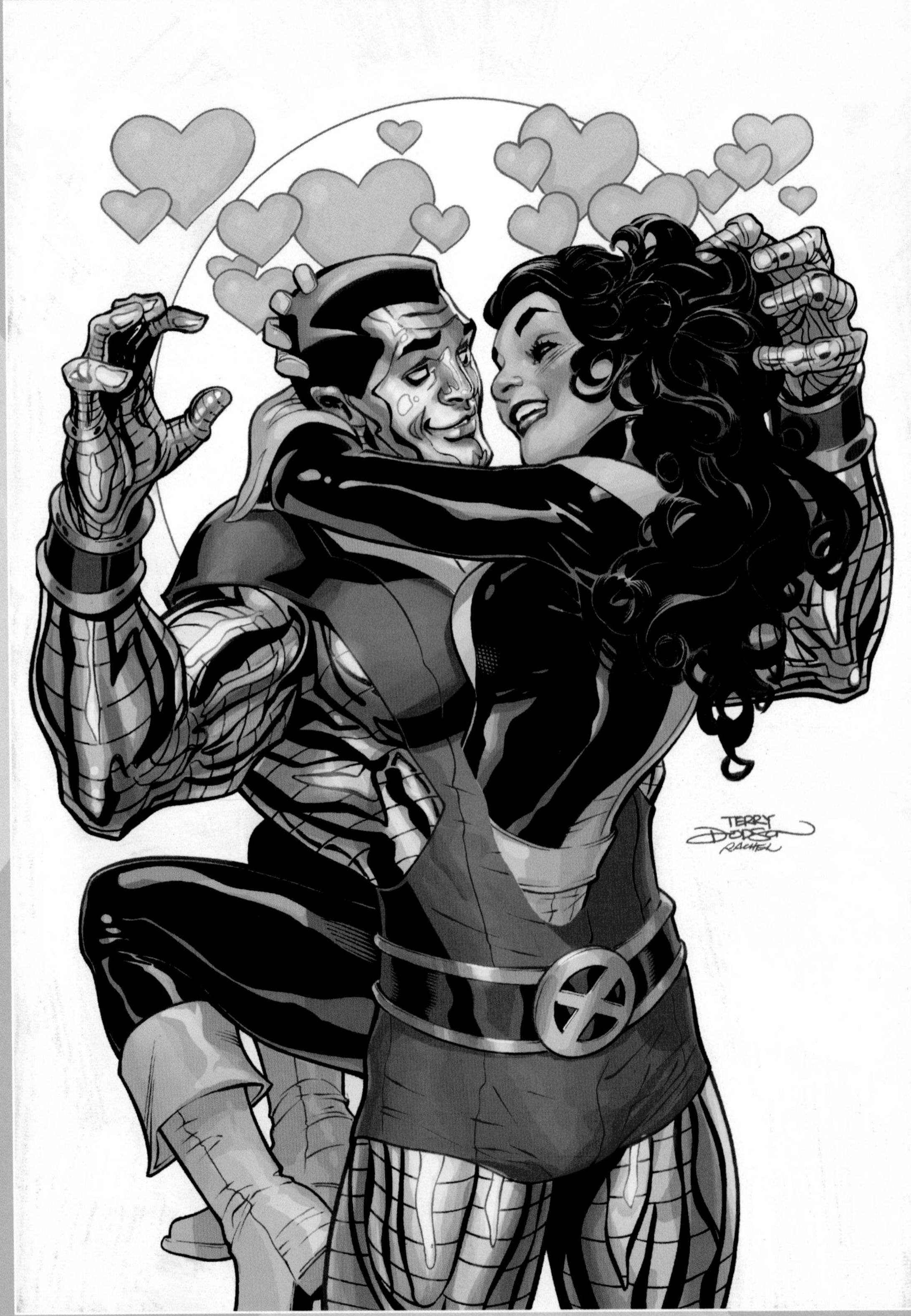

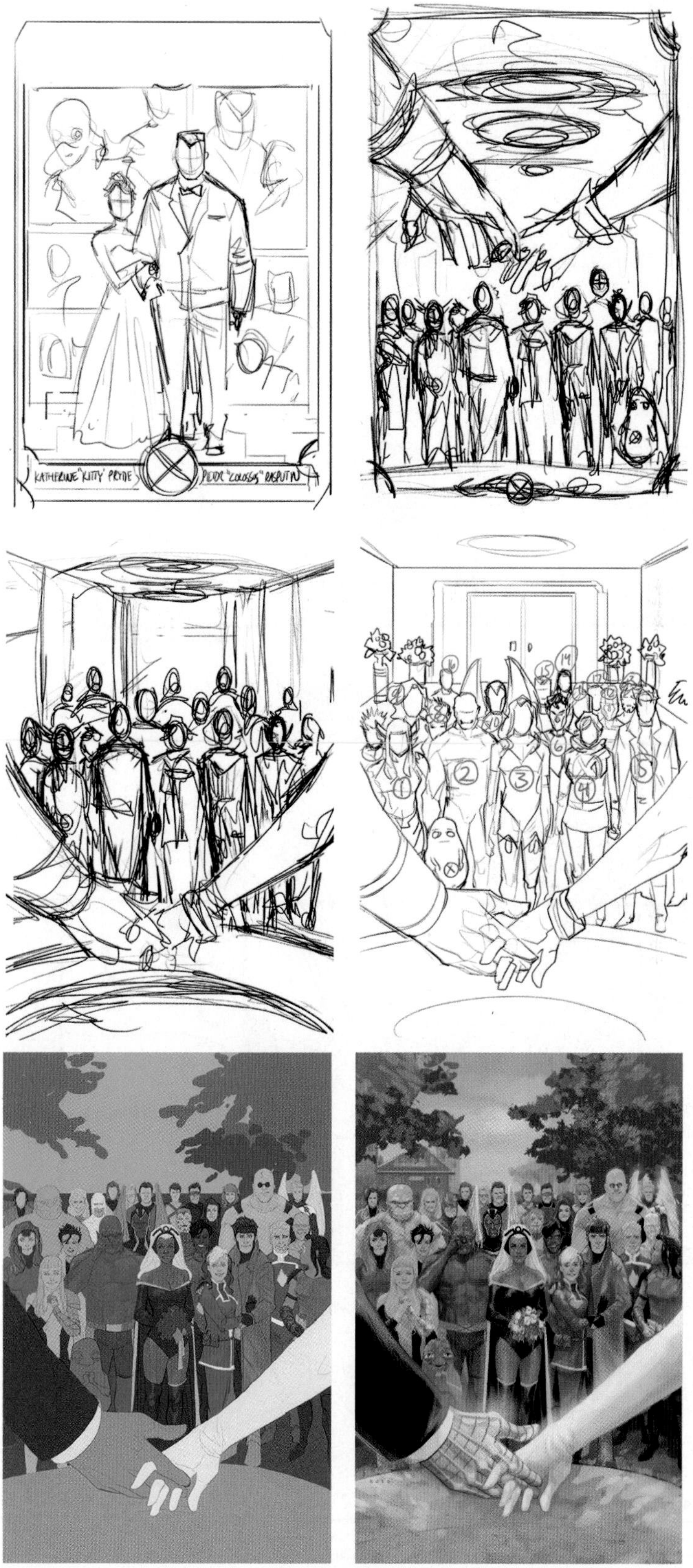
KATHERINE "KITTY" PRYDE

#30 COVER PROCESS BY **PHIL NOTO**

ART PROCESS BY **DAVID MARQUEZ**

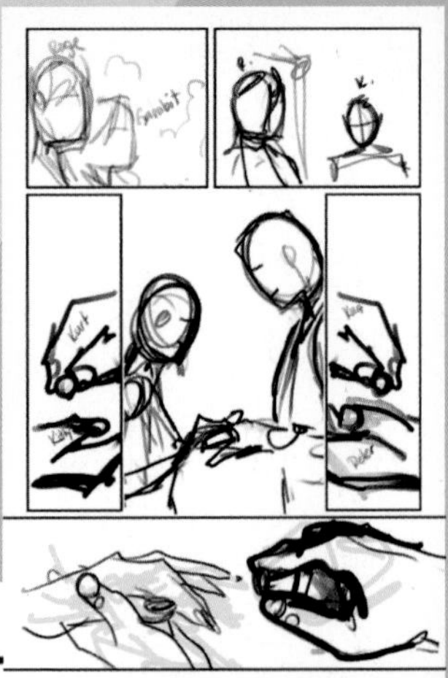

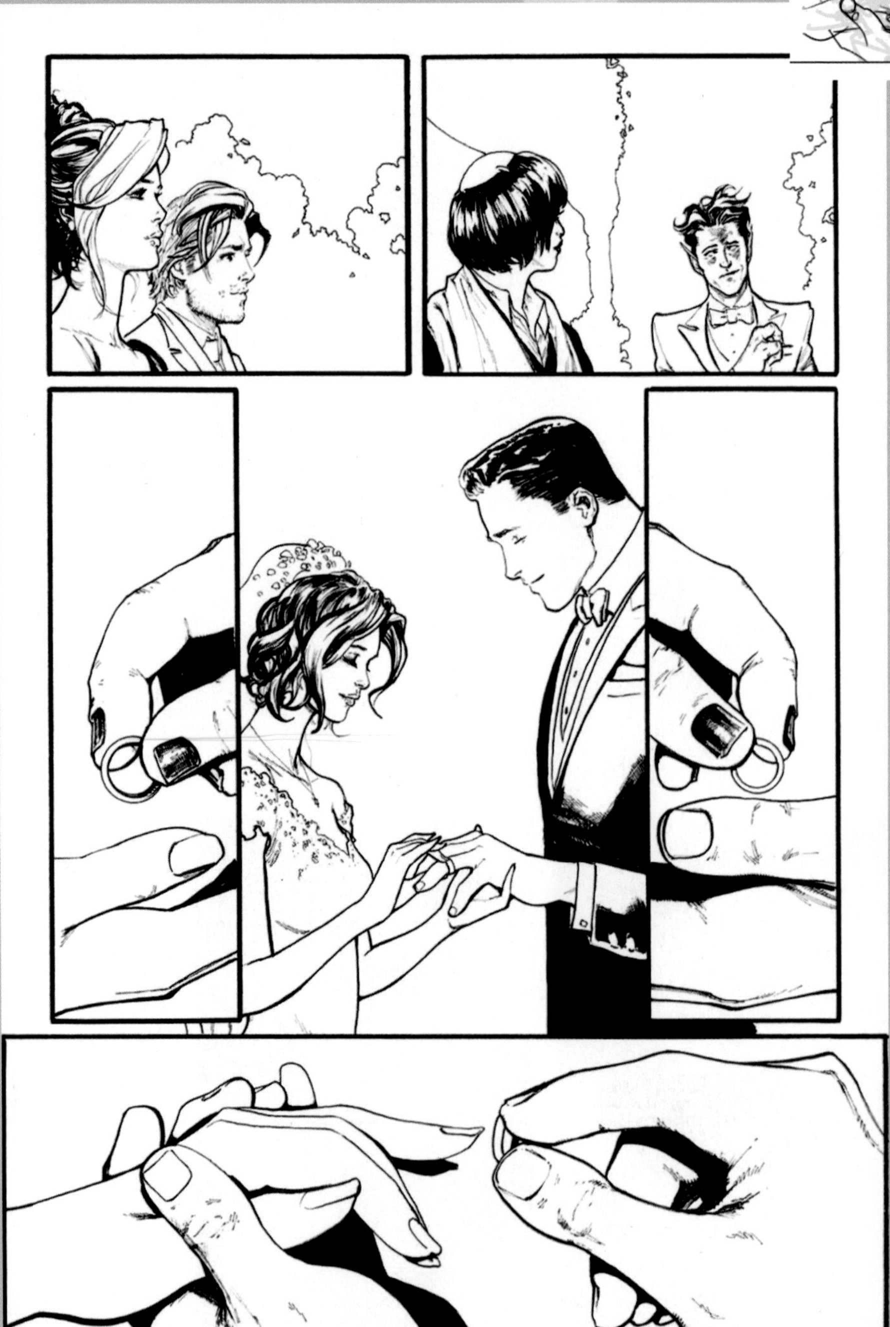

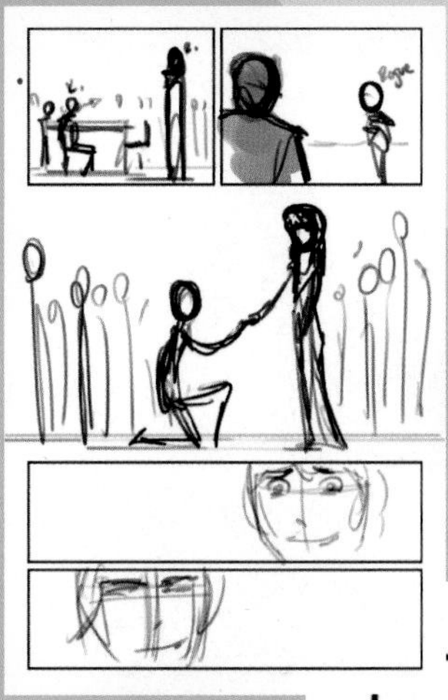

ART PROCESS BY **DAVID MARQUEZ**

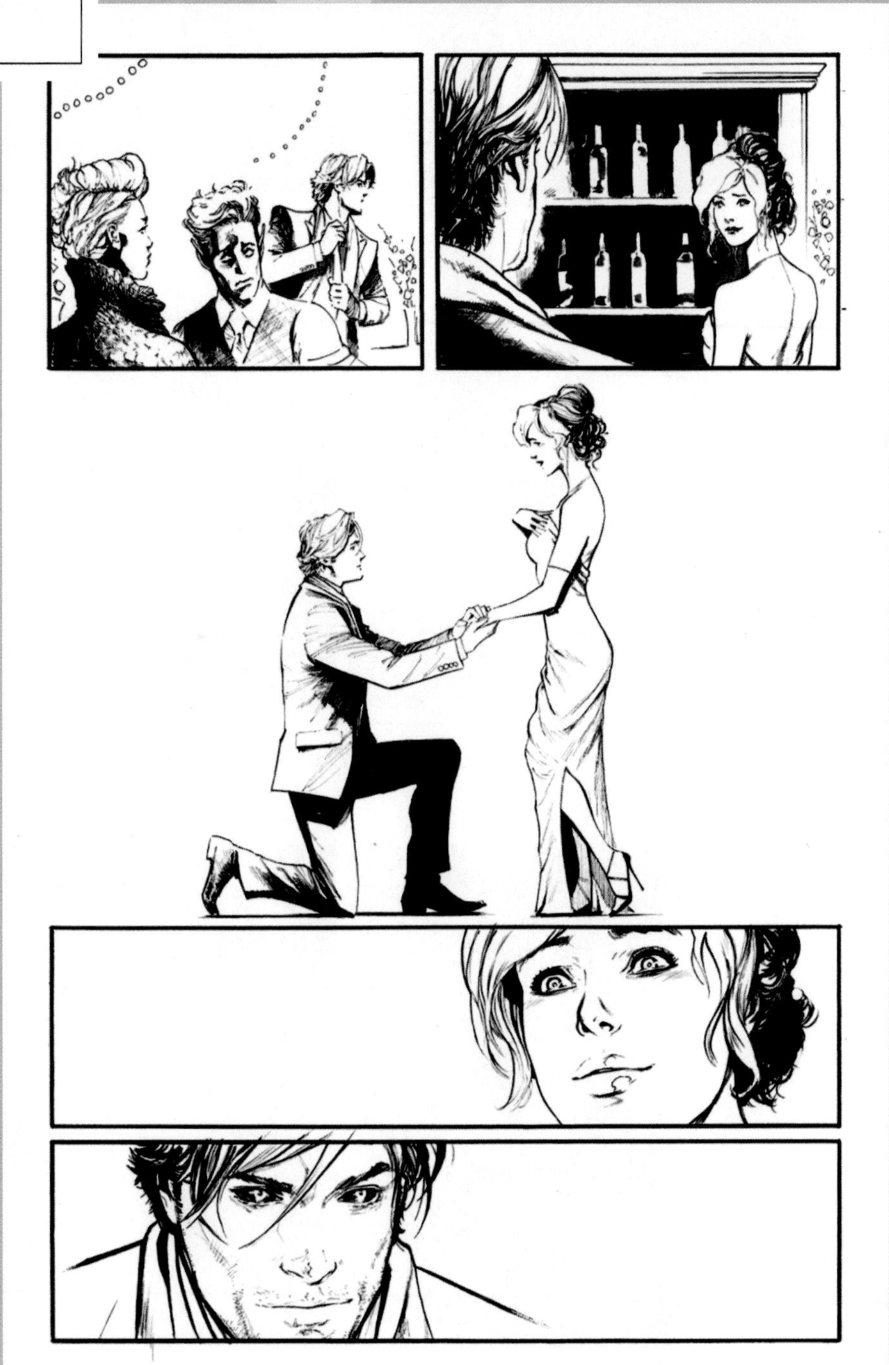

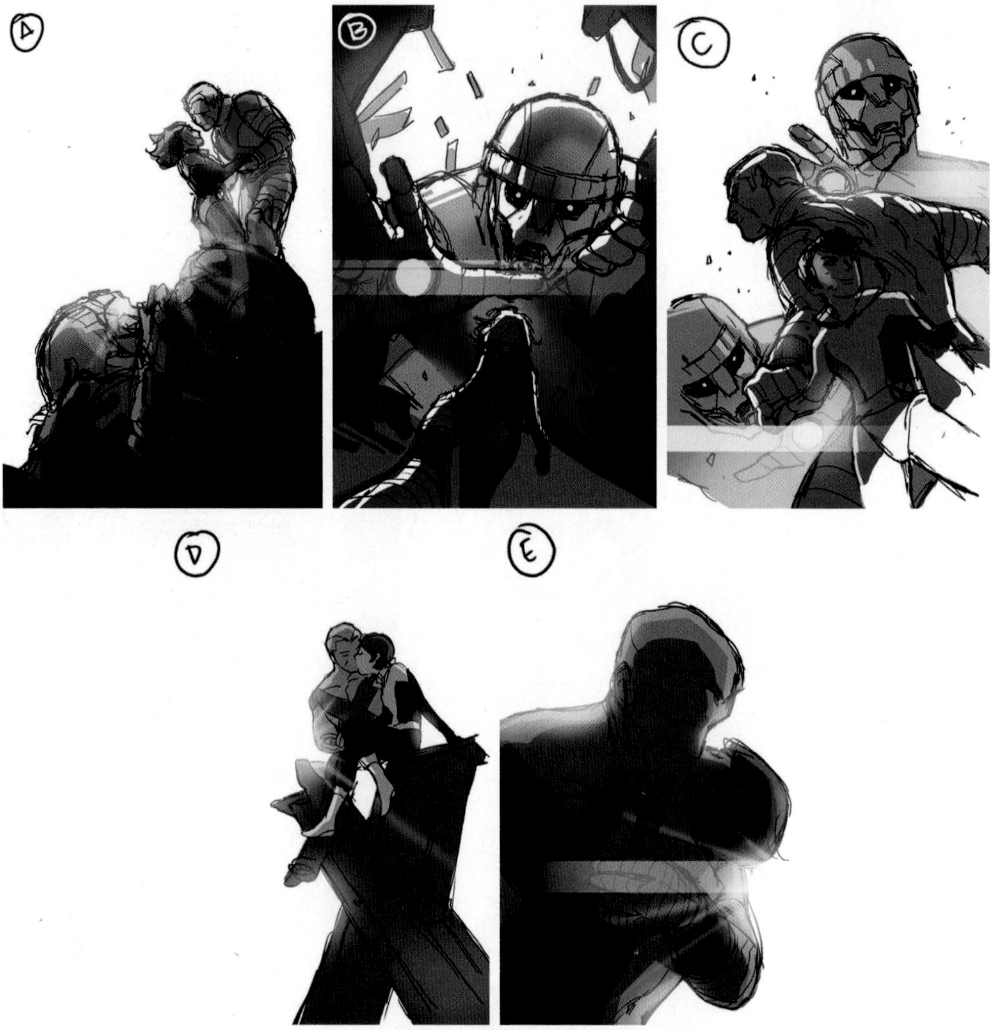
A
B
C
D
E

#30 VARIANT COVER PROCESS BY **YASMINE PUTRI**

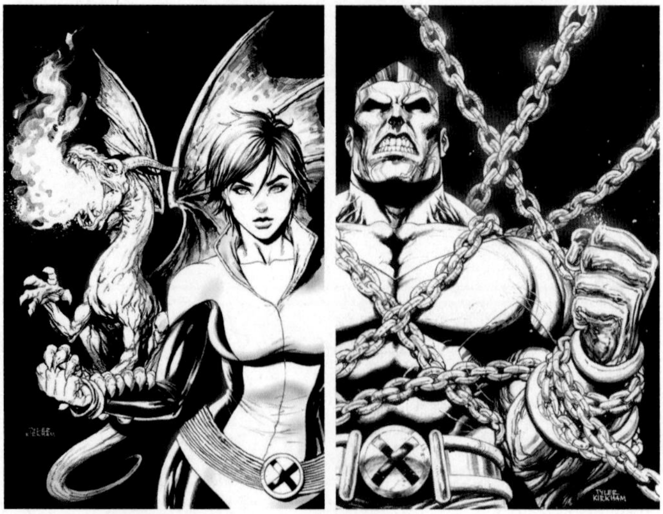
TYLER KIRKHAM

#30 VARIANT INKS BY **TYLER KIRKHAM**